Talking Business German

(G)NVQ Edition

Andy and Ulrike Yeomans

Peter Lupson   Doug Embleton   Elspeth Eggington

Stanley Thornes (Publishers) Ltd

Acknowledgements

We would like to thank the principal of Lancashire College, Diego Garcia-Lucas, for the use of the College's extensive resource bank. Thanks are also due to the German teaching staff and students at the College for their feedback and assistance. We would like to express our sincere appreciation to family and friends for their support and generous contributions.

Andy and Ulrike Yeomans

The authors and the publishers are grateful to the following for permission to reproduce material:

Bavaria Bildagentur for the photos by PRW on p. 43, Winter on p. 94, Kappelmeyer on p. 175, Otto on pp. 214 and 215; J Allan Cash for the photos on pp. 1, 2, 5, 10, 18, 41, 63, 111, 167 and 212; Early Learning Centre for the photo on p. 7; Foto Goertz for the advertisement on p. 138; Gasthof-Hotel Krone for the advertisement on p. 90; Keith Gibson for the photos on pp. 19 (bottom) and 20; Hotel Central for the advertisement on p. 90; Hotel Coenen for the advertisement on p. 85; Intercity for the photo on p. 14; Kölnmesse for the photo on p. 23; London Buses Limited for the photo on p. 210; Lufthansa German Airlines for the photo on p. 65; Adam Opel AG for the photo on p. 195; Eugen Paternolli for the card on p. 14; Pieper for the advertisement on p. 138; Rhein-Ruhr Flughafen Düsseldorf for the logo on p. 66; Greg Smith for the photos on pp. 19 (top), 49, 67, 84, 99, 107, 118, 132, 136, 144, 156, 157, 165, 176, 177, 179, 180, 188, 189, 193, 201, 205 and 220; Stief Pictures for the photos on pp. 73, 168 and 191; Andrew Tibber for the photo on p. 36; Volkswagen AG for the photo on p. 194; Werbeamt der Stadt Düsseldorf for the photos on pp. 51, 125, 134, 202 and 207.

Every attempt has been made to contact copyright holders, but we apologise if any have been overlooked.

First published in 1992
NVQ edition published 1995 by:
Stanley Thornes (Publishers) Ltd
Ellenborough House
Wellington Street
CHELTENHAM GL50 1YW
England

99 00 01 02 03 / 10 9 8 7 6

A catalogue record for this book is available from the British Library.
ISBN 0–7487–2113–4

Typeset by Tech-Set, Gateshead, Tyne & Wear
Printed and bound in Great Britain by Redwood Books, Trowbridge, Wiltshire

Contents

v

TALKING BUSINESS GERMAN NVQ REFERENCE TABLE

Unit 1	Level1	Level 2
Ex1 p2	S1.1	
Ex2 p3	S1.1	
Comp1 p3	L1.1	
Ex6:2 p6	S1.1	
Comp2 p6 (Find out)		
Ex7 p8	W1.1	L2.2
Unit 2		
Ex2 p11	W1.1	
Ex4 p13	S1.1	
Ex5 p14	W1.1	
Comp1 p15	L1.1	
Comp2 p15 (Find out)		L2.2
Unit 3		
Comp1 p21	L1.1	
Ex8 p23	S1.1	
Comp2 p23 (Find out)		L2.2
Unit 4		
Ex1 p35	S1.2	
Ex2 p35	S1.2	
Comp2 p36 (Find out)		L2.2
Unit 5		
Ex1 p42	W1.1	
Ex3 p43	S1.2	
Comp 1 p43	L1.1	
Ex4 p44	S1.2, S1.3	
Comp2 p44 (Find out)		L2.2
Unit 6		
Ex1 p50	S1.2	
Comp1 p51	L1.1	
Ex3 p52	S1.2	
Comp3 p54 (Find out)		L2.2
Unit 7		
Ex1 p66	S1.2, S1.3	
Comp1 p68	L1.1	
Ex5 p68	S1.3	
Comp3 p70 (Find out)		L2.2
Unit 8		
Ex1 p74	S1.3	
Ex2 p74	R1.1	
Comp1 p75	L1.1	

Unit 8	Level 1	Level 2
Ex3 p76	S1.2, R1.1	
Comp2 p77		R2.2
Comp3 p78 (Find out)		L2.2
Unit 9		
Ex1 p86	L1.1	
Ex3 p87	S1.1, S1.3	
Comp1 p88	L1.1, W1.1	
Ex4 p88	S1.2, S1.3	
Comp2 p89		R2.1
Comp3 p91 (Find out)		R2.2
Unit 10		
Ex1 p95	L1.1	
Ex3 p96	R1.1	
Ex4:2 p98		R2.2
Ex4:3 p98	S1.3	
Comp1 p99		L2.2
Comp2 p99		R2.1
Comp3 p100 (Find out)		R2.2
Unit 11		
Ex2 p109		S2.1
Ex3 p110		S2.2
Comp1 p112		L2.2
Comp2 p113		R2.2
Comp3 p114 (Find out)		L2.2
Unit 12		
Ex1 p119	S1.3	
Comp1 p121	L1.1, S1.3	
Ex4 p123		S2.1
Comp2 p124		L2.2
Comp4 p125 (Find out)		L2.2
Unit 13		
Ex1 p135		S2.1
Comp1 p137		L2.2
Ex3 p138		S2.2
Comp2 p140		R2.2
Comp3 p141 (Find out)		L2.2
Unit 14		
Ex1 p145		L2.2
Ex3 p146		S2.1, S2.3
Comp 1 p148		L2.2
Comp3 p151 (Find out)		L2.2

Unit 15	Level 2
Ex1 p158	L2.2
Comp1 p161	L2.2
Comp2 p161	R2.1
Comp3 p163 (Find out)	L2.2
Unit 16	
Ex1 p166	S2.3
Ex2 p167	S2.2
Comp1 p168	L2.1, W2.2
Comp2 p169	R2.1, R2.2
Comp3 p171 (Find out)	L2.2
Unit 17	
Ex2 p178	S2.2
Ex3 p178	R2.2
Ex4 p180	S2.2
Ex5 p181	R2.2, W2.2
Ex6 p181	R2.2
Comp1 p182	L2.1
Comp3 p184 (Find out)	L2.2
Unit 18	
Ex1 p190	L2.2
Ex3 p192	L2.2
Ex4 p192	S2.2
Ex7 p195	R2.1
Comp1 p195	L2.1
Comp2 p196	R2.2
Comp3 p197 (Find out)	L2.2
Unit 19	
Ex1 p203	L2.2
Ex2 p203	S2.1
Comp1 p206	L2.1
Comp2 p206	R2.2
Comp3 p207 (Find out)	L2.2
Unit 20	
Ex1 p211	L2.2
Ex2 p211	S2.1, S2.3
Ex3 p212	L2.2
Ex4 p212	R2.2
Comp1 p214	L2.2
Comp2 p214	R2.2
Comp3 p215 (Find out)	L2.2

Introduction

How to use this course

The course has several components which are described on page x. This coursebook consists of 20 units organised into 10 sections. Each section ends with a **Summary**, including **Language structures overview**, additional exercises, **Key phrases** a **Cultural briefing** and **Pronunciation summary**. The **NVQ reference table** on page vii and **NVQ referenced progress checks** at the end of each unit offer useful support if you are working towards NVQ language units at levels 1 and 2. At the end of the book is a comprehensive **Unit Key**. The different elements of each unit are described below.

Aims   Each unit starts by outlining what you should be able to achieve by the time you have completed it. You will be able to monitor your success by means of the **Progress check** (see page x) at the end of the unit.

Time management   Time management is as important in language learning as it is in general business life/affairs. You should try to organise your time in such a way as to be able to do some language learning every day. Remember that we all learn at different speeds and have different learning styles. It is important, therefore, to be realistic about the time available to you and to pace yourself accordingly. It is generally felt that short, regular and frequent bursts of study are more effective than the occasional marathon. Try to schedule a 20-minute language learning slot into your daily routine.

Study tip   A brief study tip has been included at the start of each unit. It is designed to help you find the most effective way to learn the language.

Dialogues   Each unit contains one or more dialogues which are recorded on the Presentation Cassettes. They should be listened to once or twice, without looking at the text. This gives you a feel for the sound and rhythm of the language without your being distracted by how it is spelt. Once you begin to recognise one or two words, listen again, this time with the English version (in the **Unit key** for Units 1 and 2 only), in front of you. When you are ready, listen again with the German version so that you can begin to see how the words and phrases are divided. Once you feel you can understand the material, you are ready to study it more thoroughly.

Vocabulary, notes and key phrases   Each dialogue is accompanied by explanatory vocabulary and notes. Any word which is not clear appears under **Vocabulary** where you are given the article (**der**, **die** or **das**) and plural of each noun from Unit 4 onwards. The **notes** are helpful in understanding how the language is put together. You may want to make your own: we advise you to invest in a loose-leaf binder and to divide it up into several sections, such as vocabulary, irregular verbs, grammar, and so on. You will decide for yourself which information is important to you and how to organise it. The more active you are in your learning, the more quickly and efficiently you will learn. Language can be divided into what you need to produce (*active vocabulary*) and what you need to understand (*passive vocabulary*). Both are important, but you will find that your active vocabulary will soon be outstripped by your passive vocabulary. Try to distinguish between what is worth remembering and what is simply there as background.

Practice exercises   Don't skip these! Practising the new language is vital if you are studying alone. Try to devise different ways of approaching the exercises, such as writing down the answers, reading them out loud and trying to remember them at odd times during the day. The more senses you use while learning, the more likely your new knowledge is to stick. We give you various ideas about how to do this as you work through the course. Answers to exercises appear in the **Unit key** at the end of the book. If you are working towards NVQ accreditation, you will find the NVQ reference table on page vii useful as an indication of which exercises are most relevant.

Listening comprehension   Each unit includes at least one passage recorded on the Presentation Cassettes intended for 'gist' listening, that is, for understanding the general idea only. You are not expected to understand every word. This gives you practice in several skills: listening to native speakers at normal speed, coping with words and phrases you have not met before, sensitising yourself to accent and intonation. Listen to the passages as often as you like – the more the better! If you are really stumped, you will find a transcript at the back of the book, but don't forget that it is the general drift which is important, not each individual linguistic item. The passages make for valuable listening practice to help achieve NVQ levels 1 and 2.

Reading comprehension   Again, you don't need to understand everything in order to grasp the general idea. Try to get the broad outline first and then work down to individual words and phrases. The practice exercises will help you to do this.

Talking business extra   This consists of additional, near-authentic listening material centred on specific business situations, in which Katrina and Christian discuss various dealings between their two companies.

Accompanying exercises aim to consolidate key words and phrases, whilst bearing in mind that the most important thing at this stage is to understand more complex language, rather than produce it. The dialogues are intended for gist comprehension and can be listened to in conjunction with both transcripts and translations provided in the **Unit key**. You will find this section particularly valuable if you are actively involved in business dealings with German speakers and/or building up your NVQ portfolio at level 2. Learners with a less urgent need for business German will find these dialogues an interesting, though not essential extra.

Language structures   In each unit, you will find a section called **Language structures**. Here we pull together the newly introduced grammatical elements of each unit and, drawing on numerous examples, we present them in graphic form. The **Language structures overview** in the **Summary** sections gives you complete tables which serve as an aid, a diagram to help you put language together as you might assemble a kitchen cabinet.

Although grammatical terms are explained as they are first used, for ease of reference we have included a glossary of the most commonly used words which you may or may not be familiar with already:

- *Noun*   the name of a person or thing (*John*, the *box*, my *wife*)
- *Pronoun*   a word that replaces a noun (*I*, *he*, *it*, *them*)
- *Preposition*   a word that links nouns or pronouns to show their relationship in the sentence (we paid *with* cash, I gave it *to* you, I put sugar *in* the coffee)
- *Adjective*   a word which describes a noun (*red*, *beautiful*, *small*)
- *Verb*   a doing word (you *are*, I *look*, he *ran*)

- *Infinitive* the name of the verb – in English it is preceded by *to*, (e.g. *to see, to write*)
- *Tense* the form of the verb which expresses time – future, past, or present
- *Past participle* second part of the verb indicating the past tense in phrases like 'I have *done*', 'he has *gone*'.

Progress check Each unit has a short NVQ-referenced self-assessment test. If you complete this successfully you can feel satisfied that you have learned the language points introduced in the unit. If you find it difficult, it would be a good idea to run through the material again before going any further. For self assessment of listening skills select the appropriate items listed in the NVQ reference table.

Pronunciation Good pronunciation will come naturally if you listen carefully to and imitate what you hear on the cassettes. However, in each unit on the Presentation Cassettes we have focused on some of the trickier words to help you sound as authentic as possible. In addition you will find a **Pronunciation** section in each of the ten **Summaries** in the Coursebook.

Cultural briefing You may have acquired language skills, but can you strike the right note? These sections are designed to give you insights into the cultural context and to supply you with essential background information on how things are done in German-speaking countries.

Unit key This includes answers to exercises, transcripts of listening comprehensions and translations of **Talking business extra** transcripts. In addition, you will also find a list of **Irregular verbs** and a complete **Vocabulary list** at the back of the book.

Symbols

When you see this symbol, you should listen to the appropriate material on the Presentation Cassettes.

Course components

Coursebook This book, whose contents are described on pages viii–x.

Presentation Cassettes 1 and 2 These are closely linked to the coursebook and contain dialogues, new vocabulary, listening material, and pronunciation.

Consolidation Cassettes 1 and 2 These contain extensive and varied additional listening and practice material based on the key phrases, vocabulary and structures introduced in the Coursebook.

The Resource and Assessment File Although the course can be used for self-study, this file contains unit-by-unit notes for teachers whose students are using the Talking Business course. 47 worksheets provide extra practice in all four skill areas, listening, speaking, reading and writing, and can be accessed independently by students, or photocopied and distributed by tutors. The file also has transcripts of the first example of each exercise on the Consolidation cassettes, and a full transcript of the material on the cassette which accompanies the listening worksheets. The file can also be used as a resource for Open Learning departments and as preparation towards NVQ assessment. A general introduction to Language NVQs is also included.

UNIT **1** Besuch aus Deutschland

In this unit, you will learn how to …

- greet someone and introduce yourself
- give simple information about yourself
- say what your job is and where you work
- say that something is not the case.

STUDY TIP

All new words are presented on the tape. Listen several times before reading aloud. This helps to ensure correct pronunciation from the start.

Dialogue 1: Guten Tag

At a trade fair in Birmingham Herr Müller introduces himself to a fellow German, Frau Roth.

Herr Müller	Guten Tag. Hans Müller aus München.
Frau Roth	Guten Tag Herr Müller, freut mich. Mein Name ist Helga Roth.
Herr Müller	Freut mich auch.

Vocabulary

Besuch *visit*
aus *from*
Deutschland *Germany*
Herr *Mr*

Frau *Mrs, Ms*
guten Tag *hello* (literally *good day*)*
München *Munich*

freut mich *pleased to meet you* (literally *pleases me*)*
mein Name ist *my name is*
auch *also, too*

*The word-for-word translation in brackets may be helpful at the beginning. However, the important thing is to memorise the German phrase as a whole.

Notes

Müller, München Two dots over **a**, **o** or **u** are called an **Umlaut**. This changes the sound of the vowel. Listen carefully to the way these are pronounced on the cassette.

| Exercise 1 | **1** Respond to Herr Müller in this short exchange. Write in your answers. |

| | *Herr Müller* | Guten Tag, Hans Müller aus München. |
| | *Sie (you)* | (*Say hello and that you are pleased to meet him. Give your name.*) |

_____

| | *Herr Müller* | Freut mich auch. |

2 Now you start.

| | *Sie (you)* | (*Greet Frau Roth and introduce yourself.*) |

_____

| | *Frau Roth* | Guten Tag, freut mich. Mein Name ist Helga Roth. |
| | *Sie (you)* | (*You are pleased too.*) |

_____

Dialogue 2: Wie geht es Ihnen?

Here is Mr. Lloyd welcoming his German colleague, Frau Kahn. Everybody here is putting their German into practice! The **Empfangsdame** knocks at his office door:

Mr. Lloyd	Herein!
Empfangsdame	Mr. Lloyd, der Besuch aus Deutschland ist hier.
Mr. Lloyd	Ach, guten Tag Frau Kahn. Bitte, kommen Sie herein!
Frau Kahn	Guten Tag, Mr Lloyd. Wie geht es Ihnen?
Mr. Lloyd	Gut, danke. Und Ihnen?
Frau Kahn	Auch gut, danke.
Mr. Lloyd	Trinken Sie eine Tasse Tee, oder Kaffee?
Frau Kahn	Ja bitte. Kaffee, mit Milch und ohne Zucker.
Mr. Lloyd	Mrs Brown, zwei Tassen Kaffee bitte!

Vocabulary

Herein! *come in*
Empfangsdame *receptionist*
der *the*
ist *is*
hier *here*
ach! *oh!*
bitte *please*
Kommen Sie herein! *Do come in!*
Wie geht es Ihnen? *How are you?* (literally *How goes it to you?*)

gut *well, fine*
danke *thank you*
und *and*
und Ihnen? *and you?*
trinken Sie …? *would you like to drink …?*
Sie *you*
eine Tasse Tee *a cup of tea*
oder *or*
Kaffee *coffee*
ja *yes*
mit *with*

Milch *milk*
ohne *without*
Zucker *sugar*
zwei *two*
Tassen Kaffee *cups of coffee*

Notes

1 **Empfangsdame – Empfang** *reception*
Dame *lady* German has a reputation for producing long words out of two or more short ones. These words are often joined together by an **s**.

2 **Kommen Sie herein. Wie geht es Ihnen?**
Sie *you* and **Ihnen** *(to) you* Both words have a capital letter and are explained more fully on page 82.

Exercise 2

Complete this dialogue by giving the appropriate response in German.

Mrs Brown Wie geht es Ihnen?
Sie (you) (*Fine, thank you, and you?*)

Mrs Brown Auch gut, danke.
 Trinken Sie eine Tasse Tee?
Sie (you) (*Yes, please.*)

Mrs Brown Mit Milch?
Sie (you) (*Yes, without sugar please.*)

Comprehension 1: Bei Anglia Chemicals 1

The buyer and the production manager of a German company, Sasshofer AG in Mönchengladbach, have come to visit a British company, Anglia Chemicals plc. The scene takes place at reception. Read the questions first, listen a few times to the conversation and then answer in English.

Vocabulary

bei *at*   **erwartet** *expects*   **gleich** *right away, just*

1 Where do Herr Weidmann and Frau Meyer come from?
2 Is Mr. Newby expecting them?
3 Will he be long?
4 Is he pleased to meet them?

Exercise 3

Frau Meyer is introducing herself at a morning working party, whilst Herr Weidmann's turn comes in the evening.

'Guten Morgen. Ich heiße Lotte Meyer und ich komme aus Krefeld. Ich arbeite bei der Firma Sasshofer in Mönchengladbach. Ich bin Einkaufsleiterin.'

'Guten Abend. Mein Name ist Ewald Weidmann. Ich wohne in Neuß bei Düsseldorf und ich bin Produktionsleiter bei der Firma Sasshofer.'

Vocabulary

guten Morgen *good morning*
ich *I*
ich heiße *I am called*
ich komme *I come (or I am coming)*
ich arbeite *I work (am working)*
bei *at, near*

bei der Firma Sasshofer *at Sasshofer's (literally at the Sasshofer firm)*
in *in*
bin *am*
Einkaufsleiterin *chief buyer, purchasing manageress*
guten Abend *good evening*

ich wohne *I live (i.e. reside)*
Neuß bei Düsseldorf *Neuß near Düsseldorf*
Produktionsleiter *production manager*

Notes

1 **Ich heiße Lotte Meyer** The letter ß is called **scharfes s** and is equivalent in sound to the double *s* in English, as in *hiss*. See page 9 for details.

2 **Ich bin Sekretärin** *I am a secretary.* There is no *a* before professions in German.

Fill in the blanks in the following sentences.

Mein NAME ist Lotte MEYER und ich VOHNEN in Krefeld. Ich BIN Einkaufs LEITER in. Ich trinke CAFE mit MILCH. Ich HEISSE Ewald WEIDMANN. Ich KOMMEN aus Deutschland. Ich ARBEITE in Mönchengladbach bei der FIRMA Sasshofer. Ich BIN Produktions LEITER. Ich TRINKE Kaffee MIT Zucker.

Exercise 4

Make the following sentences negative.

Example: Ich wohne in Krefeld.
　　　　　Ich wohne **nicht** in Krefeld. (*I don't live in Krefeld.*)

1 Ich heiße Ewald Weidmann.
2 Ich komme aus Deutschland.
3 Ich arbeite bei der Firma Sasshofer.
4 Ich bin Produktionsleiter.

Exercise 5

Now it's your turn to give some information about yourself. You may find the following selection of jobs useful, but there is no need to learn them all. Note the difference between male and female, and learn what is relevant to you.

Man	Woman	English
Student	**Studentin**	*student*
Telefonist	TELEFONISTIN	*telephonist*
INGENIEUR	**Ingenieurin**	*engineer*
Betriebsingenieur		*works engineer*
	Elektronikerin	*electronics engineer*
LKW-Fahrer		*lorry driver*
GESCHÄFTSFÜHRER	**Geschäftsführerin**	*manager, managing director*
Betriebsleiter		*works (general) manager*
	Einkaufsleiterin	*purchasing manager*
Verkaufsleiter		*sales manager*
	Programmiererin	*computer programmer*
Vertreter		*sales representative*
	Dolmetscherin	*interpreter*
Lagerverwalter		*warehouse manager*
	Chefsekretärin	*personal assistant*
Pförtner		*porter*
	Empfangsdame	*receptionist*
Angestellter	**Angestellte**	*(salaried) employee, clerk*

1 Now give some information about yourself:

Ich heiße (mein Name ist) _____

Ich komme aus (ich wohne in) _____

Ich arbeite bei _____

Ich bin _____

2 Supply the male/female version of jobs left out in the summary above.

Exercise 6	The following conversation takes place between two people on a flight to Germany.

Herr Müller	Guten Tag, Müller aus Duisburg.
Frau Williams	Tag, mein Name ist Williams. Es freut mich, Sie kennenzulernen.
Herr Müller	Sind Sie Deutsche?
Frau Williams	Nein, ich bin Schottin.
Herr Müller	Ach so, das ist interessant. Und woher kommen Sie?
Frau Williams	Ich komme aus Edinburgh. Ich bin Exportleiterin bei der Firma Tartan Textiles. Und Sie? Was sind Sie von Beruf?
Herr Müller	Ich bin Verkaufsleiter bei der Firma Edelmetall in Oberhausen bei Duisburg.

Vocabulary

Es freut mich, Sie kennenzulernen *Pleased to meet you*
Sind Sie Deutsche? *Are you German? (speaking to a woman)*
nein *no*
Schottin *Scotswoman*

ach so *oh, I see*
interessant *interesting*
woher? *where from?*
Was sind Sie von Beruf? *What do you do for a living? (literally: what are you by profession?)*
Edelmetall *precious metal*

richtig *true*
falsch *false*

                                            Richtig   Falsch

1 Which statements are correct? Tick the appropriate box.

  a) Frau Williams comes from England. ☐ ☐

  b) She works at Tartan Textiles. ☐ ☐

  c) Herr Müller is a purchasing manager. ☐ ☐

  d) He works in the city centre of Duisburg. ☐ ☐

2 Now complete this dialogue:

Herr Schmidt	Guten Tag, mein Name ist Gerhard Schmidt.
Sie	*(Say hello, you are pleased to meet him and introduce yourself.)*

_____

Herr Schmidt	Woher kommen Sie?
Sie	

_____

Herr Schmidt	Ach, das ist interessant. Ich komme aus Deutschland. Ich bin Programmierer. Was sind Sie von Beruf?
Sie	

_____

Talking business extra

Comprehension 2

Christian Holzhauser, from the publishing company **Verlag Germania,** has invited Katrina Stein, from an educational toy company **Spieltechnik GmbH**, for an initial meeting.

In the course of this book we're going to be listening in to their conversations, as they work closely together on the support literature for the launch of **Spieltechnik's** latest product onto the British market.

When you first listen to the conversations, there'll be parts you don't understand. Don't worry, because as you work through the course and revise previous units, things will become much clearer. If you really feel you might be missing something, read through the translations in the **Unit key**, but only after you have listened thoroughly.

Key vocabulary

Einladung *invitation*	**Büro** *office*	**Fragebogen** *questionnaire*
Zweigstelle *branch office*	**Stelle** *job*	**Betreuung** *care*
leiten *to manage*	**Ausland** *countries abroad*	**überall** *everywhere*

Key phrases

Herzlich willkommen!	*Welcome*
Darf ich vorstellen?	*May I introduce (you to …)*
Beginnen wir am Anfang	*Let's start at the beginning*
für die Kunden verantwortlich	*responsible for the customers*
Wir haben Besuch	*We have visitors*
Das kann man schon sagen	*You could say that*
Das klingt interessant	*That sounds interesting*

Find out:

1 what Frau Herz's job is
2 where the visitors come from.

Exercise 7

Fill in the details in the form below:

Vorname   Katrina

Nachname   _____

Wohnort   _____

Beruf   _____

Firma   _____

Puzzle
1 welcome
2 customers
3 visit
4 to manage
5 foreign countries

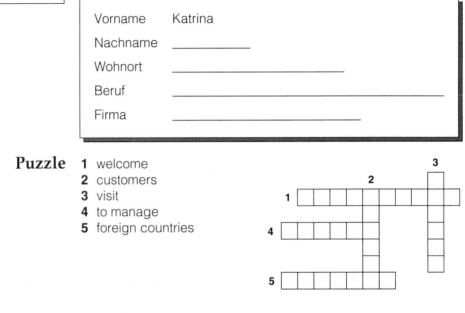

Language structures

Capitals

> **Ich** komme aus **Krefeld.**
> Trinken **Sie** eine Tasse **Kaffee?**
> guten **Tag**
> mit **Milch**
> eine Tasse **Kaffee**

All nouns begin with a capital letter in German.

> ich   *I*
> **Sie**   *you*

The word **ich** only has a capital at the beginning of a sentence.
Sie (meaning *you*) always has a capital.

Verbs   Present tense and infinitive

> ich wohn**e**   *I live*
> ich heiß**e**   *I am called*
> ich komm**e**   *I come*

As a rule, verbs used with **ich** end in **e**.

wohnen	*to live*
heißen	*to be called*
kommen	*to come*

The 'neutral' form of a verb, called the *infinitive*, consists of the stem + ending **en** (sometimes **ern** or **eln**). This is how verbs appear in the dictionary.

Exceptions to the rule are called *irregular* verbs:

sein	*to be*
ich bin	*I am*

Saying that something is not the case:

Ich komme aus Krefeld.
Ich komme **nicht** aus Krefeld.

There is no equivalent of *does not, do not* in German. Instead of saying *I don't come from Krefeld*, say *I come not …* **ich komme nicht …**

Nouns   Feminine ending on nouns

Leiter	Leiter**in**	*manager/manageress*
Telefonist	Telefonist**in**	*telephonist male/female*
Student	Student**in**	*student male/female*

The female version of jobs, professions and nationalities ends with **in**. There are occasional exceptions (**Deutsche, Angestellte**).

The letter ß   This is another way of writing **ss**. There are rules for when to use ß instead of **ss**, but it's not necessary to learn them. For now, just try to remember which words ß occurs in.

Progress check

1 NVQ S1

How would you greet somebody, ask how he/she is, and give some information about yourself in German?
a) Hello   Good morning   Good evening
b) Pleased to meet you.
c) How are you?
d) Fine, thank you.
e) I drink tea with milk.
f) My name is … (*two options*)
g) I come from …
h) I am a sales manager.
i) I don't live in Hamburg.

2 What do the following requests, statements and questions mean?
a) Ich erwarte Sie.
b) Ich arbeite nicht bei der Firma Edelmetall.
c) Woher kommen Sie?
d) Was sind Sie von Beruf?
e) Ich bin für die Betriebsleitung verantwortlich.
f) Bitte füllen Sie diesen Fragebogen aus.

UNIT 2 Sprechen Sie Deutsch?

In this unit, you will learn how to ...

- ask questions
- answer both positively and negatively
- talk about countries, nationalities and languages
- wish somebody a pleasant stay.

Dialogue 1: Auf der Konferenz

During a break at an international gathering in London delegates are getting to know each other.

Teilnehmer A	Sprechen Sie Deutsch?
Teilnehmer B	Ja, ich komme aus Österreich. Und Sie?
Teilnehmer A	Ich bin Deutscher, und meine Kollegin hier ist Schweizerin.
Teilnehmer B	Ach, wie interessant. Ich habe auch eine Kollegin aus der Schweiz. Sie spricht Deutsch, Französisch und Italienisch, und lernt auch Englisch bei der Firma. Aber sie ist nicht hier in London.

Vocabulary

auf der Konferenz *at the conference*
Teilnehmer *participant*
Sprechen Sie ...? *Do you speak ...?*
Deutsch *German (language)*
Österreich *Austria*
Deutscher *German (man)*

Kollegin *colleague (woman)*
Schweizerin *Swiss (woman)*
wie *how*
haben *to have*
aus der Schweiz *from Switzerland*
sprechen *to speak*
sie spricht *she speaks*

Französisch *French*
Italienisch *Italian*
Englisch *English*
lernen *to learn*
aber *but*
ist *is*
nicht *not*

Notes

Sprechen <u>Sie</u> Deutsch?
Aber <u>sie</u> ist nicht hier in London.

Sie *you*
sie *she* (see Summary 1, page 29)

| Exercise 1 |

Answer the questions about delegates at that conference, using the words in the box beside them.

Turn to page 16 for a selective list of countries, their languages and nationalities.

Example: Ist Herr Richoux Deutscher? (F) Nein, Franzose.

Österreicher
Schweizerin
Australier
Französin
Kanadier
Britin

1 Ist Frau Smith Amerikanerin? (GB) _____
2 Ist Herr Jones Ire? (AUS) _____
3 Ist Frau Müller Deutsche? (F) _____
4 Ist Herr Schäfer Deutscher? (A) _____
5 Ist Frau Klein Italienerin? (CH) _____
6 Ist Herr Duchêne Belgier? (C) _____

| Exercise 2 |

Your company has advertised a job for which a German speaker is required. Look at this information sent by one of the applicants.

Vorname	Hans-Dieter
Familienname	Schulz
Staatsangehörigkeit	deutsch
Wohnort	Frankfurt
Beruf	Ingenieur
Sprachen	Deutsch, Englisch

Vocabulary

Vorname *first name*
Familienname *surname*

Staatsangehörigkeit *nationality*

Wohnort *domicile*
Sprachen *languages*

Your company is sending you to work in Germany, and you must complete the same form.

Vorname	_____
Familienname	_____
Staatsangehörigkeit	_____
Wohnort	_____
Beruf	_____
Sprachen	_____

Exercise 3

Study this map, then fill in the missing European countries. Listen to the tape to hear the correct pronunciation of the more difficult ones.

Europa	F_____	Luxemburg	die S_____
Albanien	G_____	Norwegen	Slowenien
B_____	Holland	Ö_____	Sp_____
Dänemark	Ir_____	Polen	Tschechoslowakei
Deutschland	It_____	Portugal	Ungarn
Finnland	(*former*) Jugoslawien	Schweden	

Dialogue 2: Bei Anglia Chemicals 2

Michael Newby takes his two German visitors on a tour of Anglia Chemicals. He introduces them to some of his colleagues, including David Jones, the Sales Director.

David Jones	Guten Tag. Es freut mich, Sie kennenzulernen. Sind Sie zum ersten Mal in England?
Frau Meyer	Ja, ich bin zum ersten Mal hier, aber Herr Weidmann kommt oft nach England.
David Jones	Ich wünsche Ihnen einen guten Aufenthalt.
Ewald Weidmann	Sie sprechen sehr gut Deutsch. Lernen Sie es hier bei Anglia Chemicals?
David Jones	Nein, meine Frau ist Deutsche. Sie kommt aus Dortmund. Wir sprechen Deutsch zu Hause.
Frau Meyer	Entschuldigen Sie, sind Sie vielleicht Waliser? Ihr Name ist walisisch, nicht wahr?
David Jones	Ja, das stimmt, aber ich selbst bin Engländer.

Vocabulary

zum ersten Mal *for the first time*
oft *often*
nach *to*
wünschen *to wish*
Ich wünsche Ihnen einen guten Aufenthalt *I wish you a good stay*

sehr gut *very well*
es *it*
meine Frau *my wife*
zu Hause *at home*
Entschuldigen Sie *Excuse me, sorry*
vielleicht *perhaps*
Ihr *your*

nicht wahr? *isn't that so?*
das stimmt *that's right*
ich selbst *I myself*

Notes

1 **Ich bin zum ersten Mal hier** *I'm here for the first time.*

2 **Herr Weidmann kommt oft nach England** *Mr Weidmann comes to England often.*

3 **Sie sprechen sehr gut Deutsch** *You speak German very well.*

The word order differs from English – this will be discussed in more detail on page 46, Unit 5.

Exercise 4

On the train to a business appointment in London you notice that the passenger next to you has been reading a German newspaper. You seize the opportunity to try out your German. (For details on how to ask questions, refer to page 17.)

Sie   (*Ask if your fellow traveller is German.*)

Reisender   Nein, ich bin Österreicher. Ich heiße Paternolli.
Sie   (*Ask where he comes from.*)

Reisender	Ich wohne in Dornbirn, aber ich arbeite in Feldkirch.
Sie	(*Ask what he does for a living.*)

Reisender	Ich bin Ingenieur.
Sie	(*Ask if this is his first visit to England.*)

Reisender	Ja, ich bin zum ersten Mal hier.
Sie	(*Wish him a pleasant stay.*)

Reisender	Danke sehr.

Vocabulary

Reisender *traveller (male)*

Exercise 5

Here is Mr Paternolli's visiting card for you to study. Try to draw up your own card in German. The following words may be useful.

Vocabulary

Herrn Paternollis
  Visitenkarte *Mr*
  Paternolli's visiting card
Textilwerke *textile works*
Stahlwerk Tübingen
  Tübingen steel works

Metallfabrik *metal factory*
AG (die Aktiengesellschaft)
  public limited company
GmbH (Gesellschaft mit
  beschränkter Haftung)
  limited company

Ing. Eugen Paternolli
Betriebsleiter der Spinnerei Gisingen

fmhämmerleTEXTILWERKE AG

A-6800 Feldkirch
Tel. (05522) 22008

Comprehension 1

You will hear a conversation between two businessmen who have met for the first time over lunch at a trade fair in Germany. Read the questions below first, then listen a few times to what they say. Only then should you answer the following questions.

1 Where does Richard Hill live?
2 Where does he work?
3 What is his job?
4 What does Wilhelm Jaeger do?
5 Why is Richard Hill's German so good?

Vocabulary

welcher? *which?*   **ich glaube** *I believe*

Talking business extra

Comprehension 2

Katrina and Christian need to find out more about researching markets abroad. At breaktime during a conference they discuss the translation service and their competence in the English language.

Key vocabulary

schön *nice, pleasant*
Übersetzungsdienst *translation service*
Kopfhörer *headphones*
Knopf *button*

Marktforschung *market research*
fließend *fluent(ly)*
Redakteur *editor*

Fremdsprachen *foreign languages*
Telefonat *telephone call*

Key phrases

Hoffentlich funktioniert es. — *Let's hope it works.*
Was meinen Sie? — *What do you think?*
Der nächste Programmpunkt ist wichtig. — *The next item on the programme is important*

Es geht — here: *I get by*
Ich nehme Unterricht — *I'm having lessons*
Übung macht den Meister — *practice makes perfect*
im Verlagswesen — *in publishing*
Das kann ich gut verstehen — *I can well understand that*
Ich komme gleich wieder — *I'll be back straight away*

Find out:

1 what is next on the programme
2 how good Katrina's English is.

Exercise 6	Fill in the details:

Es ist sehr <u>schön</u> hier.

Der Übersetzungsdienst ist sehr _____.

Der Programmpunkt _____ _____ _____.

Language structures

Countries, nationalities and languages

COUNTRY	MALE NATIONAL	FEMALE NATIONAL
England	Engländer	Engländerin
Wales	Waliser	Waliserin
Schottland	Schotte	Schottin
Großbritannien	Brite	Britin
Irland	Ire/Irländer	Irin/Irländerin
Amerika	Amerikaner	Amerikanerin
Australien	Australier	Australierin
Kanada	Kanadier	Kanadierin
Deutschland	Deutscher	Deutsche
Österreich	Österreicher	Österreicherin
die Schweiz	Schweizer	Schweizerin
Belgien	Belgier	Belgierin
Frankreich	Franzose	Französin
Italien	Italiener	Italienerin
Spanien	Spanier	Spanierin

Ich komme **aus** Deutschland, **aus** Italien, **aus** Amerika
but: Ich komme aus **der** Schweiz
     Kommen Sie aus **der** Schweiz?

LANGUAGES Englisch, Französisch, Deutsch

ADJECTIVES (*describing nationality*) englisch, walisisch, schottisch, britisch, irisch, amerikanisch, australisch, kanadisch, deutsch, österreichisch, schweizerisch, französisch, italienisch, spanisch

Languages begin with capitals.
Ich spreche Englisch. *I speak English.*

Adjectives don't begin with capitals.
Staatsangehörigkeit: *englisch* nationality: *English*
To express nationality German uses *I am (an) Englishman/woman* rather than *I am English.*

Examples:	Ich bin Engländer(in).	*I am English.*
	Sind Sie Deutscher/Deutsche?	*Are you German?*
	Meine Kollegin ist Irin.	*My colleague is Irish.*

Verbs

Sie wohnen	*you live*	wir wohnen	*we live*
Sie arbeiten	*you work*	wir arbeiten	*we work*
Sie lernen	*you learn*	wir lernen	*we learn*

Verbs used with **Sie** and **wir** end in **en**

Sein *to be* is irregular

> Sie sind   *you are*
> wir sind   *we are*

Questions

1 **Sprechen Sie** Deutsch?   *Do you speak/Are you speaking German?*

Lernen Sie Englisch?   *Do you learn/Are you learning English?*

Sind Sie Deutscher?   *Are you German?*

To form a question, just change the statement around, so that the verb comes first.

Example: Sie sprechen Deutsch. Sprechen Sie Deutsch?

There is no German construction like the English *Do you speak ...?*

2 **Was** sind Sie von Beruf?   *What are you by profession? (What do you do for a living?)*

Woher kommen Sie?   *Where do you come from?*
Wo arbeiten Sie?   *Where do you work?*

This is the same construction as in **1** above, but beginning with a question word.

3 Another way of asking a question is to add question tags such as *aren't you?* and *don't they?* German equivalents are **oder?** or **nicht wahr?**

Examples:
Ihr Name ist walisisch, **nicht wahr?**   *Your name is Welsh,*
Ihr Name ist walisisch, **oder?**   *isn't it?*

Sie wohnen in Frankfurt, **nicht wahr?**   *You live in Frankfurt,*
Sie wohnen in Frankfurt, **oder?**   *don't you?*

Progress check

1 What are the four main countries of the British Isles in German?
2, 3, 4, 5, 6, 7 NVQ S1
2 Ask somebody (first male, then female) about their nationality:
'Are you German, Swiss or French?'
3 Name at least four languages in German which are spoken in these countries:
England, die Schweiz.
4 Ask somebody whether this is his/her first stay in England.
5 Wish him/her a pleasant stay.
6 You have Spanish guests visiting your company. Tell them that you speak Spanish at home.

7 Ask them what they do for a living?
8 Give British equivalents for:
  a) Aktiengesellschaft
  b) Gesellschaft mit beschränkter Haftung?
9 What is the spokesperson of a German delegation telling you here?
'Entschuldigen Sie, aber wir sprechen nicht Englisch.'
10 Read these statements. What is important, and what does not work?
  a) Marktforschung ist für uns sehr wichtig.
  b) Der Übersetzungsdienst funktioniert nicht.

3 Haben Sie eine Familie?

In this unit, you will learn how to …

- talk about your family situation
- ask somebody to spell something
- spell out information on the telephone
- say that you do not have something.

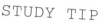

STUDY TIP

Whenever you are working at an exercise where personal information is required and therefore no key can be provided, try to get together with a German speaker to receive feedback on the correctness of your work.

Dialogue: **Beim Essen**

Mr. Lloyd takes his guests out for dinner, and the conversation turns to family life.

Frau Kahn	Haben Sie Kinder, Herr Lloyd?
Mr Lloyd	Ja, wir haben eine kleine Tochter und erwarten im Sommer ein Baby.
Frau Kahn	Das ist ja sehr schön. Unsere Kinder gehen schon zur Schule.
Mr Lloyd	Welche Sprachen lernen sie denn?
Frau Kahn	Ute lernt Englisch und Französisch. Sie ist elf Jahre alt. Jürgen ist neun und spricht auch ein wenig Englisch.

Vocabulary

die Familie *family*	**schön** *nice*	**Jahre** *years*
beim Essen *over dinner*	**gehen** *to go*	**alt** *old*
Kinder *children*	**schon** *already*	**neun** *nine*
kleine Tochter *little daughter*	**zur Schule** *to school*	**ein wenig** *a little*
im Sommer *in the summer*	**welche** *which*	
unsere *our*	**elf** *eleven*	

Notes

1 **Das ist ja sehr schön.** Note the different meanings of **schön** and **schon**.

2 **Welche Sprachen lernen sie denn?** *So which languages are they learning?*

Exercise 1

Here is a family tree of David Johnson's immediate family:

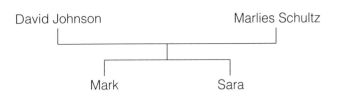

David Johnson   Marlies Schultz

Mark   Sara

Study this description and listen to the recording.

David Johnson ist Engländer. Er ist verheiratet. Seine Frau heißt Marlies und ist Deutsche. Er hat auch einen Sohn und eine Tochter. Der Sohn heißt Mark, und die Tochter heißt Sara.

Vocabulary

verheiratet *married*
seine Frau *his wife*
Er hat einen Sohn *He has a son*

Er hat eine Tochter *He has a daughter*
der Sohn *the son*
die Tochter *the daughter*

1 Now study the following family tree. Then fill in the gaps in the sentences below.

Heinz Preissler   Chantal Dupont

Anneliese

Heinz Preissler _____ Deutscher. Er ist auch

_____. Seine _____ heißt Chantal

und ist _____. Er hat keinen Sohn, nur

_____ Tochter. _____ Tochter heißt

_____.

Vocabulary

Er hat keinen Sohn *He hasn't got a son He has no son*

nur *only*

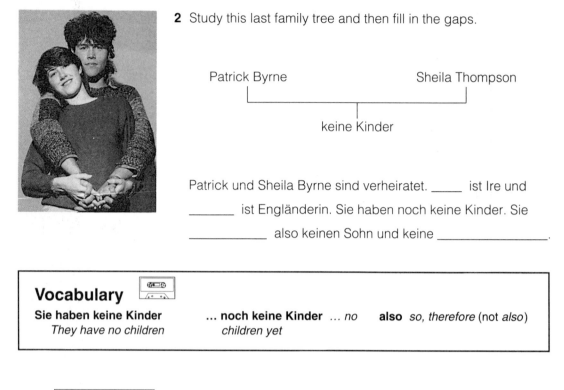

2 Study this last family tree and then fill in the gaps.

Patrick Byrne   Sheila Thompson

keine Kinder

Patrick und Sheila Byrne sind verheiratet. _____ ist Ire und

_____ ist Engländerin. Sie haben noch keine Kinder. Sie

_____ also keinen Sohn und keine _____.

Vocabulary

Sie haben keine Kinder **... noch keine Kinder** ... no **also** so, therefore (not also)
 They have no children   *children yet*

Exercise 2

Here is some information about Frank Lohmann:

Frank wohnt in Köln und arbeitet als Fahrer bei der Firma Schmidt-Möbel. Er ist verheiratet und hat vier Kinder, zwei Söhne und zwei Töchter.

Vocabulary

arbeitet als Fahrer *works as* **vier** *four*   **Töchter** *daughters*
 a driver   **Söhne** *sons*

Now make up similar descriptions for these people:

Name	Wohnort	Beruf	Firma	Familie
Stefan	Bern	Elektroniker	Schmidt AG	verheiratet keine Kinder
Petra	Salzburg	Sekretärin	Deutsche Textilien GmbH	verheiratet 1 Tochter
Sabine	Kiel	Geschäftsführerin	Jung und Sohn GmbH	ledig
Jürgen	Mannheim	Ingenieur	Schäfer-Autowerke AG	verheiratet 2 Söhne

Vocabulary

ledig (unverheiratet) *single, unmarried*

Comprehension 1

Now you'll hear Wolfgang Schüßler and Gudrun Schneider talking about themselves. While listening, try to establish the following information.

1 Is Wolfgang married?
2 Does he work?
3 Where does he live?
4 Is he an architect?
5 Is Gudrun German?
6 What nationality is Gudrun's husband?
7 What does Gudrun do for a living?
8 Is she learning French?
9 Where does her husband work and what does he do?

Vocabulary

Student *student*
unverheiratet *unmarried*
studieren *to study*
Architektur *architecture*
Taxifahrer *taxidriver*
mein, meine *my*

Mutter *mother*
Vater *father*
zu Hause *at home*
jetzt *now*
Mann *husband, man*
ein, eine *a*

Kind *child*
in der Firma *in the firm*
Vertreter *salesman, representative*

Exercise 3

Now it's your turn. With the help of these phrases say as much as you can about yourself.

Ich heiße … Ich wohne … Ich komme aus …
Ich arbeite als … bei …
Ich bin … ich habe …
Ich spreche … ich lerne …
Mein Mann/meine Frau ist …

Exercise 4

Here are some questions about Wolfgang Schüßler and Gudrun Schneider. You may find it useful to listen again to what they say, before completing the answers.

1 Ist Wolfgang Architekt?

   Nein, er_____

2 Ist er verheiratet?

   Nein, er_____

3 Arbeitet er?

Ja, er _____

4 Wo wohnt Wolfgang?

Er _____

5 Wie heißt Gundruns Mann?

Er _____

6 Ist Gudrun Deutsche?

Nein, sie _____

7 Was ist sie von Beruf?

Sie ist _____

8 Lernt Gudrun Französisch?

Nein, sie _____

Exercise 5

Spelling

You may at some time have to spell aloud (**Buchstabieren**) in German. Listen to the pronunciation of the alphabet in German, then repeat each letter.

A Ä B C D E F G H I J K L M N O Ö P Q R S T U Ü
V W X Y Z

For practice at spelling refer to the sounds suggested below and listen carefully to their pronunciation on the tape.

A	ah	**K**	kah	**U**	uh
B	beh	**L**	ell	**V**	fow (as in *now*)
C	tseh	**M**	emm	**W**	veh
D	deh	**N**	enn	**X**	iks
E	eh	**O**	oh	**Y**	ipsilon
F	eff	**P**	peh	**Z**	tsett
G	geh	**Q**	kuh	**Ä**	Ah Umlaut
H	hah	**R**	airr	**Ö**	Oh Umlaut
I	ee	**S**	ess	**Ü**	Uh Umlaut
J	yott	**T**	teh	**ß**	scharfes ess *or* ess-tsett

Exercise 6

The following conversation takes place at the reception desk of a conference centre in Munich. Practise spelling out the names of the British delegates and the places they come from, referring to the taped version to check pronunciation.

Mr Williams   Guten Morgen, John Williams aus Cardiff, in Wales.

Empfangsdame   Guten Morgen, Herr Williams. WILLIAMS, stimmt das?

Mr Williams	Ja, aus Cardiff, ich buchstabiere, CARDIFF.
Empfangsdame	Großbritannien, danke schön.
Mr Williams	Meine Kollegen sind Chris Ryder aus Exeter, Mrs. Janet McGuire, Inverness, und Shaun Reynolds aus Newry in Nordirland.
Empfangsdame	Moment, bitte buchstabieren Sie das …
Mr Williams	CHRIS RYDER, EXETER
	JANET MCGUIRE, INVERNESS
	SHAUN REYNOLDS, NEWRY

Vocabulary

buchstabieren *to spell*
Kollegen *colleagues*

Bitte buchstabieren Sie das **langsam** *slowly*
Please spell that

Exercise 7

Practise these German abbreviations:

DB	**Deutsche Bundesbahn**	*German Railways*
EG	**Europäische Gemeinschaft**	*European Community*
GmbH	**Gesellschaft mit beschränkter Haftung**	*Limited (liability) company, Ltd*
AG	**Aktiengesellschaft**	*Public limited company, plc*
ADAC	**Allgemeiner Deutscher Automobilclub**	*German Automobile Association*
VW	**Volkswagen**	
BMW	**Bayerische Motorenwerke**	

Exercise 8

Now give this personal information:

1 Wie buchstabieren Sie Ihren Familiennamen?
2 Wie buchstabieren Sie Ihren Vornamen?
3 Wie heißt Ihre Firma/Ihre Schule/Ihre Universität? Buchstabieren Sie das.
4 Wie heißt die Stadt, wo Sie wohnen? Buchstabieren Sie das.

Note **Ihr, Ihre, Ihren** *your* (the endings depend on the grammatical context; details on page 60).

Vocabulary

Stadt *city, town*

Talking business extra

Comprehension 2

After an intense meeting with the management at **Spieltechnik GmbH**, the conversation over lunch in the staff canteen is a bit more relaxing. Talking about relatives abroad seems to bring out Christian's sense of humour.

Key vocabulary

Schifahren *skiing*
Verwandte *relatives*

Onkel *uncle*
schnell *fast*

Stunde *hour*
doppelt *double*

Key phrases

aus dem Ausland — *from abroad*
in der Nähe von — *near*
Stimmt! — *(That's) correct!*
Was für ein Zufall — *What a co-incidence*
Wie lange fährt man dahin? — *How long does it take to get there?*
Das ist kein Problem für mich — *That's no problem for me*
nicht einmal — *not even*
Das war nur ein Scherz — *That was only a joke*

Find out:

1 what is said about relatives in Austria
2 how long it would take Christian to drive from Frankfurt to Lienz.

Exercise 9

Fill in the details:

Katrinas Familie

Ihre Mutter ist _____.

Ihr Vater _____ _____.

_____ Mann _____ _____.

Puzzle

All words have double letters in the shaded spaces.

1 (they have) met
2 double
3 correct
4 mother
5 co-incidence
6 fast

Language structures

Articles   *The* and *a*

der Sohn	*the son*
die Tochter	*the daughter*
das Kind	*the child*

The word *the* can be **der**, **die** or **das** in German. Which one to choose depends on what is called the *gender* of the word it goes with. Is it masculine, feminine or neuter? There are very few rules – you simply have to learn the gender with every new noun.

This is how it might look in the dictionary:

Besuch m,	*visit*	m	masculine	i.e. **der** Besuch
Firma f,	*firm*	f	feminine	i.e. **die** Firma
Taxi n,	*taxi*	n	neuter	i.e. **das** Taxi

the   *definite* article
a   *indefinite* article

ein Beruf, **ein** Kind, **ein** Stahlwerk   *a profession, a child, a steelworks*
eine Tochter, **eine** Familie   *a daughter, a family*

a	**ein**	masculine and neuter nouns
	eine	feminine nouns

einen is a different form of the masculine **ein** (details on page 81).

The negative of *a* is **kein**

Whenever **ein**, **eine** is used, you negate simply by putting a **k** in front.

David Johnson hat **eine** Tochter.
David Johnson hat **keine** Tochter (*has no daughter, hasn't a daughter*).
The endings of **kein** are the same as for **ein**. (See Language structures overview, page 27.)

Plurals   Nouns

Unsere Kind**er** gehen zur Schule.	*Our children go to school.*
Welche Sprach**en** lernen sie?	*Which languages are they learning?*
Meine Kolleg**en** sind Chris Ryder Shaun Reynolds und J. McGuire.	*My colleagues are Chris Ryder etc.*

Plural nouns in English usually end in *s* or *es*. In German there are rather more possibilities. Some guidelines are provided in the Language structures overview, page 28, but the safest thing to do is to learn every new noun complete with its gender and plural.

This is how it might look in the dictionary:

Sohn m, (⁻e)	son	der	Sohn	die	Söhne
Tochter f, (⁻)	daughter	die	Tochter	die	Töchter
Sprache f, (-n)	language	die	Sprache	die	Sprachen
Kind n, (-er)	child	das	Kind	die	Kinder

Definite article

The plural of **der**, **die** and **das** is always **die**.

Kein

The plural of **kein** and **keine** is **keine**:
Patrick und Sheila Byrne haben **keine** Kinder *(have no/haven't any)*.

Note that the opposite of *yes* is **nein** as in **nein danke** *no thanks*.

Verbs 1

Ute	**lernt**	Englisch.
Herr Weidmann	**kommt**	oft nach England.
Mein Name	**ist**	Ewald Weidmann.
Patrick Byrne	**hat**	keine Kinder.

Most verbs used with **er**, **sie** (*he, she*), and people or things in the singular end in **t**.

Where the stem of a verb already ends in **t**, the added ending is **et**.

Example: Frau Meyer arbeit**et** bei der Firma Sasshofer.

REGULAR		
heiß**en**	er, sie heißt	*he, she is called*
wohn**en**	er, sie wohnt	*he, she lives, is living*
lern**en**	er, sie lernt	*he, she learns, is learning*
arbeit**en**	er, sie arbeit**et**	*he, she works, is working*

IRREGULAR		
sprechen	er, sie spricht	*he, she speaks, is speaking*
haben	er, sie hat	*he, she has*
sein	er, sie ist	*he, she is*

Jürgen **spricht** Englisch.
Frank **hat** vier Kinder.
Mein Name **ist** Ewald Weidmann.

2

Unsere Kinder	**gehen**	zur Schule.
Herr und Frau Kahn	**haben**	zwei Kinder.
Sie	**heißen**	Ute und Jürgen.

Verbs used with **sie** meaning *they* add **en** to their stem, as with **wir** (*we*) and **Sie** (*you*):

gehen	sie gehen	*they go*
sprechen	sie sprechen	*they speak*
arbeiten	sie arbeiten	*they work*

Exception: **sein** sie sind *they are*

Progress check

1 NVQ W1
You have been asked to supply some personal information. Jot down whether you are married/single/have any children or not. (For numbers see page 38.)

2, 3, 4 and 5 NVQ S1
2 Ask a new business acquaintance about his/her family situation:
a) married?
b) any children?

3 Your company has changed hands and someone new has taken over. Answer a colleague's questions:
a) He is a Scotsman and lives in Glasgow.
b) He is married and has a daughter.

c) He speaks French and is learning German.

4 On a business trip tell your German host about the colleagues with you:
'My colleagues are also here in Frankfurt. They come from Northern Ireland, and work at Northern Metal plc in Bolton near Manchester'.

5 How would you ask somebody to spell something out?

6 NVQ R1
Read these extracts from notes you have received, and supply a rough translation.
a) Ich spreche ein wenig Italienisch, aber meine Verwandten sprechen doppelt so gut.
b) Das ist kein Problem, ich arbeite in der Nähe von Ihnen.

Summary 1
Language structures overview

Articles

	SINGULAR			PLURAL
	MASCULINE	FEMININE	NEUTER	ALL GENDERS
DEFINITE ARTICLE	**der** Mann	**die** Frau	**das** Kind	**die** Fabriken
INDEFINITE ARTICLE	**ein** Mann **kein** Mann	**eine** Frau **keine** Frau	**ein** Kind **kein** Kind	**keine** Fabriken

Ich habe **ein** Kind.   *I have a child*
Ich habe Kinder.   *I have children.*
There is no plural for the indefinite article **ein**, **eine**.

Ich habe **kein** Kind.   *I have no child*
Ich habe **keine** Kinder.   *I have no children.*
The negative form **kein**, **keine** does have a plural – **keine**.

Gender of nouns

1 Male persons are usually *masculine:* **der** Exportleiter
Female persons are usually *feminine:* **die** Tochter
but note: **das** Mädchen (*girl*), **das** Fräulein (*Miss*)

2 Otherwise, the gender of each noun has to be learnt individually. The following guidelines may help.

Most nouns ending in **e** are *feminine*.
All nouns ending in **ung**, **schaft**, **keit**, **heit**, **erei** and **in** are *feminine*.
Most nouns ending in **er** are *masculine*.
Nouns ending in **chen** and **lein** are *neuter*.
Nouns formed from the *infinitive* of verbs are *neuter*.
das Essen *food* (from **essen** *to eat*)

Compound nouns

die	Empfangs**dame**	der Empfang	**die**	Dame
der	Produktions**leiter**	die Produktion	**der**	Leiter
das	Stahl**werk**	der Stahl	**das**	Werk

When nouns are strung together, the last one determines the gender of the whole word.

Plural of nouns

As with gender, there are some guidelines to help:

Most nouns ending in **e** add **n**	**die** Schul**e**	die Schul**en**
Most other *feminine* nouns add **en**	**die** Fabrik	die Fabrik**en**

Feminine nouns ending in **in** add **nen**	**die** Kolleg**in**	**die** Kolleg**innen**
Masculine nouns ending in **er** don't change	**der** Fahr**er**	**die** Fahr**er**
Most foreign nouns commonly used in German add **s**	das Auto	die Auto**s**
Nouns ending in **chen** and **lein** don't change	das Mäd**chen**	die Mäd**chen**

There are several other ways of forming plurals:

add **e**	das Jahr	die Jahr**e**
add an Umlaut	die Tochter	die T**ö**chter
add an Umlaut + **e**	der Zug	die Z**ü**g**e**
add **er**	das Kind	die Kind**er**
add an Umlaut + **er**	das Haus	die H**äu**s**er**

Personal pronouns

SINGULAR		PLURAL	
ich	I	wir	we
du	you (familiar)	ihr	you (familiar)
er, sie, es	he, she, it	sie	they
		Sie	you (formal) sing + plural

You – familiar and formal

There are two new words included in the table above: **du** and **ihr**. Both mean *you*. **Du** is used when the speaker is on close terms with the person addressed, or when speaking to a child. **Ihr** is the same as **du**, but used when speaking to more than one person.

You already know **Sie**. This means *you* (singular or plural) when speaking to adults you only know on a formal level. **Sie** is always the one to use, unless changing to **du** has already been suggested and accepted. (See also cultural briefing on page 32.)

Sie
When pronounced, it sounds as if **sie** could be one of three things: *she, they* or *you*. In practice it is clear from the context or verb ending which is meant.

Das ist Frau Müller. **Sie** lernt Englisch.	This can only be *she*; the context makes it clear, and so does the verb ending **t**.
Herr und Frau Müller sind hier. **Sie** lernen auch Englisch.	**Sie** clearly refers to **Herr und Frau Müller**. It must mean *they*.
Lernen **Sie** Englisch, Herr Müller?	In context **Sie** can only mean *you*, and when you read it, you can also see the capital **S**.

Er, sie, es

Hier ist Herr Weidmann. **Er** wohnt in Neuß.	*He lives in Neuß.*
Das ist Frau Meyer. **Sie** ist Einkaufsleiterin	*She is chief buyer.*
Das ist meine Firma. **Sie** ist in Düsseldorf.	*It is in Düsseldorf.*
Das ist mein Name. **Er** ist französisch.	*It is French.*
Hier ist das Taxi. **Es** ist ein VW.	*It is a VW.*

Er and **sie** refer not only to male and female persons, but also to all masculine and feminine nouns. The word **es** only refers to neuter nouns (**das Kind, das Hotel, das Auto**).

Thus **es** means: *he, she,* or *it* depending on the noun it refers to;
        it when not referring back to a noun.
        (e.g. **Wie geht es Ihnen? Es gibt da Einzelzimmer**.)
        See also Unit 6, page 50.

The present tense

So far we have only met verbs in the present tense, expressing things that are happening now, or which usually happen, or which are true as general statements:

Herr Schmidt **trinkt** (*drinks/is drinking*) Kaffee.
Die Österreicher **sprechen** Deutsch.

The full present tense of a typical regular verb is as follows:

lernen *to learn*	ich lern **e**	wir lern **en**
	du lern **st**	ihr lern **t**
	er, sie, es lern **t**	sie lern **en**
		Sie lern **en**

Most German verbs follow this pattern. The stem stays the same and the relevant ending is added.

Summary 1

Irregular verbs

	sprechen *to speak*	fahren *to travel, to go*	haben *to have*	sein *to be*
ich	spreche	fahre	habe	bin
du	**sprichst**	**fährst**	**hast**	**bist**
er, sie, es	**spricht**	**fährt**	**hat**	**ist**
wir	sprechen	fahren	haben	sind
ihr	sprecht	fahrt	habt	seid
sie	sprechen	fahren	haben	sind
Sie	sprechen	fahren	haben	sind

Almost all so-called irregular verbs are actually regular, except when **du** or **er**, **sie** and **es** are used. The irregularity is then usually a change of vowel, as in **sprechen – er spricht**, or an Umlaut on the **a** or **o** in the stem, as in **fahren – er fährt**. When you learn an irregular verb, it is this change that you need to remember for now. Later on you will learn more about irregularity in different tenses.

Sein is an exception.

Additional exercises

1   Insert the correct verb forms in the following sentences.

a Was _____ Sie von Beruf? (sein)

b Wir _____ in Manchester. (wohnen)

c Ewald Weidmann _____ aus Neuß. (kommen)

d Die Sekretärin _____ für Mr Newby. (arbeiten)

e Mr und Mrs Jones _____ Deutsch. (sprechen)

f Mr Newby _____ Italienisch. (lernen)

g Ich _____ Engländer. (sein)

h Ich _____ Kinder. (haben)

i Ich _____ als Ingenieur. (arbeiten)

j Anneliese _____ Studentin. (sein)

k Mark _____ in London. (wohnen)

l Herr Mannheim _____ zwei Söhne. (haben)

2   **der**, **die** or **das**? Complete the gaps.

a _____ Geschäftsführer heißt Herr Newby.

b _____ Frau heißt Ingrid.

c _____ Kind heißt Eva.

d _____ Sekretärin ist verheiratet.

e _____ Fahrer ist Waliser.

f _____ Kinder gehen zur Schule.

g _____ Engländer kommt aus London.

h _____ Amerikanerinnen sind zum ersten Mal in England.

i _____ Taxi kommt gleich.

3 *You, she* or *they*? Decide which is meant.
a Unsere Kinder gehen schon zur Schule. **Sie** lernen Deutsch.
b Lernen **Sie** ein wenig Italienisch?
c Meine Tochter heißt Susanne. **Sie** ist Exportleiterin.
d Arbeiten **sie** bei Siemens?
e Fährt **sie** morgens zur Arbeit?
f **Sie** trinken Kaffee, Herr Williams, oder?

4 Make these sentences negative.

Example A: Wir haben **ein** Kind.
Wir haben **kein** Kind.

a Herr und Frau Richards haben einen Sohn.
b Herr Müller hat eine Sekretärin.
c Ich habe Kinder.

Example B: Gertraud Reiter arbeitet als Sekretärin
Gertraud Reiter arbeitet **nicht** als Sekretärin

d Die Empfangsdame lernt Spanisch.
e Rainer studiert in Hamburg.
f Mein Mann kommt aus der Schweiz.
g Unsere Angestellten sprechen Französisch.

Key phrases

Greeting people	Guten Morgen, guten Tag, guten Abend
Introducing oneself and others	Ich heiße… Mein Name ist…
	Es freut mich, Sie kennenzulernen
	Es freut mich auch
Saying where someone comes from	Ich komme aus…
	Ich wohne in…
	Ich bin Engländer/Engländerin
Giving information about one's work	Ich bin Dolmetscher/Dolmetscherin
	Ich arbeite als Sekretärin…
	Ich arbeite bei der Firma…
Asking how someone is and replying	Wie geht es Ihnen? Danke, gut, und Ihnen?
	Danke, auch gut
Paying and receiving a compliment	Sie sprechen sehr gut Deutsch
	Danke (schön)
Saying how often one has been somewhere	Ich bin zum ersten Mal hier
	Ich komme oft nach England
Wishing someone a pleasant stay	Ich wünsche Ihnen einen guten Aufenthalt

Cultural briefing

Wir sollten zum 'Du' kommen!

Sie and du

German distinguishes between a formal *you* **Sie**, and an informal *you* **du**. Use **Sie** for all formal contacts and only change to **du** when it is suggested. If you have got to know somebody more personally and you are senior, you may wish to suggest it yourself over a meal or a glass of wine. Normally the older person suggests changing to **du** to the younger, the woman to the man.

Du is also used with children (up to around 16), and family pets.

First names

Germans remain formal much longer than the British. Don't expect to use first names with business counterparts any sooner than a change from **Sie** to **du**. But once this change has been made, you know you've gained a friend!

Fräulein

Fräulein (abbreviated to **Frl.**) means *Miss*. Nowadays it is mainly used for teenage girls. From around 18 years onwards women can be addressed as **Frau**, carrying the neutral idea of Ms; in more traditional usage, any unmarried woman is addressed as **Fräulein**.

Pronunciation

ä ö ü

These vowels all have a short or long version.

ä	short like *e* in *men*	Engländer, Geschäftsführer
	long like *air*	Sekretärin
ö	short like *e* in *father*	Töchter
	long like *i* in *firm*	schön, Österreich, Französisch
		Söhne
ü	no English equivalent	try to say *i* as in *hit*, but with your lips rounded
	short	München, Düsseldorf, wünschen
	long	Tübingen, Geschäftsführer

English equivalent sounds are only approximations – the only way to come close to the German is by imitating exactly what you hear.

UNIT

4 Wann fahren Sie?

In this unit, you will learn how to …

- count in German and ask for the date
- arrange dates for a business trip
- start a telephone conversation
- ask to speak to somebody on the telephone.

STUDY TIP

There are lots of ways to learn new vocabulary, some of which may suit you more than others. When you learn a new noun, for example, say **der Zug**, **die Züge**, preferably aloud and several times over. Find where the word was used and say the whole sentence several times. If you can change the sentence, do so, or produce a completely new version with the new word in it and say the new version aloud. LEARN NEW WORDS IN A CONTEXT.

Dialogue: **Am Telefon 1**

The negotiations between Sasshofer AG and Anglia Chemicals plc were a great success and a promising business relationship has begun. Very shortly after the visit of the Germans to England, Michael Newby is invited by his opposite number, Herbert Walter, to visit Sasshofer AG. The respective secretaries make the necessary arrangements on the telephone. Here is part one of their conversation.

Telefonist	Sasshofer AG. Guten Tag.
Andrea Morgan	Guten Tag. Hier Anglia Chemicals. Ich möchte bitte Frau Steiner sprechen.
Telefonist	Augenblick bitte. Ich verbinde.
Frau Steiner	Steiner. Guten Tag.
Andrea Morgan	Guten Tag, Frau Steiner. Hier Andrea Morgan von der Firma Anglia Chemicals. Ich bin die Sekretärin vom Geschäftsführer, Mr. Michael Newby.
Frau Steiner	Ach ja. Mr Newby kommt bald zu Besuch, nicht wahr?
Andrea Morgan	Ja richtig.
Frau Steiner	Gut. Wann kommt Mr Newby nach Deutschland?

Andrea Morgan	Er möchte am vierten Oktober kommen und drei Tage in Mönchengladbach bleiben. Geht das?
Frau Steiner	Moment bitte … (*She checks in her diary*) Ja, das geht.

Vocabulary

fahren *to travel*
ich (er, sie) möchte *I (he, she) would like* (from **mögen** – *to like*)
wir, sie, Sie möchten *we, they, you would like*
Augenblick bitte *Just a moment please*
verbinden *to connect*
von der Firma Anglia Chemicals *from Anglia Chemicals*

vom = von dem *of the*
bald *soon*
zu Besuch kommen *to come for a visit*
ja richtig *that's right*
wann? *when?*
nach Deutschland *to Germany*
am vierten Oktober *on the 4th of October*
drei *three*
der Tag, -e *day*

bleiben *to stay*
Moment bitte *One moment, please*
Geht das? *Is that OK?*
Ja, das geht *Yes, that's fine (OK)*

Notes

1 **Ich möchte Frau Steiner sprechen.** When there are two verbs in a sentence, the second one goes to the end.

2 **Er möchte am vierten Oktober kommen und (er möchte) drei Tage in Mönchengladbach bleiben.** **Möchte** in this sentence refers to **kommen** as well as **bleiben**, i.e. … *would like to come … and to stay …*

Turn to pages 38–40 and work through the language notes before you attempt the next four exercises.

Comprehension 1

Listen to the following questions and answers and pick out the answer in each one. The first has been done for you.

1 Wann kommt Herr Schmidt?   Am 4. Mai

2 Wann fliegt Herr Johnson nach Deutschland?
3 Wann besuchen Sie die Firma Sasshofer?
4 Wann kommen Sie nach Düsseldorf?
5 Wann fährt Frau Young nach Mönchengladbach?
6 Wann kommen Sie zu Besuch?

Note: **4. Mai**   *4th of May*

Vocabulary

fliegen *to fly*

fahren (er, sie, es fährt) *to travel*

| **Exercise 1** | Here are the plans of some of the personnel of Anglia Chemicals. Frau Steiner's queries on staff arrangements are printed out below. Take the part of Andrea Morgan and answer each question with the help of the table. |

Example: Wann kommt Mr. Smith nach Altrincham, und wie
lange möchte er bleiben? Drei Tage? Eine Woche?
You   Er kommt am Freitag, dem vierten November,
und möchte drei Tage bleiben.

Vocabulary

wie lange? *how long?*   **die Woche, -n** *week*

Mr Smith	visit to Germany	Friday 4.11.	3 days
Mrs Johnson	flight to Düsseldorf	Thursday 9.6.	5 days
Mr Turner	visit to Sasshofer	Monday 1.2.	2 days
Miss Thompson	visit to Germany	Wednesday 6.7.	1 week

1 Wann fliegt Mrs Johnson nach Düsseldorf und wie lange
möchte sie bleiben?

_____

2 Wann besucht Mr Turner die Firma Sasshofer und wie lange
möchte er bleiben?

_____

3 Wann kommt Miss Thompson nach Deutschland und wie
lange möchte sie bleiben?

_____

| **Exercise 2** | Use the above table to answer these questions. |

Example: Wie lange bleibt Mr Smith in Deutschland?
           You   Vom vierten bis zum siebten November.

1 Wie lange bleibt Mrs Johnson in Düsseldorf?

_____

2 Wie lange bleibt Mr Turner bei der Firma Sasshofer?

_____

3 Wie lange bleibt Miss Thompson in Deutschland?

_____

| **Exercise 3** | Listen to the cassette and write down the dates as they are dictated to you. |

Vocabulary

die Messe, -n *trade fair*　　　**zur Messe** *to the trade fair*

| **Exercise 4** | These are the dates of some public holidays in all or some parts of Germany, Austria and Switzerland. |

Feiertage	Tag	Monat	Holidays
Silvester	31	12	New Year's Eve
Tag der Arbeit	1	5	May Day
Weihnachten	25	12	Christmas
Zweiter Weihnachtstag	26	12	Boxing Day
Neujahr	1	1	New Year's Day
Allerheiligen	1	11	All Saints' Day

Die Jahreszeiten	The seasons
der Frühling	spring
der Sommer	summer
der Herbst	autumn
der Winter	winter

1 Practise reading each date in German.
　Example: Silvester ist *am* einunddreißigst*en* Dezember.
2 Practise saying in which season the holidays occur.
　Example: Silvester ist *im* Winter.

Talking business extra

Comprehension 2　Christian phones to arrange a date to finalise the design of **Spieltechnik's** English language brochure. They soon realise how tight their time schedule is, and Katrina needs it finished soon.

Key vocabulary

die Exportabteilung, -en
　export department
die Gestaltung, -en *layout, design*
die Broschüre, -n *brochure*

der Kunde, -n *customer*
besprechen *to discuss*
die Sitzung, -en *meeting*
das Werbematerial
　advertising material

fertig *ready*
eventuell *possibly*

Key phrases

am Apparat	*speaking* (on the phone)
Wann hätten Sie Zeit?	*When would you have time?*
Das wäre möglich	*That would be possible*
im Haus	*in the office*
Ich habe frei	*I'm off (free)*
aus den Vereinigten Staaten	*from the United States*
So lange können wir nicht warten	*We can't wait as long as that*
ganz meine Meinung	*I agree entirely*
Ich rufe Sie zurück	*I'll call you back*
Geht in Ordnung	*That's fine*

Find out:

1 why this week is out for Katrina
2 whether Katrina has a little time this afternoon.

Exercise 5

Fill in the details:

Am 28. April hat Katrina Zeit.

_____ _____ _____ ist Christian nicht im Haus.

_____ _____ _____ fährt Christian nach München.

_____ ____ _____ ist Feiertag.

_____ ____ _____ hat Katrina frei.

_____ ____ _____ da geht's, aber ....

Puzzle
1 export department
2 to discuss
3 advertising material
4 meeting
5 design
6 clue: all done

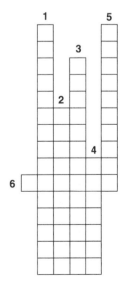

Language structures

**Numbers 0–1000
(die Zahlen)**

Note that numbers in bold type do not follow the usual rules.

CARDINAL NUMBERS	ORDINAL NUMBERS
0 null	
1 eins	1st **erste**
2 zwei (zwo)	2nd zweite (zwote)
3 drei	3rd **dritte**
4 vier	4th vierte
5 fünf	5th fünfte
6 sechs	6th sechste
7 sieben	7th **siebte**
8 acht	8th achte
9 neun	9th neunte
10 zehn	10th zehnte
11 elf	11th elfte
12 zwölf	12th zwölfte

When **eins** does not stand alone or come at the end of a number, it loses the **s**, e.g. **einundzwanzig** but **hunderteins**

	-th = **-te**
13 dreizehn	13th dreizehnte
14 vierzehn	14th vierzehnte
15 fünfzehn	15th fünfzehnte
16 **sechzehn**	16th sechzehnte
17 **siebzehn**	17th siebzehnte
18 achtzehn	18th achtzehnte
19 neunzehn	19th neunzehnte

-teen = **-zehn**	*-teenth* = **-zehnte**
20 **zwanzig**	20th zwanzigste
21 einundzwanzig	21st einundzwanzigste
22 zweiundzwanzig	22nd zweiundzwanzigste
23 dreiundzwanzig	23rd dreiundzwanzigste

-ty = **-zig**	*-tieth* = **-zigste**
30 **dreißig**	30th dreißigste
31 einunddreißig	31st einunddreißigste

-ßig is an exception

40 vierzig	40th vierzigste
50 fünfzig	50th fünfzigste
60 **sechzig**	60th sechzigste
70 **siebzig**	70th siebzigste
80 achtzig	80th achtzigste
90 neunzig	90th neunzigste

100	hundert (einhundert)	100th	hundertste (einhundertste)
101	hunderteins		
102	hundertzwei		
200	zweihundert	200th	zweihundertste
300	dreihundert	300th	dreihundertste
1000	tausend	1000th	tausendste

1992 tausendneunhundertzweiundneunzig *or* im Jahr(e)
neunzehnhundertzweiundneunzig (*in the year 1992*).
German numbers are written as one single word.

The date
(das Datum)

Der wievielte ist heute?	*What is the date* today?
Der wievielte is morgen?	What is the date tomorrow?
Der wievielte war gestern?	What was the date yesterday?
Heute ist der erste Januar.	*Today* is the 1st of January.
Morgen ist der zweite Januar.	*Tomorrow* is the 2nd of January.
Übermorgen ist der dritte Januar.	*The day after tomorrow* is the 3rd of January.
Gestern war der einunddreißigste Dezember.	*Yesterday* was the 31st of December.
Vorgestern war der *dreißigste* Dezember.	The day before yesterday was the 30th of December.
Wann kommt Herr Newby zu Besuch?	*When* is Mr Newby coming for a visit?
Wie lange bleibt er?	*How long* is he staying?
Er kommt *am* fünfte*n* Februar.	He is coming *on the* 5th of February.
Er bleibt *bis* (*zum*) siebte*n* Februar.	He is staying *till* the 7th of February.
Er ist *vom* fünfte*n bis* (*zum*) siebte*n* in Deutschland.	He is in Germany *from the* 5th *to the* 7th.
Er ist *von* Montag *bis* Freitag in München.	He is in Munich *from* Monday *till* Friday.
Wann haben Sie Geburtstag?	When is your birthday?
Am zwanzigste*n* August.	*On the* 20th of August.

DAYS OF THE WEEK
(die Wochentage)

Montag	*Monday*	**Samstag**	*Saturday*
Dienstag	*Tuesday*	(or **Sonnabend**, in northern
Mittwoch	*Wednesday*	Germany)
Donnerstag	*Thursday*	**Sonntag**	*Sunday*
Freitag	*Friday*		

MONTHS OF THE YEAR (die Monate des Jahres)	
Januar	*January*
Februar	*February*
März	*March*
April	*April*
Mai	*May*
Juni	*June*
Juli	*July*
August	*August*
September	*September*
Oktober	*October*
November	*November*
Dezember	*December*

The days of the week and names of months are masculine: **der Montag, der Mai** and so on.

Note the following:

am Montag	*on Monday*	**montags**	*every Monday*	**im März**	*in March*
am Dienstag	*on Tuesday*	**dienstags**	*every Tuesday*	**im April**	*in April*

Vocabulary

die Zahl, -en *number*
das Jahr, -e *year*
das Datum, Daten *date*
heute *today*
morgen *tomorrow*

übermorgen *the day after tomorrow*
gestern *yesterday*
vorgestern *day before yesterday*

bis *till*
der Geburtstag, -e *birthday*
der Feiertag, -e *national holiday*
die Jahreszeit, -en *season*

Progress check

1, 2 and 3 NVQ S1
1. How would you introduce yourself and your firm on the phone?
2. Ask to speak to Mrs Blohm.
3. Inquire about Mr Grün's forthcoming business trip (the line is not very clear and your questions have to be very detailed):
   a) When is he coming to England?
   b) How long is he staying?
   c) Would he like to stay for a week?
   d) Is he staying till Wednesday?

4 NVQ W1
The following points need to be faxed today:
   a) You would like to come in March.
   b) You would like to come on Tuesday, 5th March.
   c) You would like to stay from the 5th to the 7th.

5. Answer the following in German:
   a) Wann haben Sie Geburtstag?
   b) Der wievielte ist heute?
6. You need to draw up a year planner in German. Make a list of the following:
   a) the days of the week
   b) the months of the year.
7. Give these phone numbers in German:
   12–19–04   22–35–16   57–93–01

8 NVQ R2
Read these messages which have been faxed through to you, and translate them for your colleague.
   a) Wir möchten das Werbematerial in der Sitzung besprechen.
   b) Die Broschüre ist eventuell übermorgen fertig.

5 Ich möchte ein Zimmer reservieren

In this unit, you will learn how to ...

- make travel arrangements on the telephone
- arrange hotel accommodation by telephone
- read a telex
- end a telephone conversation.

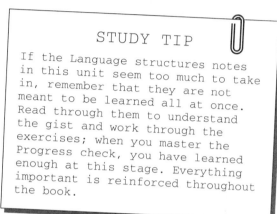

STUDY TIP

If the Language structures notes in this unit seem too much to take in, remember that they are not meant to be learned all at once. Read through them to understand the gist and work through the exercises; when you master the Progress check, you have learned enough at this stage. Everything important is reinforced throughout the book.

Dialogue: Am Telefon 2

Frau Steiner has checked in her diary and established that the 4th of October is convenient for Mr. Newby's proposed visit to Sasshofer. Here is the continuation of her conversation with Andrea Morgan on the telephone from pages 33–4.

Frau Steiner	Ja, das geht. Soll ich ein Hotelzimmer für ihn reservieren?
Andrea Morgan	Ein Einzelzimmer, bitte.
Frau Steiner	Mit Bad oder Dusche?
Andrea Morgan	Mit Bad, bitte.
Frau Steiner	Fliegt er nach Düsseldorf?
Andrea Morgan	Ja, er fliegt von Manchester ab. Er kommt um zehn Uhr am Flughafen an. Dann fährt er mit der Bahn weiter. Der Zug ist um halb zwölf in Mönchengladbach.
Frau Steiner	Ja gut. Herr Walter holt ihn dann vom Bahnhof ab.
Andrea Morgan	Danke für Ihre Hilfe.
Frau Steiner	Gern geschehen. Auf Wiederhören.
Andrea Morgan	Auf Wiederhören.

Vocabulary

Soll ich ...? *Should I ...?*
das Hotelzimmer, - *hotel room*
für ihn *for him*
reservieren *to reserve*
das Einzelzimmer, - *single room*
das Bad, ⁻er *bath*
die Dusche, -n *shower*
abfliegen *to leave (by air)*
ankommen *to arrive*

um zehn Uhr *at 10 o'clock*
die Uhr, -en *clock, watch*
am Flughafen *at the airport*
weiterfahren *to continue (by means of transport)*
weiter *further*
mit der Bahn *by rail*
die Bahn, - *railway*
der Zug, ⁻e *train*
um halb zwölf *at half past eleven*

abholen *to fetch, to meet*
vom Bahnhof *from the station*
der Bahnhof, ⁻e *station*
Danke für Ihre Hilfe *Thank you for your help*
Gern geschehen *You're welcome*

Notes

1 **Er fliegt von Manchester ab.**
Abfliegen, ankommen, weiterfahren, abholen are separable verbs (see page 45).

2 **Danke für Ihre Hilfe** *Thank you for your help.* Remember that *you* and *your* (polite form) begin with a capital in German.

Exercise 1

The arrangements for Mr. Newby's visit are later confirmed by telex. Read the telex, then answer the questions.

> BESUCH VON MR M NEWBY. 4.–7. OKTOBER.
> ANKUNFT AM FLUGHAFEN 10.00 UHR.
> FLUG NR. LH 322. HOTELRESERVIERUNG: HOTEL COENEN.
> EINZELZIMMER MIT BAD. 4.–7.OKTOBER.
> ERWARTE MR NEWBY AM MONTAG, 4. OKTOBER, UM 11.30 UHR.
> MFG STEINER

Vocabulary

das Fernschreiben, - *telex*
die Ankunft, ⁻e *arrival*
Flug Nr. *flight number*

der Flug, ⁻e
die Nummer, -n (Nr.) *number*

die Reservierung, -en *reservation*
MFG *with kind regards*

Notes

1 **11.30 Uhr** read **elf Uhr dreißig**.
2 **MFG** This abbreviation is the standard ending to a telex. It is short for **mit freundlichen Grüßen**.
3 Umlauts cannot be used, therefore you

insert **e** after the vowel, e.g. **fuer, faehrt, Coenen**.
4 The telex is still widely used in Germany, although fast being replaced by the fax (**Das Telefax** or simply **das Fax**).

1 How is Mr. Newby travelling to Düsseldorf?
2 At what time will he arrive there?
3 At what time will he arrive in Mönchengladbach?
4 What two things do we know about his hotel accommodation?

Exercise 2	Complete the sentences of the first column with an item from the second column.

1 Die Sekretärin holt Herrn Kranz …

2 Herr und Frau Kaiser kommen …

3 Der Vertreter fährt am Mittwoch …

4 Ich fahre mit dem Auto zur …

a) um halb drei am Flughafen an.

b) Firma in London.

c) vom Bahnhof ab.

d) nach Wien weiter.

Exercise 3	The table below outlines the travel plans of some of your colleagues who will be attending business meetings at your parent company in Germany. Using the information in the table, advise the parent company of their plans.

Examples: **1** Doug Jones fährt am Samstag von London Euston ab.

2 Die Ingenieure fahren am Donnerstag mit dem Auto nach Deutschland.

You will need the following prepositions: **mit, in, von, am, nach, zur.**

(Details of prepositions can be found on pages 47–8.)

		Time	Manner (der or dem)	Place
1 Doug Jones	abfahren	Samstag	–	London/Euston
2 Die Ingenieure	fahren	Donnerstag	mit … Auto	Deutschland
3 Kate Wilson	abfliegen	Montag	–	London/Heathrow
4 Sue Evans	ankommen	Dienstag	mit … Bahn	Heidelberg
5 John Ward	ankommen	Mittwoch	–	Flughafen
6 Mike Wood	fliegen	Freitag	–	Berlin
7 Ann Smith	fahren	Samstag	mit … Taxi	Firma in Goßlar

Comprehension 1   Look at the following questions before you listen to the telephonist at the Hotel Bergerhof in Düsseldorf, who has just received a call from England.

Vocabulary

nächste *next*   **wie viele?** *how many?*   **werden** *will*

1 What type of hotel accommodation does Mrs Smith require?

2 For how many people?

3 When will they arrive?

4 How long will they be staying for?

5 How are they travelling to Germany?

6 What does the telephonist recommend?

| Exercise 4 | Now it's your turn to make the arrangements. Take the part of an export assistant who has telephoned the Maschinenfabrik Rieter AG in Winterthur to arrange for her boss's forthcoming visit. |

Rieter AG   Wann möchte Mr Hodgkins in die Schweiz kommen?

Sie   (*Say he would like to come on the 14th of June and to stay in Winterthur for two days. Ask if that is possible.*)

_____

Rieter AG   Moment mal … Ja, das geht. Soll ich ein Hotel-zimmer für ihn reservieren?

Sie   (*Say yes please.*)

_____

Rieter AG   Ich empfehle das Hotel Reinhart. Da gibt es Einzel- und Doppelzimmer mit Bad oder mit Dusche. Was soll ich reservieren?

Sie   (*Say a single room with a bathroom.*)

_____

Rieter AG   Fliegt Herr Hodgkins nach Zürich?

Sie   (*Say yes, he is flying from Manchester to Zürich. Then he will continue his journey by rail. He will arrive at the airport at 15.30.*)

_____

Talking business extra

Comprehension 2

Katrina can't get hold of Christian and has to leave a message. A secretary at **Verlag Germania** promises to confirm the arrangements.

Key vocabulary

der Termin, -e *appointment*
vorher *beforehand*

die Produktliteratur, - *product literature*

bestätigen *to confirm*
zurückrufen *to call back*

Key phrases

im Moment nicht zu sprechen   *not available at the moment*
mitten in einer Betriebsführung   *in the middle of a tour of the company*
Worum geht es?   *What is it about?*
Es geht um …   *It's about …*
Kann ich ihm (ihr) etwas ausrichten?   *Can I pass on a message to him (her)?*

mit dem Wagen unterwegs	*out in the car*
gegen zwei	*around two (o'clock)*
zwischen zwei und drei	*between two and three (o'clock)*

Find out:

1 why Katrina can't stay later than 3.00 p.m

2 what Katrina is asking Frau Koller to do before lunch.

> **Exercise 5**

Fill in the details:

Um vier Uhr bin ich am Flughafen.

Gegen _____ _____ komme ich zu Ihnen.

Bis _____ _____ habe ich Zeit.

Zwischen _____ und __ _____ ist die Besprechung.

Vor _____ _____ rufe ich zurück.

Language structures

Verbs One verb in a sentence

Herr Newby **kommt** bald zu Besuch.
Hier **ist** Mr. Newby (*or* Mr. Newby **ist** hier).
Am Abend **bin** ich in Düsseldorf.
Ich **bin** am Abend in Düsseldorf.

The verb stands as the *second idea* in a statement.
(Remember that in a question the verb goes to the beginning, unless it is preceded by a question word, see Unit 2, page 17.)

Two verbs in a sentence

Herr Newby **möchte** am 4. Oktober **kommen**.
Soll ich ein Hotelzimmer **reservieren**?
Was **soll** ich **reservieren**?

If there are two verbs in a sentence, the second goes to the end of the sentence, as an infinitive.

Separable verbs

Er **fliegt** von Manchester **ab**.
Er **kommt** um zehn Uhr in Düsseldorf **an**.
Herr Walter **holt** ihn vom Bahnhof **ab**.

These are verbs with prefixes such as **ab**, **an**, **auf**, **aus**, **mit**, **nach** and **zu**.
In sentences with only a separable verb, the prefix separates from the verb and goes to the end of the sentence. From now on, (*sep*) will appear after a separable verb in the vocabulary lists.

Word order Die Ingenieure fahren am Donnerstag mit dem Auto nach Köln.
                                    Time   *Manner*   *Place*

The order of ideas in German sentences is:
Time (when?)   *Manner* (how?)   *Place* (where?)

Cases Some examples of how English uses cases:

Between you and *me* (from *I*)
The secretary*'s* voice (*of* the secretary)
We follow *him* in the car (from *he*)
To *whom* shall we refer the matter? (from *who*)

The German language makes greater use of case endings than English. For example, whereas *the* always remains *the*, even when used in different cases, the German **der**, **die** and **das** often take on a different form when used in a different case.

There are four cases in German, two of which, the nominative and accusative, are explained on the opposite page.

NOMINATIVE CASE
Ich fahre nach Deutschland.   subject
Mark ist **der Sohn**.   after **sein**
Meine Kollegin spricht Deutsch.   subject
Wann kommt **er** zu Besuch?   subject

ACCUSATIVE CASE
Der Direktor erwartet **mich**.   direct object
Die Mutter holt **den Sohn** vom   direct object
  Bahnhof ab.
Haben Sie **eine Kollegin** in der   direct object
  Schweiz?
Soll ich **ein Zimmer** für **ihn**   direct object
  reservieren?   and after **für**

DATIVE CASE
(see Unit 8, pages 79–80)
Die Sekretärin wünscht **mir**   indirect object
  einen guten Aufenthalt.
Der Vater fährt mit **dem Sohn**   after **mit**
  nach Schottland.
Hier ist das Auto von **einer**   after **von**
  Kollegin.
Fliegen Sie mit **ihm**?   after **mit**

GENITIVE CASE
(see Unit 9, pages 92–3)

The nominative case

Uses:

1 As the *subject* of a sentence (*who or what is doing* something).
2 After the verb **sein** (**bin, ist, sind**).
   Just as an equals sign = commands an equal amount on either side, so the word *is* needs a nominative case before as well as after it.

The accusative case

Uses:

1 As the *direct object* of a sentence (the object of an action, the thing or person having something done to it, him or her).
2 After certain prepositions (**für, ohne, um**, etc.)

FORMATION

der Mann	*becomes*	de**n** Mann
ein Moment		eine**n** Moment
kein Tag		kein**en** Tag
mein Sohn		mein**en** Sohn
ich		mich
er		ihn
wir		uns

Other words we have used stay the same
(die, das, eine, ein [*neuter*], sie, Sie, es).

There are a few masculine nouns which add **n** or **en** in *all cases* except the nominative singular (e.g. der Herr, **den** Herr**n**). For more examples see Unit 8, page 80.

For a summary of case endings see Language structures overview, page 81.

Prepositions   Kaffee **mit** Milch und **ohne** Zucker.
Frau Meyer arbeitet **bei** der Firma Sasshofer.
Sind Sie **zum** ersten Mal in England?
Soll ich ein Hotelzimmer **für** ihn reservieren?

Prepositions are linking words which usually come just before nouns or pronouns and determine their case, although this is not always obvious (e.g. Kaffee **ohne** Zucker, **zu** Hause). The following have been met so far:

1 Prepositions followed by the accusative case

für	*for*	für mich und meine Kollegen
ohne	*without*	Kaffee ohne Zucker
		Wir fliegen ohne den Verkaufsleiter
um	*at (time)*	um zehn Uhr

2 Prepositions followed by the dative case

aus	*from*	Besuch aus Deutschland, aus der Schweiz
mit	*with*	Tee mit Milch
		Ich fahre mit der Bahn weiter
bei	*at (place)*	bei der Firma Sasshofer
	near	Neuß bei Düsseldorf
zu	*at*	Wir sprechen Deutsch zu Hause
	to	Ich gehe zu den Taxis
von	*of*	Andrea Morgan von der Firma Sasshofer
auf*	*on, at*	Er ist in München auf Besuch
		Auf der Konferenz
in*	*in*	Ich wohne in der Nähe von der Grenze
nach	*to, after*	Er fliegt nach Deutschland
		Nach dem Essen

3 Some prepositions can be joined with the definite article to make one word.

zur	**zu der**	Unsere Kinder gehen zur Schule
vom	**von dem**	die Sekretärin vom Geschäftsführer
zum	**zu dem**	vom Bahnhof zum Flughafen
am	**an (*) dem**	Er kommt am Freitag, dem 4.Oktober

*Can also be used with the accusative, see page 59.

Note: Er fliegt am Montag **nach** Deutschland … *to Germany*
Sie fährt mit dem Taxi **zur** Firma … *to the firm*

to **nach** in conjunction with countries and place names (**nach London**)

to **zu** in conjunction with a location within town, city or village (**zum Bahnhof**)

See the summary of prepositions on pages 58–9.

Progress check

1, 2 and 4 NVQ S1

1 What would you say to reserve a single room with bathroom?

2 On the phone to a German colleague, ask about his/her travel arrangements:
  a) When are you coming for a visit?
  b) Are you flying from Munich?
  c) When are you arriving in London?
  d) Shall I reserve a hotel room?

3 NVQ W1

  Send a telex/fax with the following information:
  a) He is leaving from Heathrow on 12th December.
  b) Arrival at Zürich airport at 11.00 a.m.

  c) The train arrives at Winterthur in the evening.
  d) Miss Evans will fetch him from the station.
  e) They are going to the firm by car.

4 NVQ S1

  Ending a telephone conversation with a German colleague, thank her for her help and say good-bye.

5 What does **MFG** mean in a telex?

6 NVQ R2

  You can't help reading a large note on the PA's desk. What is the information on it?
  a) Der Betriebsleiter telefoniert im Moment und ist leider nicht zu sprechen.
  b) Es geht um die Zimmerreservierung.

UNIT **6** Wie spät ist es?

In this unit, you will learn how to …

- ask and tell the time
- discuss a time schedule
- talk about the future.

> ### STUDY TIP
>
> Questions on recorded items you're asked to listen to are not intended to test you. They should focus your mind on the most important elements, and give you clues about what in particular to listen for. So it's often useful to study the questions carefully *before* you listen. Don't be annoyed with yourself if you need to listen several times before you have the answer.

Dialogue: Im Auto

David Jones, the sales director of Anglia Chemicals, is on a business trip in Germany. His German colleague is taking him to a one-day conference. On the way they discuss the programme.

David Jones	Ich glaube, meine Uhr stimmt nicht. Wie spät ist es denn?
Petra Winkler	Es ist jetzt fast halb neun. Die Konferenz beginnt um Viertel nach neun.
David Jones	Und wie lange brauchen wir noch zum Tagungszentrum?
Petra Winkler	Ach, nur ungefähr fünfzehn Minuten.
David Jones	Gut, wir werden also noch rechtzeitig ankommen.
Petra Winkler	Am Vormittag gibt es zwei Vorträge und dann eine Stunde Mittagspause.
David Jones	Wie lange dauert das Nachmittagsprogramm? Ich muß noch auf die Bank.
Petra Winkler	Das wird kein Problem sein. Die Tagung endet schon um Viertel vor vier.

Vocabulary

Meine Uhr stimmt nicht *My watch is wrong*
Wie spät ist es? *What is the time?*
jetzt *now*
fast *almost*
die Konferenz, -en *conference*
beginnen *to begin*
um Viertel nach *at a quarter past*
brauchen *to need*
noch *still*
das Tagungszentrum *conference centre*
die Tagung, -en *conference*

das Zentrum, Zentren *centre*
nur *only*
ungefähr *approximately, about*
die Minute, -n *minute*
wir werden ... ankommen *we will arrive (future tense page 57)*
rechtzeitig *in time*
am Vormittag *in the morning*
der Vortrag, ̈-e *talk, presentation*
die Stunde, -n *hour*
die Mittagspause, -n *lunch break*
der Mittag *midday*

die Pause, -n *pause, break*
dauern *last*
das Nachmittagsprogramm *afternoon programme*
der Nachmittag, -e *afternoon*
das Programm, -e *programme*
Ich muß auf die Bank (gehen) *I must go to the bank*
das Problem, -e *problem*
enden *to end*
Viertel vor *a quarter to*

Note

Am Vormittag gibt es zwei Vorträge. Es gibt *there is, there are.* This is a very useful phrase, in the singular as well as the plural. e.g. **Es gibt hier ein Hotel.** *There is a hotel here.* **Es gibt dort Einzel- und Doppelzimmer.** *There are single and double rooms available there.*

Exercise 1

Ewald Weidmann, of Sasshofer AG, has arranged a meeting with some business colleagues. He wishes to check on their arrival times, and also on the arrangements of other members of the company. How will his assistant answer his questions?

Example: Wann kommt Frau Schaft an? Um neun Uhr.

1 Wann kommt Herr Zimmermann an?
_____

2 Wann holen wir Hans-Jürgen Braun vom Bahnhof ab?
_____

3 Wann kommt Frau Fischer zu Besuch?
_____

4 Wann erwarten Sie Mr Hodgkins?
_____

5 Wann beginnt die Besprechung mit dem Verkaufsleiter?
_____

6 Wann fährt Herr Schmidt nach Österreich?
_____

7 Wann fliegt der Produktionsleiter nach England?

_____

Exercise 2

Now look at these examples of how to use the 24-hour clock and read them aloud.

Then pretend it is five minutes later and read out the times accordingly.

Example: **1** 11.10   Es ist elf Uhr zehn.
                              Es ist jetzt elf Uhr fünfzehn.

(You will find a summary of how to tell the time on pages 55–7.)

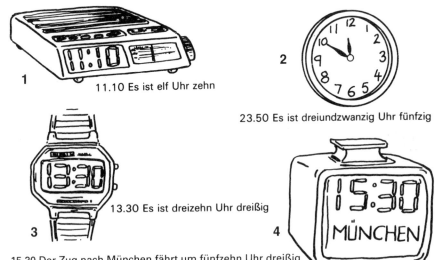

1 11.10 Es ist elf Uhr zehn

2 23.50 Es ist dreiundzwanzig Uhr fünfzig

3 13.30 Es ist dreizehn Uhr dreißig

4 15.30 Der Zug nach München fährt um fünfzehn Uhr dreißig

Comprehension 1

You will hear a telephone conversation between Frau Bauer and Herr Schneider who are arranging to meet at the Igedo Messe, a fashion fair in Düsseldorf. Read the following questions before listening and giving your answers.

Vocabulary

auch *also*
sicher *sure, certain*
das Wochenende, -n *weekend*

der Freund, -e *friend*
na, gut *alright then*

Schönes Wochenende!
Have a nice weekend!

1 When is the fair taking place?
2 How are the two people travelling to Düsseldorf?
3 From which cities and on which days are they leaving?
4 What will Herr Schneider be doing in Duisburg?
5 How is he getting to Düsseldorf on the Monday?
6 At what time will he arrive there?
7 Where will Frau Bauer be meeting him?

| Exercise 3 | You want to meet a business acquaintance at a conference in Zürich. You phone him or her to make the necessary arrangements. What do you say to your acquaintance? |

Vocabulary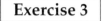

ein Bekannter *acquaintance*
eine Bekannte *female*
  acquaintance

bis Donnerstag *till Thursday*
auf eine Tagung *to a*
  conference

Sie
(*Say you are going to the conference in Zürich on Friday. Ask if he or she is going too.*)

_____

Bekannte(r) Ja sicher.
Sie (*Ask when he or she is travelling.*)

_____

Bekannte(r) Ich fahre am Donnerstag mit der Bahn von Basel.
Sie (*Ask when his or her train arrives in Zürich.*)

_____

Bekannte(r) Um halb zehn.
Sie (*Say you will meet him or her at the station. The conference begins at 11.00 and you will arrive in time.**)

_____

Bekannte(r) Und wann endet das Nachmittagsprogramm?
Sie (*Say at 5.30.*)

_____

Bekannte(r) Also gut. Bis Donnerstag.
Sie (*Say goodbye.*)

_____

*Note: Read the Language structures on page 57 for an explanation of the future tense.

Comprehension 2: Deutschland

Deutschland liegt mitten in Europa und hat sechzehn Länder (Siehe die Landkarte gegenüber). Die Hauptstadt heißt Berlin. Für Touristen und Besucher aus aller Welt ist Berlin sehr interessant. Diese Stadt hat eine lange und faszinierende Geschichte.

Deutschland ist ein sehr wichtiger Handelspartner von Großbritannien. Die Hauptexporte sind Autos, Chemikalien und Maschinen. Deutschland ist Mitglied der Europäischen Gemeinschaft (EG) und treibt großen Handel mit den anderen

EG-Ländern (Großbritannien, Irland, Belgien, Dänemark, Frankreich, Griechenland, die Niederlande, Italien, Luxemburg, Portugal, Spanien und bald Österreich).

Großbritannien importiert auch Güter aus Österreich und der Schweiz, zum Beispiel Stahl und Lebensmittel. In diesen Ländern spricht man natürlich auch Deutsch.

Vocabulary

liegen *to lie*
mitten in ... *in the middle of ...*
das Land ¨-er *(here) federal state*
die Landkarte, -n *map*
die Hauptstadt ¨-e *capital city*
der Tourist, -en *tourist*
der Besucher, - *visitor*
aus aller Welt *from all over the world*
interessant *interesting*
lang *long*

faszinierend *fascinating*
die Geschichte -n *history, story*
wichtig *important*
der Handelspartner - *trading partner*
die Hauptexporte *(pl) main exports*
das Auto, -s *car*
Chemikalien *(pl) chemicals*
die Maschine, -n *machine*
die Europäische Gemeinschaft *European Community*

das Mitglied, -er *member*
treiben here: *to carry on*
groß *big, great*
der Handel *trade*
der, die, das andere *the other*
importieren *to import*
Güter *(pl) goods*
zum Beispiel *for example*
der Stahl *steel*
die Lebensmittel *(pl) foodstuffs*
natürlich *of course*

When you feel you have understood the passage and noted the words and phrases which seem important or useful, see if you can fill in the gaps in the following:

Deutschland _____ mitten in _____ und hat

_____ Länder. Die _____

heißt Berlin. Für _____ und Besucher aus aller

Welt ist Berlin sehr _____. Deutschland

ist ein sehr wichtiger _____ von

Großbritannien. Die Hauptexporte _____ Autos, Chemikalien

und _____. Großbritannien

_____ auch Güter aus Österreich und der

_____, zum Beispiel Stahl und

_____. In diesen Ländern

_____ man natürlich _____ Deutsch.

Talking business extra

Comprehension 3

Both firms will be involved in a seminar on new marketing strategies for the single European market. **Verlag Germania** is introducing new publications on the theme, and **Spieltechnik GmbH** will exhibit some of the products, all of which are on special offer.

Key vocabulary

das Programmheft, -e
    programme booklet
der Markt, ⁻e *market*
der Binnenmarkt, ⁻e *internal (single) market*
die Tagesordnung, -en
    agenda

die Arbeitsgruppe, -n
    working group
die Serie, -n *series*
die Wirtschaft, -en *economy*
der Sitzungsraum, ⁻e
    meeting room
das Muster, - *sample*

das Ausstellungsstück, -e
    exhibition item (exhibit)
kaufen *to buy*
das Erzeugnis, -se *product*
bestellen *to order*
die Sache, -n *thing*

Key phrases

mit allen Einzelheiten	*with all the details*
eine Serie/ein Produkt präsentieren	*to present a series/product*
einen Beitrag leisten	*to make a contribution*
eine Auswahl unserer Produkte	*a selection of our products*
im Sonderangebot	*on special offer*
zum Sonderpreis angeboten	*offered at a special price*

Find out:

1 what is happening in the mornings and afternoons
2 whether exhibited items can be bought there directly.

Exercise 4

Fill in the details:

Tagung „Neue Märkte im neuen Binnenmarket"

Die Serie ist über _____ ____ _____

Das Buch heißt: Geschichte der _____

_____

Das Referat bespricht _____ ____

_____ _____

Die Ausstellung zeigt _____ zum Thema

_____ _____

Puzzle

1 exhibition
2 contribution
3 product
4 offer
5 markets
6 clue: introducing a new product

Language structures

The time (die Uhrzeit)

Wie spät ist es?   *What is the time?*
Wieviel Uhr ist es?

		12-HOUR CLOCK	24-HOUR CLOCK
ON THE HOUR			
	a.m.*	Es ist **ein Uhr.**	Es ist ein Uhr.
	p.m.	Es ist ein Uhr.	Es ist dreizehn Uhr.

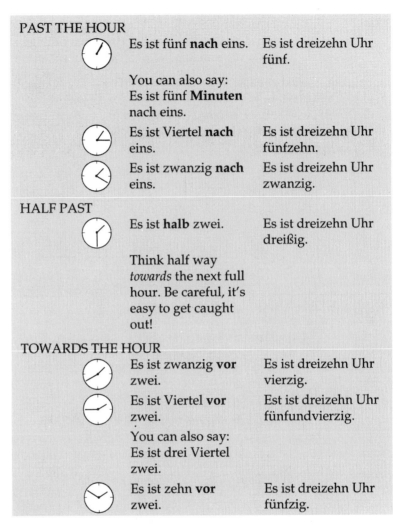

PAST THE HOUR

Es ist fünf **nach** eins.   Es ist dreizehn Uhr fünf.

You can also say:
Es ist fünf **Minuten** nach eins.

Es ist Viertel **nach** eins.   Es ist dreizehn Uhr fünfzehn.

Es ist zwanzig **nach** eins.   Es ist dreizehn Uhr zwanzig.

HALF PAST

Es ist **halb** zwei.   Es ist dreizehn Uhr dreißig.

Think half way *towards* the next full hour. Be careful, it's easy to get caught out!

TOWARDS THE HOUR

Es ist zwanzig **vor** zwei.   Es ist dreizehn Uhr vierzig.

Es ist Viertel **vor** zwei.   Est ist dreizehn Uhr fünfundvierzig.

You can also say:
Es ist drei Viertel zwei.

Es ist zehn **vor** zwei.   Es ist dreizehn Uhr fünfzig.

*Note that there is no direct equivalent of a.m. and p.m. in German. If you have to be specific, use:

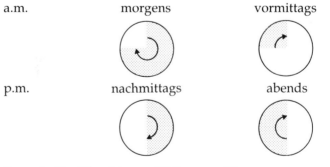

a.m.   morgens   vormittags

p.m.   nachmittags   abends

Example: Der Flug ist um elf Uhr vormittags.

These words are also used to talk about a regular action or occurrence in the day.

Example: Ich komme morgens um neun Uhr zur Arbeit.

am Morgen, **am** Vormittag	*in the morning*
am Nachmittag, **am** Abend	*in the afternoon, evening*
zu Mittag	*at noon, midday*
in der Nacht	*at night*

Note that *hours* can be **Uhr** or **Stunden**, depending on the context.

Es ist achtzehn **Uhr**.	*It is eighteen hundred hours.*
Der Vortrag dauert zwei **Stunden**.	*The presentation lasts for two hours.*
Der Vertreter bleibt eine halbe **Stunde**.	*The representative is staying for half an hour.*

Uhr is used when telling the time (as in o'clock).
Stunde indicates the duration of time.

Verbs   The future tense

There are two ways of expressing the future in German:

1 Ich **hole** Sie morgen vom Bahnhof **ab**.	*I will fetch you tomorrow …*
Er **kommt** um zehn Uhr am Flughafen **an**.	*He will arrive at …*
Der Zug **ist** um halb zwölf in Mönchengladbach.	*The train will be …*

Use the ordinary PRESENT TENSE (see pages 26–7) as long as there is a clear indication when the action is going to happen. This is the usual way of expressing the future. The actual future tense as below is used far less in German than in English.

2 Wann **werden** Sie **ankommen**?	*When will you arrive?*
Wir **werden** rechtzeitig **ankommen**.	*We shall arrive in time.*
Das **wird** kein Problem **sein**.	*That will not be a problem.*

Use WERDEN PLUS THE INFINITIVE OF THE VERB (see Language structures overview, page 60). Because there are two verbs, the infinitive has to go to the end of the sentence.

Adjectives   **Meine** Kollegin ist Schweizerin.   *My colleague is Swiss.*
Ihr Name ist walisisch, nicht wahr?   *Your name is Welsh, isn't it?*
Unsere Kinder gehen zur Schule.   *Our children go to school.*
Meine Uhr stimmt nicht.   *My watch is wrong.*

These are called *possessive adjectives*. They show, as their name implies, whom (or to what) something belongs. Their endings change in the same way as the indefinite article does.

For a full table see Language structures overview, page 60.

Progress check

1 How would you ask the time?
2 Give the following times, first in the 24-hour clock, then in the 12-hour clock:
   a.m. 10.00   11.55   *p.m.* 12.15   12.30
   13.00   14.25   18.30   21.45

3 and 5 NVQ S1

You are only partly informed about a day conference. Give/ask for more information as appropriate.
   a) The presentation starts in the morning and lasts for two hours.
   b) How long is the lunch break?
   c) When does the afternoon programme finish?
   d) Is the production manager coming in the evening?

4 NVQ W1

Somebody has asked about your daily work routine. Leave a note of your answers in writing.
   a) Wann kommen Sie morgens zur Arbeit?
   b) Gibt es in Ihrer Firma eine Mittagspause und wie lange dauert sie?
   c) Wann fahren Sie abends nach Hause?

5 NVQ S1

Give the following information in German:
   a) I will fetch you from the station.
   b) We will arrive in time.
   c) That will not be a problem.
   d) My watch is wrong.
   e) Your name is German, isn't it?

6 NVQ R2

Here are some written notes for you. **a)**, **b)** and **c)** were left by your boss when he left early on Friday lunchtime, **d)** and **e)** are from a new supplier with whom you are working out a deal.
   a) Meine Kollegin muß heute noch auf die Bank.
   b) Unsere Vertreter gehen morgen auf eine Tagung.
   c) Bis übermorgen also, und schönes Wochenende!
   d) Die Einzelheiten über den Sonderpreis besprechen wir später.
   e) Bitte schön, hier sind die Muster, und die Waren bestellen Sie direkt bei uns.

Summary 2

Language structures overview

Prepositions

As in English, German prepositions usually have one main meaning and a further one or two less obvious or less frequent meanings. Only the more common uses are summarised here.

1 Prepositions always followed by the *Accusative:*

durch	through	Wir gehen **durch** die Altstadt.
für	for	Der Tisch ist **für** den Besuch reserviert.
gegen	against	England spielt **gegen** Deutschland im Finale.
ohne	without	Ich arbeite heute **ohne** meinen Kollegen.
um	around	Wir fahren **um** den See.

2 Prepositions always followed by the *Dative:*

aus	from	Er kommt **aus** der Schweiz.
	out of	Gehen Sie **aus** dem Geschäft, dann rechts.
außer	except	Ich habe alles **außer** meiner Uhr.
bei	at	**bei** der Arbeit, **bei** der Firma Sasshofer
	at the house of	**bei** uns (*at our house*)
	near	Oberhausen **bei** Duisburg.
	with	Ich habe kein Geld **bei** mir.
mit	with	Fliegen Sie **mit** Ihrer Kollegin?
	by	Fahren Sie **mit** dem Auto?

nach	after	Ich komme **nach** der Konferenz zurück.
	to (with villages, towns, cities, countries)	Fliegen Sie morgen **nach** New York? Exception: feminine nouns – Fliegen Sie **in** die Schweiz? Note: Fahren wir **nach Hause** (Let's go *home*).
seit	for	Ich arbeite **seit** sieben Jahren bei Siemens (see page 164 for this use of **seit**).
	since	**seit** gestern
von	of	die Betriebsleiterin **von** meiner Firma
	from	ein Brief **von** einem Geschäftspartner
zu	to	Gehen Sie **zum** (zu dem) Hotel zurück?
	at	Zwei Briefmarken **zu** DM 1,50 Morgen abend bin ich **zu** Hause.
gegenüber	opposite	Das Museum liegt **gegenüber** dem Bahnhof.

3 Prepositions followed by the *Accusative* (when movement is implied) or the *Dative* (when no movement is implied):

an	to, at
auf	on, onto, to, at
hinter	behind
in	in, into
neben	next to, beside
über	over, across; about (always with accusative)
unter	under, among
vor	in front of, outside, before
zwischen	between

Ich muß **auf die** Bank gehen.	*I must go to the bank.*
Er ist **auf der** Bank.	*He is at the bank.*
Der Direktor kommt **in den** Sitzungsraum.	*The director comes into the meeting room.*
Die Ausstellung ist **im (in dem)** Sitzungsraum.	*The exhibition is in the meeting room.*
Wir gehen **über die** Straße.	*We walk across the road.*
Die Verkehrsampel hängt **über der** Straße.	*The traffic light hangs above the street.*
Eine Diskussion **über den** Europäischen Binnenmarkt.	*A discussion about the Single European Market.*
Ich fahre nächste Woche **ins** (in das) Ausland.	*I'm going abroad next week.*
Herr Müller ist diese Woche **im** (in dem) Ausland.	*Mr. Müller is abroad this week.*

The future tense

ich	werde	
du	wirst	
er, sie, es	wird	
wir	werden	rechtzeitig in München **ankommen**
ihr	werdet	
sie	werden	
Sie	werden	

When the action is *clearly* (e.g. **morgen**, **nächste Woche**) happening in the future, the ordinary present tense is frequently used instead of the future tense.

Possessive adjectives

mein	*my*	unser	*our*
dein	*your (familiar)*	euer	*your (familiar), plural*
sein	*his, its*	ihr	*their*
ihr	*her, its*	Ihr	*your (formal), singular + plural*

Each one of these has endings exactly like the indefinite article **ein**, and **kein** in the plural (see page 27).
Here are three examples:

		SINGULAR		PLURAL
	MASCULINE	FEMININE	NEUTER	ALL GENDERS
My				
Nominative	mein	meine	mein	meine
Accusative	meinen	meine	mein	meine
Dative	meinem	meiner	meinem	meinen
Genitive	meines	meiner	meines	meiner
Our				
Nominative	unser	unsere	unser	unsere
Accusative	unseren	unsere	unser	unsere
Dative	unserem	unserer	unserem	unseren
Genitive	unseres	unserer	unseres	unserer
Your				
Nominative	Ihr	Ihre	Ihr	Ihre
Accusative	Ihren	Ihre	Ihr	Ihre
Dative	Ihrem	Ihrer	Ihrem	Ihren
Genitive	Ihres	Ihrer	Ihres	Ihrer

Examples:
Möchten Sie ein Zimmer für Ihr**en** Kollegen reservieren?
Ich fliege mit mein**er** Kollegin nach Deutschland.
Wir erwarten unser**en** Geschäftsführer.

Adjectives must 'agree', which means they must have the same case and gender as the noun they refer to.

für Ihr**en** Kollegen	**für** requires *accusative*
	Kollege *masculine*
mit mein**er** Kollegin	**mit** requires *dative*
	Kollegin *feminine*
unser**en** Geschäftsführer	direct object *accusative*
	Geschäftsführer *masculine*

Additional exercises

1 Complete the sentences, using the following separable verbs:
abfliegen, abholen, ankommen, weiterfahren

a Ich __ __ __ __ Sie vom Bahnhof __ __.

b Wir __ __ __ __ __ __ um fünf Uhr __ __.

c __ __ __ __ __ __ __ Sie von München __ __?

d Wir __ __ __ __ __ __ am 10. Mai __ __ und __ __ __ __ __ __ am 12. Mai

__ __ __ __ __ __.

e __ __ __ __ __ Sie Frau Kohl vom Flughafen __ __ ?

f Wann __ __ __ __ __ __ Ihre Kollegen am Flughafen __ __?

g Der Geschäftsführer __ __ __ __ __ __ von London __ __.

2 Complete these sentences.

a Herr Schmidt kommt z____ Messe (*f*).

b Frau Schneider ist die Sekretärin v____ Geschäftsführer (*m*).

c Ingrid kommt um 11.00 z____ Bahnhof (*m*).

d Mr. Newby fährt mit d____ Bahn (*f*) nach Mönchengladbach.

e Danke für d____ Kaffee (*m*).

f Ich arbeite für d____ Stahlwerk (*n*).

3 **Nach** or **zum(zur)**?

a Mr. Newby fliegt morgen _____ Deutschland.

b Herr Bauer fährt nächsten Montag _____ Düsseldorf _____ Messe.

c Ich komme um halb sechs _____ Hotel.

d Wir fahren am Wochenende _____ Paris.

e Wann kommt Frau Kaiser _____ England?

f Die Kinder gehen am Morgen _____ Schule.

g Kommen wir noch rechtzeitig _____ Nachmittagsprogramm?

Summary 2

[4] Put into the future tense.

a Die Konferenz beginnt um Viertel vor neun.
b Der Vortrag am Nachmittag dauert ungefähr zwei Stunden.
c Das ist kein Problem.
d Ich gehe morgen auf die Bank.
e Er ist heute nachmittag nicht in der Firma.
f Wie lange bleiben Sie in Düsseldorf?
g Wann kommen wir am Flughafen an?
h Ich hole Sie um 16.00 vom Bahnhof ab.

[5] Replace the words in bold type with the words in brackets.

a **Meine** Sekretärin hat **mein** Programm für den Nachmittag.
   Unser Kollege aus Deutschland kommt heute in **unsere** Firma.
   Holt **seine** Frau **ihren** Bekannten am Flughafen ab?
   (**Ihr, Ihre, Ihren** *your*)
b Ich fahre mit **Ihrem** Verkaufsleiter zu einer Konferenz mit **unseren**
   Handelspartnern.
   Ihr Auto ist am Bahnhof. **Seine** Uhr stimmt nicht.
   (**mein, meine, meinem, meinen** *my*)
c Wann ist **mein** Flug nach Zürich?
   Ihr Taxi kommt nicht rechtzeitig bei **ihrer** Firma an.
   Ihre Besprechung wird ohne mich und **meinen** Kollegen beginnen.
   (**Unser, unsere, unseren, unserer** *our*)

[6] Which sentences include an accusative: **a** as a direct object?
                                          b after a preposition?

1 Soll ich ein Doppelzimmer reservieren?
2 Danke für Ihre Hilfe.
3 Ich möchte eine Telefonnummer für meinen Geschäftsführer.

Key phrases

Expressing a desire	Ich möchte bitte Frau Steiner sprechen
Asking someone to wait	Augenblick bitte
	Moment bitte
Enquiring/replying about possibility	Geht das?
	Ja, das geht
Thanking someone and responding to thanks	Danke für Ihre Hilfe
	Gern geschehen!
Enquiring about travel times	Wann kommt er nach Deutschland?
	Wann fahren Sie?
	Wann kommen Sie in Düsseldorf an?
Giving travel information	Er fliegt von Manchester nach Düsseldorf
	Er fährt mit der Bahn weiter
	Er kommt um neun Uhr am Flughafen an
	Ich fahre nächsten Montag nach Düsseldorf
Arranging to meet	Ich hole Sie vom Bahnhof ab. Bis dann!

Expressing confirmation	Also gut!
	Ganz bestimmt!
	Abgemacht!
Enquiring about accommodation arrangements	Soll ich ein Hotelzimmer reservieren?
Recommending something	Ich empfehle das Hotel Reinhart
Saying goodbye (on telephone)	Auf Wiederhören

Cultural briefing

The 24-hour clock
The 24-hour clock is used for all official purposes, such as railway timetables, TV and radio schedules, and public announcements. It is as well to be prepared for this, so as to avoid confusion.

Punctuality
Punctuality is important in Germany, whether for business appointments or when invited to somebody's home for dinner. Only a very good reason for lateness is acceptable.

Nationalfeiertage
When trying to make business contacts or arrangements with counterparts in Germany, Austria or Switzerland, the **Nationalfeiertage** have to be avoided, as well as May Day and important religious festivals.

The following dates are celebrated in German-speaking countries:

Germany: 3rd of October
Free movement between East and West Germany finally began when travel restrictions were lifted and the Berlin Wall was opened at midnight on the 9th/10th of November 1989. But the formal reunification of Germany, and with it the abolition of the German Democratic Republic (**Deutsche Demokratische Republik**) took place on the 3rd of October, 1990.

Austria: 26th of October
This date celebrates the signing of the Austrian constitution in 1955, and in particular the unanimous vote on the 26th of October in the Austrian parliament for the Neutrality Law (**Neutralitätsgesetz**), which secured the country's release from post-war occupation and required complete neutrality.

Switzerland: 1st of August
A proud day for the Swiss, commemorating the oath in 1291 (**Rütli Schwur**) by three farmers from the cantons of Uri, Unterwalden and Schwyz (the three **Urkantone**), promising to free their people from oppression.

Pronunciation

a – o – u
These vowels all have short and long versions.

a	short like *a* in *man*	danke, Tasse, Kaffee, alt
	long like *a* in *father*	Name, Arbeit, Dame, Jahr
o	short like *o* in *got*	von, Tochter, kommen, Woche
	long like *o* in *role*	but with the lips well rounded – Sohn, Moment, Bahnhof, ohne
u	short like *u* in *pull*	muß, Tagung, hundert
	long like *oo* in *pool*	Uhr, Schule, Architektur

An **h** after **a, o, u** has the effect of lengthening the sound: Jahr, Sohn, Uhr

7 Unterwegs

In this unit, you will learn how to ...

- enquire about trains
- buy tickets
- ask for change
- deal with German money
- say you must do something.

Dialogue 1:   An der Auskunft

Michael Newby flies from Manchester to Düsseldorf. On arrival at the airport he asks the way to the station so that he can catch a train to Düsseldorf main station.

Newby	Entschuldigen Sie, bitte. Ich will vom Flughafen zum Hauptbahnhof. Wo fährt die S-Bahn ab?
Angestellte	Dort drüben ist die Rolltreppe zur S-Bahn.
Newby	Danke schön.
Angestellte	Bitte schön.

(*An der S-Bahn Station*)

Newby	Wann fährt denn der nächste Zug zum Hauptbahnhof?
Beamter	Um elf Uhr dreiundzwanzig von Gleis eins. Er kommt um elf Uhr fünfunddreißig am Hauptbahnhof an.
Newby	Was kostet das?
Beamter	Eine Mark achtzig. Die Fahrkarte bekommen Sie vom Automaten dort drüben.
Newby	Vielen Dank.
Beamter	Bitte schön.

Vocabulary

unterwegs *out on a journey*
die Auskunft, ̈e *information,*
information office
Entschuldigen Sie, bitte
Excuse me, please
der Hauptbahnhof, ̈e *main*
station
die S-Bahn *local train*
der Angestellte, -n,

die Angestellte, -n *male,*
female employee, clerk
dort drüben *over there*
die Rolltreppe, -n *escalator*
das Gleis, -e *platform*
kosten *to cost*
Was kostet das? *How much*
is that?
die Mark, - *German Mark*

die Fahrkarte, -n *ticket*
bekommen *to get*
der Automat, -en *automatic*
machine
vielen Dank *many thanks*

Notes

Ich will vom Flughafen zum Hauptbahnhof.
Ich will *I want* (*to get to* is understood). Do
not confuse these two:

I want a coffee. **Ich will einen Kaffee.**
I will come tomorrow. **Ich werde morgen**
kommen.

Exercise 1	You've just landed at Düsseldorf airport. You need to get from the airport to Düsseldorf main station. You don't know where the station is, so you enquire at the information desk. What do you say in German?

Sie	(*Say 'excuse me' and ask where local trains depart from.*)
Angestellte	Dort drüben ist die Rolltreppe zur S-Bahn.
Sie	(*Thank the person for this information.*)
Angestellte	Bitte schön.

(*You take the escalator to the station, then find an official who gives you further instructions.*)

Sie	(*Ask when the next train goes to the main station.*)
Beamter	Um dreizehn Uhr zwanzig von Gleis eins. Er kommt um dreizehn Uhr dreiunddreißig an.
Sie	(*Ask how much it costs.*)
Beamter	Eine Mark achtzig. Die Fahrkarte bekommen Sie dort drüben.
Sie	(*Thank the official.*)
Beamter	Bitte schön.

| Exercise 2 |

You ask for some travel information, and receive the following responses. Extract the details needed to fill in the table below.

1 Der nächste Zug nach München fährt um sieben Uhr dreißig von Gleis zwei ab und kommt um zehn Uhr zwanzig in München an.

2 Der Zug nach Hannover fährt um neun Uhr fünfundvierzig von Gleis drei ab und kommt um dreizehn Uhr zehn in Hannover an.

3 Der nächste Zug nach Lübeck fährt um elf Uhr vierundzwanzig ab und kommt um sechzehn Uhr sechsundfünfzig an. Abfahrt in zwei Minuten von Gleis 6.

4 Der Zug auf Gleis eins fährt um fünfzehn Uhr neununddreißig ab und kommt um zweiundzwanzig Uhr sechzehn in Bonn an.

Vocabulary

die Richtung, -en *direction*   **das Gleis, -e** *platform*
die Abfahrt, -en *departure*   **die Ankunft, ⁻e** *arrival*

	Richtung	Abfahrt	Gleis	Ankunft
1	München	07.30	2	10.20
2				
3				
4				

Dialogue 2:   Am Fahrkartenschalter

A tourist travelling through Germany decides to visit Rothenburg. This is part of her conversation at Munich main station.

Reisende	Einmal nach Rothenburg, bitte.
Beamter	Einfach oder hin und zurück?
Reisende	Hin und zurück.
Beamter	Erster oder zweiter Klasse?
Reisende	Zweiter Klasse.
Beamter	Zweiundsiebzig Mark, bitte.
Reisende	Können Sie wechseln? Ich habe nur einen Fünfhundertmarkschein.

Vocabulary

der Fahrkartenschalter *the ticket office*
der Schalter, - *counter*
die Reisende *female traveller*
einmal here: *one ticket*

einfach *single*
hin und zurück *return* (literally: *there and back*)
erster Klasse *first class*
können *to be able to*
Können Sie ...? *Can you ...?*

wechseln *to change*
nur *only*
der Fünfhundertmarkschein *500 Mark note*

Notes

Einmal nach Rothenburg.
Einmal, zweimal, dreimal literally *once,*
twice, three times. When buying tickets,
however:

einmal *one ticket*
zweimal *two tickets*
dreimal *three tickets* etc.

Exercise 3

Answer these questions about the previous conversation in German.

1 Kauft die Reisende eine oder zwei Fahrkarten?
2 Fährt sie erster oder zweiter Klasse?
3 Was kostet ihre Fahrkarte?
4 Warum muß der Beamte wechseln?
5 Wieviel Geld bekommt die Reisende zurück?

Vocabulary

kaufen *to buy*
warum? *why?*

wieviel? *how much?*
zurück *back*

DM 20,– zurück *20 Marks*
change

Exercise 4

Express the following amounts in German:

| *Examples:* | DM 1,70 | Eine Mark siebzig |
| | DM 2,50 | Zwei Mark fünfzig |

1 DM 9,60
2 DM 8,80
3 DM 5,49

Example: DM 35,– Fünfunddreißig Mark

4 DM 27,–
5 DM 74,–
6 DM 51,–
7 DM 63,–
8 DM 1,–

Vocabulary

das Geld *money*
die Münze, -n *coin*

der Schein, -e *banknote*

das Fünfmarkstück, -e
5 Mark coin

Comprehension 1

For more practice, listen to the cassette and write down the telephone numbers as they are dictated to you.

Exercise 5

Now it's your turn to buy train tickets. Using the following table as a guide, take up your part in the conversations opposite:

Richtung	Preis	Fahrt	Wie viele?	Klasse
1 Köln	DM 5, –	→	2	2
2 Hauptbahnhof	DM 20, –	→	2	1
3 Nürnberg	DM 34, 26	⇄	1	1
4 Mannheim	DM 69, 35	⇄	3	2

1 *Sie* (*Say how many tickets you want and where you are going.*)

_____

Angestellte Erster oder zweiter Klasse?

Sie _____

Angestellte Einfach?

Sie _____

Angestellte Zehn Mark, bitte.

2 *Angestellte* Guten Tag, bitte schön?

Sie _____

Angestellte Einfach oder hin und zurück?
Sie (*Answer and say which class you want.*)

_____

Angestellte Zwanzig Mark pro Person, bitte.
Sie (*Offer a 50 Mark note.*)

_____

Angestellte Danke schön, und zehn Mark zurück.

3 *Sie* (*Say excuse me, how much is a ticket to Nürnberg?*)

_____

Angestellte Einfach?

Sie _____

Angestellte Welcher Klasse?

Sie _____

Angestellte Vierunddreißig Mark sechsundzwanzig.
Sie (*Say thank you, one ticket please.*)

_____

4 *Sie* (*Say how many tickets you want and where you are going. Ask how much it is.*)

_____

Angestellte	Erster oder zweiter Klasse?
Sie	_____
Angestellte	Einfach oder hin und zurück?
Sie	_____
Angestellte	Zweihundertacht Mark fünf, bitte.
Sie	(*Say you only have a 500 Mark note. Can she change it?*)
	_____
Angestellte	Natürlich, und zweihunderteinundneunzig Mark fünfundneunzig zurück. Bitte schön …
Sie	(*Say 'Thank you. Goodbye.'*)
	_____

Vocabulary

der Preis, -e *price*
die Fahrt, -en *journey*

pro Person *per person*
die Person, -en *person*

Comprehension 2: Zur Information

RT-Fahrausweis
für eine Fahrt
R 1   13,00   Erw.
Preiszone   DM
Nur gültig mit Entwerteraufdruck
0090719
Regionalverkehr Rhein-Ruhr

Für die U-Bahn und die S-Bahn kaufen Sie Ihre Fahrkarte normalerweise vom Automaten. Bevor Sie in die Bahn einsteigen, müssen Sie die Fahrkarte entwerten. Der Entwerter stempelt das Datum und die Uhrzeit auf die Fahrkarte.

Vocabulary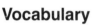

zur Information *for information*
die U-Bahn *underground train*
entwerten *cancel (tickets)*

bevor *before*
einsteigen (sep) *board, enter*
der Entwerter *ticket-punching machine*

stempeln *to stamp*
der Fahrausweis, -e *ticket*
gültig *valid*
der Entwerteraufdruck *date stamp*

Complete the following statements:

Zuerst _____ Sie Ihre Fahrkarte. Dann _____

Sie die Fahrkarte entwerten. Jetzt _____ Sie in die

Bahn einsteigen.

Talking business extra

Comprehension 3

In the fast train connection between Frankfurt main station and the airport, Katrina and Christian discuss parking fees as well as the merits of travelling by train.

Key vocabulary

weg *away*
die Parkgebühr, -en *parking fee*
günstig *reasonable*

billiger *cheaper*
die Verbindung, -en *connection*
die Großstadt, ¨e *city*

bequem *comfortable*
überprüfen *to check over*

Key phrases

Großartiges leisten	*to achieve great things*
im Stundentakt	*hourly*
auf die Minute pünktlich	*punctual to the minute*
Ich kann nur beistimmen!	*I can only agree!*
Reisen mit der Bahn	*travelling by rail*
sonst etwas	*something else*
Das weiß ich!	*I know that !*

Find out:

1 what Katrina finds impressive about the German railways
2 why Christian likes to travel by rail.

Exercise 6

Fill in the details:

Flughafen Frankfurt-Main

Parkgebühren – 20 Mark pro Tag

– _____ _____ für 1 Woche

– _____ _____ für 2 Wochen

Zum Flughafen sind es ungefähr _____ Kilometer.

Circa _____ Leute arbeiten am Flughafen.

Puzzle

1 to check over
2 airport
3 parking fees
4 out on your journey
5 cheaper
6 reasonable
7 clue: not always, but usually

'Auf die Minute pünktlich'

Language structures

Verbs   Müssen, können, wollen (have to, be able to, want to)

Sie **müssen** die Fahrkarte **entwerten**.
Können Sie bitte **wechseln**?
Mr. Newby **will** vom Flughafen zum Bahnhof **fahren**.

They are called *modal verbs* and are irregular, but easy to remember. There are six of them in all (see Language structures overview, page 81 and Unit 16, page 172).

They are called *modal verbs* and are irregular, but easy to remember. There are six of them in all (see Language structures overview, page 8 and Unit 16, page 172).

Question words

Wann kommt der Zug an?	*When ...?*
Was kostet es?	*What ...?*
Wo ist die S-Bahn?	*Where ...?*
Woher kommen Sie?	*Where ... from?*
Wie geht es Ihnen?	*How ...?*
Wieviel Geld bekommt der Reisende zurück?	*How much ...?*
Wie viele Fahrkarten kauft er?	*How many ...?*
Warum muß der Angestellte wechseln?	*Why ...?*
Wer kommt zu Besuch?	*Who ...?*
Welche Sprachen sprechen Sie?	*Which ...?*

These words are called *interrogatives* and stand at the beginning of a sentence, with the verb following in second place.

Progress check

1 and 2 NVQ S1

1   At a station in Germany, ask for the following information:
   a)   where the escalator is
   b)   where the underground leaves from
   c)   when the next train to the main station departs
   d)   how much something is
   e)   for one second class return ticket to Berlin
   f)   whether somebody can give you change.
2   You need change for an automatic machine. Say that you:
   a)   don't have a 2-Mark coin
   b)   only have a 10-Mark note
   c)   would like to change money.
3   Handing over money and giving change, say the following in German: DM5,- plus DM13,55… here we are DM20,-,… and DM1,45 change.

4 a) NVQ W2
   Leave a note with instructions about where to get a ticket in two different situations:
   You can buy the ticket at the ticket office.
   You must buy the ticket from the automatic machine.
   b)   Still at the station, a German passer-by is trying to assist you. What is he saying?
   Wollen Sie mit der U-Bahn oder mit der S-Bahn fahren?
   Warum wollen Sie nicht mit dem Taxi fahren?
   Dort drüben ist die Auskunft.

5 NVQ R2
   What do the following extracts from a letter mean?
   a)   Mit der britischen Bahn kommen Sie nicht immer pünktlich ans Ziel.
   b)   Ich kann Ihnen nur beistimmen.

UNIT 8 Wann fährt der nächste Zug?

In this unit, you will learn how to …

- ask about changing trains
- express personal thanks
- read German timetables
- use an automatic ticket machine.

Dialogue: Am Bahnhof

Liz Young, a translator working in Germany, goes to the information desk at Frankfurt main station to enquire about trains to Aachen.

Übersetzerin	Wann fährt der nächste Zug nach Aachen?
Angestellter	Um elf Uhr siebenundvierzig.
Übersetzerin	Fährt der Zug direkt nach Aachen?
Angestellter	Nein, Sie müssen in Köln umsteigen.
Übersetzerin	Wann kommt der Zug in Köln an?
Angestellter	Um vierzehn Uhr. Um vierzehn Uhr acht fahren Sie dann von Köln nach Aachen weiter.
Übersetzerin	Und wann bin ich in Aachen?
Angestellter	Um fünfzehn Uhr drei.
Übersetzerin	Von welchem Gleis fährt der Zug nach Köln?
Angestellter	Von Gleis zwei.
Übersetzerin	Ich danke Ihnen für die Auskunft.
Angestellter	Gern geschehen.

Vocabulary

die Übersetzerin, - *female translator*
direkt *direct(ly)*

umsteigen *(sep) change (trains, buses)*

von welchem Gleis …? *from which platform …?*

Note

Ich danke Ihnen für die Auskunft.
Ihnen *you* in the dative case.   **Danken,**

helfen etc. are always followed by a dative
case. See Language structures, pages 79–80.

| **Exercise 1** | You are going to a business conference in Berlin and you need to get a train ticket from Frankfurt to Berlin. What do you say in German? |

Sie (*Ask when the next train to Berlin leaves.*)

_____

Angestellter Um neun Uhr dreiundzwanzig.
Sie (*Ask if it is a direct train.*)

_____

Angestellter Nein, Sie müssen in Hannover umsteigen.
Sie (*Ask when the train arrives in Hannover.*)

_____

Angestellter Um zwölf Uhr achtunddreißig. Um dreizehn Uhr vier fahren Sie dann von Hannover nach Berlin weiter.
Sie (*Ask when you will get to Berlin.*)

_____

Angestellter Um siebzehn Uhr vierundzwanzig.
Sie (*Ask which platform the Hannover train leaves from.*)

_____

Angestellter Von Gleis drei.
Sie (*Say thank you for the information.*)

_____

(*You then make your way to the ticket counter.*)
Sie (*Ask for one ticket to Berlin.*)

_____

Beamter Einfach oder hin und zurück?
Sie (*Ask for a second class return ticket.*)

_____

Beamter Zweihundert Mark, bitte.

| **Exercise 2** | Look at the return ticket opposite, then answer the questions. You might need to have a guess at some of them; try that first, before looking at the word list. |

1 When is the ticket valid from?
2 What does **Rückseite** mean?
3 Which class are you travelling?
4 Which word tells you that this is a return ticket?
5 What does **halber Preis** mean?
6 From where to where are you travelling?
7 Via which town?
8 Where was the ticket sold?
9 What does **HBF** mean?
10 How far is the journey?
11 What is the price of the ticket?

Vocabulary

die Hinfahrt, -en *outward journey*
die Rückfahrt, -en *return journey*

die Rückseite, -n *back page*
der Preis, -e *price*
halb *half*
über *via*

Comprehension 1   Look at the table below before listening to the four dialogues on cassette. Fill in each line after the corresponding conversation. The first one has been done for you.

Vocabulary

der Zielort, -e *destination*

das Gespräch, -e *conversation*

die Nummer, -n (Nr.) *number*

Gespräch Nr.	Zielort	Abfahrt	Gleis	Umsteigen	Ankunft am Zielort
1	Frankfurt	8.30	4	Stuttgart	11.45
2					
3					
4					

Exercise 3

Here is an extract from a German Rail timetable.
It lists all trains from Frankfurt to Düsseldorf between midnight and mid-afternoon.

DB

Fahrplanauszug

Winter 1992/93

Frankfurt(M) → Düsseldorf   264 Km

Verkehrszeiten	ab	Zug	an	Service	Umsteigen in	an	ab	Zug
Sa, So- u Feiertage	0.42	Ⓢ	5.30		Mainz	1.19	2.30	D218
					Köln	4.32	4.56	E5001
werktags außer Sa,	0.42	Ⓢ	5.35		Mainz	1.19	2.30	D218
nicht 24., 31.XII.					Köln	4.32	5.03	E5003
Mo bis Sa, nicht 25.XII.	0.42	Ⓢ	5.59		Mainz	1.19	2.30	D218
bis 3.I., 2. bis 4.IV., 23.V.					Köln	4.32	5.35	IC633
	0.42	Ⓢ	7.44		Mainz	1.19	2.30	D218
					Köln	4.32	5.00	N3101
					Hagen	6.36	6.48	E3172
	4.39	D824	8.05 ♇					
	6.49	IC631	9.34					
	7.26	D222	10.15 ♇					
	7.47	IC668	10.28		Köln	10.00	10.04	IC518
Mo bis Sa, nicht 25.XII.	7.49	IC639	10.34					
bis 3.I., 2. bis 4.IV., 23.V.								
	8.47	IC666	11.28		Köln	11.00	11.04	IC500
	8.49	EC31	11.34		Kobl	10.56	11.03	IC616
	9.14	D2020	12.34		Köln	11.54	12.10	IC608
	9.14	D2020	13.03					
Mo bis Sa, auch 17.IV.,	9.47	IC526	12.28					
nicht 25.XII. bis 3.I., 2.								
bis 4.IV., 23.V.								
Mo bis Sa, nicht 25.XII.	9.49	IC608	12.34					
bis 3.I., 2. bis 4.IV., 23.V.	10.47	IC664	13.28		Köln	13.00	13.04	IC516
	10.49	IC606	13.34					
Mo bis Sa, nicht 25.XII.								
bis 3.I., 2. bis 4.IV., 23.V.	11.47	IC524	14.28					
Mo bis Sa, nicht 25.XII.								
bis 3.I., 2. bis 4.IV., 23.V.	11.49	IC531	14.34		Köln	15.00	15.04	EC8
	12.47	IC628	15.28					
	12.49	IC602	15.34					
	13.47	EC26	16.28					
	13.49	IC600	16.34					
	14.47	IC522	17.28					

This word list will help familiarise you with German railway timetables.

Vocabulary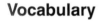

der Fahrplan, ⁝e *timetable*
der Auszug, ⁝e *extract*
die Verkehrszeit, -en
operating time
Sa, So- u. Feiertage
*Samstag, Sonntag und
Feiertage*
werktags *on weekdays*
außer *except*

Frankfurt ab *depart
Frankfurt*
Düsseldorf an *arrive
Düsseldorf*
Zug:
  S-Zug (Schnellzug)
  express train
  D-Zug *through express train*
  IC-Zug *Inter City*

Umsteigen: *gives you
information about where,
when and into which train
you have to change*

While studying this timetable at the station in Frankfurt, you are approached by someone who has forgotten his glasses and asks you to decipher the timetable. Answer his questions:

1 Ich fahre um 07.47 nach Düsseldorf. Kann ich direkt fahren, oder muß ich umsteigen?
2 Ist das ein D-Zug?
3 Wann komme ich in Düsseldorf an?

Write down three similar conversations, using the timetable and the sample questions above.

Comprehension 2: Der Fahrausweisautomat – Bedienungsanleitung

1 Wählen
Benutzen Sie den Automaten für Reisen bis 60 Kilometer. Die Zielbahnhöfe stehen alphabetisch auf einer Liste. Wählen Sie zuerst Ihr Ziel. Neben dem Ziel ist eine Tastatur. Drücken Sie die Taste von Ihrem Zielbahnhof.

2 Zahlen
Der Fahrpreis erscheint über der Tastatur. Unter dem Fahrpreis ist der Münzeinwurf. Werfen Sie das Geld hier ein.

3 Nehmen
Der Automat funktioniert schnell und einfach.
Sie erhalten Ihren Fahrausweis innerhalb von zwei Sekunden.

Vocabulary

die Bedienungsanleitung, -en *instructions for use*

1
wählen *to select, dial*
benutzen *to use*
bis 60 Kilometer *up to 60 kilometers*
das Ziel, -e *target, destination*
stehen *to stand*
alphabetisch *alphabetically*

die Liste, -n *list*
zuerst *first*
die Tastatur *key pad*
drücken *to press*
die Taste, -n *key*

2
zahlen *to pay*
der Fahrpreis, -e *ticket price*
erscheinen *to appear*
über *(+ Dat/Acc.) above*
unter *(+ Dat/Acc.) below*

der Münzeinwurf *coin slot*
einwerfen *(sep) insert*

3
nehmen *to take*
funktionieren *to function*
schnell *fast*
einfach *simply*
erhalten *to receive*
innerhalb von *(+ Dative) within*

Fill in the missing words:

Zuerst müssen Sie Ihren Zielbahnhof _____. Dann

müssen Sie die Taste _____. Jetzt können Sie das

Geld _____, Sie müssen also _____.

Innerhalb von zwei Sekunden können Sie Ihren Fahrausweis

_____.

| **Exercise 4** | A visitor to Germany uses a ticket machine for the first time. Read the following account, then re-write or re-tell it, starting with **Er ist** … |

Ich <u>bin</u> in Deutschland und <u>will</u> eine Fahrkarte von Düsseldorf nach Mönchengladbach lösen. <u>Ich muß</u> den Automaten benutzen, aber es ist nicht einfach, und ein Beamter muß <u>mir</u> helfen. <u>Ich drücke</u> die Taste für Mönchengladbach. Dann <u>werfe ich</u> den Fahrpreis ein und <u>erhalte</u> den Fahrausweis. <u>Ich entwerte</u> den Fahrausweis, bevor <u>ich</u> in die Bahn <u>einsteige</u>.

Vocabulary

lösen *to buy (a ticket)*   **helfen** *to help*

These verbs are irregular:

ich bin,	er ist
ich will,	er will
ich muß,	er muß
ich werfe … ein,	er wirft … ein
ich erhalte,	er erhält

When you feel confident, try the exercise again without referring to the above notes.

Talking business extra

Comprehension 3

On a flight to the UK, we overhear Christian and Katrina's ideas on the English weather, traffic and driving.

Key vocabulary

der Mietwagen, - *hire car*
der Linksverkehr *traffic on the left*
das Einbahnstraßensystem, -e *one way system*
die Stoßzeit, -en *rush hour*

das Stadtzentrum, -zentren *town centre*
der Experte, -n *(male) expert*
die Expertin, -nen *(female) expert*
glücklicherweise *luckily*

das Unternehmen, - *firm*
die Autobahnausfahrt, -en *motorway exit*
die Aktentasche, -n *briefcase*

Key phrases

stark bewölkt	*heavily clouded*
Vielen Dank für Ihre Aufmerksamkeit	*Thank you for your attention*
Das ist typisch englisch	*That's typically English*
Das stört mich nicht	*That doesn't bother me*
Wir machen das immer so	*We always do it like that*
das alles	*all that*
Würden Sie mir den Mantel reichen?	*Would you please pass me the coat?*
neben Ihnen	*next to you*

Find out:

1 what Katrina makes of the English weather
2 what Christian thinks of the traffic in Birmingham city centre, and what he prefers to it.

| **Exercise 5** | Fill in the details: |

Wir werden in _____ Minuten _____ Flughafen

landen.

Es ist stark bewölkt _____ einer Temperatur von _____ __

Grad.

Das Wetter ist _____ Winter recht mild.

Die Stoßzeit ist frühmorgens und _____ späten Nachmittag.

Das Unternehmen liegt direkt an _____ Autobahnausfahrt.

Ich bleibe bei _____ englischen Chauffeur.

Würden Sie _____ meinen Mantel reichen?

Die Aktentasche ist neben _____ auf dem Sitz.

Puzzle

1 typically
2 traffic
3 hire car
4 left
5 briefcase
6 clue: she knows things extremely well

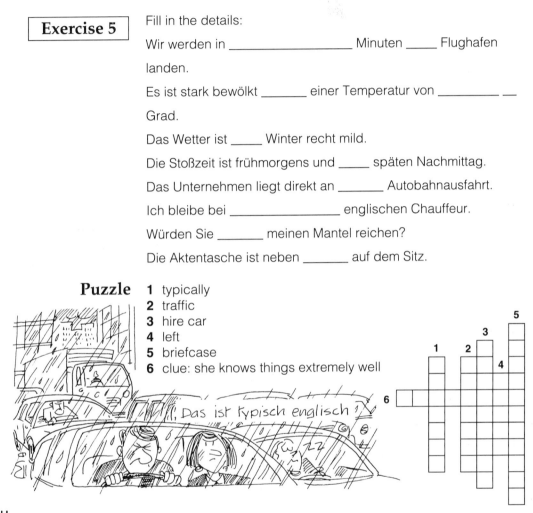

Das ist typisch englisch!

Language structures

Cases The dative case

Uses:

Der Reisende gibt **dem** Beamten einen Fünfhundertmarkschein.

For the *indirect object* in a sentence,
i.e. when something is given, said, wished etc. *to somebody*

Unter **dem** Fahrpreis …

After certain *prepositions* (**aus**, **mit**, **von**, etc. see page 48)

Ich danke **Ihnen**.

Wie **geht** es **Ihnen**? Danke, gut, und **Ihnen**?
Können Sie **mir** bitte **helfen**?
(**helfen** and **danken** go with the dative)

Certain *phrases* and *verbs* require the use of dative as a rule.

FORMATION

der Zug	**dem** Zug
das Gleis	**dem** Gleis
die Fahrkarte	**der** Fahrkarte
die D-Züge	**den** D-Zügen

ein, kein, mein Mann   ein**em**, kein**em**, mein**em** Mann
eine, keine, meine Frau   ein**er**, kein**er**, mein**er** Frau

ich	**mir**
er, es	**ihm**
sie (*she*)	**ihr**
sie (*they*)	**ihnen**
Sie (*you*)	**Ihnen**

ALL NOUNS add **n** in the *dative plural*, unless the plural already ends in **n**, or **s**.

Examples: Herr Bauer fährt mit seinen Kinder**n** nach Wien.
Wie komme ich zu den Gleise**n**?

Nouns   der Herr   Ich möchte Herr**n** Newby sprechen.
der Name   Wie buchstabieren Sie Ihren Name**n**?
der Beamte   Ich danke dem Beamte**n** für seine Hilfe.
der Bekannte   Er fährt mit seinem Bekannte**n** zur Firma.
der Kollege   Ich erwarte meinen Kollege**n**.
der Kunde   Ich muß mit einem Kunde**n** sprechen.
der Polizist   Sehen Sie den Polizist**en** dort drüben?
der Automat   Benutzen Sie den Automat**en**.

A small number of *masculine nouns* add **n** (**en**) in all cases except the nominative singular. They are called *weak nouns*.

Progress check

1 NVQ S1

At the station information office you ask for the following in German:
a) Is the train to Munich direct?
b) Do I have to change in Frankfurt?
c) From which platform is the train to Leipzig?
d) How do I get to the trains?

2 NVQ W2

Write down the following requests, instructions and statements:
a) I would like to buy a ticket.
b) He must use the automatic ticket machine.
c) Now you must pay the money.
d) Then you can take the return ticket.
e) Mr Newby is at the information desk.
f) My colleague is talking to (**mit**) the clerk.

3 NVQ S1

How would you:
a) thank somebody for information
b) ask somebody for help?

4 Explain the following in English:
a) die Fernrückfahrkarte
b) die Ankunft, die Abfahrt
c) die Bedienungsanleitung
d) das Telefongespräch.

5 NVQ R2

In a letter a German colleague comments on his experience of traffic in England. What are the points he makes?
a) In der Stoßzeit ist der Verkehr im Stadtzentrum sehr stark.
b) Der Linksverkehr und das Einbahnstraßensystem stören mich immer sehr.

Summary 3
Language structures overview

Modal Verbs

	müssen *must, to have to*	**können** *can, to be able to*	**wollen** *to want to*
I	ich muß	ich kann	ich will
you (familiar)	du mußt	du kannst	du willst
he	er	er	er
she	sie } muß	sie } kann	sie } will
it	es	es	es
we	wir müssen	wir können	wir wollen
you (pl. familiar)	ihr müßt	ihr könnt	ihr wollt
they	sie müssen	sie können	sie wollen
you (formal)	Sie müssen	Sie können	Sie wollen

The remaining three modal verbs are listed on page 173.

Articles

Definite article

	SINGULAR			PLURAL
	MASCULINE	FEMININE	NEUTER	ALL GENDERS
Nom.	der Tag	die Firma	das Zimmer	die Tage, Firmen, Zimmer
Acc.	den Tag	die Firma	das Zimmer	die Tage, Firmen, Zimmer
Dat.	dem Tag	der Firma	dem Zimmer	den Tage**n**, Firmen, Zimmer**n**
Gen.	des Tag**es**	der Firma	des Zimmer**s**	der Tage, Firmen, Zimmer

Indefinite article

Nom.	ein	Tag	eine	Firma	ein	Zimmer
Acc.	einen	Tag	eine	Firma	ein	Zimmer
Dat.	einem	Tag	einer	Firma	einem	Zimmer
Gen.	eines	Tag**es**	einer	Firma	eines	Zimmer**s**

Note: the ending **n** on *plural nouns* in the dative
the ending **es** or **s** on *masculine* and *neuter nouns* in the *genitive singular*.

For details on the genitive case, see Language structures, Unit 9 pages 92–3.

Personal pronouns

Some examples to show how pronouns replace the noun:

	NOUN	PRONOUN
Nom.	**Der Kollege**	**er**
Acc.	Ich hole **meinen Kollegen** vom Flughafen ab.	Ich hole **ihn** vom Flughafen ab.
Dat.	Ich fahre mit **meinem Kollegen** zur Messe.	Ich fahre mit **ihm** zur Messe.
Nom.	**Die Beamtin**	**sie**
Acc.	Mr. Smith erwartet **die Beamtin**.	Mr. Smith erwartet **sie**.
Dat.	Mrs. Gee spricht mit **der Beamtin**.	Mrs. Gee spricht mit **ihr**.
Nom.	**Die Besucher**	**sie** (*they*)
Acc.	Das Buch ist für **die Besucher**.	Das Buch ist für **sie**.
Dat.	Wir helfen **den Besuchern**.	Wir helfen **ihnen**.
Nom.	**...** (*your name*)	**ich**
Acc.	Die Sekretärin möchte **...** (*your name*) sprechen.	Die Sekretärin möchte **mich** sprechen.
Dat.	Herr Kain arbeitet mit **...** (*your name*).	Herr Kain arbeitet mit **mir**.

Table of *personal pronouns:*

	NOMINATIVE	ACCUSATIVE	DATIVE
I	ich	mich	mir
you (familiar)	du	dich	dir
he	er	ihn	ihm
she	sie	sie	ihr
it	es	es	ihm
we	wir	uns	uns
you (familiar plural)	ihr	euch	euch
they	sie	sie	ihnen
you (formal)	Sie	Sie	Ihnen

Additional exercises

1 Insert the correct form of **müssen**, **können** or **wollen**.

a Fährt der Zug direkt, oder _____ ich umsteigen? (müssen)

b Sie _____ umsteigen. (müssen)

c Der Reisende _____ die Fahrkarte entwerten. (müssen)

d Entschuldigen Sie, wo _____ ich eine Fahrkarte kaufen? (können)

e _____ Mr. Newby direkt nach London fliegen? (können)

f Wann _____ Sie mich abholen? (können)

g Ich _____ nach Bremen fahren. (wollen)

h _____ Sie zum Hauptbahnhof? (wollen)

i Wir _____ Deutsch sprechen. (wollen)

[2] Can you identify the datives in these sentences **a** as an indirect object
b after a preposition?

1 Andrea Morgan ist die Sekretärin vom Geschäftsführer von der Firma Anglia
  Chemicals.
2 Ich wünsche Ihnen einen guten Aufenthalt.
3 Am Wochenende besucht er Freunde in der Stadt.
4 Wie geht es Ihnen und Ihrer Familie?
5 Der Beamte muß mir helfen.

[3] Complete the gaps in these sentences with the correct form of *the*.

a Wie heißt _____ Hotel am Bahnhof?

b Wir erwarten _____ Geschäftsführer um elf Uhr.

c Können Sie _____ Empfangsdame helfen?

d Kommen Sie mit _____ Auto oder mit _____ Zug?

e Nach _____ Konferenz fahren wir nach Hause.

f _____ Taxi steht vor _____ Hotel.

g Wo ist _____ Uhr?

h Die Besucher erhalten morgen _____ Fahrausweis.

i Bitte wechseln Sie _____ Hundertmarkschein.

j Jetzt müssen Sie _____ Ziel wählen.

k Was kostet _____ Rückfahrkarte?

[4] Replace the nouns in bold print with the correct personal pronoun.

Example: Funktioniert **der Automat** schnell und einfach?
      Funktioniert **er** schnell und einfach?

a **Meine Sekretärin** wird **das Zimmer** reservieren.
b **Der Zug** kommt um halb eins in Hannover an.
c **Herr Kaiser** kann **das Fünfmarkstück** nicht wechseln.
d Erwarten Sie **Herrn Newby** heute?
e Wann sprechen Sie mit **Ihren Freunden**?
f Ich kaufe von **Frau Müller** ein Auto.
g **Meine Kollegen** lernen mit **Herrn Schwarz** Deutsch.
h Ich muß **das Geld** von der Bank abholen.
i Wir danken **unserer Kollegin**.

Key phrases

Enquiring about train times	Wann fährt der nächste Zug nach/zum/zur ...?
	Wann kommt der Zug in ... an?
Asking if you have to change	Muß ich umsteigen?
	Fährt der Zug direkt nach ...?
Enquiring about platforms	Von welchem Gleis fährt der Zug nach ...?
Enquiring about cost	Was kostet das?
Buying tickets	Einmal/zweimal/dreimal nach ...
	Einmal einfach
	Einmal hin und zurück
	Erster/zweiter Klasse
Asking for change	Können Sie bitte wechseln?
Saying 'you're welcome'	Bitte schön
	Gern geschehen
	Nichts zu danken

Cultural briefing

Public transport in Germany

German railways are very impressive; they are punctual, comfortable and reasonably priced. Beware of the **Zuschlag**, or supplement, on fast Intercity trains. The efficient local train/tram service linking important places is called the **S-Bahn**. Tram services are common in larger towns. An **H** sign indicates a **Haltestelle**, a tram or bus stop. Taxis are readily available, usually charging quite moderate rates, but drivers expect around ten per cent of the fare as a tip.

For help at smaller railway stations, etc., look out for the word **Auskunft**, an alternative to **Information**.

Pronunciation

e – i

Like **a**, **o**, **u** these vowels have short and long versions

e	short like *e* in *men*	Essen, elf, Student
	long like *a* in *mate*	pronounced as with a Scottish accent
		wenig, gehen, zehn, Problem

In an unstressed syllable, *e* is like the *e* in father
Kinder, Schule, bitte, Besuch

i	short like *i* in *bit*	Kind, richtig, Firma
	long like *ee* in *see*	ihn, Ihnen, wir

An **h** after **e** or **i** has the effect of lengthening the sound:
gehen, Ihnen

UNIT **9** Unterkunft

In this unit, you will learn how to …

- book into a hotel
- fill in a registration form
- ask somebody to sign a form
- extract information from hotel brochures.

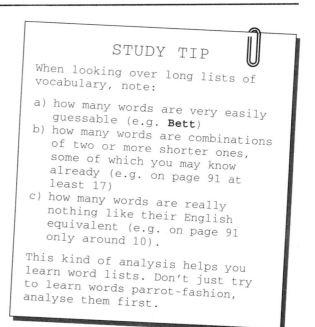

STUDY TIP

When looking over long lists of vocabulary, note:

a) how many words are very easily guessable (e.g. **Bett**)
b) how many words are combinations of two or more shorter ones, some of which you may know already (e.g. on page 91 at least 17)
c) how many words are really nothing like their English equivalent (e.g. on page 91 only around 10).

This kind of analysis helps you learn word lists. Don't just try to learn words parrot-fashion, analyse them first.

Dialogue: **Am Empfang**

On arrival at the Hotel Coenen Michael Newby deals with registration formalities at the reception desk.

Empfangsdame	Guten Tag, mein Herr.
Newby	Guten Tag. Ich habe ein Zimmer reserviert.

Empfangsdame	Ihr Name bitte?
Newby	Ich heiße Michael Newby.
Empfangsdame	Ach ja, Sie sind auf Geschäftsreise von der Firma Anglia Chemicals, nicht wahr?
Newby	Ja, stimmt. Ich bin Geschäftsführer der Firma Anglia Chemicals.
Empfangsdame	Bitte füllen Sie diese Seite des Anmeldeformulars aus, Herr Newby.
Newby	Selbstverständlich. Also, Tag meiner Ankunft … der vierte Oktober.
Empfangsdame	So, Zimmer Nummer neun – Einzelzimmer mit Bad im ersten Stock. Hier ist Ihr Schlüssel. Es ist sehr schön. Einen Fahrstuhl haben wir auch. Er ist gleich um die Ecke. Wir bringen Ihr Gepäck nach oben, wenn Sie wollen.
Newby	Danke, das geht schon.

Vocabulary

der Empfang *reception*
westlich von *to the west of*
Ich habe … reserviert *I have reserved …*
ausfüllen *(sep) to fill in*
diese *this*
die Seite, -n *page*
des *of the (* for masculine and neuter nouns*)*
das Anmeldeformular, -e *registration form*

(die Anmeldung, -en *registration)*
das Formular, -e *form*
selbstverständlich *of course*
meiner *of my (* for feminine nouns)*
im ersten Stock *on the first floor*
hier *here*
der Schlüssel, - *key*
sehr *very*

der Fahrstuhl, ¨e *lift*
um die Ecke *around the corner*
die Ecke, -n *corner*
bringen *to take, bring*
das Gepäck *luggage*
nach oben bringen *to take upstairs*
wenn *if*

Notes

1 **Guten Tag, mein Herr.** This is the equivalent of *sir*, whilst *madam* is **gnädige Frau**.

2 **Danke, das geht schon.** This is a useful phrase for saying that you can manage by yourself. In reply to a question whether you want something, say **danke** when you mean *no, thank you*, and **ja, bitte** for *yes please*.

3 **Einen Fahrstuhl haben wir auch.** *Einen Fahrstuhl* is emphasised and therefore is put to the beginning of the sentence. Note that the verb is still the second idea in the sentence, so that *wir* comes after the verb.

Exercise 1

Answer these questions on Mr Newby's arrival at the hotel.

1 After giving his name, what is Newby asked to do?
2 Where is his room situated?
3 What does the receptionist point him to?
4 Where will he find this?
5 What does he decline?

| **Exercise 2** | Put the following words in the correct spaces in the sentences below. |

dieser, diesen, diesem, dieses, welches, welche, welchem, welcher (**welcher** and **dieser** take the same endings as **der**, **die**, **das**, see page 103.)

_____ Zimmer ist sehr schön.

Bitte nehmen Sie _____ Schlüssel.

In _____ Stock ist das Zimmer?

_____ Nummer hat mein Zimmer?

Ihr Zimmer ist in _____ Stock.

_____ Hotel ist dort drüben?

_____ Fahrstuhl funktioniert nicht.

_____ Tag ist der Tag Ihrer Ankunft?

| **Exercise 3** | You have just arrived at the reception desk of a hotel in Frankfurt. What do you say in German? |

| *Empfangsdame* | Guten Tag, mein Herr/gnädige Frau. |
| *Sie* | (*Greet the receptionist and say you have reserved a single room with a bath.*) |

_____

| *Empfangsdame* | Ihr Name, bitte? |
| *Sie* | (*Give your name.*) |

_____

| *Empfangsdame* | Ach ja, Sie kommen aus England, nicht wahr? |
| *Sie* | (*Say that you do.*) |

_____

| *Empfangsdame* | Bitte füllen Sie dieses Anmeldeformular aus, Herr/Frau … |
| *Sie* | (*Say yes, of course you will. Ask what number your room is.*) |

_____

| *Empfangsdame* | Also, Zimmer Nummer dreiundvierzig im dritten Stock. |
| *Sie* | (*Ask where the lift is.*) |

_____

| *Empfangsdame* | Er ist da drüben, sehen Sie? Wir bringen Ihr Gepäck nach oben, wenn Sie wollen. |
| *Sie* | (*Say thank you, but you can manage.*) |

_____

Comprehension 1

Listen to the passage about the visitor to the Arabella Hotel in Duisburg, then fill in the registration form on her behalf.

```
                        Anmeldeformular
 Name_____

 Vorname_____

 Staatsangehörigkeit_____

 Straße/Nr._____

 Wohnort_____

 Paß-Nr_____

 Ankunft_____        Abreise_____

 Zimmer-Nr_____

 Firma_____

 Unterschrift_____
```

Vocabulary

reisen *to travel*
bekommen *to get, receive*
unterschreiben *to sign*

der Paß, ¨sse *passport*
die Abreise, -n *departure*

viel *much*
zu tun *to do*

Exercise 4

Use the symbols below to complete the dialogues.

Vocabulary

das Doppelzimmer, - *double room*

eine Nacht, ¨e *night*

der Hotelbesitzer, - *hotel owner*

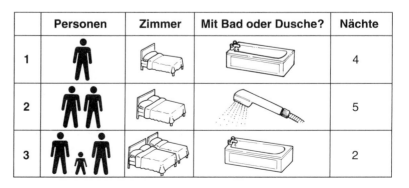

	Personen	Zimmer	Mit Bad oder Dusche?	Nächte
1				4
2				5
3				2

1 *Empfangsdame*   Guten Tag, gnädige Frau.

Dame   _____

Empfangsdame   Ein Einzelzimmer? Ja. Für wie viele Nächte?

Dame   _____

Empfangsdame   Mit Bad oder Dusche?

Dame   _____

Empfangsdame   Also, Nummer sechzehn ist noch frei.

2 *Hotelbesitzer*   Guten Tag, bitte schön?

Herr   _____

Hotelbesitzer   Ja. Möchten Sie ein Doppelzimmer?

Herr   _____

Hotelbesitzer   Für wie viele Nächte?

Herr   _____

Hotelbesitzer   Möchten Sie ein Zimmer mit Bad oder Dusche?

Herr   _____

3 *Empfangsdame*   Guten Abend.

Herr   _____

Empfangsdame   Ja, für wie viele Personen?

Herr   _____

Empfangsdame   Also, ein Doppelzimmer und ...?

Herr   _____

Empfangsdame   Und möchten Sie auch Bad oder Dusche?

Herr   _____

Empfangsdame   Für wie viele Nächte bitte?

Herr   _____

Comprehension 2

Your company plans to hold a residential conference in southern Germany for 30 guests in order to promote a new product. You have been entrusted with the task of finding a suitable hotel at which to stage the conference. After much inquiry and consultation you draw up a shortlist of the three shown over the page.

The final choice must satisfy the following conditions:

1 All rooms must have a bath or shower.
2 All rooms must have a radio, TV and a telephone.

3 An evening meal must be available until 22.00.
4 There must be parking facilities.
5 The hotel must offer a range of recreational facilities.

Which of the three do you decide on?

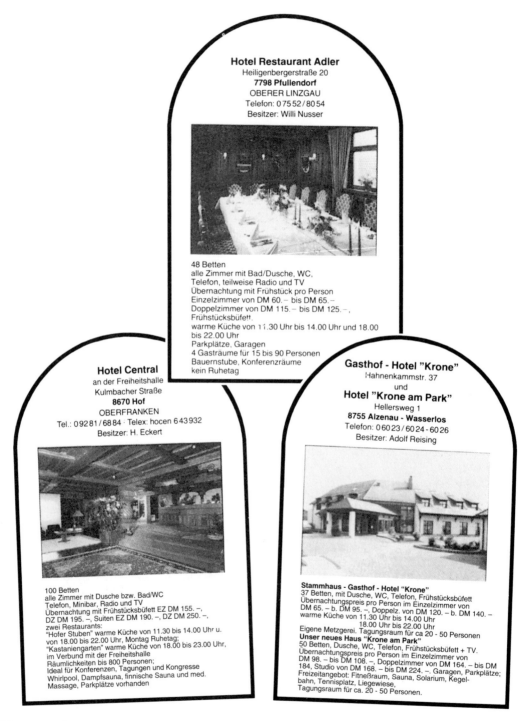

Hotel Restaurant Adler
Heiligenbergerstraße 20
7798 Pfullendorf
OBERER LINZGAU
Telefon: 0 75 52 / 80 54
Besitzer: Willi Nusser

48 Betten
alle Zimmer mit Bad/Dusche, WC,
Telefon, teilweise Radio und TV
Übernachtung mit Frühstück pro Person
Einzelzimmer von DM 60. – bis DM 65. –
Doppelzimmer von DM 115. – bis DM 125. –,
Frühstücksbüfett.
warme Küche von 11.30 Uhr bis 14.00 Uhr und 18.00
bis 22.00 Uhr
Parkplätze, Garagen
4 Gasträume für 15 bis 90 Personen
Bauernstube, Konferenzräume
kein Ruhetag

Hotel Central
an der Freiheitshalle
Kulmbacher Straße
8670 Hof
OBERFRANKEN
Tel.: 0 92 81 / 68 84 · Telex: hocen 6 43 932
Besitzer: H. Eckert

100 Betten
alle Zimmer mit Dusche bzw. Bad/WC
Telefon, Minibar, Radio und TV
Übernachtung mit Frühstücksbüfett EZ DM 155. –,
DZ DM 195. –, Suiten EZ DM 190. –, DZ DM 250. –,
zwei Restaurants:
"Hofer Stuben" warme Küche von 11.30 bis 14.00 Uhr u.
von 18.00 bis 22.00 Uhr, Montag Ruhetag;
"Kastaniengarten" warme Küche von 18.00 bis 23.00 Uhr,
im Verbund mit der Freiheitshalle
Räumlichkeiten bis 800 Personen;
Ideal für Konferenzen, Tagungen und Kongresse
Whirlpool, Dampfsauna, finnische Sauna und med.
Massage, Parkplätze vorhanden

Gasthof - Hotel "Krone"
Hahnenkammstr. 37
und
Hotel "Krone am Park"
Hellersweg 1
8755 Alzenau - Wasserlos
Telefon: 0 60 23 / 60 24 - 60 26
Besitzer: Adolf Reising

Stammhaus - Gasthof - Hotel "Krone"
37 Betten, mit Dusche, WC, Telefon, Frühstücksbüfett
Übernachtungspreis pro Person im Einzelzimmer von
DM 65. – b. DM 95. –, Doppelz. von DM 120. – b. DM 140. –
warme Küche von 11.30 Uhr bis 14.00 Uhr
18.00 Uhr bis 22.00 Uhr
Eigene Metzgerei. Tagungsraum für ca 20 - 50 Personen
Unser neues Haus "Krone am Park"
50 Betten, Dusche, WC, Telefon, Frühstücksbüfett + TV.
Übernachtungspreis pro Person im Einzelzimmer von
DM 98. – bis DM 108. –, Doppelzimmer von DM 164. – bis DM
184, Studio von DM 168. – bis DM 224. –. Garagen, Parkplätze;
Freizeitangebot: Fitneßraum, Sauna, Solarium, Kegel-
bahn, Tennisplatz, Liegewiese,
Tagungsraum für ca. 20 - 50 Personen.

Vocabulary 🔲

Hotel Restaurant Adler *The Eagle Hotel and Restaurant*
das Bett, -en *bed*
alle *all*
teilweise *partly*
das Radio, -s *radio*
die Übernachtung, -en *overnight stay*
das Frühstück, -e *breakfast*
die Person, -en *person*
das Frühstücksbüfett *breakfast buffet*
warme Küche *hot cuisine, food*
der Parkplatz, ̈e *car park*
die Garage, -n *garage*
der Gastraum, ̈e *guest dining room*
die Bauernstube, -n *rustic style lounge*

der Konferenzraum, ̈e *conference room*
der Ruhetag, -e *closing day*
bzw.= beziehungsweise *or*
EZ, DZ = Einzel-, Doppelzimmer
'Kastaniengarten' *chestnut tree garden*
im Verbund mit *in association with*
Räumlichkeiten *room, capacity*
bis *up to*
ideal *ideal*
der Kongreß, -sse *congress*
die Dampfsauna *steam sauna*
med.= medizinische *medical*
die Massage, -n *massage*
vorhanden *available*

Gasthof-Hotel 'Krone' *The Crown Inn and Hotel*
Hotel 'Krone am Park' *The Crown Hotel by the Park*
das Stammhaus *original building*
eigen *own*
die Metzgerei, -en *butcher*
neu *new*
das Freizeitangebot, -e *recreational facilities*
der Fitneßraum, ̈e *gymnasium*
die Kegelbahn, -en *9-pin bowling facility*
der Tennisplatz, ̈e *tennis court*
die Liegewiese, -n *sunbathing lawn*

Talking business extra

Comprehension 3

🔲 When Christian and Katrina compare notes on their accommodation, their experiences are very different. Whether in English or in German we'll never know, but Katrina did complain!

Key vocabulary

erstklassig *first class*
das Messegelände, - *trade fair complex*
die Heizung *heating*
wunderschön *beautiful*

die Wärmeregulierung, -en *temperature regulation*
sich beschweren *to complain*
die Beschwerde, -n *complaint*

verärgert *annoyed*
bekommen *to get*
der Messestand, ̈e *trade fair stand*

Key phrases

mit der Unterkunft zufrieden
Ist etwas nicht in Ordnung?
Das ist nicht so einfach
bei der Hotelleitung reklamieren
Das weiß ich nicht genau
keine Sorge
ein anderes Zimmer
Viel Glück!
Bis später!

happy with the accommodation
Is anything wrong?
That's not so straightforward
to complain to the hotel management
I don't exactly know
don't worry
a different room
Good luck!
See you later !

Find out:

1 what Christian did before breakfast

2 what Katrina did before breakfast.

Exercise 5

Fill in the details:

Reklamation

Die Wärmeregulierung _____ nicht.

Haben Sie sich _____?

Ich habe bei der Hotelleitung _____.

Ich war sehr _____.

Die Hotelleitung hat alles sofort überprüft.

Puzzle

1 complaint
2 trade fair stand
3 basis
4 window
5 heating
6 clue: extremely good

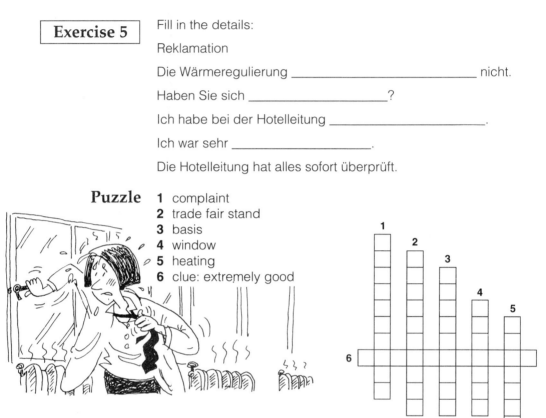

Language structures

Verbs Imperative

Füllen Sie dieses Anmeldeformular **aus**.	*Fill in this registration form.*
Wählen Sie Ihr Ziel.	*Choose your destination.*
Drücken Sie die Taste.	*Press the button.*
Werfen Sie das Geld **ein**.	*Insert the money.*

The imperative form is used when giving instructions or orders. Just as in a question, the **Sie** follows the verb.

Cases The genitive case

Die Sekretärin **des** Verkaufsleiters	*The sales manager's secretary*
Der Geschäftsführer **der** Firma	*The managing director of the firm*
Diese Seite **des** Anmeldeformulars	*This page of the registration form*

Uses:
1 To indicate possession. English frequently uses *of* for this purpose, as well as the apostrophe *s*, e.g. *the firm's managing director*. German uses the genitive forms of the article, or whatever is in place of the article. Remember to add the **(e)s** on the end of a masculine or neuter noun in the genitive (see below).
2 After certain prepositions, the most common of which are:
   während   *during*
   wegen   *because of*

FORMATION
Refer to the relevant tables (articles on page 27, **dieser** on page 103, possessive adjectives on page 60, etc.)

Masculine and neuter nouns
   add **es** if they have one syllable or if they end in **s**.
   add **s** if they have more than one syllable.

der Mann   des Mann**es**   der Fahrstuhl   des Fahrstuhl**s**
das Gleis   des Gleis**es**   das Formular   des Formular**s**

Feminine nouns add no ending

die Firma   der Firma
die Frau   der Frau

Note also the use of **s** added to people's names to indicate possession:

Gudrun**s** Mann   *Gudrun's husband*
Wolfgang**s** Eltern   *Wolfgang's parents*
Herrn Paternolli**s** Visitenkarte   *Mr. Paternolli's business card*

Progress check

1 NVQ S1
At reception, what would you say if you wanted to:
a) book a double room with a bath for three nights
b) ask the receptionist for a registration form
c) enquire on which floor your room is
d) ask where the lift is
e) ask the porter to take your luggage upstairs
f) return your keys?

2 NVQ S2
Give the following instructions in German:
a) Fill in this form please.
b) Please sign here.
c) Take a taxi from the airport to the firm.
d) Choose a hotel with a car-park and a restaurant.

3 NVQ W1
Make a list of your requirements in German:

ten single rooms with shower, toilet, telephone and TV; two conference rooms; hot food at lunchtime; and a tennis court.

4 What is this receptionist telling you about her hotel?
'Selbstverständlich haben wir Räumlichkeiten für fünfzig Personen. Hier ist eine Liste der Übernachtungspreise. Unser Freizeitangebot ist ideal für Tagungen und Kongresse. Jetzt brauche ich noch das Datum Ihrer Ankunft und Abreise, und Ihre Unterschrift hier unten, bitte.'

5 NVQ R2
These two notes relate to two separate complaints. What are they telling you?
a) Ich verstehe Ihre Beschwerde, aber ich kann Ihnen leider nicht helfen.
b) Ich habe reklamiert, und jetzt ist alles in bester Ordnung.

UNIT 10 Was kostet Halbpension?

In this unit, you will learn how to …

- ask for availability and prices of accommodation
- specify your accommodation requirements
- compare things with each other
- ask for sights and amenities in town.

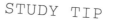

Dialogue: Im Gasthof Lehen

Mr Saunders has business to do in Munich. He has decided to combine this with a family holiday in Austria. He makes enquiries at the **Gasthof Lehen** which features in the list of local hotels (**Zimmernachweis**).

Mr Saunders	Guten Tag. Haben Sie noch Zimmer frei?
Inhaber	Für wie viele Personen?
Mr Saunders	Für zwei Erwachsene und zwei Kinder. Ich möchte ein Doppelzimmer und zwei Einzelzimmer für drei Nächte.
Inhaber	Ja, das geht.
Mr Saunders	Haben Sie Zimmer mit Bad?
Inhaber	Nein, Zimmer mit Bad haben wir nicht, nur mit Dusche. Auch mit Fernsehen und Balkon, wenn Sie wollen. Alle Zimmer sind schön.
Mr Saunders	Gut. Ihr Gasthof hat ja eine herrliche Aussicht auf die Berge. Die ist wirklich sehr schön. Ich finde es hier sehr angenehm.

(*He then discusses with his family whether they require full or half-board, when meals are served, and the hotel's charges.*)

Inhaber	Möchten Sie Voll- oder Halbpension?
Mr Saunders	Lieber Halbpension. Tagsüber möchten wir die Sehenswürdigkeiten der Umgebung besichtigen. Wann gibt es Frühstück und Abendessen?

Inhaber	Frühstück ab sieben Uhr, Abendessen gibt es um halb sieben.
Mr Saunders	Was kostet Halbpension?
Inhaber	Für die Erwachsenen zweihundertvierzig Schilling, für die Kinder ist es billiger, hundertsiebzig Schilling pro Nacht.
Mr Saunders	Können wir die Zimmer sehen?
Inhaber	Ja, gern. Kommen Sie bitte mit …
Mr Saunders	Die Zimmer sind prima. Die nehmen wir.

Vocabulary

der Inhaber, - *owner*
Zimmer frei *rooms available*
der Erwachsene, -n *adult*
das Fernsehen *television*
der Balkon, -s *balcony*
schön *beautiful*
herrlich *magnificent, splendid*
die Aussicht, -en *view*
der Berg, -e *mountain*
Aussicht auf die Berge *view of the mountains*

wirklich *really*
finden *to find*
die Vollpension *full board*
die Halbpension *half board*
lieber *preferably*
tagsüber *during the day*
die Sehenswürdigkeit, -en *sight, thing worth seeing*
die Umgebung *surrounding area*
besichtigen *to view*

ab *(+ Dative) from*
das Abendessen, - *dinner*
der Schilling, -e *Austrian shilling*
billig *cheap*
billiger *cheaper*
ja, gern *yes, (I'll) gladly (show you)*
prima *super*

Notes

1 **Ihr Gasthof hat ja eine herrliche Aussicht. Die ist sehr schön.**
Ja is for emphasis … *does have a splendid view.*
Die refers to **Aussicht.** You could say
Sie ist sehr schön, but using the definite article gives it more emphasis.

2 **Wann gibt es Frühstück?**
Gibt es *there is, there are* (see Unit 6, page 50).

Exercise 1

Complete the phrases in the first column with an appropriate phrase from the column opposite, according to the information in the dialogue.

1 Frühstück gibt es …
2 Alle Zimmer haben …
3 Für ein Kind kostet …
4 Für die Kinder gibt es …
5 Der Vater und die Mutter möchten …
6 Sie können ein Zimmer mit Fernsehen und Balkon haben, …
7 Vollpension möchte …
8 Die Aussicht vom Balkon …

a) die Familie nicht.
b) zwei Einzelzimmer.
c) wenn Sie wollen.
d) ist auf die Berge.
e) ein Zimmer mit Halbpension AS170,-.
f) ein Doppelzimmer.
g) ab 07.00.
h) Dusche.

Exercise 2	You work at a tourist office. A German client is making preliminary enquiries about a hotel before booking a room. Complete the gaps with the appropriate pronoun.

(Remember *it* is either **er**, **sie** or **es**, depending on the gender of the noun it refers to. See Language structures overview, page 29.)

Example: Ist das Zimmer noch frei? Ja, **es** ist noch frei.

1 Wie ist das Hotel? _____ ist klein, sehr ruhig und liegt am Stadtrand.

2 Hat das Hotel einen Parkplatz? Ja, und _____ hat auch eine Garage.

3 Was kostet die Garage? _____ kostet DM 6,- pro Nacht.

4 Hat man eine gute Aussicht vom Hotel? Ja, _____ ist ganz wunderbar.

5 Hat das Hotel einen Garten? Ja, _____ ist sehr schön und auch sonnig.

6 Gibt es auch einen Fahrstuhl? Ja, _____ ist ganz neu.

Exercise 3	A colleague at work wants to rent a flat in Switzerland during the summer. She has asked you to read the following advertisement which she found in a Swiss accommodation leaflet, and also to answer some questions for her.

> In der Wohnung: ein Schlafzimmer, zwei Kinderzimmer, Eßzimmer, Wohnzimmer, Küche, Badezimmer, Balkon mit wunderbarer Aussicht auf Berge und See, Fahrstuhl im Haus, Parkplätze, Garten (leider keine Tiere).
> Zehn Minuten mit dem Auto/Bus von Stadtmitte und Bahnhof. In der Stadt: modernes Schwimmbad, bunte Parks, römisches Museum, großer Zoo, alter Dom.
> Für nähere Informationen telefonieren oder schreiben Sie an: Schneider-Appartements, Bachstr. 4, Zürich, Tel: 01/202 39 47.

Vocabulary

die Wohnung, -en *flat*
das Schlafzimmer, - *bedroom*
das Eßzimmer, - *dining-room*
das Wohnzimmer, - *living-room*
die Küche, -n *kitchen*
das Badezimmer, - *bathroom*
der See, -n *lake*
leider *unfortunately*

das Tier, -e *animal (here: pet)*
der Bus, -se *bus*
die Stadtmitte, -n *town centre*
modern *modern*
das Schwimmbad, ¨er *swimming pool*
bunt *colourful*
der Park, -s *park*

römisch *Roman*
das Museum, die Museen *museum*
der Zoo *zoo*
alt *old*
der Dom, -e *cathedral*
nähere Informationen *more information*

Now answer your colleague's questions.

1 What are the views like?
2 I'm not taking the car. Can we reach the town centre easily?
3 Is there a lift?
4 Is there a railway station there?
5 What are the main tourist attractions?
6 How do I find out more information?

| Exercise 4 |

Mrs. Johnson is to travel to Bavaria on business to discuss the purchase of some machinery. She receives the following letter from the company she will be visiting, confirming her accommodation.

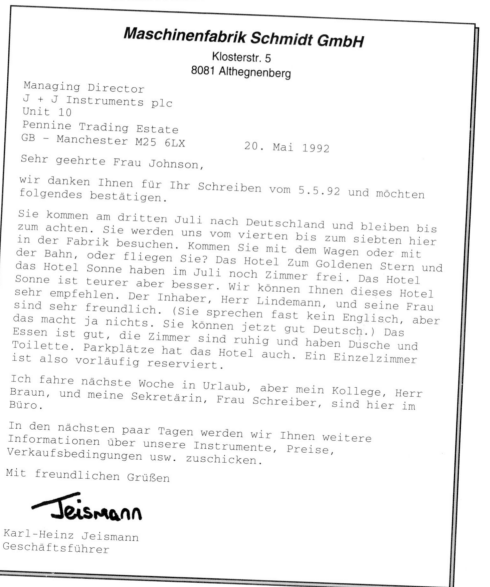

Maschinenfabrik Schmidt GmbH

Klosterstr. 5
8081 Althegnenberg

```
Managing Director
J + J Instruments plc
Unit 10
Pennine Trading Estate
GB - Manchester M25 6LX          20. Mai 1992
```

Sehr geehrte Frau Johnson,

wir danken Ihnen für Ihr Schreiben vom 5.5.92 und möchten folgendes bestätigen.

Sie kommen am dritten Juli nach Deutschland und bleiben bis zum achten. Sie werden uns vom vierten bis zum siebten hier in der Fabrik besuchen. Kommen Sie mit dem Wagen oder mit der Bahn, oder fliegen Sie? Das Hotel Zum Goldenen Stern und das Hotel Sonne haben im Juli noch Zimmer frei. Das Hotel Sonne ist teurer aber besser. Wir können Ihnen dieses Hotel sehr empfehlen. Der Inhaber, Herr Lindemann, und seine Frau sind sehr freundlich. (Sie sprechen fast kein Englisch, aber das macht ja nichts. Sie können jetzt gut Deutsch.) Das Essen ist gut, die Zimmer sind ruhig und haben Dusche und Toilette. Parkplätze hat das Hotel auch. Ein Einzelzimmer ist also vorläufig reserviert.

Ich fahre nächste Woche in Urlaub, aber mein Kollege, Herr Braun, und meine Sekretärin, Frau Schreiber, sind hier im Büro.

In den nächsten paar Tagen werden wir Ihnen weitere Informationen über unsere Instrumente, Preise, Verkaufsbedingungen usw. zuschicken.

Mit freundlichen Grüßen

Jeismann

Karl-Heinz Jeismann
Geschäftsführer

Vocabulary

sehr geehrter Herr ... *dear Mr ... (formal)*
sehr geehrte Frau ... *dear Mrs ...*
danken *(+ dative) to thank*
das Schreiben, - *letter*
folgendes *the following*
bestätigen *to confirm*
Hotel zum Goldenen Stern *The Golden Star Hotel*
Hotel Sonne *The Sun Hotel*
teurer *more expensive, dearer*

besser *better*
freundlich *friendly*
fast kein Englisch *hardly any English*
das macht nichts *that doesn't matter*
das Essen *food*
ruhig *peaceful, quiet*
vorläufig *provisionally*
in Urlaub fahren *to go on holiday*
das Büro, -s *office*
paar *few*

weiter *further*
die Verkaufsbedingungen *sales conditions*
usw.= und so weiter *and so on*
zuschicken *(sep) to send*
mit freundlichen Grüßen *with best regards*

1 Can you pick out two uses of the German future tense?
2 Translate the letter into English.
3 Since some of the arrangements have changed, you have decided to ring Schmidt GmbH. Take your part in this conversation with Herr Jeismann's secretary.

You	(*Thank her for the letter to Mrs Johnson.*)
	_____
Frau Schreiber	Bitte sehr.
You	(*Say Mrs Johnson will be bringing her husband, so please reserve a double room at the Hotel Sonne.*)
	_____
Frau Schreiber	Ach so, ja, das mache ich sofort. Wie lange werden Frau und Herr Johnson denn hier bleiben?
Sie	(*They will be staying until the 10th of July and travelling by car. So please reserve a parking space.*)
	_____
Frau Schreiber	Gut, geht in Ordnung. Vielen Dank für Ihren Anruf. Ich werde Ihnen morgen alles per Telex bestätigen.
Sie	(*Thank her for her help and say goodbye.*)
	_____
Frau Schreiber	Gern geschehen. Auf Wiederhören.

Comprehension 1 While travelling through Austria a couple stop at a tourist information office (**Verkehrsverein**) to enquire about accommodation. Listen to the cassette and answer the following questions.

Vocabulary

in zentraler Lage *in a central location*
außerhalb *(+ genitive) outside*

sogar *even*
fahren wir hin *let's go there*
der Stadtplan, ̈e *map of the town*

der Zimmernachweis, -e *list of hotels*

---

1 In what kind of location do the couple want accommodation?
2 How is the Parkhotel described?
3 How do prices at the Gasthof Huber compare with those of the Parkhotel?
4 What is situated behind the Gasthof?
5 What does the tourist ask for?
6 What else is he given?

Comprehension 2: ## Unterkunft in Deutschland

Deutschland bietet eine Unterkunft für jeden Geschmack. Geschäftsleute, Familien und Studenten können alle eine geeignete Unterkunft finden. In fast allen Städten gibt es Hotels, Appartements, Ferienwohnungen, Privatzimmer, Campingplätze und auch Jugendherbergen.

Viele Leute zelten gern. Im Zelt kann man sehr billig und auch bequem übernachten. In Deutschland gibt es rund 1000 Campingplätze mit fließend Wasser, Toiletten, Duschen, Stromanschluß und Lebensmittelgeschäften. Studenten und auch andere Leute, z.B. Familien und sogar alte Leute wohnen gern in Jugendherbergen. Hier ist man ziemlich frei, und eine Übernachtung ist billig, circa zehn Mark inklusive Frühstück. Die Übernachtungspreise sind niedrig, denn die Jugendherbergen haben wenig Personal. Die Arbeit machen die Gäste. Sie müssen zum Beispiel abwaschen oder die Fenster putzen.

Die großen Luxushotels bieten oft sehr viel, zum Beispiel: mehrere Restaurants, Konferenz- oder Tagungsräume, Garagen, eigenes Schwimmbad, Sauna und Fitneßräume. Hier kann man bequem und mit allem Komfort wohnen beziehungsweise arbeiten. Es gibt auch billigere Hotels und Gasthöfe. Man kann Halb- oder Vollpension nehmen oder in einem Hotel garni wohnen.

Vocabulary

bieten *to offer*
jeder *every*
der Geschmack, ⸚e *taste*
die Leute *people*
geeignet *suitable*
fast *almost*
die Ferienwohnung, -en *holiday flat*
der Campingplatz, ⸚e *camp site*
die Jugendherberge, -n *youth hostel*
zelten *to camp*
... zelten gern *like to camp*

das Zelt, -e *tent*
rund *around*
fließend Wasser *running water*
der Stromanschluß, ⸚sse *electricity point*
das Lebensmittelgeschäft, -e *food shop*
z.B = zum Beispiel
wohnen gern *like to live*
hier ist man ... *here one is ...*
inklusive *inclusive of*
wenig *little*
das Personal *staff*

die Arbeit, -en *work*
der Gast, ⸚e *guest*
abwaschen *(sep) to wash up*
das Fenster, - *window*
putzen *to clean*
das Luxushotel, -s *luxury hotel*
mehrere *several*
hier kann man *here one can*
bequem *comfortable*
der Komfort *comfort*
das Hotel garni *bed and breakfast hotel*

Summarise each of the three paragraphs in English.

Talking business extra

Comprehension 3

Katrina and Christian are finalising terms and conditions to appear on an information leaflet supporting the marketing campaign for their new **Päda-Computer**.

Key vocabulary

die Währung, -en *currency*
die Tabelle, -n *(statistical) table*
die Zahlungsmethode, -n *method of payment*
die Nachnahme *cash on delivery*

die Banküberweisung, -en *bank credit transfer*
die Lieferung, -en *delivery*
die Größenordnung, -en *scale, size*
die Spedition, -en *haulage*
die Garantie, -n *guarantee*

der Mangel, ⸚ *fault*
schiefgehen *(sep) to go wrong*
die Wartung *servicing*
Halt! *Hold on, stop!*

Key phrases

Allgemeine Geschäftsbedingungen (AGB)	*General terms and conditions*
der nächste Punkt	*the next point*
Lassen wir das im Moment	*Let's leave that for the moment*
Es kann etwas schiefgehen	*Something can go wrong*
letzter Punkt	*last point*

Find out:

1 in which currencies prices will be given
2 how deliveries are sent to England.

Exercise 5

Fill in the details:

Verschiedene Zahlungsmethoden

per Post	mit	_____
per Telefon ⎫ per Telefax ⎭	mit	_____

per Nachnahme
per Banküberweisung

Puzzle

Words **1** to **5** all end in **ung**.

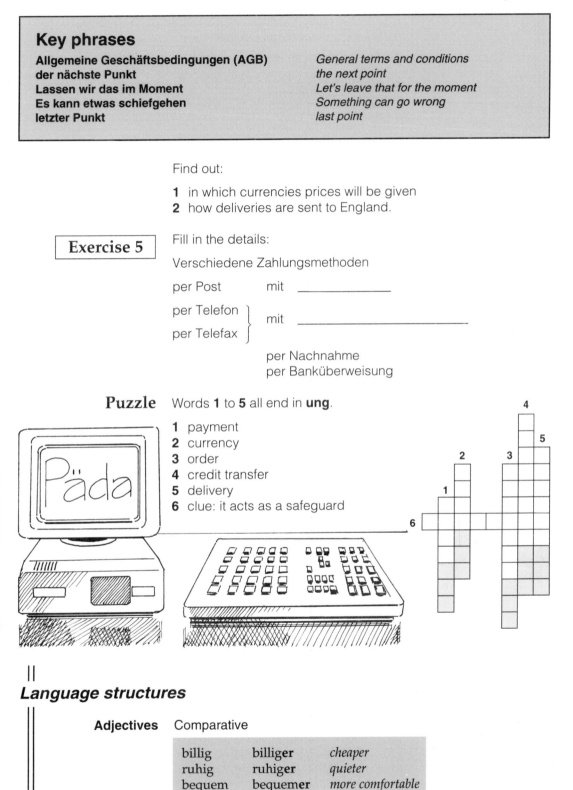

1 payment
2 currency
3 order
4 credit transfer
5 delivery
6 clue: it acts as a safeguard

‖ Language structures

Adjectives   Comparative

billig	billi**ger**	*cheaper*
ruhig	ruhi**ger**	*quieter*
bequem	bequem**er**	*more comfortable*

The comparative is formed by adding **er** to the adjective or adverb. If a word has *one syllable*, an *umlaut* is usually added to the **a**, **o** or **u**, unless the word already has an umlaut.

alt	**älter**
groß	**größer**
früh	**früher**

There are some irregular comparatives, for example:

gut	**besser**	*good, better*
viel	**mehr**	*much, more*
hoch	**höher**	*high, higher*
teuer	**teurer**	*dear, dearer*

Adjective endings

Hier gibt es eine **herrliche** Aussicht.
Die **großen** Luxushotels bieten viel.
Dieses Hotel hat ein **eigenes** Schwimmbad und eine Sauna.
Dieses Hotel hat **moderne** Konferenzräume

Words *describing a noun* are called adjectives. They have to *agree*, which means that the adjective has to take the *same gender* and *case* as the noun it describes.

There are three groups of adjective endings.

1 The adjective comes *after* **der**, **die**, **das** (and **dieser**, **welcher**, etc.)
2 The adjective comes *after* **ein**, **eine** (and **kein**, **mein**, etc.)
3 The adjective stands *on its own* before a noun.

For a full table of adjective endings see Language structures overview, pages 103–4; if the prospect of learning them all seems a little daunting, leave it till later. You will be understood, even if your adjective endings are wrong. However, it is important to remember at this stage that *adjectives used before nouns* must have an ending. Why not look at the tables and learn when to add **en**, then just use **e** for all other instances, till you're ready to memorise them all? The longer and more intensively your mind has been involved in German, the more readily it will jump to the endings which sound right.

Man This is the equivalent of *one* in English (as in *one can't say*) but is more commonly used in German.

Im Zelt kann **man** billig übernachten.
Frühstück bekommt **man** ab 7.00 Uhr.
Man muß zuerst das Anmeldeformular ausfüllen.

Do not confuse **man** with **der Mann** (*the man*)!

Progress check

1 NVQ S1

Arranging accommodation, what would you say if you wanted to:

a) ask if there are any rooms free
b) reserve a double room for two nights
c) ask when breakfast is
d) ask to see a room with balcony
e) say that full board is too expensive
f) ask when you can see the sights
g) say you will take the rooms, they are superb?

2a) and 2b) NVQ S2

State your preferences:

a) That (this) inn over there is larger and cheaper.
b) A quiet room is better.

2c), d), e) and f) NVQ W2

Look through literature on accommodation, you write down notes to be faxed later:

c) The hotel has a marvellous view onto the old cathedral.
d) One can have a flat with a kitchen, a bathroom and two bedrooms.
e) One can also visit a lake and a large zoo there.
f) There is a modern swimming pool in the town centre. It is very big. There is also a tourist information office. It is at the main station.

3 How would you explain these words in English?

a) Inhaber, vorläufig, Verkaufsbedingungen
b) Zimmernachweis, Verkehrsverein
c) Strom, Lebensmittel, Geschäfte

4 NVQ R2

A German customer is concerned about delivery and terms of business. What exactly has he written?

a) Hoffentlich geht mit der Lieferung nichts schief.
b) Die Größenordnung unserer Bestellung hängt von Ihren Geschäftsbedingungen ab.

Summary 4

Language structures overview

Dieser and welcher

Dieser, **diese**, **dieses** *this* and **welcher**, **welche**, **welches** *which?* have the same endings as **der**, **die** and **das**.

	MASCULINE	FEMININE	NEUTER	PLURAL
Nom.	dieser	diese	dieses	diese
Acc.	diesen	diese	dieses	diese
Dat.	diesem	dieser	diesem	diesen
Gen.	dieses	dieser	dieses	dieser

Adjective agreement

1 After **der**, **die**, **das** (and **dieser**, **welcher**) the adjective takes the following endings:

	MASCULINE	FEMININE	NEUTER	PLURAL
Nom.	der gute Wagen	die neue Firma	das große Hotel	die alten Gäste
Acc.	den guten Wagen	die neue Firma	das große Hotel	die alten Gäste
Dat.	dem guten Wagen	der neuen Firma	dem großen Hotel	den alten Gästen
Gen.	des guten Wagens	der neuen Firma	des großen Hotels	der alten Gäste

2 After **ein**, **eine**, **ein** and **kein**, **mein**, **Ihr**, etc. (for possessive adjectives, see page 60) the adjective takes the following endings:

Summary 4

	MASCULINE	FEMININE	NEUTER
Nom.	ein gut**er** Wagen	eine neu**e** Firma	ein groß**es** Hotel
Acc.	einen gut**en** Wagen	eine neu**e** Firma	ein groß**es** Hotel
Dat.	einem gut**en** Wagen	einer neu**en** Firma	einem groß**en** Hotel
Gen.	eines gut**en** Wagens	einer neu**en** Firma	eines groß**en** Hotels

Note: The horizontal lines in the previous two tables should help you remember that all adjectives below them end in **en**.

In the plural (after **keine**, **meine**, **Ihre**, etc.) the adjective takes the same endings as in table 1.

	PLURAL
Nom.	keine neu**en** Firmen
Acc.	meine alt**en** Freunde
Dat.	unseren neu**en** Vertretern
Gen.	Ihrer englisch**en** Kollegen

3 When an adjective stands *on its own*, it takes the following endings:

	MASCULINE	FEMININE	NEUTER
Nom.	gut**er** Stahl	interessant**e** Information	gut**es** Essen
Acc.	gut**en** Stahl	interessant**e** Information	gut**es** Essen
Dat.	gut**em** Stahl	interessant**er** Information	gut**em** Essen
Gen.	gut**en** Stahls	interessant**er** Information	gut**en** Essen

	PLURAL	
Nom.	wichtig**e**	Lebensmittel
Acc.	wichtig**e**	Lebensmittel
Dat.	wichtig**en**	Lebensmitteln
Gen.	wichtig**er**	Lebensmittel

Additional exercises

1 Your colleague has a habit of going one better than you. Complete his answers.

Example: Ich habe ein großes Haus. Ja, aber mein Haus ist größer.

a Meine Arbeit ist interessant. Ja, aber meine Arbeit ist

_____.

b Hier hat man eine schöne Aussicht auf die Berge. Ja, aber diese Aussicht ist

noch _____.

c Dieses Hotel ist teuer. Ja, aber dieses Hotel ist noch _____.

d Wir importieren viel aus der Schweiz. Ja, aber wir importieren _____ aus Frankreich.

e Der Automat ist kompliziert. Ja, aber dieser Automat ist noch

_____.

f Dieses Zimmer ist ruhig. Ja, aber dieses Zimmer ist noch _____.

g Mein Vater ist schon alt. Ja, aber mein Vater ist _____.

h Diese Berge sind sehr hoch. Ja, aber die Berge dort drüben sind noch viel

_____.

i Ich fliege oft nach Deutschland. Ja, aber ich fliege _____ nach Amerika.

j Unsere Instrumente kosten wenig. Ja, aber unsere kosten noch

_____.

2 Complete the following sentences with the correct form of **dieser, diese, dieses**.

a _____ Gegend ist sehr schön.

b _____ Zimmer ist groß.

c _____ Firma hat ein Büro in Frankreich.

d Der Vertreter von _____ Firma heißt Herr Maily.

e Fahren Sie mit _____ Zug?

f _____ Zimmer sind sehr schön.

g _____ Bus fährt zum See.

h Sehen Sie _____ Fahrplan?

3 Complete the gaps in the following sentences with the genitive form of **der, die, das**.

a Wie heißt der Geschäftsführer _____ Firma?

b Der Leiter _____ Fabrik heißt Herr Kostner.

c Der Preis _____ Fahrausweises ist DM2, –.

d Ich möchte die Sehenswürdigkeiten _____ Umgebung besichtigen.

e Die Sekretärin _____ Geschäftsführers heißt Frau Morgan.

f Die Namen _____ Kinder sind Lotte und Jürgen.

g Ich schicke Ihnen morgen die Preise _____ Hotels.

h Wo ist das Gepäck _____ Geschäftsleute?

4 Do the adjectives in the following sentences have the ending **e, en**, or do they have no ending at all?

a Das billig__ Hotel hat keine Sauna.

Dieses Hotel ist sehr billig__.

b Sehen Sie den schön__ Dom dort drüben?

Der Kölner Dom ist sehr schön__, nicht wahr?

c Wo ist der neu__ Stadtplan?

Ich habe einen neu__ Stadtplan für Sie.

Dieser Stadtplan ist leider nicht neu__.

d Diese alt__ Firma hat sehr gut__ Verkaufsbedingungen.

Unsere Firma ist schon sehr alt__.

Heute besuche ich eine alt__ Firma.

e Die groß__ Luxushotels bieten sehr viel.

Man kann in den groß__ Luxushotels auch Fitneßräume

finden. Die Luxushotels sind manchmal sehr groß__.

f Wie hoch__ ist dieser Berg?

Ist die Umgebung schön__?

Warum sind die Übernachtungspreise so teuer__?

g Dieser alt__ Fahrstuhl funktioniert nicht.

Wo gibt es einen ruhig__ Park?

Wann ist die wichtig__ Tagung in Bonn?

Welche bequem__ Unterkunft gibt es hier?

Wollen Sie eine interessant__ Firma besuchen?

Key phrases

Saying you have reserved a room	Ich habe ein Zimmer reserviert
Saying that something is correct	Ja, (das/es) stimmt
Saying 'of course'	Selbstverständlich
	Natürlich
Saying you can manage	Danke, das geht schon
Asking if rooms are available	Haben Sie noch Zimmer frei?
Asking for particular rooms and facilities	Ich möchte ein/zwei Einzelzimmer/
	Doppelzimmer mit Bad/Dusche/Balkon/
	Fernsehen/Telefon
Asking about meal times	Wann gibt es Frühstück und Abendessen?
Asking about prices	Was kostet Halbpension?
Asking to see rooms	Können wir die Zimmer sehen?
Saying you like something	Die Zimmer sind sehr schön
Saying you will take the rooms	Die nehmen wir
Asking someone to recommend you something	Können Sie uns einen/eine/ein ... empfehlen?
Saying your prefer something	Lieber ein(e)(en) ...
Saying something is acceptable	Das geht

Cultural briefing

Accommodation

If you're not heading straight for the five-star hotel, or the town doesn't boast one, you may be bemused by the range of accommodation available. If so, the local **Verkehrsverein**, or tourist information office, can do more than point you in the right direction. The staff will arrange your booking for you, having established whether rooms are free in the required combinations of bath/shower, balcony and so on.

Here, as elswhere in the service sector, don't be surprised at the ease with which staff can express themselves in English, frustrating your attempts to practise your German! They are often highly motivated and trained in what is after all an international language, and their expectation will be that you don't speak German adequately. Keep trying to prove them wrong!

Pronunciation

j – r – v – w – z – y

j	like English *y* – ja, jetzt
r	very like French *r*, rolled in the throat
	Straße, Rolltreppe, der Reisende
v	like English *f* – Vormittag, vier, von
w	like English *v* – Wochenende, Welt, wichtig
z	like *ts* in *cats* – Zucker, Zug, Zentrum, Französisch
y	same as **ü** sound – typisch

UNIT **11** Wie war die Reise?

In this unit, you will learn how to …

- talk about how you are feeling
- express your likes and preferences
- talk about hobbies and spare time activities
- choose where to eat
- talk about things which have happened in the past.

STUDY TIP

Saying what you like, don't like, prefer or like best is something you do surprisingly often. Relate German phrases for expressing likes and dislikes as much as possible to your own circumstances and lifestyle. Go through the things you typically do in the course of the day, both at work and leisure, and express all these things in terms of how much you like and dislike them, what you prefer to what, and so on. Look up whatever you need in a dictionary.

Dialogue: **Im Hotel Coenen**

Herbert Walter, Lotte Meyer and Ewald Weidmann arrive at the Hotel Coenen to take Michael Newby to one of their factories and then out to lunch.

Walter	Guten Morgen, Herr Newby. Wie geht es Ihnen?
Newby	Gut, danke. Ich war gestern abend sehr müde, aber jetzt geht es mir besser. Ich habe sehr gut geschlafen.
Walter	Sie kennen schon meine Kollegin Frau Meyer und meinen Kollegen Herrn Weidmann?

Newby	Ja, wir haben uns in Altrincham kennengelernt. Tag, Frau Meyer, Tag, Herr Weidmann. Es freut mich sehr, Sie wiederzusehen.
Meyer	Gleichfalls, Herr Newby. Haben Sie eine gute Reise gehabt?
Newby	Ziemlich gut, danke.
Weidmann	Sind Sie zum ersten Mal in Mönchengladbach?
Newby	Ja.
Walter	Wir können Ihnen später die Sehenswürdigkeiten der Stadt zeigen, wenn Sie Lust haben.
Newby	Ja, das möchte ich gerne. Ich habe so viel von Mönchengladbach gehört. Bekannte von mir sind oft auf Geschäftsreise hier gewesen.

Vocabulary

war *was*
müde *tired*
ich habe … geschlafen *I (have) slept …*
wir haben uns … kennengelernt *we have met …*

gleichfalls *likewise*
Haben Sie … gehabt? *Did you have …?*
zeigen *to show*
… wenn Sie Lust haben *if you like*
hören, gehört *to hear, heard*

sind … gewesen *have been …*

Notes

1 **Ich war … sehr müde** *I was very tired.*
Ich habe … gut geschlafen *I slept well.*
You are now learning different ways of speaking about what happened in the past. Sometimes the word order is very different from English. You'll find fuller explanations in the Language structures.

2 **Das möchte ich gern** *I would like that a lot.*

Gern is normally used with a verb to say that the speaker likes doing something (details in Language structures, page 117).

3 **Es freut mich, Sie wiederzusehen** *Pleased to see you again.* **Wiedersehen** is a separable verb. Therefore the **zu** *(to)* goes in between the two separable parts.

Exercise 1

Complete the phrases in the first column with an appropriate phrase from the column opposite, according to the information in the dialogue.

1 Es freut Michael Newby …

2 Michael Newby hat …

3 Michael Newby ist …

4 Michael Newby kennt schon …

5 Heute ist Michael Newby …

a) sehr gut geschlafen.
b) nicht mehr müde.
c) Herrn Weidmann und Frau Meyer wiederzusehen.
d) zum ersten Mal in Mönchengladbach.
e) Frau Meyer und Herrn Weidmann.

Exercise 2

You are being taken out to lunch by your German host on the first day of a business trip to Hamburg. You are collected at your hotel in Hamburg. What do you say in German?

Gastgeber	Guten Morgen, Herr/Frau ... Wie geht es Ihnen?
Sie	(*Say you had a good sleep. You were very tired but now you are better.*)

_____

Gastgeber	Sie kennen meinen Kollegen, Herrn Desch?
Sie	(*Say yes, you met at a conference in Munich. Tell Herr Desch you are pleased to see him again.*)

_____

Desch	Gleichfalls, Herr/Frau ... Haben Sie eine gute Reise gehabt?
Sie	(*Say thank you, you have had quite a good one.*)

_____

Gastgeber	Sind Sie zum ersten Mal in Hamburg, Herr/Frau ...?
Sie	(*Say yes, that's right.*)

_____

Gastgeber	Wir zeigen Ihnen später die Sehenswürdigkeiten, wenn Sie wollen.
Sie	(*Say you would like that, you have heard so much about Hamburg.*)

_____

Vocabulary

der Gastgeber, - *host*

Exercise 3	You have been sent by your company to gain work experience in their German office. This morning your boss left you this list of tasks to be done in his absence. When you have familiarised yourself with its contents, look at the Language structures on pages 115–16, on the past tense, so that you can carry out the task set opposite.

> Flughafen-Reisebüro anrufen und Flugkarte bestellen
> Marketing-Zeitschrift kaufen
> Hotelzimmer in Bremen für nächsten Dienstag reservieren
> Mit dem Restaurant Schloßhof sprechen
> Tisch für zwei Leute für 13.00 reservieren
> Export-Formulare ausfüllen
> Brief an die Firma Mann GmbH tippen
> Hans Schoening um 11.45 vom Bahnhof abholen

Vocabulary

das Reisebüro, -s *travel agency*

die Zeitschrift, -en *magazine*
bestellen *to order*

tippen *to type*

You have had a busy morning. On your boss's return give him a quick résumé of your activities.

Example: Ich **habe** das Flughafen-Reisebüro **angerufen**.
Ich **habe** ...

The past participles are listed here to help you along, but once you have studied them, you should try the exercise again without referring to the list.

Separable verbs	**Regular verbs**	**Irregular verbs**
angerufen	gekauft	gesprochen
ausgefüllt	getippt	
abgeholt	bestellt	
	reserviert	

Exercise 4

Read the following sentences about somebody's spare time activities and his/her preferred sports in summer and winter.

In meiner Freizeit gehe ich **gern** ins Kino, und ich höre auch **gern** Musik. Ich treibe **sehr gern** Sport. Im Winter spiele ich Fußball, aber im Sommer gehe ich **lieber** schwimmen. **Am liebsten** lese ich.

Now write similar sentences saying what your hobbies are. Use the words **gern** and **lieber** and some of the following words and phrases (see Language structures on **gern**, **lieber**, **am liebsten** on page 117 for more details):

– in die Oper/ins Theater/in die Stadt/auf die Jagd/zur Disko gehen
– ins Ausland/ans Meer/nach Schottland fahren
– zu Hause bleiben, fernsehen, Radio hören, basteln
– Tischtennis/Golf spielen, trampen, zelten, das Auto reparieren

Vocabulary

die Freizeit *free/leisure time*
das Kino, -s *cinema*
die Musik *music*
der Sport *sport*
Sport treiben, getrieben *to do sports*
Fußball spielen *to play football*
schwimmen, geschwommen (sein) *to swim*
lesen, gelesen *to read*

die Oper, -n *opera*
das Theater, - *theatre*
auf die Jagd gehen, gegangen (sein) *to go hunting*
ins Ausland fahren *to go abroad*
ans Meer fahren, gefahren (sein) *to go to the seaside*
zu Hause *at home*

fernsehen, ferngesehen (sep) *to watch TV*
Radio hören *to listen to the radio*
basteln *to make things with one's hands*
Tischtennis spielen *to play table tennis*
trampen *to hitch-hike*
reparieren *to repair*

Comprehension 1

Next week you are visiting a company in Gladbeck and you have rung your German office to enquire about accommodation. Listen to your German colleague's information and check whether he has answered all your queries.

Your queries:

1 Sie möchten ein Zimmer mit Bad. Geht das?
2 Wo können Sie parken?
3 Am Dienstag abend wollen Sie mit Kollegen im Restaurant essen. Geht das?
4 Wann ist das Restaurant nicht geöffnet?

In the afternoon the fax arrives and you can have a closer look at the **Hotel Schultenhof**.

Hotel-Restaurant-Café
mit dezenter Unterhaltungsmusik

Unser Hotel ist durch-gehend (warme Küche) geöffnet von 11.30 bis 1.00 Uhr nachts.

— Kein Ruhetag —

Wir sind ein Spezialitäten-Restaurant (Wild, Fisch und Balkan-Grill). Internationale und bürgerliche Küche. Ausreichender Park-platz am Hause. Hotelzimmer mit Dusche, WC und Telefon. (Gäste-Garagen und Hofparkplatz). 2 Bundeskegel-bahnen im Hause. Wir erwarten Sie — und danken für Ihren Besuch.

Familie Šime Jović

Restaurant mit gemütlichen Sitznischen

Vocabulary

dezente Unterhaltungsmusik
*discreet musical entertain-
ment*
die Spezialität, -en *speciality*
das Wild, - *game, venison*

der Fisch, -e *fish*
bürgerliche Küche *good
plain home cooking*
ausreichend *sufficient*
der Hof, ⁻e *courtyard*

gemütlich *cosy*
die Sitznische, -n *corner
seats*
der Telefax *fax*

Comprehension 2

Die R^{PIAZZA}OMAN A ist von 12.00 – 15.00 Uhr und von 18.00 – 24.00 Uhr geöffnet. Lassen Sie sich über die Telefon-Nr. 7 rechtzeitig einen Tisch reservieren. Ob Sie elegant oder leger kommen – Sie sind uns immer liebe Gäste.

Französisches Flair (im Sommer auch auf der Straße) offeriert **Die Brasserie**. Aber natürlich auch alles, was genußvoll satt macht: Fisch und Fleisch vom Grill, zahlreiche verschiedene Delikatessen und Leckerbissen von unserem Gourmet-Buffet (die leckeren Desserts nicht gezählt), Weine und Champagner offen. Bedienen Sie sich oder lassen Sie sich bedienen. Wir richten uns ganz nach Ihren Wünschen.

Die Brasserie ist durchgehend von 12.00 bis 01.00 Uhr nachts geöffnet. Ab 07.00 Uhr finden Sie in unserer Brasserie unser berühmtes Frühstücksbuffet. Damit fängt der Tag wahrhaftig elysisch an.

Eilige Gäste können von 06.15 bis 12.30 Uhr auf dem **BOULEVARD** unser Pariser Boulevard-Frühstück mit ofenfrischen Croissants, mehreren Sorten Brötchen, frischgepreßtem Orangensaft und duftendem Kaffee einnehmen.

Vocabulary

Lassen Sie sich einen Tisch reservieren *Have a table reserved*
ob ... oder *whether ... or*
leger *casual*
liebe Gäste *dear guests*
offerieren *to offer*
genußvoll *enjoyable*
satt machen *to satisfy*
Ich bin satt *I am full*
das Fleisch *meat*
zahlreiche *(pl)* = **viele** *many, numerous*
verschiedene *(pl)* *various*
die Delikatesse, -n *delicacy*

der Leckerbissen, - *something tasty to eat, a delicacy*
lecker *tasty, delicious*
zählen, gezählt *to count, counted*
offen *open*
Bedienen Sie sich! *help yourself*
der Wunsch, ¨e *wish*
berühmt *famous*
damit (da + mit) *with it*
anfangen, angefangen *(sep) to begin*
wahrhaftig *truly*

eilig *in a hurry*
ofenfrisch *fresh from the oven*
mehrere *(pl)* *several*
die Sorte, -n *kind*
das Brötchen, - *bread-roll*
frischgepreßt *freshly squeezed*
der Saft, ¨e *juice*
duftend *aromatic*
einnehmen, eingenommen *(sep) to eat*

Answer these questions in German:

1 Wann kann man in der Piazza Romana essen?
2 Wo kann man im Sommer sitzen, wenn man in der Brasserie ißt?
3 Was kann man dort trinken?
4 Kann man dort um Mitternacht essen?
5 Um wieviel Uhr kann man auf dem Boulevard frühstücken?
6 Was kann man dort essen? Und trinken?

Talking business extra

Comprehension 3

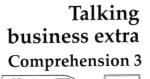

Katrina and Christian have met to complete work on their information leaflet. The quality of **Spieltechnik's** products is reflected in the awarding of the **TÜV** symbol for passing stringent safety tests, and the **VDE** symbol, which assures conformity with specifications laid down by the Association of Electrical Engineers.

Key vocabulary

die Werbeschrift, -en *publicity leaflet*
vollständig *complete*
die Qualitätsgarantie, -n *quality assurance*
das VDE (Verband deutscher Elektrotechniker) Zeichen *VDE symbol*

das TÜV (Technischer Überwachungsverein) Zeichen *TÜV symbol*
unterstreichen, unterstrichen *to underline, stress*
betonen *to emphasise*
der Vorschlag, ¨e *suggestion*

Key phrases

Bedienen Sie sich!	*Help yourself!*
An die Arbeit	*(Down) to work*
Moment!	*Just a moment!*
Das ist Geschmacksache	*It's a question of taste*
von elektronischen Geräten überschwemmt	*flooded with electronic equipment*
minderwertige Güte	*lesser quality*
Wie wär's mit einem Werbespruch?	*How about an advertising slogan?*

Find out:

1 where Katrina and her husband went on holiday
2 on what note **Spieltechnik's** brochure is going to end.

Exercise 5

Fill in the details:

Qualitätsgarantie

Sie verkaufen nur erstklassige _____.

Es gibt viele Importe von minderwertiger _____.

Ich finde, das ist _____.

Haben Sie einen _____?

Am Ende der Broschüre kommt unsere

_____ und unser

_____.

Puzzle

1 much
2 merchandise
3 taste
4 imports
5 suggestion
6 to the right
7 clue: it sticks in one's mind

Language structures

Verbs Talking in the past

Ich **habe** gut **geschlafen.**
Herr Newby **hat** viel von Mönchengladbach **gehört.**
Ich **war** gestern sehr müde.

THE PERFECT TENSE

This is the most common tense used to talk about the past. It is formed by using **haben** (or sometimes **sein** see page 127) with a so-called *past participle*, which goes at the end of the sentence.

PAST PARTICIPLE

Take the infinitive of a verb, put **ge** at the beginning and replace **en** with **t**.

machen	gemacht
hören	gehört
haben	gehabt

IRREGULAR VERBS

Many verbs are irregular, and have their own particular past participle. Because they do not follow the rule, they have to be learnt separately. Those introduced in this book are given with their past participles in the vocabulary lists from now on. Refer to the list of irregular verbs on page 221 to check up on the irregularities of verbs introduced in previous chapters.

For a full summary of the formation of the perfect tense, and exercises, see Language structures overview, pages 128–9.

THE IMPERFECT TENSE

This tense is mainly used for writing in the past and will not be introduced till Unit 20. However, two forms occur very commonly.

ich	war		ich	hatte	
du	warst		du	hattest	
er, sie, es	war		er, sie, es	hatte	
wir	waren	*was, were*	wir	hatten	*had*
ihr	wart		ihr	hattet	
sie	waren		sie	hatten	
Sie	waren		Sie	hatten	

Word order

MAIN CLAUSE	SUBORDINATE CLAUSE
Wir **zeigen** Ihnen später die Stadt,	**wenn** Sie Lust **haben**.
Ich **sende** Ihnen einen Telefax,	**wenn** Sie **wollen**.

The first part of the above sentences is called the *main clause*. (Remember, the verb is always the second idea, unless the main clause is a question.)

The second part of the sentence, starting with **wenn**, is called a *subordinate clause*. In subordinate clauses the verb stands at the end. Main clauses and subordinate clauses are *always* separated by a comma.

Other words introducing subordinate clauses, called *subordinating conjunctions*, are:

weil	**als**	**da**	**obwohl**	**obgleich**	**ob**

(see Language structures overview, page 129)

Adverbs **Gern, lieber, am liebsten**

Ich höre **gern** Musik.   *I like to listen to music.*
Gern (literally *gladly*) is normally used with a verb to mean the speaker *likes* doing something.

Ich gehe **lieber** schwimmen.   *I prefer to go swimming.*
The comparative form (i.e. *to prefer to do something*) is **lieber**.

Ich lese **am liebsten** Shakespeare.   *I like to read Shakespeare best.*
The superlative form **am liebsten** is used to indicate what the speaker likes doing most/best.

Ja, das möchte ich **gern(e)**.   *Yes, I would like (to have, to do) that.*
Gern on its own means *Yes, I would like to.*

Progress check

1 NVQ S1

Tell a friend how you are feeling:
I was very tired last night, but I slept very well. Now I am feeling better.

2 NVQ S2

How would you tell your German colleague that:
a) the hotel restaurant is only open from 12.00 to 2.00 p.m.
b) the inn (fish specialities) is open non-stop from lunchtime to midnight
c) you thank him for his visit
d) you can show him/her the sights of the town later, if he/she likes?

3 NVQ W2

In your diary, make a note of what you did yesterday:
a) I met Mr and Mrs Schwarz from Rheinland AG.
b) I ordered a flight ticket to London.
c) I bought a German book for my colleague.
d) I booked a table for three at the Crown restaurant.

4 NVQ S2

Answer these questions about your spare time:
a) Fahren Sie oft ins Ausland?
b) Was machen Sie lieber: zu Hause bleiben und fernsehen, oder in die Stadt fahren und ins Theater gehen?
c) Spielen Sie gern Golf?
d) Hören Sie lieber Musik, oder reparieren Sie lieber Ihr Auto?
e) Was essen und trinken Sie am liebsten?

5 What does this person enjoy?
'Wenn ich Zeit habe, esse ich zum Frühstück gerne ofenfrische Brötchen.'

6 NVQ R2

Regarding the quality of goods, what is said in these extracts from a potential German customer's letter?
a) Ich möchte betonen, daß wir an Waren minderwertiger Güte nicht interessiert sind.
b) Für eingeführte Produkte kann man in Deutschland um die VDE und TÜV Zeichen ansuchen.

UNIT 12 Essen und Trinken

In this unit, you will learn how to ...

- order food and drink
- say how the food tastes and ask others whether they are enjoying their meal
- request and deal with the bill.

> ### STUDY TIP
>
> Expressing what has happened in the past is very important, and deserves lots of attention and practice. Spend some time every study session putting present tense sentences into the past. Look up past participles you don't know. Say the sentence over, preferably aloud, substituting **er**, **sie**, **wir**, etc. for whatever you started with. Make questions out of statements, all ending with that past participle.

Dialogue: Im Restaurant

A little while later Walter, Meyer, Weidmann and Newby arrive at the restaurant of the Hotel Schultenhof. Here is part of their conversation.

Walter	Guten Tag, wir haben einen Tisch für vier Personen reserviert.
Kellner	Ja. Bitte schön, meine Herrschaften. Dort in der Ecke.
Walter	Können Sie mir bitte die Speise- und Getränkekarte bringen? Wir möchten bestellen.
Kellner	Ja, sofort ...
Walter	(Später) Haben Sie schon gewählt? ... Herr Ober.
Kellner	Bitte sehr, was darf es sein?
Newby	Ich möchte bitte Wiener Schnitzel mit Röstkartoffeln, Gemüse und Salat.
Kellner	Möchten Sie eine Vorspeise?
Newby	Ja, vielleicht doch. Bringen Sie mir einen kleinen Salat.
Kellner	Und zu trinken?
Newby	Eine Flasche Bier, bitte, König Pilsener. Und als Nachtisch bekomme ich einen Pfannkuchen mit Zitrone. Das schmeckt mir immer so gut.
Meyer	Ich möchte gern eine Ochsenschwanzsuppe, und als Hauptgericht rheinischen Sauerbraten mit Kartoffeln

und Rotkohl. Das esse ich sehr gern. Als Nachspeise
bekomme ich Apfelkompott.

Kellner	Und was trinken Sie?
Meyer	Ein Glas Weißwein.

Vocabulary

der Kellner, - *waiter*
die Herrschaften (*pl*) *ladies and gentlemen*
die Speisekarte, -n *menu*
die Getränkekarte *wine list*
bestellen *to order*
Herr Ober *waiter*
Was darf es sein? *What may I get you?*
das Wiener Schnitzel, - *fillet of veal or pork fried in breadcrumbs*
die Röstkartoffeln (*pl*) *roast or fried potatoes*

das Gemüse, - *vegetables*
der Salat, -e *salad*
die Vorspeise, -n *starter*
die Flasche, -n *bottle*
das Bier *beer*
der Nachtisch *dessert*
der Pfannkuchen, - *pancake*
die Zitrone, -n *lemon*
schmecken (*+ dative*) literally *to taste*
Das schmeckt mir gut *I like that*
die Ochsenschwanzsuppe, -n *oxtail soup*

das Hauptgericht, -e *main dish*
rheinischer Sauerbraten *stewed, marinated beef speciality from the Rhineland*
der Rotkohl *red cabbage*
als Nachspeise *for a pudding*
das Apfelkompott *stewed apples*
das Glas, ¨er *glass*
der Weißwein, -e *white wine*

Notes

1 **Das schmeckt mir immer so gut.**
Schmecken is followed by a dative (see Language structures on page 127).

2 **Kellner** means *waiter* but when you call for the waiter you address him as **Herr Ober**.

3 **Ein Glas Weißwein** *A glass of white wine.* There is no *of* here in German. **Für mich ein Glas Orangensaft, bitte.**

Exercise 1

You are in a restaurant in Germany with a colleague. You order a meal. What do you say in German?

Sie	(*Ask if they have a table for two.*)

_____

Kellner	Jawohl, mein Herr/gnädige Frau. Dort in der Ecke.
Sie	(*Ask for the menu and wine list.*)

_____

Kellner	Ich bringe sie sofort …
Sie	(*Tell the waiter you have made your choice.*)

_____

Kellner	Bitte sehr, was darf es sein?
Sie	(*Say you would like oxtail soup for starters, followed by Wiener Schnitzel with roast potatoes, vegetables and salad.*)

_____

| Kellner | Etwas zu trinken dazu? |
| Sie | (*Say you would like a glass of red wine.*) |

| Kellner | Möchten Sie eine Nachspeise? |
| Sie | (*Say yes, you would like a pancake and a cup of coffee.*) |

Exercise 2 | Study this menu, then make up a conversation similar to the one above.

Hotel zum Adler

Speisekarte

Vorspeisen
Französische Zwiebelsuppe
Ochsenschwanzsuppe

☆ ☆ ☆ ☆ ☆

Hauptgerichte
Süßsaure Matjes
mit Salzkartoffeln und Tomaten

Heilbutt mit
Kartoffelpüree und Salat

Wiener Schnitzel
mit Pommes frites, Champignons und Erbsen

Pfeffersteak (sehr scharf)
mit Reis und Karotten

☆ ☆ ☆ ☆ ☆

Nachspeisen
Obstsalat
Birne Hélène
Gemischtes Eis
Haselnußcreme

Vocabulary

die Zwiebel, -n *onion*
süß *sweet*
sauer *sour*
der Matjeshering, -e *salted herring fillet*
das Salz *salt*
die Tomate, -n *tomato*
der Heilbutt *halibut*
das Kartoffelpüree *mashed potatoes*

die Pommes frites *chipped potatoes*
der Champignon, -s *button mushroom*
die Erbse, -n *peas*
der Pfeffer *pepper*
scharf *hot, spicy*
der Reis *rice*
die Karotte, -n *carrot*
das Obst *fruit*

die Birne, -n *pear*
gemischt *mixed*
das Eis *ice cream*
die Haselnußcreme *hazelnut cream*

Comprehension 1 Listen to this dialogue between a waiter and a couple in a café. When you are confident of understanding everything, study the words as well as the following price list. Then make up a similar conversation, allowing the couple to indulge in various items from the price list!

Preistafel

Warme Getränke	
Tasse Kaffee	2,50
Tasse Tee mit Zitrone oder Milch	2,50
Tasse Espresso	2,60
Tasse Kakao	2,60
Torten und Kuchen	
Erdbeertorte mit Sahne	3,75
Apfelstrudel	3,00
Schokoladenkuchen	2,50
Käsekuchen	2,50
Eisspezialitäten	
Vanille, Erdbeer, Schokolade	2,00
Gemischtes Eis mit Sahne	3,75
Eis-Kaffee	4,00
Schwarzwaldbecher	4,50

Vocabulary

Sonst noch etwas?
   Anything else?
das Stück, -e *piece*
die Rechnung, -en *bill*
alles zusammen *all together*
die Preistafel, -n *price list*
der Espresso *strong, black coffee*

der Kakao *cocoa*
die Torte, -n *gateau*
der Kuchen, - *cake*
der Käse *cheese*
Vanille *vanilla*
die Erdbeere, -n *strawberry*
die Schokolade, -n *chocolate*

die Sahne *cream*
der Schwarzwaldbecher
   black forest cup
Stimmt so *That's correct*
(see Cultural briefing, page 132)

<table>
<tr><td>

Exercise 3

</td><td>

Sie sind mit einem Kollegen im Restaurant Bommersheim, und der Kellner bringt Ihnen die Rechnung:

</td></tr>
</table>

1 Welche Nummer hat Ihr Tisch?
2 Haben Sie eine Vorspeise gegessen?
3 Sie haben Filet Stroganoff gewählt. Was hat es gekostet?
4 Was hat Ihr Kollege als Hauptgericht bekommen?
5 Und als Nachtisch?
6 Was haben Sie getrunken?
7 Was ist der Gesamtbetrag?
8 Was steht auch im Gesamtbetrag?
9 Welches Datum steht auf der Rechnung?

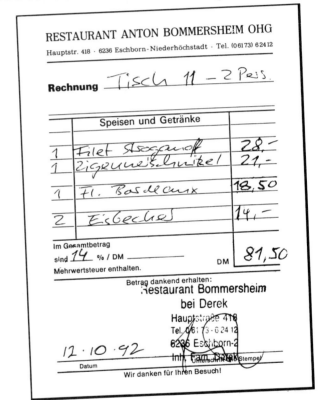

Vocabulary

das Zigeunerschnitzel, - *gypsy steak*
der Eisbecher, - *ice-cream cup*

der Gesamtbetrag, ¨e *total amount*
die Steuer, -n *tax*
die Mehrwertsteuer *VAT*

enthalten, enthalten *to include*
der Betrag, ¨e *amount*
erhalten, erhalten *to receive*
der Stempel, - *stamp*

Note

Was steht denn hier? *What does it say here?*
Das steht nicht drauf *It's not on here*

Stehen, gestanden is used frequently to express that something is to be read.

| **Exercise 4** | While working in Germany you go to the 'Enka Restaurant' one day for your lunch. Tell your colleagues back at work about the restaurant and your meal. Here is the beginning of your report: |

> Heute mittag **habe** ich in einem neuen Restaurant **gegessen**.
> Ich **bin** in die Stadt **gefahren** und **habe** am Rheinufer **geparkt**.
> Dann **bin** ich zu Fuß zum Restaurant 'Enka' **gegangen**. Es **war**
> sehr nett und auch nicht sehr teuer.

The following words might be useful:
Die Speise-/Getränkekarte, Weiß-/Rotwein, als Vorspeise/
Hauptspeise/Nachspeise, die Rechnung
bringen (gebracht), bestellen (bestellt), wählen (gewählt), trinken
(getrunken), essen (gegessen), bekommen (bekommen),
bestellen (bestellt), schmecken (geschmeckt), kosten (gekostet).

Remember to use the perfect tense and try to memorise the
above past participles.

Speiseplan

ENKA ENKA ENKA ENKA
Enka
Kasino

vom	9.11.92–13.11.92
MONTAG	Geflügelcremesuppe Gefüllte Wirsingroulade mit magerer Fleischfüllung Würfelkartoffeln Eichblatt-Radieschensalat Dessert
DIENSTAG	Suppe Wiener Schnitzel mit Pommes frites Farmer Salat Dessert
MITTWOCH	Suppe Geschnitzeltes Schweinefleisch in Rahmsauce m. Champignons und Tomaten, Gabelspaghetti Kopf- u. Selleriesalat Dessert
DONNERSTAG	Grüne Erbsensuppe mit geräucherter Bockwurst Brötchen Schokoladencreme mit Birne
FREITAG	Selleriecremesuppe Bayrischer Leberkäse mit Spiegelei, Röstkartoffeln Chinakohl- u. Wachsbrechbohnensalat Dessert

Vocabulary

das Geflügel *poultry*	**das Eichblatt** *oakleaf lettuce*	**geräuchert** *smoked*
gefüllt *filled*	**das Radieschen, -** *radish*	**die Bockwurst, -̈e** *hard*
die Wirsingroulade, -n	**geschnitzelt** *shredded*	*German sausage*
stuffed, rolled cabbage	**das Schweinefleisch** *pork*	**bayrischer Leberkäse**
dish	**der Rahm = die Sahne**	*Bavarian meatloaf*
mager *lean*	*cream*	**das Ei, -er** *egg*
die Fleischfüllung, -en *meat*	**die Gabel, -n** *fork*	**das Spiegelei** *fried egg*
stuffing	**der Kopfsalat, -e** *lettuce*	**der Chinakohl** *chinese*
Würfelkartoffeln *cubed*	**der Sellerie** *celery*	*leaves*
potatoes	**grün** *green*	**die Bohne, -n** *bean*

Comprehension 2

During the course of the meal Michael Newby and his colleagues talk about the restaurant and different cuisine. Look at these questions before you listen to the dialogue. Then give the answers in English.

1 What does Newby say about the restaurant and the food? Give as much information as possible.
2 Why is Newby so familiar with German cuisine?
3 What was significant about his first trip to Linz?
4 Why does Walter prefer German to English food?
5 For what does Weidmann have a weakness?

Vocabulary

hierher *(to) here*	**übrigens** *by the way*	**etwas Süßes** *something*
gut verstehen, verstanden	**gar nicht so schlecht** *not so*	*sweet*
to understand well	*bad at all*	**Das merkt man** *One can see*
das Gericht, -e *dish*	**etwas Einmaliges**	*that*
ich bin gewesen *I have*	*something unique*	**Was ist aus ... geworden?**
been	**gut gewürzt** *well seasoned,*	*What has happened to ...?*
seitdem *since then*	*spicy*	

Comprehension 3: Das Essen

Die drei Mahlzeiten in Deutschland sind das Frühstück, das Mittagessen und das Abendessen. Zum Frühstück ißt man normalerweise Brötchen, Brot oder Toast mit Butter, Marmelade oder Honig. Viele Leute essen auch ein gekochtes Ei. Man trinkt Tee oder Kaffee. Oft nimmt man ein zweites Frühstück zur Arbeit mit, wenn man sehr früh zu Hause gefrühstückt hat.

Für viele Leute ist das Mittagessen die Hauptmahlzeit. Dann ißt man entweder zu Hause oder in einem Restaurant, wenn man in der Stadt arbeitet. Das Mittagessen besteht meistens aus Fleisch, Gemüse, Kartoffeln und Salat. Manchmal ißt man vorher eine Suppe und danach Eis, Pudding oder Obst als Nachtisch.

Mittags hört man sehr oft im Büro den Ausdruck ‚Mahlzeit'. Das sagt man zu seinen Kollegen und Kolleginnen, wenn man essen geht, und wenn man zurückkommt.

Nachmittags trinkt man oft Tee oder Kaffee, aber auch Mineralwasser. Manchmal ißt man auch Kuchen.

Das Abendessen ist etwas einfacher. Man ißt zum Beispiel Brot mit Schinken, Käse, Wurst, Salat oder Tomaten. Abends trinken viele Deutsche ein Glas Wein oder Bier.

Vocabulary

die Mahlzeit, -en *meal*
'Mahlzeit' = 'guten Appetit'
  said when wishing someone an enjoyable meal
das Mittagessen, - *lunch*
das Abendessen, - *dinner*
normalerweise *normally*
die Butter *butter*
die Marmelade, -n *jam, marmelade*

der Honig *honey*
gekocht *cooked, boiled*
mitnehmen, mitgenommen *(sep) to take with you*
früh *early*
die Hauptmahlzeit, -en *main meal*
danach *afterwards*
der Pudding *blancmange*
das Obst *fruit*
der Ausdruck, ̈e *expression*

zurückkommen, zurückgekommen *(sep, sein) to return*
einfach *simple*
das Brot, -e *bread, loaf*
der Schinken *ham*
der Käse *cheese*
die Wurst, ̈e *sausage*

1 Was ißt man in Deutschland normalerweise zum Frühstück?
2 Woraus besteht das Mittagessen für viele Deutsche?
3 Wie ist das Abendessen in Deutschland?

Talking business extra

Comprehension 4

Christian and Katrina have bumped into each other at the **Frankfurter Buchmesse** and are comparing notes on the competition. **Spieltechnik** are newcomers to a very competitive market with their **Päda-Computer**, but another branch of their products is well established and unrivalled abroad.

Key vocabulary

die EDV (elektronische Datenverarbeitung) Anlage *electronic data processing system*
zusätzlich *additional*
das Lehrmaterial, -ien *teaching material*
ausrüsten *(sep) to equip*

die Konkurrenz *competition, competitors*
ähnlich *similar*
der Konkurrenzkampf, ̈e *competition*
der Wettbewerb, -e *competition, competitive game*

konkurrenzfähig *competitive*
erwerben, erworben *to gain*
das Teil, -e *part, component*
die Bildungsserie, -n *educational series*

Key phrases

komplett mit Unterrichtsbüchern	*complete with teaching manuals*
den gesamtdeutschen Markt beherrschen	*to dominate the all-German market*
ein Marktanteil von 35%	*a market share of 35%*
neu in dieser Branche	*new to this business sector*
Marktlücken füllen	*to fill gaps in the market*
neue Interessensgebiete	*new areas of interest*
ein beachtlicher Marktanteil	*a significant market share*
in der selben Preislage	*in the same price category*
Ich wünsche viel Erfolg!	*I wish you a lot of success*

Find out:

1 what **Vetti's** new product consists of
2 what Katrina has to say about their toy series **Deutsches Automobil**.

Exercise 5

Fill in the details:

Der Konkurrenzkampf

Die Firma Vetti hat einen Marktanteil von _____.

Spieltechnik ist noch neu in dieser _____.

Der Verlag Germania füllt die _____.

Nur so ist der Verlag _____.

Spieltechnik hat im Ausland einen beachtlichen

_____.

Puzzle

1 market share
2 business sector
3 competitive
4 success
5 price bracket
6 clue: it spurs you on

Marktlücken füllen

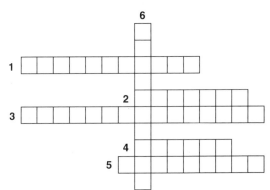

Language structures

Verbs   The perfect tense

Ich **bin** in die Stadt **gefahren**.
Er **ist** ins Hotel **gegangen**.
Sie **sind** oft auf Geschäftsreise in Deutschland **gewesen**.

Verbs which suggest *movement* from one location to another, or a change of state, use **sein** with the past participle. Usually the ending of a past participle with **sein** is **en**. See Language structures overview, page 128 for full details.

Use of the dative

Here are some more phrases with the dative case:

Gehen   Es geht **mir** besser.
Es geht **ihm** gut.
Geht es **Ihnen** schlecht?

Schmecken   Schmeckt es **Ihnen**?
Eis schmeckt **mir** immer so gut.

(See also Unit 8, pages 79–80.)

Progress check

1 NVQ S2
In the restaurant you want to say the following to the waiter:
a) I have booked a table for two.
b) Please bring us the menu and the wine list.
c) We have already made our choice and would like to order.
d) I am having vegetable soup for a starter.
e) I would like pork, roast potatoes and a salad for a main course.
f) For me a piece of apple cake for a pudding, please.
g) We would like a bottle of red wine, please.
h) Waiter, the bill please.
i) It tasted very nice.

2 NVQ W2
On a postcard to your colleagues back in Britain you give a short account of your trip. Use the perfect (past) tense to make the following points:
a) Wir fahren mit dem Auto zum Flughafen.
b) Heute gehen wir zu Fuß vom Hotel zur Firma.
c) Ich bin jetzt zum ersten Mal am Bodensee.
d) Meine Kollegen essen im Gasthaus 'Blauer Stern' zu Mittag und trinken am Nachmittag im Kaffeehaus Gerti eine Tasse Tee.

3 NVQ S2
Enquire after your German colleague and ask him some questions:
a) How are you?
b) Did you enjoy the soup?
c) How do you like the beer here?
d) How is Miss Redman?
e) May I help you with your case?
f) Have you brought me the bill?
g) May I thank you for your visit?

4 NVQ R2
A potential new supplier from Germany is trying to sell his goods in Britain. Read these leaflet extracts and pass on the information in English.
a) Unser Marktanteil im gesamtbritischen Markt liegt ungefähr bei 25 %.
b) Alle Produkte in dieser Preislage sind bei uns billiger und besser als bei der Konkurrenz!

Summary 5

Language structures overview

The perfect tense

This is used to talk about what happened in the past. To form it, put the appropriate form of **haben** or **sein** in the place of the verb, and the verb in the form of its past participle to the end of the main clause.

1 Regular verbs with **haben**:

ich	habe	... gehört
du	hast	... gehört
er, sie, es	hat	... gehört
wir	haben	... gehört
ihr	habt	... gehört
sie	haben	... gehört
Sie	haben	... gehört

I heard, I have heard

2 Verbs with **sein** for verbs of movement or a change of state (and a very few others, such as **bleiben** – Ich **bin** drei Tage in München geblieben):

ich	bin	... gefahren
du	bist	... gefahren
er, sie, es	ist	... gefahren
wir	sind	... gefahren
ihr	seid	... gefahren
sie	sind	... gefahren
Sie	sind	... gefahren

I went (by vehicle), drove
I have been travelling

3 Separable or compound verbs

Ich habe Herrn König am Bahnhof ab**ge**holt.
Herr Newby hat das Anmeldeformular aus**ge**füllt.
Wir haben uns schon in Altrincham kennen**ge**lernt.
Er hat seinen Kollegen heute wieder**ge**sehen.

The **ge** goes in between the prefix and verb.

4 Verbs *beginning* with **be**, **ge**, **emp**, **ent**, **er**, **ver**, **zer**, or *ending* with **ieren**

Wir haben Wiener Schnitzel **bestellt**.
Man hat mir das Hotel **empfohlen** (*from* empfehlen).
Ich habe den Besuch gestern **erwartet**.
Die Sekretärin hat mein Zimmer **reserviert**.

There is no **ge** at the beginning of these past participles.

5 Many verbs are irregular and have their own particular past participle. (See list of irregular verbs on page 221.)

gehen	Er ist um 5.30 nach Hause	**gegangen**.
bringen	Herr Meyer hat das Gepäck nach oben	**gebracht**.
sprechen	Ich habe mit dem Restaurant Schloßhof	**gesprochen**.

Word order in subordinate clauses

Wir möchten morgen kommen,	**wenn**	Sie ein Zimmer frei	**haben**.
Wir werden hier übernachten,	**weil**	die Preise billig	**sind**.
Ich finde es schön,	**daß**	wir uns	**wiedersehen**.
Ich bin müde,	**obgleich**	ich gut geschlafen	**habe**.

Here are some common words which introduce subordinate clauses and send the verb to the end of the sentence:

daß	*that*
weil	*because*
wenn	*if, when*
als	*when (in the past)*
ob	*if, whether*
obwohl	*although*
obgleich	*although*
nachdem	*after*

Additional exercises

1 Complete the gaps in the following sentences with **weil**, **obgleich**, **wenn** or **daß**:

a Ich fahre zum Flughafen, _____ wir nach Österreich fliegen.

b Wir finden es sehr interessant, _____ dieses Hotel schon so alt ist.

c Sie müssen das Restaurant Bommersheim besuchen, _____ das Essen dort sehr gut ist.

d Wir möchten essen, _____ das Restaurant noch offen ist.

e Sie können im Restaurant ‚Zur Eule' essen, _____ es ziemlich spät ist.

f Ich bekomme einen Apfelstrudel, _____ der Kellner das empfohlen hat.

g Ich kann heute nachmittag kommen, _____ Sie Zeit haben.

2 Put the following sentences into the perfect tense.

a *Example:* Ich wohne nicht in Bonn.
Ich habe nicht in Bonn gewohnt.
(**haben** + *regular* past participle)

Ich wähle immer eine Vorspeise.
Im Hotel Stern kostet ein Zimmer DM 72,- pro Nacht.
Der Ingenieur drückt die Taste.

Summary 5

Ich zahle mit einem Fünfhundertmarkschein.
Wir kaufen oft eine Rückfahrkarte.
Meine deutschen Kollegen danken mir für das Mittagessen.

b haben + past participle ending in **en**

Die Messe heißt 'Interlang 92'.
Ich sehe das Geschäft leider nicht.

c haben + past participle *without* **ge**

Herr Klaus telefoniert jeden Tag mit der deutschen Firma.
Die Gäste reservieren ein Doppelzimmer mit Bad und Fernsehen.
Studieren Sie Wirtschaft an der Universität?
Was produzieren Sie in Ihrer Firma?
Er bekommt einen Zimmernachweis im Reisebüro.
Besuchen Sie heute das römische Museum?

d haben + **ge** between separable prefix and past participle

Zuerst fülle ich das Anmeldeformular aus.
Meine Bekannten in der Schweiz holen mich vom Flughafen ab.
Sie lernen sich auf der Ausstellung in Bonn kennen.
Ich werfe das Zweimarkstück in den Automaten ein. (werfen, geworfen)

e haben + *irregular* past participles (see the list of irregular verbs, page 221)

Wir nehmen die S-Bahn zum Hauptbahnhof.
Es gibt hier ein sehr gutes Restaurant.
Herr Kramer hilft mir mit dem Gepäck.
Ich finde die Aussicht auf den See sehr schön.
Sprechen Sie in Deutschland immer Deutsch?

f sein + past participle

Der Vertreter kommt am 15. März nach Essen.
Sie fährt oft mit der Bahn nach Belgien.
Sie gehen zu Fuß nach Hause, nicht wahr?
Wann fliegen Sie in die Schweiz?
Wo steigen Sie in die S-Bahn um?
Ich bleibe eine Woche im Hotel Schultenhof.

3 Put the following sentences into the past.
Using **ich, war, du warst,** etc. is the simplest, but you can also use the perfect
tense: ich **bin**, du **bist**, etc. **gewesen.**

Example: Die Ausstellung ist sehr interessant.
Die Ausstellung war sehr interessant.
Die Ausstellung ist sehr interessant gewesen.

a Ich bin auf einer Tagung in Mönchengladbach.
b Die Übernachtungspreise sind ziemlich teuer.
c Die Information über Ihre Verkaufsbedingungen ist sehr interessant.

d Sind Sie zum ersten Mal in Stuttgart?
e Die Besucher aus Deutschland sind heute im Schwimmbad.
f Im Gasthaus 'Am Fluß' ist es sehr gemütlich.
g Sie sind im Januar auf Geschäftsreise in Wien, nicht wahr?

4 Put the following into the past.
Using **hatte** is simpler than **habe ... gehabt.**

a Ich habe viel Gepäck.
b Herr und Frau Klein haben eine Rückfahrkarte nach Manchester.
c Das Café Zentral hat heute frische Erdbeertorte mit Sahne.
d Leider haben wir für dieses Zimmer keinen Schlüssel.

5 Put the following sentences into the perfect tense.

a Ich fahre oft nach Deutschland.
b Wir lösen die Fahrkarten am Hauptbahnhof.
c Herr Schaaf reserviert ein Zimmer.
d Der Zug fährt um 13.00 Uhr ab.
e Die Sekretärin ruft das Restaurant an.
f Wir essen heute im Restaurant.
g Ich bestelle ein Glas Weißwein.
h Mr Newby schläft sehr gut.

Key phrases

Saying how you feel	Ich bin sehr müde
	Es geht mir jetzt besser
Asking if someone is known	Sie kennen schon Herrn/Frau ...?
Saying you have already met	Wir haben uns schon in ... kennengelernt
Saying you are pleased to see someone again	Es freut mich sehr, Sie wiederzusehen
Saying you'd like something	Das möchte ich (gerne)
Saying you have heard a lot about a place, a person	Ich habe viel von ... gehört
Saying you have a table reserved for four	Ich habe einen Tisch für vier Personen reserviert
Asking for the menu and wine list	Können Sie mir bitte die Speise- und Getränkekarte bringen?
Asking what somebody would like	Was darf es sein?
Ordering food and drink	Ich möchte bitte ...
	Bringen Sie mir ...
	Ich möchte gern ...
	Ein Glas Weißwein, bitte
Asking how someone likes the food	Wie schmeckt Ihnen das Essen?
Saying you like the food	Das Essen schmeckt prima
Asking for the bill	Die Rechnung, bitte!
	Darf ich bitte die Rechnung haben?

Cultural briefing

Eating and drinking

For a quick snack, look out for a **Schnellimbiß** or **Imbißstube**, a café or snack-bar in the English sense. A **Konditorei**, or café/cake-shop will provide coffee and numerous examples of typical German **Kuchen**, **Strudel**, etc. Having ordered a drink in a bar or café you are entitled to stay as long as you like without further obligation, lovely if you can sit outside in the sunshine and watch the world go by!

For something more substantial, but still short of an expensive restaurant, one of the many **Gasthäuser (das Gasthaus)** or **Gasthöfe (der Gasthof)** will prove more than adequate, offering good quality meals, often including local dishes, at very reasonable prices.

Whilst a waiter/waitress is a **Kellner/Kellnerin**, you never address them as such. To call the waiter say **Herr Ober**, and for the waitress **Fräulein**. Even if the service charge is included in the price, it's usual to give a small tip. If you don't want any change say **Stimmt schon** (or **Stimmt so**) as you hand over your money. Otherwise decide how much you want to give, add it to the total, and tell the waiter/waitress the new figure. You'll be thanked and given the appropriate change. It's worth remembering that Germans still tend to use cash, especially in restaurants, and credit cards are still not accepted everywhere. Eurocheques are a pretty safe bet, however.

Pronunciation

 b – d – g

b	like English *b* **bringen, oben**
	but like English *p* when the last letter of a word or syllable
	außerhalb
d	like English *d* **dreißig**
	but like English *t* when the last letter of a word or syllable
	Schwimmbad, duftend
g	like *g* in *glass* **Glas, Gespräch**
	but as the last letter of a word or syllable often closer to
	k **Tag**
	or a sound between *sh* and the *h* of *hue* **ruhig, eilig**

UNIT **13** Ich suche die Königsallee

In this unit, you will learn how to …

- give and ask for directions
- find out about shops and opening times
- understand advertisements.

Dialogue: Auf der Straße

Charlotte Stewart, a computer programmer on business in Düsseldorf, needs to find her way around the city. She asks the way to the Königsallee and enquires about shops.

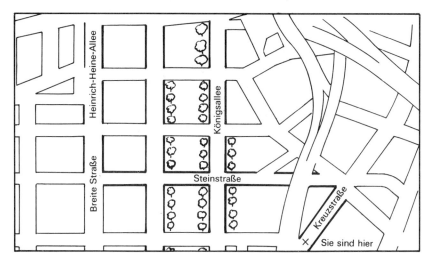

Programmiererin	Entschuldigen Sie bitte. Ich suche die Königsallee.
Passant	Ach, die Kö ist gar nicht so weit. Gehen Sie hier geradeaus bis zur Kreuzung, dann nehmen Sie die erste Straße links, die Steinstraße. Sie führt direkt zur Kö.
Programmiererin	Herzlichen Dank. Können Sie mir auch ein Geschäft in der Königsallee empfehlen, wo ich Geschenke für meine Familie in England kaufen kann?
Passant	Was für Geschenke wollen Sie denn?
Programmiererin	Na ja, Parfüm, T-Shirts, Bücher, … Ich weiß nicht genau.
Passant	Also, bei Habitus finden Sie bestimmt das Richtige. Dann gibt's noch Benetton und das Modehaus Heinemann, wenn Sie Bekleidung suchen. Parfüm kriegen sie in der Parfümerie Douglas. Auf der Kö gibt's sehr viele Geschäfte. Es gibt da fast alles.
Programmiererin	Aber die Preise …
Passant	Das stimmt. Wenn Sie etwas billiger einkaufen wollen, müssen Sie in ein Kaufhaus oder in die Altstadt gehen.
Programmiererin	Die Altstadt, wie komme ich am besten dahin?
Passant	Gehen Sie die Steinstraße entlang, bis Sie zur Königsallee kommen. Dann gehen Sie immer noch geradeaus bis zur Breite Straße. Dort geht es rechts weiter. Gehen Sie die Breite Straße hinunter bis in die Heinrich-Heine-Allee. Die Altstadt liegt dann auf der linken Seite.
Programmiererin	Ich danke Ihnen für Ihre Hilfe.
Passant	Nichts zu danken. Gern geschehen. Auf Wiedersehen.

Vocabulary

suchen *to look for*
der König, -e *king*
die Allee, -n *avenue*
gar nicht *not at all*
weit *far*
geradeaus *straight ahead*
die Kreuzung, -en
  crossroads
nehmen, genommen *to take*
führen *to lead*
direkt *direct(ly)*
herzlichen Dank *thank you*
  very much
das Geschäft, -e *shop*
empfehlen, empfohlen *to*
  recommend
das Geschenk, -e *present*
kaufen *buy*
was für ...? *what kind of ...?*
wollen *to want*

na ja, ... *oh well, ...*
das Parfüm *perfume*
das T-Shirt, -s *T-shirt*
das Buch, ̈-er *book*
ich weiß nicht genau *I don't*
  know exactly
finden, gefunden *to find*
bestimmt *certainly*
das Richtige *the right thing*
das Modehaus, ̈-er *fashion*
  store
die Bekleidung *clothing,*
  clothes
kriegen *to get*
die Parfümerie, -n *perfumery*
fast alles *almost everything*
der Preis, -e *price*
das Kaufhaus, ̈-er
  department store

die Altstadt *older part of the*
  town
entlanggehen,
  entlanggegangen (*sep,*
  sein) *to go along*
immer noch *still*
bis *until*
Dort geht es rechts weiter
  There you carry on right
  (literally: *it goes on the*
  right further)
hinuntergehen,
  hinuntergegangen (*sep,*
  sein) *to go down*
auf der linken Seite *on the*
  left-hand side
danken (+ *dative*) *to thank*
Nichts zu danken *Don't*
  mention it

Notes

1 **Wie komme ich am besten dahin?**
  What's the best way to get there?
  Am besten *at, for the best,*
  da/dahin *there.* The word **hin** is added
  because *motion is implied,* making the
  phrase *to there.* **Dort** and **dorthin** mean
  the same as **da** and **dahin**.

2 **München ist sehr schön. Ich wohne
  dort. Morgen fahre ich dorthin.** *Munich is*

  *very beautiful. I live there. Tomorrow I am
  going (to) there.*

3 **Dann gibt's noch Benetton ...** *Then
  there's Benetton ...*
  Gibt es can be shortened to **gibt's**.
  Es gibt da fast alles can be shortened to
  Da gibt's fast alles.
  See also page 50.

| **Exercise 1** | You want to buy some presents for your family before travelling home from a congress in Innsbruck. You stop someone in the street to ask the way. What do you say in German? |

Sie   (*Say 'excuse me', you want to buy presents for your
          family in England. Ask if they can recommend a
          shop.*)

Passant   Was für Geschenke wollen Sie denn eigentlich?
Sie   (*Say you don't know exactly yet, possibly books,
            perfume or T-shirts.*)

Passant	Also, in den kleinen Gassen in der Altstadt finden Sie viele Geschenkartikel in den Andenkengeschäften.
Sie	(*Say you know, but they are rather expensive.*)

_____

Passant	Dann müssen Sie zur Maria-Theresien-Straße gehen. Dort finden Sie Warenhäuser. Die verkaufen fast alles.
Sie	(*Ask what is the best way to get there.*)

_____

Passant	Also, gehen Sie hier die Universitätsstraße entlang bis zum Burggraben. Gehen Sie dann links bis zur Kreuzung. Rechts sehen Sie den Verkehrsverein und links die Maria-Theresien-Straße.
Sie	(*Thank the passer-by for his help.*)

_____

Passant	Nichts zu danken.

Vocabulary

der Geschenkartikel, - *gift item*

das Andenkengeschäft, -e *souvenir shop*

das Warenhaus, ⸚er *department store*

Exercise 2	You are visiting Germany. While in the tourist office you hear the following conversation. With the help of the map complete the gaps with a suitable word or phrase.

1 Ich suche die Hochstraße. Wie komme ich am besten dahin? Gehen Sie hier geradeaus, dann nehmen Sie die erste Straße

_____ .

2 Ich suche die Berliner Straße. Wie komme ich am besten dahin?

Gehen Sie hier _____ bis zur

_____ . Dort gehen Sie nach _____, und

dann nehmen Sie die _____ _____ .

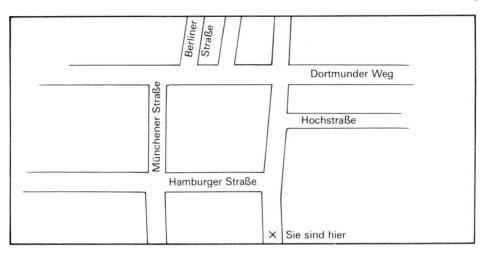

3 Wie komme ich am besten zur Münchener Straße, bitte?

Gehen Sie _____ bis zur

_____ _____, dann gehen Sie die

Hamburger Straße _____. Die Münchener Straße

ist _____ _____ rechts.

4 Now answer the following question:
Wie komme ich am besten zum Dortmunder Weg?

_____

Comprehension 1 Listen to the information on shop opening times in Germany and answer the following questions in German.

Vocabulary

normalerweise *normally*
öffnen *to open*
offen *open*
das Postamt, ̈er *post office*

zwischen *between*
schließen, geschlossen *to shut*
zu *closed*

bleiben, geblieben (sein) *to remain, stay*
sogenannt *so-called*
lang *long*

---

1 Von wann bis wann sind deutsche Geschäfte montags bis freitags offen?
2 Wann schließen sie normalerweise am Samstag?
3 Wie lange dürfen sie am 'langen Samstag' offen bleiben?
4 Welcher Samstag im Monat ist der sogenannte 'lange Samstag'?

Exercise 3

While visiting Germany an English businessman wishes to buy a few presents for his family and colleagues. Look at the advertisements below, then say what a German colleague might reply to his queries.

Foto Goertz Service:
Farbbilder über Nacht!
Bis 18.00 Uhr gebracht –
um 11.00 Uhr gemacht!

150 Jahre Fotografie
65 Jahre Foto Goertz

FOTO GOERTZ
Das Fotohaus mit dem Parkplatz

zu kaufen bei

mössinc
Ihr Uhren- u. Schmuckfachgeschäft

Düsseldorf
Schadowstr./Ecke Blumenstr.
Tel. 13 41 12

Heyne-Taschenbücher erhalten Sie bei Ihrer Buchhandlung:

Die große Buchhandlung
im Bahnhof Düsseldorf
GRAUERT

Der Weinmann Tscharke
Unsere Liebe gehört dem Wein

Düsseldorfs führender Fachhandel. Über 1000 Sorten Weine und Spirituosen ständig vorrätig.
Fachliche Beratung und Probiermöglichkeit.
Wein in Fässern – Präsentdienst
Kaiserswerther Straße 150–152 · ☎ 02 11 / 45 09 11
Parkplatz vorhanden   AN84881

Stadtparfümerie Pieper
Ihr führendes Haus für
Schönheit + Mode
Jetzt 10 x im Ruhrgebiet

- BOCHUM Huestraße 14
- BOCHUM Kortumstraße 65
- CASTROP-RAUXEL Am Markt 1
- GELSENKIRCHEN Bahnhofstraße 22
- GELSENK.-BUER Blindestraße 2
- HERNE Bahnhofstraße 38
- HERTEN Antoniusstraße 31
- RECKLINGHAUSEN Kunibertistraße 4
- WANNE-EICKEL Hauptstraße 249
- WATTENSCHEID Oststraße 20

Example: Für meine Frau will ich eine Halskette kaufen.
Dann gehen Sie am besten zum Schmuckfachgeschäft Mössing.

DER GESCHENK-TIP
in der Engel-Drogerie

1 Für meine Frau will ich eine Flasche Parfüm kaufen.
2 Für meine Sekretärin will ich ein Buch kaufen.
3 Wo kann ich für meinen Chef eine Flasche Weißwein kaufen?
4 Für meine Tochter möchte ich ein schönes Geschenk kaufen.
5 Für meinen Sohn möchte ich eine Uhr kaufen.
6 Für meine Kamera muß ich einen Film kaufen.

Vocabulary

das Farbbild, -er *colour picture*
bringen, gebracht *to bring, to take*
machen, gemacht *to make, to do*
der Schmuck *jewellery*
das Fachgeschäft, -e *specialist shop*
führend *leading*
die Schönheit, -en *beauty*

die Mode, -n *fashion*
die Buchhandlung, -en *book shop*
das Taschenbuch, ¨er *paperback*
erhalten, erhalten *to get, receive*
der Fachhandel *specialist trade*
die Sorte, -n *kind*
Spirituosen *spirits*

ständig *continuously*
vorrätig *in stock*
fachlich *specialist*
die Beratung *advice*
die Probiermöglichkeit, -en *sampling opportunity*
das Faß, Fässer *barrel*
vorhanden *available*
die Drogerie, -n *drug store, non-dispensing chemist*

| **Exercise 4** | Study this plan of a German department store (**Kaufhaus**) and then answer the following questions. |

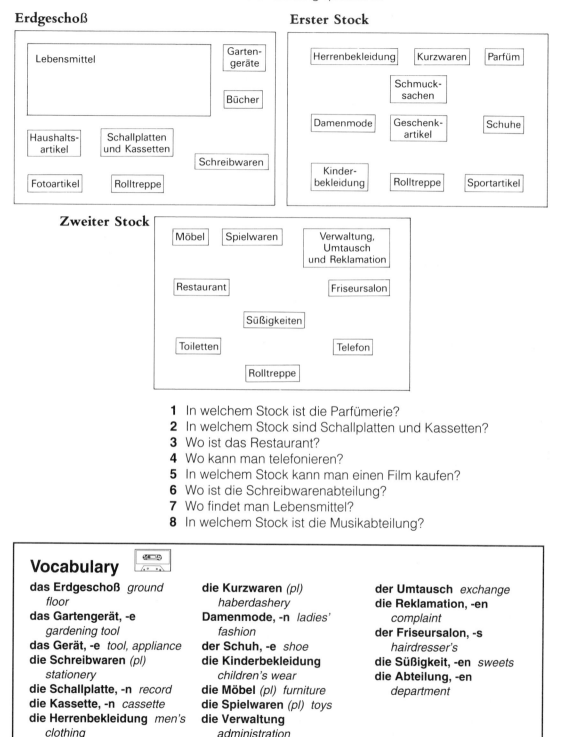

Erdgeschoß

Lebensmittel

Garten-geräte

Bücher

Haushalts-artikel

Schallplatten und Kassetten

Schreibwaren

Fotoartikel

Rolltreppe

Erster Stock

Herrenbekleidung | Kurzwaren | Parfüm

Schmuck-sachen

Damenmode | Geschenk-artikel | Schuhe

Kinder-bekleidung | Rolltreppe | Sportartikel

Zweiter Stock

Möbel | Spielwaren | Verwaltung, Umtausch und Reklamation

Restaurant | Friseursalon

Süßigkeiten

Toiletten | Telefon

Rolltreppe

1 In welchem Stock ist die Parfümerie?
2 In welchem Stock sind Schallplatten und Kassetten?
3 Wo ist das Restaurant?
4 Wo kann man telefonieren?
5 In welchem Stock kann man einen Film kaufen?
6 Wo ist die Schreibwarenabteilung?
7 Wo findet man Lebensmittel?
8 In welchem Stock ist die Musikabteilung?

Vocabulary

das Erdgeschoß *ground floor*
das Gartengerät, -e *gardening tool*
das Gerät, -e *tool, appliance*
die Schreibwaren *(pl) stationery*
die Schallplatte, -n *record*
die Kassette, -n *cassette*
die Herrenbekleidung *men's clothing*

die Kurzwaren *(pl) haberdashery*
Damenmode, -n *ladies' fashion*
der Schuh, -e *shoe*
die Kinderbekleidung *children's wear*
die Möbel *(pl) furniture*
die Spielwaren *(pl) toys*
die Verwaltung *administration*

der Umtausch *exchange*
die Reklamation, -en *complaint*
der Friseursalon, -s *hairdresser's*
die Süßigkeit, -en *sweets*
die Abteilung, -en *department*

Comprehension 2: Limbach

While visiting Mannheim on business you look out for some publicity material about the district. A friend of yours has asked you for information, since he wants to go for a holiday in rural Germany. What can you tell him about Limbach? You might find the following outline helpful.

Limbach ist ein kleines Dorf im Odenwald mit 2200 Einwohnern. Es liegt im südlichen Odenwald. Wegen der guten Luft ist es ein Luftkurort. Zu allen Zeiten, im Sommer wie im Winter, im Frühling wie im Herbst, kommen deshalb viele Leute von Mannheim und Frankfurt, um dort in der guten Luft Spaziergänge zu machen. Zu diesem Zweck gibt es viele Wanderwege in den vielen schönen Wäldern.

Limbach selbst liegt in einem Tal. Von weitem sichtbar ist die schöne Kirche mitten im Dorf. Obgleich Limbach in einem Tal liegt, ist es dennoch 500 Meter über dem Meeresspiegel. Auf den Höhen ringsum sind Wälder und Felder. Ja, Limbach ist noch ein Agrardorf. Es gibt deshalb viele Bauernhöfe. Limbach besitzt allerdings auch zwei Fabriken: eine Lampenschirm- und eine Steppdeckenfabrik.

Für die ärztliche Versorgung der Einwohner hat Limbach einen Arzt, einen Zahnarzt und eine Apotheke.

Brot, Brötchen und Kuchen kann man in den zwei Bäckereien kaufen, und Fleisch in den zwei Metzgereien. Es gibt auch zwei Lebensmittelgeschäfte, sowie eine Gärtnerei, wo man Obst und Gemüse kaufen kann, und eine Gaststätte natürlich. Zeitungen und Zeitschriften findet man im Schreibwarengeschäft. Für die Schönheit sorgen zwei Friseure.

Schulen und Unterhaltung, zum Beispiel Sport, Kino, Theater und so weiter, findet man in der nächsten Stadt.

Vocabulary

das Dorf, ¨er *village*
der Einwohner, - *inhabitant*
südlich *southern*
wegen *because of*
die Luft *air*
der Kurort, -e *health resort*
deshalb *therefore*
der Spaziergang, ¨e *walk*
zu diesem Zweck *for this purpose*
der Wanderweg, -e *footpath*
der Wald, ¨er *wood*
selbst *itself*
das Tal, ¨er *valley*

sichtbar *visible*
die Kirche, -n *church*
mitten in *in the middle of*
der Meeresspiegel *sea-level*
die Höhe, -n *hill, height*
ringsum *all around*
das Feld, -er *field*
der Bauernhof, ¨e *farm*
besitzen, besessen *to possess*
der Lampenschirm, -e *lamp shade*
die Steppdecke, -n *quilt*
der Arzt, ¨e *doctor*

der Zahnarzt, ¨e *dentist*
die Apotheke, -n *dispensing chemist*
die Bäckerei, -en *baker's*
die Metzgerei, -en *butcher's*
die Gärtnerei, -en *garden centre*
die Zeitung, -en *newspaper*
die Zeitschrift, -en *magazine*
die Unterhaltung *entertainment*
zum Beispiel *for example*

1 What can you tell your friend about Limbach's size, population, situation and surroundings?
2 What is it well known for?
3 What is a favourite activity for visitors?
4 What is worth seeing?
5 What shops are there?
6 Are there other things to do?
7 What if you're ill during your stay?

Talking business extra

Comprehension 3

Katrina has received a bill from **Verlag Germania**. She gives Christian a ring and says she's a bit puzzled. They are talking through the problem.

Key vocabulary

die Rechnungsnummer, -n *invoice number*

die Unterlage, -n *paper, document*

die Bestellung, -en *order*

die Teillieferung, -en *part delivery*

das Handbuch, ⁻er *manual*

beinhalten *to include*

die Materialkosten *(pl) materials costs*

der Rabatt, -e *regular discount*

abziehen, abgezogen *(sep) to deduct*

der/das Skonto, Skonti *cash discount*

Key phrases

Kommen wir zur Sache	*Let's get straight down to business*
laut Ihrer Offerte	*according to your offer*
pro Stück	*each, per piece*
der Preis war auf ... festgesetzt	*the price was fixed at ...*
eins Komma fünf Prozent	*1.5 %*
prompte Zahlung	*prompt payment*
Davon weiß ich nichts	*I know nothing about that*
Wir haben offensichtlich einen Fehler gemacht	*We have obviously made a mistake*
Das kann passieren	*It can happen*
Es hat keine Eile	*There's no hurry*

Find out:

1 who arranged the cash discount
2 what is going to be done about the error.

Exercise 5

Fill in the details:

Rechnungsnummer _____

Bestellungsdatum _____

monatl. Teillieferung _____ Broschüren

Preis pro Stück _____

_____ Handbücher

Betrag _____

- _____ Rabatt

+ 15%   Mehrwertsteuer

Telefongespräch, Datum _____

prompte Zahlung _____ Skonto

Puzzle
1 manual
2 part delivery
3 materials costs
4 regular discount
5 mistake
6 cash discount
7 clue: no businessman or woman is without them

Language structures

Verbs Wissen and kennen

Wissen is an irregular verb which has endings just like **müssen**, **können** and **wollen** (see Language structures overview, page 81). In the singular the verb is irregular, but the plural forms are regular.

ich weiß	wir wissen
du weißt	ihr wißt
er, sie, es weiß	sie wissen
	Sie wissen

Der Programmierer **weiß** nicht, wo die Altstadt ist.

The computer programmer doesn't know (i.e. does not have the facts) where the old centre of the town is.

Der Programmierer **kennt** die Altstadt nicht.

The computer programmer doesn't know (is not acquainted with) the old centre of the town.

To know is either **wissen** or **kennen**, depending on whether it means to know as a fact, or to know personally, being acquainted with something or somebody.

Progress check

1 NVQ S1

You are asking for, as well as giving directions. Tell someone that:

a) you are looking for the tourist office

b) they should go straight ahead

c) they should take the second road on the left

d) they should walk along the **Steinstraße**

e) the department store is on the right

f) the old centre of the city lies on the left hand side.

2 NVQ W2

On a first trip to the town of your company's German subsidiary, you realise you need help. Make a note of some questions, asking somebody:

a) to recommend a souvenir shop to you

b) what the best way is to get there

c) where you can buy presents for your family

d) whether the hairdresser's is on the ground floor

e) on which floor the music department is

f) when the post office is open

g) whether the bookshop is closed at lunchtime

h) whether they know your colleague

i) whether they know where the toilets are.

3 What is the difference between an **Apotheke** and a **Drogerie**?

4 You have asked for directions to the nearest food shop and get the following reply:

'Das weiß ich leider nicht. Ich kenne diese Stadt auch nicht, ich bin nur ein paar Tage auf Besuch hier.'

You ask another passer-by and this time you are more successful:

'Ja, ich kenne ein gutes Lebensmittelgeschäft. Wissen Sie wo das Modehaus Heinemann ist? Gehen Sie dort an der Kreuzung links, dann kommen Sie direkt zu einem großen Spar Geschäft. Dort gibt's auch eine Bäckerei und eine Metzgerei.'

What have you been told?

5 NVQ R2

Your boss has left written instructions regarding an incorrect invoice. What is he saying?

a) Vom Gesamtbetrag können Sie 2% Skonto für prompte Zahlung abziehen.

b) Dieser Fehler darf nie wieder passieren.

UNIT 14 Einkaufen

In this unit, you will learn how to …

- shop for presents and food
- ask for colours and sizes of clothes
- analyse an average German income.

Dialogue: Im Kaufhaus

Angela Nicholson, a British sales representative, is in a German department store buying presents for her family at the end of her first business trip to Germany.

Verkäufer	Guten Tag. Was darf es sein?
Vertreterin	Wo bekomme ich Parfüm?
Verkäufer	Das bekommen Sie in der Parfümerie im zweiten Stock.
Vertreterin	Danke. Wo ist die Rolltreppe?
Verkäufer	Da vorne. Sehen Sie?
Vertreterin	Ach ja. Und in welchem Stock finde ich T-Shirts?
Verkäufer	Die gibt's hier im Erdgeschoß.

(*Einige Minuten später*)

Verkäufer	Kann ich Ihnen helfen?
Vertreterin	Danke. Ich weiß nicht, ob mein Sohn lieber ein T-Shirt oder Spielzeug möchte.
Verkäufer	Wie alt ist denn Ihr Sohn?

Vertreterin	Er wird dieses Jahr sechs Jahre alt.
Verkäufer	Vielleicht interessiert ihn ein T-Shirt mit Micky Maus-Motiv?
Vertreterin	Das gibt's auch in Deutschland! Das gefällt ihm ganz bestimmt. Also, ich nehme eins … Welche Farben haben Sie denn?
Verkäufer	Wir haben blau, gelb, schwarz und braun.
Vertreterin	Ja gut, ein blaues bitte.
Verkäufer	Welche Größe hat Ihr Sohn?
Vertreterin	Ach, das ist schwer. Ungefähr sechsundzwanzig inches. Ich habe hier eine Umrechnungstabelle. Mal sehen … Also, das sind ungefähr 65 Zentimeter.
Verkäufer	Das hier wird ihrem Sohn sicher passen.
Vertreterin	Was kostet es bitte?
Verkäufer	Siebzehn Mark neunzig.
Vertreterin	Bitte schön. Und für meine Tochter will ich eine Kassette kaufen. Wo ist die Musikabteilung, bitte?
Verkäufer	Die finden Sie im dritten Stock.
Vertreterin	Vielen Dank.

Vocabulary

Was darf es sein? *How can I help you? (* literally: *What may it be?)*
das Parfüm *perfume*
da vorne *there at the front*
das Spielzeug, -e *toy*
interessieren *to interest*
das Motiv, -e *motif*

gefallen, gefallen *(+ dative) to please, to like*
die Farbe, -n *colour*
blau *blue*
gelb *yellow*
schwarz *black*
braun *braun*
ein blaues *a blue one*

die Größe, -n *size*
schwer *difficult*
ungefähr *about*
die Umrechnungstabelle, -n *conversion table*
mal sehen *let's just see*

Notes

1 **In welchem Stock finde ich T-Shirts? Welche Größe hat Ihr Sohn? Welcher, welche, welches** *which* have the same endings as the definite article. For revision refer back to Language structures overview, page 103.

2 **Er wird dieses Jahr sechs Jahre alt** *He will be six years old this year.* As well as being used for the future tense (page 60) **werden** can also be used on its own to mean *will be*. Details in the Language structures overview, page 153.

Exercise 1

Answer the following questions in German.

1 Wo im Warenhaus kann man Parfüm kaufen?
2 Was weiß die Vertreterin nicht?
3 Wie alt ist der Sohn der Vertreterin im Moment?
4 Welches Motiv gefällt ihrem Sohn bestimmt?
5 Was kostet das T-Shirt?
6 Welche Größe trägt der Sohn?
7 Welche Größe ist das in England?
8 Warum geht die Vertreterin in den dritten Stock?

Exercise 2	Before completing the blanks in this exercise, turn to page 152, Language structures, for further details on how to say that you like something or somebody, and that something suits or fits you. When you feel confident enough, try the whole exercise again, but this time cover up the answers after the yes/no faces!

Example:

Gefällt Ihnen dieses Parfüm?　😊 Ja, es gefällt mir gut.

☹ Nein, es gefällt mir nicht.

1 Gefällt Ihnen diese Kassette? 😊 Ja, sie _____ __ gut.

2 Paßt mir dieses T-Shirt? ☹ Nein, __ _____ Ihnen __.

3 Gefällt Ihnen dieses Zimmer? 😊 Ja, es _____ __ __.

4 Passen Ihnen diese Schuhe? ☹ Nein, __ _____ mir __.

5 Wie geht es ihm? 😊 Es _____ ihm __.

6 Schmeckt Ihnen der Wein? ☹ Nein, __ schmeckt __ __.

Exercise 3	You are in a German department store buying a T-shirt and a toy. What do you say in German?

2·STOCK
SPIELZEUG

Verkäuferin	Was darf es sein?
Sie	(*Say you want to buy a T-shirt for your daughter.*)

_____

Verkäuferin	Wie alt ist Ihre Tochter denn?
Sie	(*Say she will be thirteen this year.*)

_____

Verkäuferin	Vielleicht gefällt ihr dieses T-Shirt mit Lufthansa Motiv. Das ist etwas typisch Deutsches. Wir haben es in verschiedenen Farben … rot, schwarz, weiß, gelb und blau.
Sie	(*Say you like the red one.*)

_____

Verkäuferin	Welche Größe, bitte?
Sie	(*Say you would like 81 centimetres and ask what it costs.*)

_____

Verkäuferin	18 Mark.
Sie	(*Ask where you can buy a toy for your son.*)

_____

Verkäuferin	Im zweiten Stock.
Sie	(*Thank the assistant and say goodbye.*)

_____

Verkäuferin	Auf Wiedersehen.

Vocabulary

etwas typisch Deutsches
  something typically German

verschieden *various*
rot *red*

Exercise 4

1 Read the following dialogue, then using the adverts over the page and other vocabulary you have learnt, make up similar dialogues asking for:

a) orange juice and pork fillet
b) apples and coffee
c) cheese, eggs and onions.

These phrases may be useful:

Sie wünschen?
Kann ich Ihnen helfen?
Wieviel möchten Sie?
Sonst noch etwas?
Ich danke Ihnen für Ihre Hilfe.
Nichts zu danken.

Verkäufer	Guten Tag. Was darf es sein?
Kunde	Ich möchte ein Kilo Pfirsiche bitte, und einen Kopfsalat.
Verkäufer	Eine Mark neunundneunzig und eine Mark neunundzwanzig. Das macht drei Mark achtundzwanzig.
Kunde	Bitte schön.
Verkäufer	Danke.

Vocabulary

Sonst noch etwas?
  Anything else?
der Pfirsich, -e *peach*
der Schinkenspeck *bacon*

der Blumenkohl *cauliflower*
das Fischstäbchen, - *fish finger*
Tafeläpfel (*pl*) *eating apples*

Gehacktes (Fleisch) *minced meat*
die Ananas, - *pineapple*

2 Try and guess from the context the meaning of the following words and phrases, consulting a dictionary if necessary:
   a) mild und mager
   b) tiefgekühlt
   c) mild gesalzen
   d) gemischt
   e) 10er Packung
   f) gezuckert
   g) 236 ml-Dose

Comprehension 1

While waiting for a business colleague at the reception desk of a large German hotel, you can hear the receptionist dealing with the queries of other guests. Listen to her instructions to each of the visitors, then using the map opposite establish the destination of each one and complete the table on the following page. **Gast A** has been done for you.

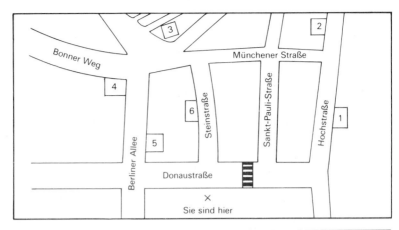

Person	Destination	
	Number on map	**Place**
Gast A	*1*	*Tourist information office*
Gast B		
Gast C		
Gast D		
Gast E		

Vocabulary

das Büro, -s *office*
gar nicht weit *not far at all*
gegenüber *(+ dative)*
   opposite
bestimmt *certainly*

die Geschäftsverbindung,
  -en *business connection*
dort geht es rechts weiter
  there you continue on the
  right

der Fußgängerüberweg, -e
  pedestrian crossing

Comprehension 2:   Wie geben deutsche Familien ihr Geld aus?

Für eine durchschnittliche Familie mit vier Personen ist das
Leben ziemlich teuer. Vom Bruttoeinkommen muß man zuerst
Steuern und Sozialversicherung abziehen.

Im Durchschnitt gibt man circa 26 Prozent seines
Nettoeinkommens im Monat für Nahrungs- und Genußmittel
aus. Für Kleidung und Schuhe ist die Ausgabe ungefähr 8
Prozent, und für Wohnungsmieten, Strom, Gas und Brennstoffe
braucht man im Durchschnitt 24 Prozent des Nettoeinkommens.
Die Kosten für andere Haushaltsgüter sind 8 Prozent. Post und
Verkehr, (also öffentliche Verkehrsmittel, Benzin, Autoreparatur,
und so weiter) sind auch nicht billig. Im Durchschnitt gibt man 16

Bruttoeinkommen
− Steuern
− Sozialversicherung
Nettoeinkommen

Körper- und Gesundheitspflege
3 %

Persönliche Ausstattung usw
7 %

Bildung und Unterhaltung
8 %

Post und Verkehr
16 %

Andere Haushaltsgüter
8 %

Nahrungs- und Genußmittel
26 %

Kleidung und Schuhe
8 %

Wohnungsmieten, Strom,
Gas und Brennstoffe
24 %

Prozent seines Einkommens dafür aus. Für Bildung (zum Beispiel Abendkurse) und Unterhaltung (Kino, Theater und so weiter) gibt man 8 Prozent seines Einkommens aus. Für Körper- und Gesundheitspflege (Seife, Zahnpasta, Gymnastik usw.) ist der Betrag 3 Prozent. Dazu kommt noch persönliche Ausstattung wie zum Beispiel Luxusgüter. Man spart also im Monat normalerweise nicht viel Geld.

Man darf auch nicht vergessen: die Wiedervereinigung kostet viel, und bedeutet höhere Steuern für alle.

Vocabulary

ausgeben, ausgegeben (sep) *to spend*
durchschnittlich *(on) average*
das Bruttoeinkommen, - *gross income*
die Steuer, -n *tax*
die Sozialversicherung, -en *national insurance*
abziehen, abgezogen (sep) *to deduct*
im Durchschnitt *on average*
das Nettoeinkommen, - *net income*
die Nahrungsmitte (pl) *food provisions*
die Genußmittel (pl) *semi-luxury goods*
die Ausgabe, -n *expenditure*

die Wohnungsmiete, -n *rent for flat, etc.*
das Öl *oil*
das Gas *gas*
der Brennstoff, -e *fuel*
die Kosten (pl) *costs*
die Haushaltsgüter (pl) *household goods*
der Verkehr *transport*
die Nachrichten (pl) *news*
die öffentlichen Verkehrsmittel (pl) *public transport*
das Benzin *petrol*
die Autoreparatur, -en *car repair*
die Bildung *education*
der Abendkurs, -e *evening class*

übrig *left over*
die Unterhaltung, -en *entertainment*
die Körper- und Gesundheitspflege *body and health care*
die Seife, -n *soap*
die Zahnpasta *tooth paste*
dazu *in addition*
die Gymnastik *gymnastics*
der Betrag, ⁻e *amount*
die Ausstattung *equipment*
Luxusgüter (pl) *luxury goods*
sparen *to save*
die Wiedervereinigung *reunification*
bedeuten *to mean*

Answer the following questions in German:

1 Wieviel Prozent ihres Nettoeinkommens gibt eine deutsche Familie für Essen und Trinken aus?
2 Wieviel braucht man für Post und Verkehr? Und Kleidung?
3 Was ist teurer, Essen und Trinken oder Wohnungsmieten?
4 Was ist billiger, Bildung und Unterhaltung oder Strom usw.?
5 Wieviel ihres Nettoeinkommens kann eine deutsche Familie sparen?

Talking business extra

Comprehension 3

Whilst waiting for Frau Haider to join their meeting, Katrina does not waste any time in asking a rather personal question. But amongst colleagues it's alright to discuss salaries, she thinks.

Key vocabulary

vergleichen, verglichen *to compare*
die Gehaltserhöhung, -en *pay-rise*
zurückweisen, zurückgewiesen *to refuse (sep)*

die Überstunde, -n *overtime*
einteilen *(sep) to organise, plan (time)*
das Betriebsgeheimnis, -se *company secret*
verdienen *to earn*

das Dienstjahr, -e *year's service*
einholen *(sep) to catch up*

Key phrases

Worum handelt es sich?
unter Kollegen
prinzipiell
die genaue Summe
Sie werden schon sehen
Das kann ich mir nicht leisten

What is it about?
between, amongst colleagues
on principle
the exact sum
You'll see
I can't afford it

Find out:

1 which one of the two seems to enjoy a better salary
2 what Christian thinks of the idea of making a bet.

Exercise 5

Fill in the details:

Christian würde eine Gehaltserhöhung nicht

_____.

Spieltechnik zahlt prinzipiell keine _____.

Die genaue Summe bleibt ein

_____.

Ich kann Sie ja noch _____.

Eine Wette kann ich mir nicht _____.

Puzzle

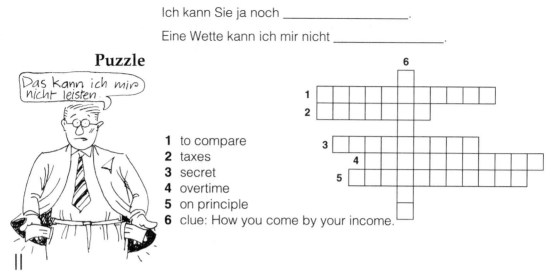

Das kann ich mir nicht leisten.

1 to compare
2 taxes
3 secret
4 overtime
5 on principle
6 clue: How you come by your income.

Language structures

Verbs **Gefallen** and **passen**

Vielleicht gefällt **ihr** dieses T-Shirt. *Perhaps she likes this T-shirt.*
Diese Schuhe gefallen **mir** nicht. *I do not like these shoes.*

Gefallen is a very useful word and like other verbs learned previously (see Unit 8 page 80 and Unit 12 page 127) it takes the dative. It is used as frequently as the English word *to like* and has the same meaning, but its grammatical use becomes clear when translated with *is pleasing to.*

Examples:
Dieses Buch **gefällt mir**. *(This book is pleasing to me.) I like this book.*

Welche Kassette **gefällt Ihnen?** *Which cassette do you like?*
Das Zimmer **gefällt den Gästen**. *The guests like the room.*
Gefällt Ihnen unser Buch? *Do you like our book?*
Gefallen Ihnen die Geschenke? *Do you like the presents?*
Diese Fotos **gefallen dem Herrn** nicht. *The gentleman doesn't like these photos.*

Passen is another verb which takes the dative.

Example:
Diese Größe **paßt Ihrem Sohn** sicher. *This size will certainly fit your son.*

Pronouns Demonstrative pronouns

In welchem Stock finde ich bitte T-Shirts?
Die finden Sie hier im Erdgeschoß. (literally) *Those you (can) find here on the ground floor.*

Möchten Sie ein großes oder ein kleines T-Shirt?
Das hier wird mir sicher passen. (literally) *This (one) here will certainly fit me.*

|| *Demonstrative pronouns* have the same form as the definite article (see page 81). They are mainly used for emphasis, as a colloquial alternative to the personal pronouns (see page 28).

Progress check

1 NVQ S2

You are buying a present for your son. Make the purchase in German.

a) I like this T-shirt.
b) Which colours do you have?
c) I'll take the blue one.
d) Do you have a conversion table?
e) This size will fit my son.
f) I want to buy a toy for my daughter.

2 NVQ W1

Make a short shopping list in German:

a) a bottle of orange juice
b) a tin of pineapples
c) 250 grams of cheese.

3 What is a **Fußgängerüberweg**?

4 Can you match the German words with their correct English equivalents?

a) income **b)** taxes **c)** national insurance
d) on average **e)** expenditure **f)** amount
g) to spend **h)** to save
A Sozialversicherung **B** sparen
C im Durchschnitt **D** Einkommen
E Ausgabe **F** ausgeben **G** Steuern
H Betrag

5 NVQ R2

You have enquired about a pay rise. What are the main points in the written reply?

a) Wir zahlen prinzipiell keine Überstunden.
b) Eine Gehaltserhöhung können wir uns erst im nächsten Jahr leisten.

Summary 6
Language structures overview

Werden

1 Used with an infinitive for the future tense (see page 60)

Where the infinitive is **sein**, it is sometimes dropped and **werden** is used on its own to mean *will be*

Mein Sohn **wird** dieses Jahr drei Jahre alt.   *My son will be 3 years old this year.*

Es **wird** bald drei Uhr.   *It will soon be 3 o'clock.*

2 *to become*
Es **wird** dunkel.   *It is dark.*
Es **ist** dunkel **geworden**.   *It has become dark.*
Die Kosten **werden** teurer.   *The costs are becoming more expensive.*

Present tense

ich	werde
du	wirst
er	
sie	wird
es	
wir	werden
ihr	werdet
sie	werden
Sie	werden

Perfect tense

ich	bin	
du	bist	
er		
sie	ist	
es		geworden
wir	sind	
ihr	seid	
sie	sind	
Sie	sind	

Summary 6

Replacing nouns with *one, some, any, none*

Hier sind die Filme. Wieviel kostet **einer**?
Wo sind die Kassetten? Ich suche **eine** für meine Tochter.
Diese T-Shirts gefallen mir. Also, ich nehme **eins**.
Diese Äpfel sind zu teuer. Ich nehme **keine**.
Ich brauche neue Geschäftsverbindungen. Haben Sie **welche?** *(any)*

	MASCULINE	FEMININE	NEUTER	PLURAL	
Nom.	(k)einer	(k)eine	(k)eins	welche,	keine
Acc.	(k)einen	(k)eine	(k)eins	welche,	keine
Dat.	(k)einem	(k)einer	(k)einem	welchen,	keinen

Additional exercises

1 **Werden** is used   **a** for the future tense
                         b to mean *will be*
                         c to mean *to become*
In each of the following sentences, decide which of the three is correct.

1 Wann werden Sie für Ihre Familie Geschenke kaufen?
2 Ich werde nächste Woche vierzig Jahre alt.
3 Unser Verkaufsleiter ist jetzt Direktor geworden.
4 Es wird spät. Sind wir bald fertig?
5 Wird Herr Walter morgen wieder anrufen?
6 Wir werden im Herbst noch mehr Steuern zahlen.

2 Fill in the following spaces with the correct form of **werden**.

a Wann _____ Herr Schmidt nach England fliegen?

b _____ die Beamten morgen hier sein?

c Meine Tochter _____ bald mit der Schule fertig.

d Gestern abend ist es leider spät _____.

e Sie _____ nächstes Jahr zwei Prozent Ihres Einkommens sparen,

nicht wahr?

f Vielleicht _____ ich bald Einkaufsleiterin.

3 **Gefallen**

a Put the following sentences into English:

1 Die Altstadt gefällt mir sehr.
2 Wie gefällt Ihnen dieses Spielzeug?
3 Diese Farben hier gefallen mir gar nicht.
4 Gefallen Ihnen diese deutschen Zeitschriften?
5 Welches T-Shirt gefällt Ihnen besser, das rote oder das blaue?
6 Das Lebensmittelgeschäft in der Hauptstraße gefällt den englischen
Besuchern nicht.

b Put the following sentences into German:

1 Do you like this book?
2 How do you like the shops in Mönchengladbach?
3 How does Mrs King like the little villages in the Odenwald?
4 Do the customers like our new product?
5 I like this souvenir shop.
6 Our guests like the evening programme.
7 Mr Newby doesn't like these shoes.
8 I don't like this newspaper at all.
9 Why don't you like the firm?

4 Revision of numbers between 100 and 1000 (see page 39).
How do you write the following numbers in German?

a 220 **b** 172 **c** 310 **d** 978 **e** 561 **f** 436 **g** 677 **h** 789

5 Revision of **welche/r/s** (see page 103).
Complete the gaps in the following sentences with the correct form of **welche/r/s**

a _____ Hotel empfehlen Sie?

b _____ Straße suchen Sie?

c _____ Brief schreiben Sie?

d _____ Bücher lesen Sie?

e _____ Firma besuchen Sie?

f _____ Wein trinken Sie?

g _____ Parfüm kaufen Sie?

Key phrases

Asking the way to somewhere	Ich suche die Königsallee
	Wo ist die?
	Wie komme ich am besten zur Münchener Straße?
	Wie komme ich am besten dahin/dorthin?
Saying you don't exactly know	Ich weiß nicht genau
Asking about prices	Ist das nicht sehr teuer?
Thanking someone for his/her help	Ich danke Ihnen für Ihre Hilfe
Asking on what floor something can be found	In welchem Stock finde ich …?
Saying you are only looking	Ich schau nur
	Ich schau mich nur um
Asking where a particular product is sold	Wo kann ich bitte Parfüm kaufen?
Asking if you can help	Kann ich Ihnen helfen?

Cultural briefing

Shopping

Many shops open earlier than in Britain, and close later. However, they tend to close for longer periods over lunchtime. Maximum opening times are quite strictly regulated and almost all shops close on Saturday afternoons. The exception is the first Saturday in the month, the **langer Samstag** or *long Saturday*, when you can shop in the afternoon. On Sundays shopping is limited to some flower-shops and newspaper kiosks, but bars, cafes and restaurants are open, and a Sunday walk to include a visit to the local **Konditorei** is common.

Shop-assistants have typically been well trained in retailing skills, and are expected to be helpful and informative. If you tell them that what you're buying is meant as a gift, **ein Geschenk**, they will wrap the article accordingly.

The use of credit cards is still less widespread than in Britain, though most shops do now accept some. Nevertheless, to be safe have cash or eurocheques handy.

Pronunciation

ei, ai – au – ie – eu, äu

ei, ai	like *i* in *bike* sein, Gesundheit, weiter, Mai
au	like *ow* in *flower*, but with rounded lips genau, geradeaus, Kaufhaus
ie	like *ee* in *feed*, pronounced with a Scottish accent Spielzeug, verschieden, Zwiebel (exceptionally pronounced as two separate vowel sounds, e.g. Familie Famili-e)
eu, äu	like *oi* in *boil* Kreuzung, Steuer, Häuser

UNIT **15** Krankheit

In this unit, you will learn how to …

- make an appointment
- ask what is wrong with someone
- explain that you are feeling ill
- name different parts of the body.

Dialogue: Beim Arzt

While on a visit to a German factory, a British engineer, John Faulkner, feels unwell. He phones a doctor's surgery and then goes to see the doctor.

Dr. med. K.H. Kietzmann

Hals-Nasen-Ohrenarzt

Sprechstunden					
Mo.	Di.	Mi.	Do.	Fr.	Sa.
9-12		9-12	9-12		9-11
15-18	15-18		15-18	15-18	

Ingenieur	Guten Tag. Ich möchte einen Termin für heute.
Stimme	Moment bitte. Ich sehe mal nach … Können Sie um elf Uhr zwanzig kommen?
Ingenieur	Ja, das geht.
Stimme	Wie ist Ihr Name, bitte?
Ingenieur	Ich heiße Faulkner.
Stimme	Wie schreibt man das?
Ingenieur	F-A-U-L-K-N-E-R. Ich bin Engländer.
Stimme	Haben Sie einen Krankenschein?
Ingenieur	Ich habe einen internationalen Krankenschein.
Stimme	Bringen Sie den bitte mit.

(*Beim Arzt*)

Arzt	Was fehlt Ihnen denn?
Ingenieur	Ich habe Kopfschmerzen und Magenweh.
Arzt	Wie lange haben Sie diese Schmerzen schon?
Ingenieur	Seit gestern abend. Ich habe gar nicht geschlafen.
Arzt	Machen Sie bitte den Mund auf … Hm, Ihr Hals ist rot und Sie haben auch Fieber … Sie haben eine Grippe. Sie müssen sofort ins Bett.
Ingenieur	Ach, wie ärgerlich!
Arzt	Ich gebe Ihnen ein Rezept. Eine Apotheke finden Sie gleich um die Ecke.
Ingenieur	Also, danke, Herr Doktor. Soll ich gleich bezahlen, oder schicken Sie mir die Rechnung?
Arzt	Die Sprechstundenhilfe erledigt das alles.
Ingenieur	Danke. Auf Wiedersehen.
Arzt	Auf Wiedersehen. Gute Besserung!

Vocabulary

die Stimme, -n *voice*
der Termin, -e *appointment*
nachsehen, nachgesehen *(sep) to check*
Ich sehe mal nach *I'll just check*
der Krankenschein, -e *medical insurance record*
mitbringen, mitgebracht *(sep) to bring along*

beim Arzt *at the doctor's*
Was fehlt Ihnen? *What is wrong with you?*
die Kopfschmerzen *(pl) headache*
das Magenweh *stomachache*
der Schmerz, -en *pain*
seit wann? *for how long, since when?*

aufmachen *(sep) to open*
der Hals, ¨e *neck, throat*
das Fieber *(high) temperature*
die Grippe *flu*
ärgerlich *annoying*
das Rezept, -e *prescription*
die Sprechstundenhilfe, -n *doctor's receptionist*
erledigen *to settle, finish off*

Notes

1 **Bringen Sie den bitte mit.**
Machen Sie den Mund auf.
Mitbringen and **aufmachen** are separable verbs. When used in an order or instruction (i.e. Imperative, see page 92, the prefix stands at the end of the sentence.

2 **Was fehlt Ihnen denn?** *What is wrong with you?* The verb **fehlen** takes the dative.

3 **Wie lange haben Sie diese Schmerzen schon?** *For how long have you had these pains?* In this construction English uses a past tense, whereas the German equivalent is a present tense. See Language structures, page 164.

Exercise 1	Answer the following questions on Mr Faulkner's visit to the doctor.

1 What time is his appointment?
2 What is he asked to do after giving his name?
3 What documentation is he asked to bring with him?
4 What pains does he complain of to the doctor?
5 Since when has he had these pains?

6 What sort of night did he have?
7 What is the doctor's diagnosis?
8 What does he tell the engineer to do?
9 What is Mr Faulkner's reaction?
10 Where is the nearest chemist?
11 Who deals with the question of the doctor's fee?

| **Exercise 2** | The morning after arriving in Vienna to attend an international conference, you feel quite unwell and decide to see a doctor. You phone the surgery to arrange an appointment. What do you say in German? |

Sie   (*Say you would like an appointment for today.*)

_____

Stimme   Moment mal, bitte … Können Sie um elf Uhr
                 dreißig kommen?
Sie   (*Say that's fine.*)

_____

Stimme   Wie ist Ihr Name, bitte?
Sie   (*Give your name, and say you're English.*)

_____

Stimme   Buchstabieren Sie das bitte.
Sie   (*Spell out your name.*)

_____

Stimme   Haben Sie eine Krankenversicherung?
Sie   (*Say you have a medical insurance form – E111.*)

_____

Stimme   Bringen Sie den bitte mit.

Vocabulary

die Krankenversicherung
medical insurance

| **Exercise 3** | Look at the pictures and tables overleaf. When you have familiarised yourself with the new words and phrases, study the dialogue that follows and make up similar ones, changing the variables as often as you can. |

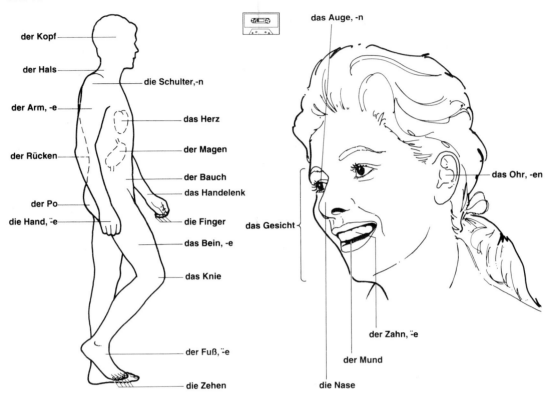

der Kopf
der Hals
die Schulter,-n
der Arm, -e
das Herz
der Rücken
der Magen
der Bauch
das Handelenk
der Po
die Hand, ¨e
die Finger
das Bein, -e
das Knie
der Fuß, ¨e
die Zehen

das Auge, -n
das Ohr, -en
das Gesicht
der Zahn, ¨e
der Mund
die Nase

Something's hurting

Mein		Kopf Mund Hals Rücken Herz Finger	tut weh.
	linker rechter	Arm Fuß	
	linkes	Bein Ohr	
	rechtes	Auge Handgelenk	
Meine	linke	Hand Nase	

Meine	Arme Füße	tun weh.
	Beine Ohren	
	Augen	

What's wrong with you?

	Kopfschmerzen. Magenschmerzen. Zahnschmerzen. einen Schnupfen.
Ich habe	eine Erkältung. Halsschmerzen. Husten. Durchfall. Ohrenschmerzen.

Vocabulary

der Schnupfen *head-cold,*
   snuffles

die Erkältung *cold*
der Husten *cough*

der Durchfall *diarrhoea*

Sekretärin	Wie geht es Ihnen?
Bekannte	Nicht gut.
Sekretärin	Was fehlt Ihnen?
Bekannte	Ich habe Halsschmerzen.
Sekretärin	Wie lange haben Sie diese Schmerzen schon?
Bekannte	Seit Montag.
Sekretärin	Am besten gehen Sie zur Apotheke/zum Arzt.
Bekannte	Ja, das mache ich.
Sekretärin	Also, gute Besserung.
Bekannte	Danke.

Comprehension 1

 Listen to this piece of information about what happens in German firms when employees are absent because of illness. Then answer the questions below. Don't forget that it may be helpful to study the questions before you start listening.

Vocabulary

der Arbeitnehmer, -
   employee
der Arbeitgeber, - *employer*

die Arbeitsunfähigkeits-
   bescheinigung, -en *sick*
   note

der Lohn, ¨-e *wages*
weiterzahlen *(sep)* *to carry*
   on paying

1 How long can you be off work before seeing a doctor?
2 What do you have to do with the sick note?
3 How long must the employer pay wages if the employee has to stay off work?

Comprehension 2

While waiting to be served at the chemist's you hear the following statements. Match each of the symptoms to one of the advertisements pictured overleaf.

b)
Schnupfenspray in die Nase sprühen, und dann ist die Nase nicht mehr verstopft. Es hilft schnell und wirkt für Stunden. Am Tag und bei Nacht.

a)

Durchfall?

Dieses besonders gute Mittel bringt Ihnen rasche Besserung. Besonders gut bei Reise- und Sommerdurchfällen

c)
Bei Kopfschmerzen, Zahnschmerzen, Grippe usw. nehmen Sie 2–3 Tabletten.

e)
Vividrin®
antiallergische
Augentropfen

d)
Schmidt-Medikamente
Unsere Hustentropfen befreien Sie schnell von Hustenreiz.
Mit oder ohne Wasser einnehmen.

f)
frubienzym® HALSSCHMERZ-TABLETTEN

g)
Hopfen-Tabletten
Nur 2 Tabletten bringen Ihnen gesunden Schlaf und ruhige Nerven.

Vocabulary

das Mittel, - *remedy*
rasch *fast*
sprühen *to spray*
wirken *to work, have an effect*

der Tropfen, - *drop*
befreien *to free*
der Hustenreiz *throat tickle*
einnehmen, eingenommen *(sep) to take (medicines)*

die Tablette, -n *tablet*
gesund *healthy*
die Nerven *(pl) nerves*

1 Mein Kopf tut weh, und ich bin erkältet.
2 Mein Magen tut weh, und ich muß die ganze Zeit zur Toilette laufen.
3 Meine Nase ist verstopft. Ich kann kaum atmen.
4 Ich bin ganz nervös und kann nicht schlafen.
5 Mein Hals tut weh.
6 Ich huste Tag und Nacht.
7 Ich habe eine Augenentzündung.

Vocabulary

erkältet *suffering from a cold*
laufen, gelaufen (sein) *to go, run*

verstopft *blocked*
kaum *hardly*
atmen *to breathe*

nervös *nervous*
die Entzündung, -en *inflammation*

Talking business extra

Comprehension 3

Katrina wants to finish some urgent matters before her planned meeting with Christian this afternoon. She is in the middle of dictating an accompanying letter to a price quotation, when her plans are about to change.

Key vocabulary

das Begleitschreiben, - *accompanying letter*
dringend *urgent*
die Anfrage, -n *enquiry*
der Kostenvoranschlag, ⁻e *quotation*

die Akte, -n *file*
die Kundendatei *customer data-bank*
speichern *to store*
der Drucker, - *printer*

das Pauschalangebot, -e *package deal*
verlängern *to extend*

Key phrases

als Anlage — *as an enclosure*
die gewünschten Artikel — *required items*
zum Einführungspreis anbieten — *to offer at an introductory price*
das Angebot gilt bis ... — *the offer is valid until ...*
Streichen Sie das! — *Delete that!*
die Besprechung absagen — *to cancel the meeting*
nichts Ernstes — *nothing serious*
das Meeting verlegen — *to postpone the meeting*
zur gleichen Zeit — *at the same time*

Find out:

1 what is special about the package deal
2 what is going to be done about the meeting.

Exercise 4

Fill in the details:

Katrina diktiert ein _____.

Im Finanzbüro ist die _____.

Wir senden Ihnen unseren

_____.

Wir verkaufen den Computer zu einem günstigen

_____.

Bis Jahresschluß gilt dieses _____.

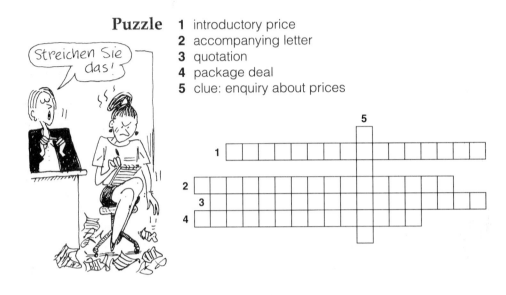

Puzzle

1 introductory price
2 accompanying letter
3 quotation
4 package deal
5 clue: enquiry about prices

‖ Language structures

Seit and **schon**

Seit wann **haben Sie** diese Schmerzen?   *How long have you*
Wie lange **haben sie** diese Schmerzen **schon**?   *had these pains?*

These are two words to show *how long* something has been *going on*. Note that the past tense is used in English, whereas German uses the *present tense*.

Progress check _____

1 Imagine you are at a doctor's surgery. Say the following to the German receptionist:
 a) I would like an appointment for today.
 b) I have had a headache since last night.
 c) I have brought the medical insurance record with me.
 d) Will you send me the bill?
2 Tell the doctor that you have a sore throat and a cough and your left ear hurts. Say also that you have a temperature and did not sleep at all last night.
3 Using the verb **abholen**, instruct your colleague to fetch your ear drops, cough medicine and throat tablets.

4 What do the following words mean?
 a) der Arbeitnehmer
 b) der Arbeitgeber
 c) der Lohn
5 What is being said here?
 a) Bitte speichern Sie den Kostenvoranschlag, der Drucker funktioniert nicht.
 b) Wir bieten Ihnen die Waren zu einem günstigen Einführungspreis an, aber dieses Angebot kann nur bis Monatsende gelten.

UNIT 16 Unfall

In this unit, you will learn how to …

- buy medicines at a chemist's
- understand a doctor's instructions
- report an accident and call an ambulance.

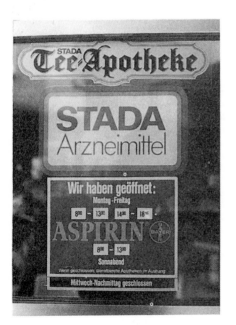

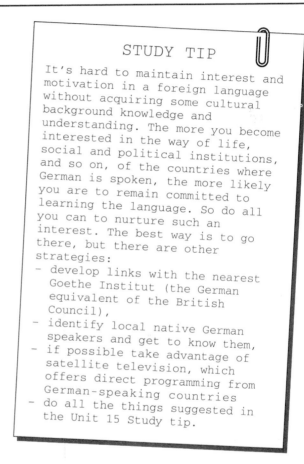
Dialogue: In der Apotheke

John Faulkner, a British engineer working in Germany, goes to the chemist to collect his medicine.

Apothekerin	Guten Morgen. Kann ich Ihnen helfen?
Ingenieur	Guten Morgen. Ich war gerade beim Arzt. Ich habe hier ein Rezept – bitte sehr.
Apothekerin	Danke … Also, Sie bekommen Tabletten.
Ingenieur	Wie oft muß ich die einnehmen?
Apothekerin	Drei Tabletten pro Tag.
Ingenieur	Muß ich die vor oder nach dem Essen einnehmen?

Apothekerin	Nehmen Sie immer vor dem Essen eine Tablette mit etwas Wasser ein.
Ingenieur	Und wie lange muß ich die einnehmen?
Apothekerin	Bis sie alle aufgebraucht sind. Und wenn die Schmerzen nicht nachlassen, informieren Sie den Arzt sofort.
Ingenieur	Also gut, ich danke Ihnen.
Apothekerin	Nichts zu danken. Ich wünsche Ihnen gute Besserung.

Vocabulary

der Apotheker, - *chemist*
gerade *just now*
einnehmen, eingenommen
  (sep) to take (tablets)

etwas *a little*
aufbrauchen, aufgebraucht
  (sep) to use up

nachlassen, nachgelassen
  (sep) to ease up

Notes

1 **Ich habe hier ein Rezept – bitte sehr.**
On presenting the prescription to the chemist, the engineer says **bitte sehr**, a standard phrase used when handing something to somebody. **Bitte sehr** is also used as a response to an expression of thanks: **Danke sehr – Bitte sehr**.

2 **Wie oft muß ich die einnehmen?**
Remember that modal verbs (**müssen, können**, etc. see page 81) send the second verb to the end. The second verb has to be in the infinitive form.

Exercise 1

After seeing the doctor in Germany, you go to the chemist with a prescription. What do you say in German?

Apotheker	Guten Morgen. Kann ich Ihnen helfen?
Sie	(*Greet the chemist. Say that you've just been to the doctor. Present your prescription.*)

Apotheker	Danke … Also, Sie bekommen Tabletten.
Sie	(*Ask how often you have to take them.*)

Apotheker	Drei Tabletten täglich.
Sie	(*Before or after meals?*)

Apotheker	Immer vor dem Essen, mit etwas Wasser.
Sie	(*How long for?*)

Apotheker	Bis sie alle aufgebraucht sind. Und wenn es Ihnen nicht besser geht, gehen Sie sofort wieder zum Arzt.
Sie	(*Thank him and ask how much the tablets cost.*)

Apotheker	Fünf Mark zehn.

Vocabulary 🔲

das Arzneimittel, - *medicine, remedy*   **täglich** *daily*

Exercise 2	**Notfälle**

Study the following dialogue about a factory accident.

Vorarbeiter	Hallo, können Sie mir bitte helfen? In der Fabrik ist ein Unfall passiert.
Chefsekretärin	Was ist denn geschehen?
Vorarbeiter	Frau Lohmann ist die Treppe heruntergefallen.
Chefsekretärin	Ist sie verletzt?
Vorarbeiter	Ja, ihre Beine und ihr Rücken tun sehr weh.
Chefsekretärin	Rufen Sie schnell einen Krankenwagen.
Vorarbeiter	Ja, das mache ich sofort.

Vocabulary 🔲

der Vorarbeiter, - *foreman*
der Notfall, ⁻e *emergency*
der Unfall, ⁻e *accident*
passieren (sein) *to happen*
geschehen, geschehen (sein) *to happen*

herunterfallen, heruntergefallen (sep, sein) *to fall down*
verletzt *injured*
verletzen *to injure*
rufen, gerufen *to call*

der Krankenwagen, - *ambulance*

One day your colleague, Herr Norwak, develops a stomach-ache and a headache and appears to be very ill. You report this to your boss, Frau Kröger. Complete the following conversation.

Sie	Frau Kröger,
	_____
Frau Kröger	Was fehlt ihm denn?
Sie	_____
Frau Kröger	Ist er sehr krank?
Sie	_____
Frau Kröger	Rufen Sie schnell einen Krankenwagen.
Sie	_____

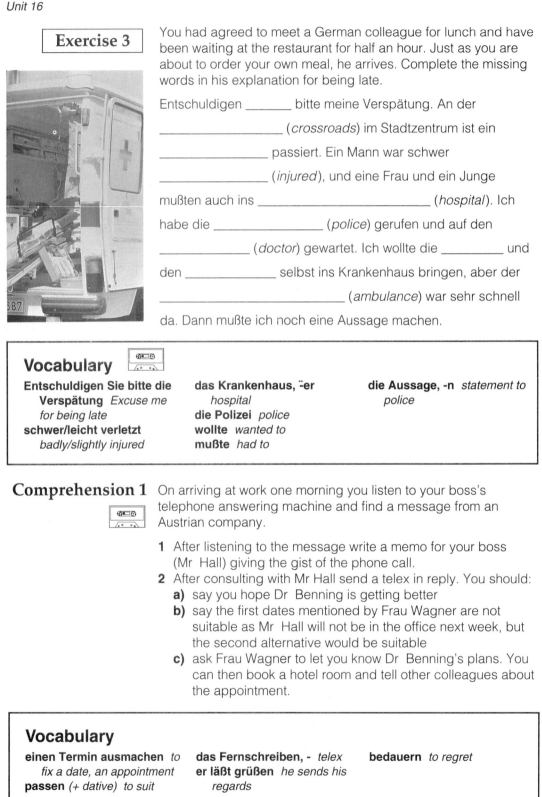

Exercise 3

You had agreed to meet a German colleague for lunch and have been waiting at the restaurant for half an hour. Just as you are about to order your own meal, he arrives. Complete the missing words in his explanation for being late.

Entschuldigen _____ bitte meine Verspätung. An der

_____ (*crossroads*) im Stadtzentrum ist ein

_____ passiert. Ein Mann war schwer

_____ (*injured*), und eine Frau und ein Junge

mußten auch ins _____ (*hospital*). Ich

habe die _____ (*police*) gerufen und auf den

_____ (*doctor*) gewartet. Ich wollte die _____ und

den _____ selbst ins Krankenhaus bringen, aber der

_____ (*ambulance*) war sehr schnell

da. Dann mußte ich noch eine Aussage machen.

Vocabulary

Entschuldigen Sie bitte die Verspätung *Excuse me for being late*
schwer/leicht verletzt *badly/slightly injured*

das Krankenhaus, ̈er *hospital*
die Polizei *police*
wollte *wanted to*
mußte *had to*

die Aussage, -n *statement to police*

Comprehension 1

On arriving at work one morning you listen to your boss's telephone answering machine and find a message from an Austrian company.

1 After listening to the message write a memo for your boss (Mr Hall) giving the gist of the phone call.
2 After consulting with Mr Hall send a telex in reply. You should:
   a) say you hope Dr Benning is getting better
   b) say the first dates mentioned by Frau Wagner are not suitable as Mr Hall will not be in the office next week, but the second alternative would be suitable
   c) ask Frau Wagner to let you know Dr Benning's plans. You can then book a hotel room and tell other colleagues about the appointment.

Vocabulary

einen Termin ausmachen *to fix a date, an appointment*
passen *(+ dative) to suit*

das Fernschreiben, - *telex*
er läßt grüßen *he sends his regards*

bedauern *to regret*

Comprehension 2: Die Republik Österreich

Allgemeines

Österreich ist einer der kleineren europäischen Staaten. Seit vielen Jahren bleibt die Einwohnerzahl bei etwa 7.5 Millionen mit zirka achtzig Einwohnern pro Quadratkilometer. Österreich ist zu 90 Prozent katholisch und zu sechs Prozent evangelisch. Die restlichen vier Prozent der Österreicher gehören zu anderen kleinen religiösen Gruppen. Von Westen nach Osten sind es 560 Kilometer mit einer maximalen Entfernung von Norden nach Süden von nur 280 Kilometern. Im Westen ist Österreich nur ungefähr 40 bis 60 Kilometer breit. Nördlich dieses Teils liegt Deutschland und südlich Italien. Im Westen liegt die Schweiz. Im Osten grenzt Österreich an die Tschechoslowakei und Ungarn, und südöstlich liegt Slowenien. Man sagt: «Österreich liegt im Herzen Europas.»

Österreich ist in neun Bundesländer eingeteilt. Jedes Land wählt seinen eigenen Landtag und Landeshauptmann. Das Bundesparlament besteht aus zwei Kammern, dem Bundesrat mit 54 Vertretern der neun Landtage und dem Nationalrat mit 165 Abgeordneten.

Die Hauptstadt Österreichs ist Wien, eine internationale Stadt und ein bekanntes Industriezentrum.

Industrie und Arbeit

Viele der österreichischen Arbeiter sind in der Schwerindustrie (zum Beispiel Eisen und Stahl, Schwermaschinenbau) beschäftigt. Die Feinmechanik (zum Beispiel Kameras und Mikroskope) ist weltberühmt. Wichtige Branchen der Industrie sind auch die Papier-, Kraftfahrzeug- und Textilienindustrien. Tourismus und die Elektroindustrie spielen außerdem eine große Rolle. Österreich produziert sehr viel elektrische Energie und exportiert sie auch in andere Länder Europas.

Auf dem Land sind heute nur 7.6 Prozent der österreichischen Arbeiter beschäftigt.

Vocabulary

allgemein *general*
Allgemeines *general information*
klein(er) *small(er)*
europäisch *European*
der Einwohner, - *inhabitant*
etwa *approximately*
der Quadratkilometer, - *square kilometre*
katholisch *catholic*
evangelisch *protestant*
restlich *remaining*
gehören (zu) *belong (to)*
religiös *religious*
der Westen *the west*
der Osten *the east*
maximal *maximum*
die Entfernung, -en *distance*
der Süden *the south*
der Norden *the north*
ungefähr *about, approximately*
breit *wide, broad*
der Teil, -e *part*
liegen, gelegen *to lie*
das Bundesland, ¨er *federal province, state*
einteilen, eingeteilt (sep) *to divide*
jede/r/s *each*

das Land, ¨er *country, province, state*
wählen, gewählt *choose, elect*
eigen *own*
der Landtag, -e *provincial government*
der Landeshauptmann, ¨er *head of government of a province (Austria)*
das Bundesparlament *federal parliament*
bestehen, bestanden (aus) *consist (of)*
die Kammer, -n *chamber, house (parliament)*
der Bundesrat *upper house (parliament)*
der Vertreter, - *representative*
der Nationalrat *lower house (parliament)*
der/die Abgeordnete, -n *member of parliament*
die Hauptstadt, ¨e *capital city*
bekannt *well-known*
die Schwerindustrie, -n *heavy industry*
das Eisen *iron*

der Stahl *steel*
der Schwermaschinenbau *heavy engineering*
beschäftigen, beschäftigt *to employ*
die Feinmechanik *precision engineering*
die Kamera, -s *camera*
das Mikroskop, -e *microscope*
weltberühmt *world-famous*
wichtig *important*
die Branche, -n *branch, area*
das Papier, -e *paper*
das Kraftfahrzeug, -e *vehicle*
die Textilien (pl) *textiles*
der Tourismus *tourism*
spielen, gespielt *to play*
außerdem *besides*
die Rolle, -n *rôle*
produzieren, produziert *to produce*
die Energie *energy*
exportieren, exportiert *to export*
andere *other*
auf dem Land *in the countryside, in farming*

1 Summarise what you can understand about the first part of the passage, **Allgemeines**, with the help of the following headings:

Size
Population
Religion
Geographical situation
Government
Capital city.

2 Answer the following questions in German.
   a) Was produziert man in der österreichischen Industrie?
   b) Zu welcher Branche der Industrie gehören Kameras?
   c) Was bedeutet ‚Tourismus und die Elektroindustrie spielen außerdem eine große Rolle'?
   d) Warum ist elektrische Energie wichtig für Österreich?

Talking business extra

Comprehension 3

Verlag Germania is involved with an Austrian company producing a collector's book on toys in the twentieth century. Christian has told Herr Suchanek about **Spieltechnik's** products, and has brought him for a visit. Katrina is introducing the company to him.

Key vocabulary

das Erzeugnis, -se *product*
sich verabschieden *to say goodbye*
die Belegschaft, -en *staff*
der Mitarbeiter, - *colleague*
die Zentrale, -n *head office*

die Produktionsanlage, -n *production plant*
die Filiale, -n *branch office*
die Kundendienststelle, -n *customer service base*

zusammenbauen *(sep) to assemble*
sogenannt *so-called*
die Montage, -r. *assembly*
das Zubehör, - *accessories*

Key phrases

Erzählen Sie mir etwas mehr! — *Tell me (some) more!*
ein mittelgroßes Unternehmen — *a medium-sized company*
vor kurzem — *a short while ago*
Sind Sie im Ausland vertreten? — *Are you represented abroad?*
Ladenketten führen unsere Produkte — *chain stores carry our products*
das reguläre Sortiment — *the regular range*
die Serie läuft noch — *the series is still going*
nach wie vor sehr beliebt — *as popular as ever*
... lassen wir uns zuliefern — *... we have supplied to us*

Find out:

1 what plans Spieltechnik have in England
2 what Katrina has to say about their very first product.

Exercise 4

Fill in the details:

Das Unternehmen Spieltechnik GmbH

Größe: _____

Belegschaft: _____ Mitarbeiter

Zentrale: _____

Produktionsanlage: _____

Filiale: _____

Geplant: _____

in Warrington/England

Erste Produktserie: _____ _____

Neuestes Erzeugnis: _____

Puzzle

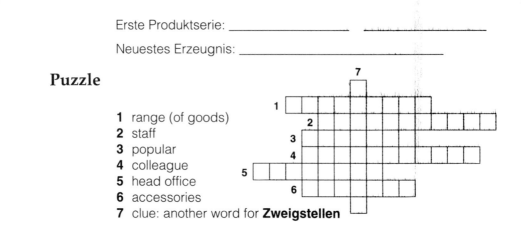

1 range (of goods)
2 staff
3 popular
4 colleague
5 head office
6 accessories
7 clue: another word for **Zweigstellen**

‖ Language structures

Verbs   Modal verbs

Der Fahrer **darf** keinen Alkohol trinken.
Soll ich einen Krankenwagen rufen?
Herr Kröger **mag** diese Tabletten nicht einnehmen.
Ich **möchte** einen Termin für heute.

dürfen	*to be allowed*
sollen	*shall, should, to be (supposed) to*
mögen	*to like*

Note:
The most commonly used form of **mögen** is **ich möchte** *I would like*.

Must not is expressed by **dürfen + nicht**:
Sie dürfen das nicht machen. *You must not do that.*
Need not is expressed by **müssen + nicht**:
Sie müssen das nicht machen. *You don't have to/needn't do that.*

For a full table of these modal verbs, see Language structures overview, opposite.

Progress check _____

1 NVQ S1

You are at the chemist. How would you say the following?

  a) I have a prescription here.
  b) How many tablets, before or after meals and how long for?
  c) How much do the tablets cost?

2 What are you told to do in these instructions?
  a) Nehmen Sie dreimal täglich zwei Tabletten ein, eine vor und eine nach dem Essen.
  b) Hier ist ein Unfall passiert. Rufen Sie schnell einen Krankenwagen.
  c) Wenn die Schmerzen nicht nachlassen, gehen Sie wieder zum Arzt.
  d) Bitte bestätigen Sie diesen Termin, wenn sie wissen, wie es Herrn Renner geht.

3 NVQ W2

In a fax to a business counterpart who has had a bout of flu mention the following points:

a) I hope you are better.

b) I want to fix an appointment for next week.

4 What do the following mean?

a) Bundesland

b) Feinmechanik

c) Kraftfahrzeug

d) weltberühmt

5 NVQ R2

You are going to open a customer service office in Germany. A letter from a new stockist over there contains a request, some confirmation and a condition. What are they?

a) Erzählen Sie mir etwas mehr über Ihre geplante Kundendienststelle im Ausland.

b) Wir werden Ihr Produkt in unserem regulären Sortiment führen, aber die Montage übernehmen Sie selbst.

Summary 7

Language structures overview

Modal verbs

DÜRFEN *to be allowed*		SOLLEN *to be (supposed) to*		MÖGEN *to like*	
ich	darf	ich	soll	ich	rnag
du	darfst	du	sollst	du	magst
er		er		er	
sie	darf	sie	soll	sie	mag
es		es		es	
wir	dürfen	wir	sollen	wir	mögen
ihr	dürft	ihr	sollt	ihr	mögt
sie	dürfen	sie	sollen	sie	mögen
Sie	dürfen	Sie	sollen	Sie	mögen

Mögen is most often used in a form which expresses *would like ...*, and in this case is as follows:

ich	möchte	wir	möchten
du	möchtest	ihr	möchtet
er		sie	möchten
sie	möchte	Sie	möchten
es			

Additional exercises

1 While travelling in Germany you are unwell and have to visit the doctor. In the waiting-room you hear the following conversations among the other patients. Complete the gaps with the correct form of one of the words in brackets.

a (können, wollen, müssen)

Ich _____ heute Herrn Dr. Braun sprechen. Ich habe seit Montag

Magenschmerzen und _____ nichts essen oder trinken. Ich _____

nur schlafen.

b (wollen, mögen, müssen, können)

Ich habe eine Grippe. Ich habe Kopfschmerzen, und meine Beine und Arme

tun weh. Ich _____ morgen nach Österreich fliegen. Wenn es mir aber

nicht besser geht, _____ ich das nicht. Ich _____ das aber, weil

ich meine österreichischen Kollegen kennenlernen _____ .

c (dürfen, können)

Mein Hals tut weh. Ich _____ Schmerztabletten nehmen, aber ich

_____ täglich nur drei nehmen. Und weil ich nicht sprechen _____,

_____ ich auch nicht arbeiten.

2 Answer the following questions using **seit** as an expression of time.

Example: Seit wann haben Sie Kopfschmerzen? (*yesterday*) Seit gestern.

a Seit wann hat Ihr Kollege Zahnschmerzen? (*last week*)
b Wie lange haben Sie schon Magenweh und Durchfall? (*this morning*)
c Wie lange haben Sie schon Halsschmerzen? (*Wednesday*)
d Seit wann hat Ihre Kollegin diese Erkältung? (*yesterday*)
e Wie lange haben Sie schon Husten? (*2 weeks*)
f Seit wann hat der Direktor Grippe? (*3 days*)

3 Here is a list of tasks to be accomplished by various people. Put their original instructions into the imperative.

Example: Frau Braun muß vor dem Essen eine Tablette einnehmen.
Nehmen Sie vor dem Essen eine Tablette ein.

a Frau Schmidt muß zur Stadtmitte weiterfahren.
b Die Sekretärin soll Herrn Müller vom Bahnhof abholen.
c Herr Ergang muß den Arzt in einer Woche wiedersehen.
d Ich muß das Fahrgeld in den Automaten einwerfen.
e Fräulein Schreiber soll in Köln umsteigen.

4 Spelling is an important skill. Look back to Unit 3, page 22 for revision, then practise spelling the following:

a your own name and address
b the name and address of your company, college, etc.
c some of your colleagues' names.

Key phrases

Making an appointment	Ich möchte einen Termin für heute
Asking someone to spell their name	Wie schreibt man das?
	Buchstabieren Sie das bitte
Asking what is wrong with someone	Was fehlt Ihnen?
	Was ist los?

Saying what is wrong with you	Ich habe Kopf-, Magen-, Ohrenschmerzen/-weh
	Ich habe Durchfall/Fieber/Husten/ Schnupfen/eine Grippe
Expressing annoyance	Ach, wie ärgerlich!
Wishing someone a speedy recovery	Gute Besserung!
Asking how often to take tablets	Wie oft muß ich die Tabletten einnehmen?
Asking if tablets should be taken before or after meals.	Muß ich die Tabletten vor oder nach dem Essen einnehmen?
Asking how long tablets should be taken	Bis wann muß ich die Tabletten einnehmen?
Asking what has happened	Was ist geschehen?
	Was ist passiert?

Cultural briefing

Illness and emergencies

Unless you have taken out private medical insurance, you will need to present your E111 form whenever you require medical treatment in Germany. This entitles you to free hospital treatment, free treatment from doctors and dentists, and 80 % off prescribed medicines. In Austria and Switzerland the bi-lateral agreements in existence at present are much less comprehensive – take out insurance!

When collecting your medicines, distinguish between a **Drogerie** and an **Apotheke** as only the latter is a dispensing chemist's.

The word **Not** attached to other words is worth special attention. The **Notruf** is the emergency telephone number used in a particular locality. The **Notarzt** is the doctor on call for emergencies. A **Notausgang** is an emergency exit, and a **Notbremse** is an emergency communication cord (emergency brake) in a train. Of course, you only pull this **im Notfall** (**der Notfall** *emergency*)!

Pronunciation

c – ch – sch

c	like English *k* before **a, o, u** Café, Campingplatz
	like German **z** before **e, i** Hotel Central
ch	like *ch* in Scottish *loch* after **a, o, u**
	Nachmittag, auch, Besuch, Buch
	otherwise between English *sh* and the *h* of *hue*
	Richtung, nicht, Bücher
sch	Always as English *sh* Dusche, Schule, Geschichte

(*sh* doesn't exist as a single sound in German.
E.g. **deshalb** is pronounced **des-halb**)

UNIT **17** Geld, Bank und Post

In this unit, you will learn how to …

- exchange traveller's cheques and foreign currency
- ask for the current exchange rate
- buy stamps and get letters and parcels posted.

Dialogue 1: **Auf der Bank**

Liz Roberts, an export manager, arrives in Germany on business. As she has had no time to obtain foreign currency in England, she goes straight to a bank on her arrival.

Angestellter	Guten Tag. Kann ich Ihnen helfen?
Exportleiterin	Kann ich hier Reiseschecks einlösen?
Angestellter	Ja, das können Sie schon. Darf ich Ihren Reisepaß sehen?
Exportleiterin	Selbstverständlich. Bitte schön.
Angestellter	Danke schön. Also, wieviel Geld möchten Sie?
Exportleiterin	Ich möchte für hundert Pfund D-Mark.
Angestellter	Haben Sie nur Reiseschecks oder auch Bargeld?
Exportleiterin	Ich habe kein Bargeld, nur Reiseschecks. Wie steht der Kurs im Moment?
Angestellter	Für ein Pfund bekommen Sie DM 2,92.
Exportleiterin	Vor einem Jahr habe ich viel mehr bekommen.
Angestellter	So, unterschreiben Sie hier, bitte. Das Geld bekommen Sie drüben an der Kasse.
Exportleiterin	Geben Sie mir bitte vier Fünfzigmarkscheine, sechs Zehnmarkscheine und etwas Kleingeld. Vielen Dank. Auf Wiedersehen.

Vocabulary

der Reisescheck, -s
  traveller's cheque
Reiseschecks einlösen *to*
  cash traveller's cheques
der Paß, ⁻sse *passport*

das Pfund, - *pound*
das Bargeld *cash*
Wie steht der Kurs? *What is*
  the current rate?
viel mehr *much more*

etwas *some*
das Kleingeld *small change,*
  coins

Notes

1 **Ja, das können Sie schon.** **Schon**
usually means *already*, but in addition has
a number of less obvious meanings, which
do not always have exact English
equivalents. Here it adds the idea *of
course; naturally; Yes, of course you can.*

2 **Ich habe kein Bargeld.** **Kein, keine,
keines** mean *no*, in the sense of *not any*.
See Unit 3, page 25 for revision.

Können Sie bitte wechseln?

Können Sie bitte diesen Zehnmarkschein in zwei Fünfmarkstücke wechseln?

Wenn Sie Geld wechseln wollen, gehen Sie zum Geldwechsel in
der Bank. Es gibt aber auch Automaten für Münzen,
'Münzwechsler'. Man wirft zum Beispiel ein Einmarkstück ein und
bekommt zweimal fünfzig Pfenning zurück.

Kleingeld

Geldscheine

Vocabulary

der Geldschein, -e *bank
note*

Geldwechsel *bureau de
change*

der Münzwechsler *small
change machine*

Exercise 1

How would you ask to change:

1 a 100-Mark note into one 50-Mark banknote and have the
remainder in ten-Mark notes?
2 a five-Mark coin into four single Mark pieces and two 50-Pfennig
pieces?

Exercise 2	You are in a bank in Germany. You would like to cash some cheques. What do you say in German?

Angestellter Guten Tag. Kann ich Ihnen helfen?
Sie (*Ask if you can cash Eurocheques here.*)

Angestellter Ja, das können wir schon machen. Darf ich Ihren Paß sehen?
Sie (*Say yes, of course. Here it is.*)

Angestellter Danke schön ... Also, wieviel Geld möchten Sie?
Sie (*Say you have £50. Ask what the exchange rate is at the moment.*)

Angestellter DM 2,90 für ein Pfund. Wie möchten Sie das Geld?
Sie (*Say you would like two 50-Mark notes and some change.*)

Angestellter Wenn Sie hier unterschreiben ... So, danke. Gehen Sie jetzt bitte zur Kasse.
Sie (*Say thank you very much. Goodbye.*)

Exercise 3	Before going to work in Germany, you write to the **Deutsche Bank** requesting information on opening an account.

Along with their reply they enclose details of customer facilities available, including the following leaflet on money dispensers.

Bargeld auch abends und am Wochenende – 🏧-Geldautomaten-Service.

An allen ec-Geldautomaten können Sie auch außerhalb der Banköffnungszeiten, zum Beispiel abends oder am Wochenende, Bargeld von Ihrem Persönlichen Konto abheben – täglich bis zu 400 DM.

Diesen Service können Sie auch zunehmend in europäischen Reiseländern (zum Beispiel in Spanien) in Anspruch nehmen. Alles, was Sie dazu brauchen, sind Ihre eurocheque-Karte und Ihre persönliche Geheimzahl.

Die ec-Geldautomaten der Deutschen Bank wie auch der anderen Kreditinstitute erkennen Sie am bekannten 🏧 Symbol.

1 How much money could you draw out in a week?
2 When is a dispenser particularly useful?
3 From what sort of account can you draw money using a dispenser?
4 Where can you use this service?

Vocabulary

der Geldautomat, -en
money dispenser, cash machine
außerhalb (+ genitive)
outside of
das persönliche Konto
personal account
das Konto, -en *account*

abheben, abgehoben (sep)
to withdraw
der Service *service*
zunehmend *increasingly*
das Reiseland, ¨-er *tourist country*
in Anspruch nehmen, genommen *to call on*

dazu *for this*
die Karte, -n *card*
die Geheimzahl, -en *secret number, PIN code*
erkennen, erkannt *to recognise*

Dialogue 2: Auf dem Postamt

While in Germany, Charles Stewart, a fitter, goes to the post office. He wants to post some letters and a parcel.

Monteur	Guten Tag. Ich möchte ein Paket schicken.
Beamtin	Ins Inland oder ins Ausland?
Monteur	Nach Hamburg. Was kostet das denn?
Beamtin	Ich muß es zuerst wiegen … So, zwölf Mark fünfzig, bitte. Hier ist der Einlieferungsschein für Ihr Paket. Sonst noch etwas?
Monteur	Und diese Briefe möchte ich nach München schicken. Geben Sie mir bitte zwei Briefmarken zu einer Mark.
Beamtin	Also, ein Paket zu zwölf Mark fünfzig und zwei Briefmarken zu einer Mark, das macht vierzehn Mark fünfzig zusammen.
Monteur	(*Hands over money*) Bitte schön. Wo kann ich meine Briefe einwerfen?
Beamtin	Den Briefeinwurf finden Sie gegenüber Schalter fünf.
Monteur	Danke schön. Auf Wiedersehen.
Beamtin	Auf Wiedersehen.

Vocabulary

der Monteur, -e *fitter*
das Paket, -e *parcel*
schicken *to send*
ins Ausland *abroad*
zuerst *first*
wiegen, gewogen *to weigh*

der Einlieferungsschein, -e
   certificate of posting
die Briefmarke, -n *stamp*
zu zwölf Mark fünfzig *at DM*
   12,50

einwerfen, eingeworfen *(sep)*
   to insert
der Briefeinwurf *letter box in*
   post office
der Schalter, - *counter*

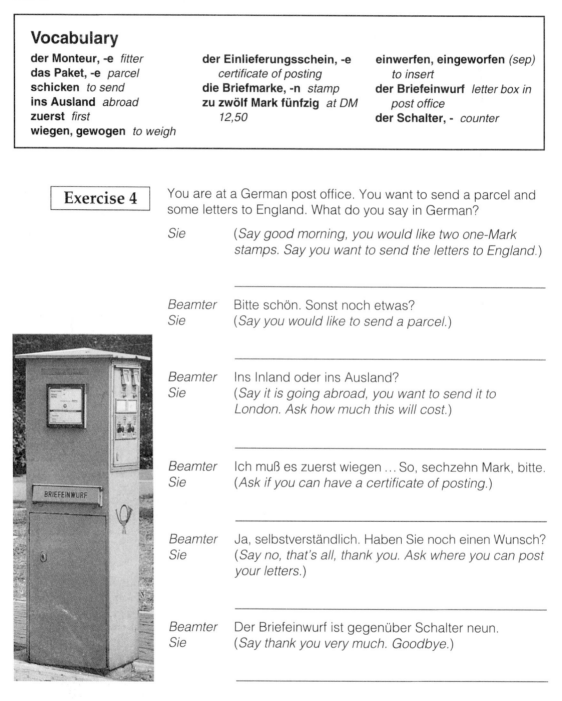

| **Exercise 4** | You are at a German post office. You want to send a parcel and some letters to England. What do you say in German? |

Sie   *(Say good morning, you would like two one-Mark stamps. Say you want to send the letters to England.)*

Beamter   Bitte schön. Sonst noch etwas?
Sie   *(Say you would like to send a parcel.)*

Beamter   Ins Inland oder ins Ausland?
Sie   *(Say it is going abroad, you want to send it to London. Ask how much this will cost.)*

Beamter   Ich muß es zuerst wiegen ... So, sechzehn Mark, bitte.
Sie   *(Ask if you can have a certificate of posting.)*

Beamter   Ja, selbstverständlich. Haben Sie noch einen Wunsch?
Sie   *(Say no, that's all, thank you. Ask where you can post your letters.)*

Beamter   Der Briefeinwurf ist gegenüber Schalter neun.
Sie   *(Say thank you very much. Goodbye.)*

Vocabulary

noch einen Wunsch?
   anything else?

Exercise 5

You work as a translator for a British engineering company. The calendars and rulers intended as gifts for your German customers and promised to your subsidiary company in Duisburg for mid-December have not arrived. You receive a telex urgently requesting them (see Unit 5 page 42 for revision).

> WIR BRAUCHEN DRINGEND 20 KALENDER UND
> ROSTFREI-LINEALE FUER UNSERE KUNDEN.
> BITTE SOFORT SCHICKEN, DIESE MUESSEN
> WIR MOEGLICHST VOR WEIHNACHTEN,
> UNBEDINGT VOR JAHRESENDE LIEFERN.
>
> MFG SCHMIDT

Reply by telex in German, explaining that you sent a parcel off yesterday. They should let you know if the parcel does not arrive as you have a certificate of posting.

Vocabulary

dringend *urgent(ly)*
der Kalender, - *calendar*
rostfrei *stainless*
das Lineal, -e *ruler*

möglichst *if possible*
unbedingt *certainly, absolutely*

vor Jahresende *before the end of the year*

Exercise 6

You and a friend go to a German post office to post some letters. Your friend does not understand this advertisement. Answer his questions.

Wenn Sie Briefmarken brauchen...

...haben Sie meistens keine zur Hand. Nehmen Sie doch gleich ein paar mehr mit. Oder wählen Sie Markenheftchen. Die gibt's auch aus dem Automaten.

Deutsche Bundespost

4 Postwertzeichen zu 10 Pf
2 Postwertzeichen zu 50 Pf
2 Postwertzeichen zu 80 Pf
Abgabepreis 3 DM

4 x A 6, Kl. 69   Weichert 2 000 000 6.82/4653   911 038 000

Notes

Markenheftchen gibt's auch aus dem Automaten. Die Marke is short for die Briefmarke, do not mix this up with **die Mark.**

Gibt's is short for **gibt es**, see page 50, Unit 6 for revision.

1 What does **Postwertzeichen** mean?
2 What is the advertisement encouraging you to do?
3 Apart from the post office, where can you buy stamps?

Vocabulary

meistens *usually*
etwas zur Hand haben *to*
have something at hand

ein paar *a few*
mitnehmen, mitgenommen
(sep) to take with you

das Markenheftchen, - *book*
of stamps

Comprehension 1

Listen to a conversation between a British tourist and a clerk at a bureau de change, then complete each sentence with the appropriate ending from the opposite column.

Vocabulary

der Wechselkurs, -e
exchange rate

die Quittung, -en *receipt*

1 Ich möchte englisches Geld …
2 Wie ist der Wechselkurs …
3 Vor zwei Jahren …
4 Geben Sie mir D-Mark …
5 Ich will fünfzig Pfund …
6 Darf ich …
7 Wollen Sie das Geld …
8 Ich möchte fünf Fünfzigmarkscheine und drei
Zehnmarkscheine …
9 Den Wechselkurs …
10 Ach, das Pfund …

a) sinkt ständig!
b) in D-Mark umwechseln.
c) Ihren Paß sehen?
d) und etwas Kleingeld, bitte.
e) für englisches Geld?
f) war das noch DM 3,38.
g) für hundert Pfund.
h) in großen Scheinen?
i) Reiseschecks einlösen.
j) finden Sie auf der Quittung.

Comprehension 2: Die Deutsche Bundespost

Die Post hat viele Berufe – das kann ein Architekt sein und ein Briefträger, ein Programmierer und ein Kraftfahrer, ein Fernmeldeingenieur und eine Dolmetscherin, ein Lehrer und ein Koch, eine Sekretärin und ein Drucker. Eine knappe halbe Million Menschen arbeiten für die Deutsche Bundespost – ein Drittel aller 'Postler' sind übrigens Postlerinnen.

Vocabulary

die Post *post office*
der Architekt, -en *architect*
der Briefträger, - *postman*
der Kraftfahrer, - *driver*
der Fernmeldeingenieur, -e
post office engineer

der Lehrer, - *teacher*
der Koch, ¨e *cook*
der Drucker, - *printer*
knapp *just under*
der Mensch, -en *person*
ein Drittel *a third*

der 'Postler' *post office*
employee

Die Bundesdruckerei

Die Bundesdruckerei hat ihren Hauptsitz in Berlin. Zu den Aufgaben dieses Großbetriebs gehören die Herstellung von Banknoten und Postwertzeichen, Sparbüchern und Reisepässen, Personalausweisen und Kraftfahrzeugbriefen.

Vocabulary

die Bundesdruckerei
federal printing works
der Hauptsitz, -e
headquarters
der Großbetrieb, -e *large company*

die Herstellung *manufacture*
die Banknote, -n *bank note*
das Postwertzeichen, -
postage stamp
das Sparbuch, ¨er *savings book*

der Personalausweis, -e
identity card
der Kraftfahrzeugbrief, -e
motor vehicle papers

Telexdienst

Der Telexdienst (oder Fernschreiberdienst) der Bundesrepublik ist sehr groß. Alle Verbindungen im Inland und fast alle im Ausland sind vollautomatisch. Ein Computer gibt Auskünfte über Telexnummern. Neben dem Telexdienst spielen auch andere Dienste (zum Beispiel das öffentliche Datennetz und das Kabelfernsehen) eine wichtige Rolle.

Vocabulary

Telex/Fernschreiberdienst
telex service
die Verbindung, -en
connection

vollautomatisch *fully automatic*
neben *(+ dative) in addition to*

das öffentliche Datennetz
public data network
das Kabelfernsehen *cable television*

Kennen Sie die Postleitzahl?

In jeder Adresse in Deutschland steht eine Postleitzahl. Mit Postleitzahlen kann man die Post schneller sortieren und zwischen Absender und Empfänger verteilen. Elektronische Sortieranlagen spielen jetzt eine große Rolle im Transport der Post zum Bestimmungsort.

Vocabulary

die Postleitzahl, -en *post code*
sortieren, sortiert *to sort*
der Absender, - *sender*

der Empfänger, - *recipient*
verteilen, verteilt *to distribute*
elektronisch *electronic*

die Sortieranlage, -n *sorting machine*
der Bestimmungsort, -e
destination

Say whether the following statements are true or false.

	Richtig	Falsch
1 Über eine halbe Million Leute arbeiten für die Deutsche Bundespost.	☐	☐
2 Mehr Frauen als Männer arbeiten für die Bundespost.	☐	☐
3 Die Bundesdruckerei druckt Briefmarken.	☐	☐
4 Telexverbindungen innerhalb Westdeutschlands sind vollautomatisch.	☐	☐
5 Computer spielen beim Telexdienst eine große Rolle.	☐	☐
6 Ohne Postleitzahl verteilt man die Post nicht so schnell.	☐	☐
7 Angestellte der Bundespost müssen jede Postleitzahl selbst lesen und jeden Brief selbst sortieren.	☐	☐

Talking business extra

Comprehension 3

Katrina is on time for a meeting with Christian at **Verlag Germania**. They need to discuss the English version of the manual.

Key vocabulary

die Zeichnung, -en *drawing*
die Brieftasche, -n *wallet, purse*
der Versand *dispatch*

die Sendung, -en *consignment*
die Verwaltung, -en *administration*

die Jacke, -n *jacket*
die Störung, -en *interruption*

Note

es ist gefallen *it has fallen, it fell*

es hat mir gefallen *I liked it*

Key phrases

etwas ganz Dummes	*something really silly*
Nachforschungen anstellen	*to make enquiries*
Kein Grund zur Aufregung	*No need to panic*
mit einigen Vorbehalten	*with some reservations*
Sehr erfreulich!	*I am delighted!*

Find out:

1 what Katrina is doing while Christian talks to Frau Koller
2 what Christian has been doing since his return to the office after lunch.

Exercise 7	Fill in the details:

Ich habe _____ vom Geldautomaten abgehoben.

Dann habe ich die Parkgebühren _____.

Ich habe meine Brieftasche _____.

Sie ist aus der Jacke _____.

Die Zeichnungen haben Katrina _____.

Frau Filz hat die Brieftasche _____.

Puzzle

1 consignment
2 administration
3 reservation (not total agreement)
4 dispatch
5 clue: usually one is not very pleased about it

Sehr erfreulich!

Language structures

Etwas	**Etwas** has three meanings:

some, a little
Geben Sie mir vier Fünfzigmarkscheine und **etwas** Kleingeld.
somewhat
In der Altstadt können Sie **etwas** billiger einkaufen.
something
Darf ich Ihnen **etwas** Neues zeigen?

After **etwas**, **nichts** and **viel**, an adjective is usually written with a capital letter, and adds the ending **es**.

Examples:
Hat er **etwas Wichtiges** gesagt?
In diesem Geschäft gibt es **nichts Schönes** zu kaufen.
Ich habe über Ihre Firma **viel Interessantes** gehört.

Einige   **Einige**, meaning *some* has the same endings as **dieser** and **welcher**, see page 103.

Examples
Nach **einiger** Zeit sind wir zum Flughafen gefahren.
In **einigen** Stunden werden wir dort sein.
In diesem Prospekt gibt es **einige** schöne Hotels.

Progress check

1 NVQ S2

How would you conduct these money matters in German?

a) Can I cash traveller's cheques here?
b) What is the exchange rate at the moment?
c) I would like marks for 80 pounds.
d) Where do I get the cash?
e) Would you like to see my passport/identity card?
f) Where is the bureau de change?
g) Would you please change this 100-mark note to a 50-mark note, some ten-mark notes and some small change?

2 NVQ W2

You have things to do at the post office. Make a note of what you are going to say at the counter. You want to:

a) send a parcel abroad

b) have a letter weighed and buy stamps for it
c) ask where you can post your letters.

3 What is:

a) **ein Einlieferungsschein?**
b) **eine Quittung?**
c) **eine Postleitzahl?**
d) **ein Empfänger?**
e) the difference between **drei Mark** and **drei Marken?**

4 NVQ R2

You have suggested what to do about a lost parcel. What does the MD say about it in her memo?

a) Ich werde sofort in der Versandabteilung Nachforschungen anstellen.
b) Mit einigen kleinen Vorbehalten ist Ihr Vorschlag ausgezeichnet.

Summary 8

Language structures overview

Kein, keine

This takes the same endings as the indefinite article in the singular; these and plural endings are outlined below (see also page 25.)

	MASCULINE	FEMININE	NEUTER	PLURAL
Nom.	kein	keine	kein	keine
Acc.	keinen	keine	kein	keine
Dat.	keinem	keiner	keinem	keinen
Gen.	keines	keiner	keines	keiner

Ich habe kein Bargeld.
Er hat kein**en** Paß.
Haben Sie kein**e** Zehnmarkscheine?

Additional exercises

1   Complete the following sentences with the correct form of **kein**.

Example: Ich bin kein Engländer, ich bin Franzose.

a   Ich bin _____ Deutsche, ich bin Engländerin.

b Das Zimmer hat _____ Balkon.

c Hier gibt es _____ U-Bahn.

d Haben Sie _____ Paß?

e Der Beamte hat _____ Zehnmarkscheine.

f Wir kaufen heute _____ Bücher.

g Das ist _____ gutes Hotel.

h Dieses Hotel hat _____ Garten.

i Hat er _____ Geld?

2 Use the words in brackets to complete the sentences below.

Example: Ich habe heute **etwas Wichtiges** gesehen. (etwas, wichtig)

a Haben Sie _____ _____ gelernt? (nichts, neu)

b Heute habe ich _____ _____ gekauft. (etwas, billig)

c Mein Kollege möchte _____ _____ essen. (etwas, heiß)

d In diesem Prospekt steht _____ _____. (viel, interessant)

3 For revision, work through the language notes on how to write dates in German in Unit 4, pages 39–40. Then complete this exercise.

Example: 4.3. Heute ist der vierte März *or* der vierte dritte.

a 7.6.
b 20.9.
c 15.1.
d 9.11.
e 21.8.
f 3.5.

Key phrases

Asking if you can cash traveller's cheques	Kann ich hier Reiseschecks einlösen?
Saying how much money you want to change	Ich möchte hundert Pfund wechseln
	Ich möchte englisches Geld in D-Mark umwechseln
Asking about the exchange rate	Wie steht der Kurs im Moment?
	Wie ist der Wechselkurs für englisches Geld?
Saying how you want the currency	Geben Sie mir bitte vier Fünfzigmarkscheine, sechs Zehnmarkscheine und etwas Kleingeld
Saying you want to send a parcel	Ich möchte ein Paket schicken
Asking for a certificate of posting	Kann ich einen Einlieferungsschein haben?
Asking for stamps	Geben Sie mir bitte zwei Briefmarken zu einer Mark/zu achtzig Pfennig
Asking where you can post your letters	Wo kann ich meine Post einwerfen?

Cultural briefing

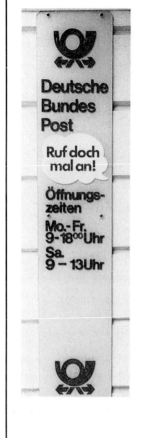

Banks and post-offices

German banks close for lunch, but open earlier in the morning and remain open longer in the afternoon than in Britain. Many banks are called **Sparkassen** (**die Sparkasse** – *savings bank*), but they offer the same general banking services.

Post offices remain open until 6.00 in the evening. Look out for the post-horn symbol on a yellow background (orange in Austria). Telephone numbers to note are: 118 **Auskunft** (*directory enquiries*), 110 **Polizei** (*police*), 00118 **Auskunft fürs Ausland** (*international directory enquiries*). Some public phone-boxes can only be used for domestic calls.

Pronunciation

 st – sp – qu

st, sp	An s followed by a **t** or **p** within the same syllable is pronounced as if it were the German **sch**
	zum Bei**sp**iel, **St**adtplan, be**st**ellen, **Sp**eck
qu	**qu** is pronounced as a combination of the English consonants *k* and *v* be**qu**em sounds like be**kv**ehm

f – k – l – m – n – p – t – x

These are very close to their English equivalents. Note that **t** is pronounced like the German **z** when in the combination **tion**

Reklama**tion**, Spedi**tion**, interna**tion**al

SECTION 9

UNIT 18 Auto und Zoll

In this unit, you will learn how to …

- deal with customs
- interpret traffic signs
- ask for service at a petrol station and garage
- discuss size and measurements
- understand a job advertisement.

> ### STUDY TIP
>
> From time to time you will probably have noted similarities between German and English. This is in fact a very useful strategy, and one you should consciously develop. By reflecting on similarities and differences between the two, you help yourself to remember vocabulary, and understand structures. Poetic or archaic English is often very close to modern German, and a realisation of how closely the two languages are related reduces the degree of strangeness of some of the concepts, and makes them easier to accept.

Dialogue 1: An der Zollgrenze

Jim Smith works for a publishing house. He often travels to book fairs, and on this occasion is returning from Hungary, via Austria. He stops at the Hungarian-Austrian border.

Zollbeamtin	Guten Tag. Ihre Papiere bitte, Paß, Führerschein und grüne Versicherungskarte.
Jim Smith	Bitte schön.
Zollbeamtin	Alles in Ordnung. Wohin fahren Sie?
Fahrer	Nach Wien, zu einer Buchmesse.
Zollbeamtin	Wie weit sind Sie heute schon gefahren?
Fahrer	So ungefähr 400 Kilometer, von Budapest.
Zollbeamtin	Haben Sie etwas zu verzollen?
Fahrer	Nein, gar nichts.
Zollbeamtin	Leider müssen wir Ihren Wagen durchsuchen.
Fahrer	Das gibt's ja gar nicht! Muß das sein?
Zollbeamtin	Tut mir leid. Wir müssen Stichproben machen. Fahren Sie bitte zum Parkplatz dort drüben.

Fahrer	Ach, wie ärgerlich. Ich soll um elf Uhr in Wien sein. Das schaffe ich jetzt nicht mehr. Wie lange dauert das denn?
Zollbeamtin	Es dauert höchstens zehn Minuten, bestimmt nicht länger.

Vocabulary

die Zollgrenze, -n *border customs post*

der Zollbeamte, -n *customs officer*

der Führerschein, -e *driving licence*

die Versicherungskarte, -n *insurance document*

verzollen *to declare (at customs)*

durchsuchen, durchsucht *to search*

Das gibt's ja nicht! *That can't be!*

Muß das sein? *Is that really necessary?*

die Stichprobe, -n *random check*

ärgerlich *annoying*

schaffen *to manage*

höchstens *at the most*

Notes

Wo ist der Geschäftsführer?
Wohin fahren Sie?
Woher kommen Sie? Aus Birmingham?
Wo *where* when no motion is implied

wohin *where (to)*, i.e. when movement towards a place is meant
woher *where from*

Exercise 1

Answer in German.

1 Wo hält Mr. Smith an?
2 Woher kommt er heute?
3 Welche Papiere will der Zollbeamte sehen?
4 Wohin fährt Mr. Smith?
5 Wie viele Kilometer ist er heute schon gefahren?
6 Hat er etwas zu verzollen?
7 Warum muß der Zollbeamte den Wagen durchsuchen?
8 Wie lange dauert die Durchsuchung?
9 Um wieviel Uhr soll Mr. Smith in Wien sein?

Vocabulary

anhalten, angehalten *(sep)* *to stop*

die Durchsuchung, -en *search*

Exercise 2

You will be travelling by car to Germany and need to understand certain road signs. Match each sentence below with a corresponding sign.

1 Der Verkehr darf nur in eine Richtung fahren.

a)

2 Hier dürfen Sie nicht fahren.

Your right of way

b)

3 Hier dürfen Fahrzeuge über 10 m Länge nicht fahren.

c)

No entry

4 Wenn ein Auto von der linken Seite kommt, müssen Sie halten. (Links hat Vorfahrt.)

d)

e)

Einbahnstraße

5 Sie dürfen nicht schneller als 60 km pro Stunde fahren.

f)

6 Sie haben auf dieser Straße Vorfahrt.

g)

7 Straßenbahnhaltestelle.

Haltestelle

h)

8 Hier ist das Halten und Parken verboten.

i)

9 Kinder gehen über die Straße.

10 Die Straße wird enger.

j)

Give way to traffic from the left

Vocabulary

die Vorfahrt *right of way*	**die Einbahnstraße, -n** *one-way street*	**die Straßenbahn, -en** *tram* **die Haltestelle, -n** *bus stop*

Dialogue 2: ## An der Tankstelle

Andrea Brown, a British businesswoman, is driving through Germany to attend a trade fair in Hannover. En route she stops at a petrol station.

Geschäftsfrau	Volltanken, bitte.
Tankwart	Bleifrei oder verbleit?
Geschäftsfrau	Super bleifrei, bitte. Und machen Sie bitte auch den Reservekanister voll.
Tankwart	Ja, sofort. Soll ich auch den Ölstand prüfen?
Geschäftsfrau	Danke, nein. Ich habe erst vorgestern nachgesehen. Aber kontrollieren Sie bitte den Reifendruck.
Tankwart	Ich sehe mal nach … Der Luftdruck ist in Ordnung. Haben Sie noch einen Wunsch?
Geschäftsfrau	Danke, das ist alles. Was macht das, bitte?
Tankwart	Also, dreißig Liter bleifrei. Zweiundvierzig Mark, bitte.
Geschäftsfrau	Ich habe leider nur einen Fünfhundertmarkschein. Können Sie bitte wechseln?
Tankwart	Ja, natürlich.

Geschäftsfrau	Kann ich eine Quittung haben?
Tankwart	Selbstverständlich. Bitte schön.
Geschäftsfrau	Danke schön. Auf Wiedersehen.
Tankwart	Auf Wiedersehen. Gute Fahrt.

Vocabulary

volltanken *(sep) to fill up*
das Benzin *petrol*
bleifrei *lead-free*
verbleit *leaded*
Super *four star*
der Reservekanister, -
  spare can

vollmachen, vollgemacht
  (sep) to fill up
der Ölstand *oil level*
prüfen, geprüft *examine,*
  test
nachsehen, nachgesehen
  (sep) to check

kontrollieren *to check,*
  control
der Reifendruck *tyre*
  pressure
der Luftdruck *air pressure*

Exercise 3

Was ist richtig, was ist falsch?

	Richtig	Falsch
1 Der Tankwart soll den Reservekanister vollmachen.	☐	☐
2 Der Tankwart prüft den Ölstand.	☐	☐
3 Ein Mechaniker prüft die Bremsen.	☐	☐
4 Der Tankwart kontrolliert den Reifendruck.	☐	☐
5 Der Reifendruck ist in Ordnung.	☐	☐
6 Der Tankwart füllt das Wasser nach.	☐	☐
7 Der Mechaniker wechselt die Reifen.	☐	☐
8 Die Geschäftsfrau will das Auto waschen.	☐	☐
9 Ein Mechaniker muß das Auto reparieren.	☐	☐
10 Die Geschäftsfrau hat kein Kleingeld.	☐	☐

Vocabulary

reparieren *to repair*
die Bremse, -n *brake*

der Reifen, - *tyre*
nachfüllen *(sep) to fill (top up)*

waschen, gewaschen *to*
  wash

Exercise 4

You stop off at a petrol station in Switzerland before travelling back home. What do you say in German?

Tankwart	Guten Tag. Volltanken?
Sie	(*Say yes please, lead-free, and would he please check the tyre pressure?*)

Tankwart	Ja, sofort. Soll ich auch den Ölstand prüfen?
Sie	(*Say yes and ask for the water level to be checked too.*)

Tankwart	Ich werde gleich nachsehen … So, alles in Ordnung. In den linken Vorderreifen habe ich etwas Luft nachgepumpt und wir haben auch Öl nachgefüllt. Der Wasserstand war in Ordnung.
Sie	(*Say many thanks, that's all. How much ist it?*)

Tankwart	Also, fünfunddreißig Liter bleifrei und eine Dose Öl, vierundfünfzig Mark, bitte.

Vocabulary

der Vorderreifen
front tyre

nachpumpen *(sep) to pump up (top up)*

Exercise 5

Wenn man selbst tankt, bekommt man manchmal einen Beleg. Diesen Beleg nimmt man mit zur Kasse, wo man bezahlen muß.

Betrag incl. 13% MwSt. Verkauf der Kraftstoff im Namen und für Rechnung der AVIA-Liefer im Verkaufspreis für Kraftstoffe ist der gesetzliche Bevorratungsbeitrag enthalten.

AVIA

Tankstelle
WOLFGANG KLUPIEC
Königeberger Straße 78
4150 Krefeld-Linn
Telefon (02151) 572167

2 92 3 7 ℓ 0 5 4 0 1   DM 0 5 4, 4 9

Vocabulary

der Beleg, -e *voucher, slip*

Answer the following questions.

1 What is the date this transaction took place?
2 How much petrol was bought?
3 What was the price of the petrol?

Exercise 6

Welcher Wagen ist besser?

Technische Daten	VW Polo	Opel Corsa	BMW 525i
Preis	ab DM 14 485,–	ab DM 15 305,–	ab DM 48 900,–
Höchstgeschwindigkeit km/Stunde	147	153	217
Benzinverbrauch l/100 km bei 90 km/Stunde	4,9 (Normal)	4,7 (Super)	7,2 (Super)
Gewicht (kg)	750	772	1450
Abmessungen			
Breite (m)	1,58	1,53	1,75
Länge (m)	3,65	3,62	4,72

Vocabulary

die Höchstgeschwindigkeit, -en *top speed*
der Benzinverbrauch *petrol consumption*

das Gewicht, -e *weight*
die Abmessung, -en *measurement*
die Breite, -n *width*

die Länge, -n *length*

1 Read the following passage.

Der VW Polo kostet ungefähr DM 14 486. Er hat eine Höchstgeschwindigkeit von 147 Stundenkilometern und verbraucht 4,9 Liter Normalbenzin pro 100 Kilometer. Er wiegt 750 Kilo und hat eine Länge von 3, 65 Metern und eine Breite von 1,58 Metern.

Now write a similar account for the Opel Corsa.

Vocabulary

verbrauchen *to use up*

der Stundenkilometer, - *kilometre per hour*

2 The following text compares the VW and the Opel.

Der VW ist billiger als der Opel, und er fährt langsamer. Er verbraucht mehr Benzin pro 100 km als der Opel, aber Benzin für den Opel ist teurer als für den VW. Der VW ist nicht so schwer wie der Opel und ist auch etwas länger und breiter als der Opel.

Now compare the BMW with the VW. You might like to look through the Language structures on comparisons on page 199 first.

3 Describe your own car (or that of a relative or friend) briefly. Use some of the information above as a guideline.

Exercise 7

A German friend has sent you a copy of the following advertisement for a job that he has applied for. Explain to your family in general terms what the advertisement says.

Ausbildungsplätze für Berufskraftfahrer

In Westeuropa sind wir eine erfolgreiche und moderne Spedition. Qualität und Service haben uns international bekannt gemacht.

Wir brauchen jetzt junge Menschen für interessante Arbeitsplätze zum 1.1.1993 (Mindestalter: 21 Jahre). Wenn Sie Interesse haben, bitte schicken Sie uns Ihren Lebenslauf zusammen mit Lichtbild und Zeugnissen an:

Lohmann Spedition, Dortmunderstr. 7, 4400 Münster Tel. 045021/8030 Telex 862310

Vocabulary

der Ausbildungsplatz, ¨e
position with on-the-job training
die Ausbildung *training*
der Kraftfahrer, - *driver*
der Berufskraftfahrer, -
professional driver
erfolgreich *successful*
die Spedition, -en *haulage firm*

die Qualität *quality*
international bekannt
internationally renowned
der Arbeitsplatz, ¨e *post, position*
das Mindestalter *minimum age*
der Lebenslauf, ¨e
curriculum vitae
zusammen *together*

das Lichtbild, -er *photo*
das Zeugnis, -se
school/training report

Comprehension 1

You will hear a conversation between a policeman and a motorist, Herr Kramer, whose car has broken down. After you have listened to the conversation, complete the phrases in the first column with an appropriate phrase from the column opposite.

Vocabulary

das Parkverbot, -e *No parking (sign)*
Ich habe eine Panne *My car has broken down*
die Batterie, -n *battery*

die Werkstatt, ¨-e *garage, workshop*
Machen Sie schnell! *Do hurry up!*
zumachen *(sep) to shut*

der Mensch, -en *person*
innerhalb *within*
die Strafe, -n *penalty*

1 Die Batterie ist …
2 Herr Kramer hat …
3 Die Werkstatt ist …
4 In der Grünstraße darf …
5 Herr Kramer zeigt …
6 Herr Kramer wird eine Geldstrafe bekommen, …

a) in der nächsten Straße.
b) dem Polizisten seinen Führerschein.
c) wenn er innerhalb von 30 Minuten nicht zurückkommt.
d) Benzin gekauft.
e) in Ordnung.
f) man nicht parken.

Comprehension 2: Die Schweiz

Die Schweiz liegt mitten in Europa und hat als Nachbarländer Deutschland, Österreich, Italien und Frankreich. Das Land ist in 26 Kantone eingeteilt mit 3000 Gemeinden und Städten. Die meisten Städte der Schweiz sind nicht sehr groß. (Zürich hat 356 800 Einwohner, dann kommt Basel mit 177 900 Einwohnern.) Sie sind fast 'auf dem Land'. Man kommt also in wenigen Minuten beinahe immer ins Grüne.

Ein modernes Verkehrsnetz (Autobahn, andere Straßen und Bahn) verbindet die Gemeinden und Städte. Es gibt auch fünf Flughäfen; in Zürich, Genf, Basel, Bern und Lugano.

Industrie und Handel sind in der Schweiz sehr wichtig. An der Spitze der Exportliste stehen heute Maschinen, Filmapparate und chemische und pharmazeutische Produkte. Andere wichtige Ausfuhrgüter (Exportgüter) sind Textilien, Uhren und Lebensmittel.

Einwohnerzahl	6,4 Millionen
Hauptstadt	Bern
Einwohnerzahl von Bern	142 000
Fläche	41 293 km²
Länge (Norden-Süden)	220 km (137 Meilen)
Breite (Westen-Osten)	348 km (216 Meilen)
Sprachen	Deutsch Französisch Italienisch Romanisch
Religionen	katholisch evangelisch

Vocabulary

der Kanton, -e *canton*
einteilen *(sep) to divide into*
die Gemeinde, -n *community*
'auf dem Land' *out in the country*

ins Grüne kommen *arrive in open country*
das Verkehrsnetz, -e *road and rail network*

verbinden, verbunden *to connect*
der Handel *trade*
an der Spitze *at the top*
der Filmapparat, -e *camera*

Answer these questions in German, using the text and information above.

1 Wie viele Einwohner hat die Schweiz?
2 Wie heißen die Nachbarländer der Schweiz?
3 Welche Güter exportieren die Schweizer?
4 Ist Bern eine große oder eine kleine Stadt?
5 Warum ist das Verkehrsnetz sehr wichtig?
6 Wie kann man innerhalb der Schweiz reisen?
7 Welche Sprachen spricht man dort?
8 Wie heißen die zwei Hauptreligionen der Schweiz?
9 Wie viele Kilometer ist die Schweiz lang? Und breit?
10 Wie groß ist die Fläche der Schweiz?

Vocabulary

innerhalb *(+ genitive) within*   **die Güter** *goods*   **die Fläche, -n** *area*

Talking business extra

Comprehension 3

Katrina has a problem with her car. Whilst getting a lift from Christian, they touch on their firms' advertising strategies.

Key vocabulary

der Motor, -en *engine*
mitnehmen, mitgenommen
  (sep) to give a lift
die Kundschaft, -en
  customers

der Werbespot, -s
  commercial
der Abnehmer, - *customer*
der Gewinn, -e *profit*
der Verlust, -e *loss*

sich beklagen *to complain*

Key phrases

So ein Pech!
den Umsatz vergrößern
eine Werbekampagne durchführen
auf der Suche nach neuen Märkten
wir machen Reklame
Im Angebot
die Nachfrage steigt
Verluste in Kauf nehmen
das Geschäft läuft bestens

What bad luck!
to increase the turnover
carry out an advertising campaign
in search of new markets
we advertise
On special offer
demand rises
to put up with losses
business is flourishing

Find out:

1 Katrina's reasons for the business trip to Switzerland
2 how the advertising strategy in the **Deutsches Handelsblatt** leads to profit.

Exercise 8

Fill in the details:

Wir müssen den _____ vergrößern.

Wir werden eine _____ durchführen.

Das wird neue _____ bringen.

Wir müssen ständig neue _____ suchen.

Wir können in der Zeitung _____ machen.

Wir müssen auch _____ in Kauf nehmen.

Puzzle

1 commercial
2 profit
3 turnover
4 losses
5 clue: people buying from you

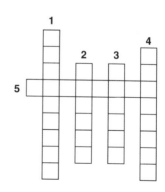

Language structures

Adjectives   Comparative

Der VW ist **billiger als** der Opel.   *cheaper than*
Der Opel verbraucht **mehr** Benzin **als** der VW.   *more than*
Der VW ist nicht **so teuer wie** der Opel.   *as expensive as*
Der Opel verbraucht nicht **so viel** Benzin **wie**   *as much as*
    der VW.

Other forms of the comparative:

lang	länger
breit	breiter
schwer	schwerer
schnell	schneller
langsam	langsamer

See also Unit 10, pages 101–2.

Word order   Subordinate clauses

Wenn man selbst **tankt, bekommt** man einen Beleg.
Wenn die Schmerzen nicht **nachlassen, informieren** Sie den Arzt.

If a subordinate clause stands at the *beginning* of a sentence, it is
immediately followed by the main verb.
Remember as a rule: verb – comma – verb.
See also Unit 11, pages 116–17.

Progress check

1 NVQ S2

At a border check-point, how would you say
that:
a) you have nothing to declare
b) your passport, driving licence and
       insurance card are in the car
c) you are annoyed
d) it will only last five minutes
e) you have driven for five hours.

2 NVQ S2

You are at a petrol station and ask the
attendant to:
a) Fill up with lead free, four-star
b) Wash the car
c) Top up the water
d) Check the tyre pressure
e) Give you a receipt.

3 NVQ W2

Write a fax to your colleague. Say that you
have checked the technical data: the new car
is longer, wider and a little heavier than the
old one, it drives faster and price and petrol
consumption are about as high as before
(**vorher**). Where do you get the key and
where should you both go for lunch?

4 NVQ R2

This advertisement has been left on your
desk. What does it say?
'Wenn Sie einen neuen Arbeits- oder
Ausbildungsplatz suchen, schicken Sie Ihren
Lebenslauf mit Lichtbild und Zeugnissen
direkt an das Hauptbüro der Spedition
Lohmann.'

5 NVQ R2

Read and analyse the comments about the
publicity efforts of two separate companies:
a) Wir machen in Zeitungen, Zeitschriften,
       Radio und Fernsehen Reklame, ja, mit
       praktisch allen Massenmedien.
b) Die Kundschaft beklagt sich, der Gewinn
       sinkt, Verluste steigen …, wir müssen
       dringend eine Werbekampagne
       durchführen.

Summary 9

Additional exercises

1 Complete the gaps in the following sentences with **als** or **wie**.

a Die Durchsuchung Ihres Lastkraftwagens dauert nicht länger _____ ein paar Minuten.

b In der Stadt darf man nicht so schnell _____ auf der Autobahn fahren.

c Hier dürfen Sie nicht schneller _____ sechzig Kilometer fahren.

d In dieser Straße darf man nicht länger _____ neunzig Minuten parken.

e An dieser Tankstelle kostet das Benzin nicht so viel _____ dort drüben.

f Kennen Sie ein größeres Hotel _____ das Schloß-Hotel?

2 Re-arrange the structure of these sentences so that they begin with **wenn**.

Example: Es kostet mehr, wenn man Superbenzin kauft.
Wenn man Superbenzin kauft, kostet es mehr.

a Ich möchte vier Fünfzigmarkscheine, wenn das geht.
b Gehen Sie zur Stadtmitte, wenn Sie Geschenke kaufen wollen.
c Wir können hier bleiben, wenn Sie müde sind.
d Man muß den ADAC rufen, wenn man eine Panne hat.
e Ich muß zur Bank gehen, wenn wir kein Geld haben.
f Wir können Ihnen unsere Stadt zeigen, wenn Sie möchten.

3 For revision look through the Language structures on the perfect tense, Unit 11, pages 115–16, Unit 12, page 127 and pages 128–9. Then put the following sentences into the perfect tense.

Examples: Wie weit **fahren** Sie?   Wie weit **sind** Sie **gefahren**?
Wo **parken** Sie?   Wo **haben** Sie **geparkt**?

a Ich gebe Ihnen eine Quittung.
b Mein Kollege prüft den Ölstand.
c Wir wechseln die Reifen.
d Der Wagen bleibt über Nacht in der Werkstatt.
e Der Zollbeamte macht eine Stichprobe.
f Es dauert nicht lange.
g Die Besucher kommen bald zurück.
h Ich löse den letzten Reisescheck ein.
i Wir brauchen die Lieferung dringend.
j Er bekommt das Bargeld am Geldwechselschalter.

Key phrases

Expressing irritation   Das gibt's ja nicht!
Saying you cannot do something anymore   Das schaffe ich nicht mehr

Asking for petrol	Volltanken bitte
	Dreißig Liter Super/Normal/bleifrei
	Bitte machen sie den Reservekanister voll
Asking for something to be checked	Bitte prüfen Sie den Ölstand
	Bitte kontrollieren Sie den Reifendruck
Saying you have checked something	Ich habe schon nachgesehen
Saying that is all	Das ist alles
Asking about the cost	Was macht das?
Asking if someone can change a banknote	Können Sie wechseln?
Asking for a receipt	Kann ich eine Quittung haben?
Asking what is wrong	Was ist denn los?

Cultural briefing

Driving

German motorways, even the two-lane ones, have no speed-limit other than a recommended 130 kilometres per hour. Expect to see some very fast driving, and be duly cautious especially when overtaking. Motorway service areas (**der Rasthof/die Raststätte**) are more frequent than in Britain, with shorter access and exit roads; again, caution is required. Look out for the word **Stau**, a jam or tail-back often announced in advance by banners strung across bridges, or flashing from police cars moving slowly along the hard shoulder (**die Notspur**).

It is normal to have all documentation relating to your car with you, and a driving licence, warning triangle and first-aid kit are compulsory. The traffic police can give on-the-spot fines. Penalties for drink-driving are severe. If drinking away from the hotel, use taxis!

Pronunciation

Compound words

Many longer German words are made up of smaller ones. In pronouncing them the constituent words should be individually recognisable, and slightly separate from each other:

geradeaus   gerade-aus
Geldautomat   Geld-automat
Briefeinwurf   Brief-einwurf
woher   wo-her
Tafeläpfel   Tafel-äpfel

Often the elements of a compound word are joined with an **s**. In pronunciation the joining **s** will belong to the element preceding it:

Jahresende   Jahres-ende
Bestimmungsort   Bestimmungs-ort
Arbeitsplatz   Arbeits-platz
Lebenslauf   Lebens-lauf

UNIT 19 Stadtbesichtigung

In this unit, you will learn how to …

- arrange a sightseeing tour
- say that you are looking forward to and are interested in something
- talk about the longest, best known, most famous, and so on.

Dialogue: Spaziergang durch die Stadt

During a business trip to a trade fair in Düsseldorf, Karen Clark, the sales director of a British company, is given a tour of the city by her opposite number, Hedwig Stingl, from the German company she has been visiting.

Stingl Sind Sie zum ersten Mal in Düsseldorf?

Clark Ja.

Stingl Möchten Sie heute die Stadt besichtigen? Heute nachmittag haben wir bestimmt etwas Zeit.

Clark Ja, gern. Düsseldorf soll sehr schön sein.

Stingl Ja, das stimmt. Es soll eine der schönsten Städte Europas sein. Wollen Sie zuerst die Königsallee sehen? Sie ist Düsseldorfs bekannteste und eleganteste Straße.

Clark Das wird bestimmt interessant.

Stingl Nachher könnten wir in der Altstadt ein bißchen spazierengehen. Dort gibt es allerlei Interessantes – einen großen Marktplatz, Spezialgeschäfte, Antiquitätenläden, Kirchen, Kneipen, angenehme Restaurants, alte Gebäude und so weiter.

Clark Ich glaube, in dieser Stadt langweilt man sich nie.

Stingl Und dann müssen wir einen Spaziergang am Rheinufer machen, wenn wir noch Zeit haben.

Vocabulary

die Besichtigung, -en *visit*
   to view something
der Spaziergang, ¨e *stroll*
besichtigen, besichtigt *to view*
der, die, das bekannteste *the most well known*
der, die, das eleganteste *the most elegant*

nachher *afterwards*
ein bißchen *a little*
spazierengehen,
   spazierengegangen (*sep, sein*) *to go for a walk*
allerlei *all sorts of*
der Marktplatz, ¨e *market square*
die Kirche, -n *church*

die Kneipe, -n *pub*
man langweilt sich *one gets bored*
nie *never*
das Rheinufer, - *banks of the Rhine*

Notes

1 **Es soll eine der schönsten Städte Europas sein** *It is said to be one of the most beautiful towns in Europe.* **Sollen** usually means *should* or *shall*. Occasionally, as here, it indicates that something is *said* or *supposed to be* something.
Schönsten, eleganteste *Most beautiful, most elegant.* Details of the superlative are in Language structures, page 209.

2 **... wenn wir noch Zeit haben ...** *if we still have time.* See Language structures, page 209 for different meanings of **wenn**.

3 **... einen großen Marktplatz, ... alte Gebäude ...** Remember that an adjective which comes directly *before* a noun must have an *ending*. For revision of adjective endings, see pages 102–4.

Exercise 1

Answer the following questions in German.

1 Wie oft ist Karen Clark schon in Düsseldorf gewesen?
2 Was wissen Sie über die Königsallee?
3 Wo genau in der Altstadt kann man einkaufen?
4 Was machen Karen Clark und ihre Kollegin in der Altstadt? Und später?
5 Was wissen Sie über Düsseldorf von diesem Dialog?
6 An welchem Fluß liegt Düsseldorf?

Exercise 2

You are on a business trip in Vienna. Your host invites you to visit the sights. What do you say in German?

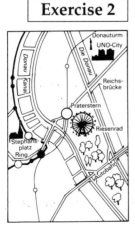

Gastgeber	Sind Sie zum ersten Mal in Wien?
Sie	(*Say yes, you are.*)

Gastgeber	Möchten Sie die Stadt besichtigen? Wir haben heute Zeit.
Sie	(*Say yes, you would like to.*)

Gastgeber	Möchten Sie zuerst die Ringstraße sehen? Sie ist Wiens eleganteste Straße und hat viele imposante Gebäude.

Sie	*(Say yes, and then you would like to see the river.)*

Gastgeber	Die Donau ist ja sehr schön. Dann könnten wir zum Prater fahren. In diesem Park befindet sich das Riesenrad, das größte der Welt.
Sie	*(Say it is very impressive. You saw it in the film 'The Third Man'.)*

Vocabulary

der Gastgeber, - host

imposant *imposing, impressive*

das Riesenrad, ¨er *big wheel*

Exercise 3	While on a language course in Düsseldorf you are taken on a conducted bus tour of the area.

Have a look at the new words and listen (several times) to the guide's introduction.

Vocabulary

an Bord *aboard*
die Rundfahrt, -en *round trip*
sich befinden, befunden *to be (situated)*
der Ausflugsbus, -se *excursion bus, coach*
sich setzen *to sit down*
sich langweilen *to be bored*
bestimmt *certainly*
sich über etwas freuen *to be glad about, take pleasure in something*
der Geschmack, ¨e *taste*
die Geschichte *history*

sich für etwas interessieren *to be interested in*
schwärmen *to be enthusiastic*
sich wohlfühlen *(sep) to feel at ease*
fast *almost*
sich verlieben in *(+ accusative) to fall in love with*
persönlich *personally*
sich auf etwas freuen *look forward to something*
der Straßenkünstler, - *street artist*

der Bummel *stroll*
die Kirmes, -se *fair, funfair*
sich amüsieren *to have fun*
das Stadion, Stadien *stadium*
die Rückkehr *return*
sich entspannen *to relax*
sich bedanken *to express thanks*
die Aufmerksamkeit, -en *attention*

The next day you are provided with a summary of the guide's introduction, but there are gaps for you to fill with reflexive verbs. The appropriate form of these have been written down below to make things a little easier, but when you feel confident enough, do the exercise again, filling in the blanks from memory.
See Language structures on reflexive verbs on pages 208–9.

sich ... interessieren, sich ... freuen, befinden sich, sich bequem, sich ... wohlfühlen, setzen ... sich, langweilen ... sich
freue mich, bedanke mich, euch ... amüsieren, verliebt sich, uns ... entspannen, euch ... unterhalten

Guten Tag, meine Damen und Herren

Willkommen an Bord

Wir machen heute eine schöne Stadtrundfahrt durch Düsseldorf und Umgebung. Sie

_____ _____ jetzt in einem Düsseldorfer Ausflugsbus. Bitte

_____ Sie _____, und machen Sie es _____ _____. Heute

nachmittag _____ Sie _____ bestimmt nicht. Sie werden

_____ über unsere elegante Stadt _____. Wir haben für jeden

Geschmack etwas, zum Beispiel wenn Sie _____ für Geschichte

_____, wird unser Schloß Benrath Ihnen sicher gefallen.

Wenn Sie aber für das Einkaufen schwärmen, werden Sie _____ im neuen

Einkaufszentrum _____.

Fast jeder Besucher _____ _____ in unsere schöne Stadt am Rhein.

Ich persönlich _____ _____ auf einen Bummel durch die Altstadt mit ihren

vielen Restaurants, Boutiquen, Kneipen und Straßenkünstlern. Ich sehe, wir haben auch

Kinder an Bord. Ihr werdet _____ auch _____. Im Rheinstadion,

auf dem Wochenmarkt und auf der Kirmes werdet ihr _____ gut

_____. Dann können wir _____ vor unserer Rückkehr zur

Stadtmitte beim Kaffeetrinken etwas _____. So, meine Damen und

Herren, ich _____ _____ für Ihre Aufmerksamkeit und wünsche Ihnen

noch einen schönen Nachmittag.

Note

Ihr werdet **euch** gut **amüsieren** *You will have a lot of fun.* The children have been addressed in the familiar plural form.

Exercise 4

During a conference in Germany you are having a day off. You decide to visit Bad Embach and while your colleague wants to go for a dip at the local swimming bath, you decide to look at the sights. You stop at the tourist office and ask:

1 how to get to the swimming baths by car
2 where to park
3 how to get from the car park to the museum
4 and from the museum to St. Pauli church.

Write down the conversation between you and the official referring to the map. The phrases below may be useful.

- **Ich bin hier fremd**
- **Wie komme ich zum/zur …?**
- **Sind Sie mit dem Auto hier?**
- **Gehen Sie zu Fuß?**
- **am Kreisverkehr geradeaus**
- **Nehmen Sie die erste Straße links.**

Vocabulary

der Kreisverkehr *roundabout*

Note

gehen, gegangen (sein) *to go on foot, walk*

fahren, gefahren (sein) *to go by car/any vehicle*

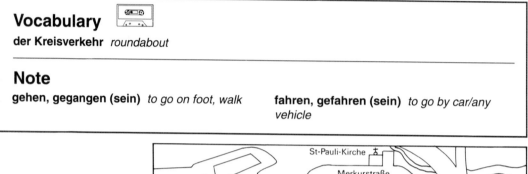

Comprehension 1

While waiting at the tourist office for information you overhear five instructions. Match each instruction with one of the following places of interest:

das Kino   das Schwimmbad   die Kunstgalerie
das Theater   das Museum

Vocabulary

die Kunstgalerie, -n *art gallery*

die Ausstellung, -en *exhibition*

Comprehension 2

You are in Düsseldorf with friends and want to go on a river trip. You have found the following leaflet, but as your friends do not understand German, you must answer their questions.

Eine Rheinfahrt

Eine Fahrt auf dem Rhein ist immer wieder ein Erlebnis – nicht nur für die Kinder. Und dieses Vergnügen sollten Sie auf keinen Fall versäumen, wenn Sie in Düsseldorf sind.

Die schmucken Passagierschiffe der Rheinbahn sind komfortabel eingerichtet. Wenn Sie Hunger oder Durst haben, dann finden Sie an Bord Bars und Restaurants.

Von Ostern bis Ende September können Sie mit uns fahren. Nehmen Sie an einer unserer zahlreichen Ausflugsfahrten teil, z.B. nach Königswinter mit dem Drachenfels oder nach Zons, einer kleinen Römerstadt am Rhein.

Fahren Sie mit uns, wir freuen uns, Sie als Gast an Bord zu haben.

Vocabulary

das Erlebnis, -se *experience*
das Vergnügen, - *pleasure*
auf keinen Fall *under no circumstances*
versäumen, versäumt *to miss*

schmuck *ornate*
eingerichtet *furnished*
teilnehmen an *(+ dative) (sep) to take part in*
zahlreich *numerous*

Drachenfels *dragon rock*
die Römerstadt, ⁝e *roman town*
der Dampfer, - *steamer*

1 Do the boats run all the year round?
2 What are the furnishings like?
3 Will we get decent food and drink?
4 What age groups are there likely to be on board?
5 Does the leaflet sound welcoming?
6 Is there a choice of excursions?

Talking business extra

Comprehension 3

Spieltechnik is represented at an educational resources exhibition in London, introducing their **Päda-Computer** and software. Katrina is answering an enquiry on dispatch and deliveries, when Christian turns up. His purpose for being here is market research, but he isn't taking things too seriously.

Key vocabulary

das Ersatzteil, -e *spare part*
der Lieferverzug, ⁝e *delay in delivery*
das Prachtexemplar, -e *fine specimen, beauty*

das Umschulungszentrum, -zentren *re-training centre*
das Mißverständnis, -se *misunderstanding*

Key phrases

den Vertrieb haben	to have the (distribution) agency
Wie steht es mit ...?	What about ...?
auf Lager	in stock
kurzfristig liefern	deliver at short notice
Die Ausnahme bestätigt die Regel	The exception proves the rule
Sie irren sich	You are wrong
ein Geschäft abschließen	to clinch a deal
Wollen Sie Genaueres wissen?	Do you want to know the details?
Wir laden Sie zu einem Glas Wein ein	We'd like you to join us for a glass of wine
Ich gratuliere!	Congratulations!

Find out:

1 how the Päda-Computer is going to be distributed in England
2 what there is to be celebrated.

Exercise 5

Fill in the details:

Educational Electronics hat den Vertrieb in England _____.

Educational Electronics kann auch kurzfristig _____.

Darf ich Ihnen unser neues Erzeugnis _____.

Darüber können Sie mir nichts Neues _____.

Wir haben soeben ein prima Geschäft _____.

Das muß ein Mißverständnis _____.

Sie haben ganz richtig _____.

||
Language structures

Verbs   Reflexive verbs

Ich wasche **mich**.
Er langweilt **sich**.
Setzen **Sie sich**.
Ich interessiere **mich** besonders für die City.

German has many verbs which are used with a reflexive pronoun. Sometimes there is an English equivalent, for example, Amüsieren Sie **sich**! *Enjoy yourself!*

However, often there is no obvious reason why the German verb is reflexive, for example,
Ich langweile **mich** hier. *I'm getting bored here.*

Exercise 3 on page 204, contains a list of useful reflexive verbs.
See page 217 for a summary of reflexive pronouns.

Adjectives   Superlative

Die Königsallee ist Düsseldorfs bekannt**este** Straße.
Düsseldorf soll eine der schön**sten** Städte Europas sein.

bekannt	der, die, das bekannt**este**	*the best known*
alt	der, die, das ält**este**	*the oldest*
groß	der, die, das größte	*the biggest*
schön	der, die, das schön**ste**	*the most beautiful*
gut	der, die, das beste	*the best*
viel	der, die, das meiste	*the most*

Word order   **Wenn** and **wann?**

Wenn wir Zeit haben   *If we have time*
In the example from this unit **wenn** means *if*. However,
depending on the context, **wenn** can also mean *when*, as in this
sentence:
Wir gehen immer spazieren, **wenn** wir Zeit haben. *We always go
for a walk when we have time.*
But for the question *when?* always use **wann?**:
Wann kommen Sie in München an? *When do you arrive in Munich?*

Note that **wenn** moves the verb to the end, whereas **wann**, being
a question word, changes round the subject and the verb.

Progress check

1 NVQ S2

Your German host is taking you for an
afternoon out. How would you ask him/her:
  a) whether you can see the town
  b) what the most famous street is called
  c) whether you have time for a walk on the
      bank of the Rhine
  d) whether he/she finds old buildings
      interesting?

2 Using reflexive verbs, how would you tell
someone:
  a) to sit down and make himself/herself
      comfortable
  b) that you are looking forward to a stroll in
      the old city
  c) thanks for his/her attention?

3 NVQ W2

Leave written instructions for a visitor, on how
to get to the hospital. Tell him/her to go
straight ahead, at the roundabout turn right,
and take the second road on the left. The

hospital is opposite the swimming pool.

4 What are you being told in the following?
  a) Wir dürfen die Ausstellung im
      Messezentrum auf keinen Fall versäumen.
  b) Vor Ihrer Rückkehr nach England müssen
      Sie unbedingt an einer Ausflugsfahrt auf
      einem Rheindampfer teilnehmen.
  c) Der Nachmittag in der Kunstgalerie war
      das größte Vergnügen.

5 NVQ R2

Read this response to your enquiry from a
German firm. What is said about the
availability of their goods in the Netherlands,
and about spare parts?
  a) Wir haben kein eigenes Büro in den
      Niederlanden, aber die Firma Van der
      Bloom hat den Vertrieb für unsere
      Erzeugnisse.
  b) Ersatzteile können wir jederzeit kurzfristig
      liefern. Genaueres finden Sie in der
      Produktliteratur.

UNIT 20 Es gibt viele Möglichkeiten

In this unit, you will learn how to ...

- express your particular interest in something
- organise entertainment for visitors
- understand detailed tourist information
- say where things are in relation to others.

Dialogue: Als Geschäftsmann ...

A flourishing business relationship has developed between Anglia Chemicals and Sasshofer AG. Today Michael Newby is entertaining the new manager of Sasshofer's purchasing department.

Newby	Wenn Sie Lust haben, können wir heute Londoner Sehenswürdigkeiten besichtigen.
Gast	Ja, gern.
Newby	Sind Sie zum ersten Mal in London?
Gast	Als Kind war ich einmal mit meinen Eltern hier, aber ich kann mich nicht so genau daran erinnern. Wir hatten kein Auto und mußten immer zu Fuß gehen. Meine Schwester studierte damals nicht weit von London.
Newby	Dann gibt es viele Möglichkeiten. Möchten Sie lieber eine Stadtrundfahrt machen oder ein bestimmtes Stadtviertel kennenlernen?

Gast	Als Geschäftsmann interessiere ich mich besonders für die City. Die möchte ich unbedingt sehen, wenn's geht.
Newby	Das geht schon. Wir können ruhig den ganzen Tag dort verbringen. Möchten Sie mit dem Bus oder mit dem Auto fahren?
Gast	Was empfehlen Sie?
Newby	Vom Bus aus kann man viel besser sehen. Wir können nämlich im Doppeldecker oben sitzen.
Gast	Also gut. Fahren wir mit dem Bus.

Vocabulary

Lust haben *to want to*
die Eltern *(pl) parents*
sich an etwas erinnern *to remember something*
zu Fuß gehen *to go on foot*
damals *then, at that time*

die Möglichkeit, -en
  possibility
die Rundfahrt, -en *round trip*
bestimmt *certain(ly)*
das Stadtviertel, - *quarter, district of the town*

unbedingt *absolutely*
den Tag verbringen,
  verbracht *to spend the day*
vom Bus aus *from the bus*
der Doppeldecker, - *double decker*

Notes

1 **Wenn Sie Lust haben ...** *If you want to ...* **Lust haben** is a commonly used phrase for saying that you want to do something. See also page 109, Dialogue.

2 **... aber ich kann mich nicht so genau daran erinnern.** *... but I can't remember it very clearly.*

3 **Mußten, studierte** *had to, studied.* The imperfect tense is explained on page 216.

4 **Wenn's geht** = **wenn es geht** *if possible.*

5 **Als Kind, als Geschäftsmann** *as a child, as a businessman.* Note the omission of the article in this phrase.

Exercise 1	Answer the following questions.

1 Wann war der Gast zum letzten Mal in London?
2 War er damals mit dem Wagen dort?
3 Was möchte der Gast gerne machen? Warum?
4 Wieviel Zeit haben Newby und sein Gast?
5 Warum nehmen sie den Bus?
6 Was für einen Bus nehmen sie?

Exercise 2	You propose taking a German visitor to see the sights of your town. What do you say in German?

Sie	*(Ask whether she is here for the first time.)*

Besucherin	Nein, ich war letztes Jahr schon einmal hier, aber nur ganz kurz, für eine Besprechung mit Herrn Jones.
Sie	*(Say in that case she must see the town this time. Would she like that?)*

Besucherin	Oh ja, sehr gern. Heute nachmittag haben wir genug Zeit.
Sie	(*Ask which is preferable, a tour of the town or looking at some of the sights.*)

Besucherin	Am liebsten möchte ich die Sehenswürdigkeiten in der Altstadt sehen. Die soll sehr schön sein.
Sie	(*Which would she prefer, going by bus, car or on foot?*)

Besucherin	Wenn es nicht zu weit ist, können wir zu Fuß gehen. Ein Spaziergang in der Altstadt wäre wirklich sehr angenehm.

Vocabulary

wäre *would be*

Exercise 3

Your company is holding a three-day conference for representatives from its European subsidiary companies, and you are helping to organise entertainment during the daytime for the representatives' spouses. Your boss dictates a letter to the German subsidiaries giving an outline of possible activities. Listen to the letter and write down a complete version of it.

Vocabulary

der Ehepartner, - *spouse*
dreitägig *three-day*
abwechslungsreich *varied*

für folgendes *for the following*

die Modefabrik, -en *fashionwear factory*
zur Hand sein *to be on hand*

Exercise 4

You are working for an international organisation in Switzerland and have been asked to translate into English a leaflet to be issued to foreigners coming to work in Switzerland.

Touristische Informationen hören Sie über Telefonnummer 120, Wetterberichte über Nummer 162. Teletext und Videotext informieren ebenfalls laufend über das Neuste. Nützliche Rufnummern: Pannenhilfe 140, Polizei 117, Feuerwehr 108, Straßenzustand 163. Diese und weitere Nummern können Sie in allen offiziellen Telefonbüchern auf den blauen Seiten finden. Ladenöffnungszeiten: Montag bis Freitag in der Regel 08.00 – 18.30 Uhr, am Samstag meistens bis 16.00 Uhr. Auf den wichtigen Bahnhöfen sind Lebensmittel-Automaten installiert. Allgemeine Feiertage

sind: Neujahr, Ostern, Auffahrt, Pfingsten und Weihnachten.
Der 1. August ist Nationalfeiertag. Über kantonale und
lokale Feiertage geben die örtlichen Verkehrsbüros
Auskunft. In allen Restaurants ist Service inbegriffen. Ein
Bedienungsgeld ist für Gepäckträger, an Tankstellen mit
Kundendienst und in einigen Städten für Taxichauffeure
üblich.

Vocabulary

der Wetterbericht, -e
  weather report
ebenfalls *also, likewise*
laufend *continually*
die Rufnummer, -n
  telephone number
die Pannenhilfe *breakdown
  service*
die Feuerwehr
  fire brigade

der Straßenzustand, ⁻e *road
  condition*
der Laden, ⁻ *shop*
in der Regel *as a rule*
allgemeine Feiertage
  *general (i.e. public)
  holidays*
Auffahrt *Ascension Day*
Pfingsten *Whitsun*
örtlich *local*

Auskunft geben, gegeben
  give information
**das Bedienungsgeld
  (Trinkgeld)** *tip*
der Gepäckträger, - *porter*
der Kundendienst *customer
  service*
üblich sein, gewesen (sein)
  to be customary

Exercise 5

For revision of prepositions read through pages 47–8, Unit 5.
Then study the picture overleaf and complete the following
sentences. To help you, a list of required prepositions, as well as
the gender of the relevant nouns, has been included. When you
feel confident, try the exercise again without looking at the clues.

Example: In dem (im) *Auto* (n) *auf der* linken Straßenseite (f)
        sitzen drei Passagiere.

1 _____ _____ Auto (n) _____ _____ rechten Straßenseite (f)
   steht eine Politesse.

2 _____ _____ rechten Ecke (f) vorne stehen zwei Leute und
   sprechen miteinander.

3 _____ _____ Bürgersteig (m) _____ _____ Kaufhaus (n)
   Meyer sind drei Leute.

4 _____ _____ Kreuzung (f) ist eine Verkehrsampel.

5 _____ _____ Kaffeehaus (n) stehen einige Tische.

6 _____ _____ Café (n) ist eine Kirche.

7 _____ _____ Bus (m) sieht man Bäume.

Prepositions: **gegenüber, in, neben, hinter, auf, an, vor**

Vocabulary

die Politesse, -n *traffic
  warden*

der Bürgersteig, -e
  pavement

der Baum, ⁻e *tree*

Comprehension 1

The representative of a British company is in Recklinghausen on a business visit. While there, she is given a tour of the town. Listen to the conversation, then answer the questions below.

Vocabulary

nicht mehr *no longer*
das Jahrhundert, -e *century*
die Burg, -en *castle*
bieten, geboten *to offer*
außer *besides*

das Ruhrfestspielhaus *Ruhr Festival Hall*
jährlich *yearly*
der Tierfreund, -e *animal lover*

lebendig *lively*
kaum *hardly*
(Das) meine ich auch *I think so, too*

1 How often has the representative been to Recklinghausen before?
2 What is the oldest building there?
3 Where is an interesting art gallery housed?
4 Apart from museums and art galleries, which other three attractions are mentioned?

Comprehension 2: Solingen – Klingenstadt Deutschlands

Seit über 700 Jahren stellt man in Solingen Schneidwaren her. Diese Tradition begann mit dem Schwert, dann kamen Messer und später Gabel und Löffel mit Griffen aus Silber und Porzellan, Werkzeuge, Scheren und andere Schneidegeräte, jetzt hauptsächlich aus rostfreiem Stahl. Heute, mit 170 000 Einwohnern und eine knappe halbe Stunde mit dem Auto von Düsseldorf entfernt, ist Solingen eine moderne Industriestadt. Ungefähr 350 hauptsächlich kleine oder mittlere Betriebe produzieren Schneidwaren. Der größte Teil dieser Betriebe beschäftigt weniger als 1000 Menschen, bei vielen sind weniger als 20 Mitarbeiter beschäftigt. Es gibt auch viele Heimarbeiter. Diese Leute führen Aufträge in ihren eigenen Werkstätten aus.

Die Solinger Schneidwarenindustrie ist weltbekannt. Rund 50 Prozent der Produktion verkauft man innerhalb Deutschlands. Die andere Hälfte exportiert man, zum Beispiel nach Nordamerika und Japan und in die arabischen Staaten.

In Solingen sieht man eine Mischung aus Altem und Neuem, hier eine moderne Kirche oder Fußgängerzone, dort ein altes Gebäude mit Schieferdach und Fachwerk. Die alte Tradition lebt gut mit der Gegenwart zusammen.

Vocabulary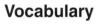

die Schneidwaren *(pl)* *cutting tools*
das Schwert, -er *sword*
kamen *came*
das Messer, - *knife*
die Gabel, -n *fork*
der Löffel, - *spoon*
das Silber *silver*
das Werkzeug, -e *tool*
die Schere, -n *scissors*
das Gerät, -e *tool, (piece of equipment)*

hauptsächlich *mainly*
der Betrieb, -e *company*
beschäftigen, beschäftigt *to occupy, employ*
der Mitarbeiter, - *work colleague, employee*
der Heimarbeiter, - *home worker*
der Auftrag, ̈e *order, commission*
innerhalb *(+ genitive) within*
arabisch *arab*

die Mischung, -en *mixture*
die Fußgängerzone, -n *pedestrian precinct*
das Schieferdach, ̈er *slate roof*
das Fachwerk *half timbering*
die Gegenwart *present time*
zusammenleben, zusammengelebt *(sep) to live together*

Answer these questions in German.

1 Seit welchem Jahrhundert stellt man in Solingen Schneidwaren her?
2 Wie lange fährt man von Düsseldorf nach Solingen?
3 Wo arbeiten Heimarbeiter?
4 Ist die Solinger Schneidwarenindustrie berühmt?
5 Wieviel Prozent der Produktion geht ins Ausland?
6 Wie sind die Gebäude in Solingen?

Talking business extra

Comprehension 3

Christian has joined Katrina and her colleagues who are manning the stall at the exhibition, for drinks to celebrate the successful launch of their new product. They take stock of what has been achieved and look confidently to the future.

Key vocabulary

der Interessent, -en *interested party*
zufrieden *satisfied, content*

nötig *necessary*
die Zusammenarbeit, -en *collaboration*

der Bericht, -e *report*

Key phrases

etwas übertrieben	*slightly exaggerated*
den Vertrag unterzeichnen	*to sign the contract*
gute Anzeichen	*good indications*
Es kommt sehr gut an	*It is well received*
Kann ich das schriftlich haben?	*May I have that in writing?*
zum 'Du' kommen	*start using the familiar form of address, as opposed to **Sie***
völlig einverstanden sein	*to be in complete agreement*
Zum Wohl allerseits! Prost!	*Cheers everybody!*

Find out:

1 what indications show that the British market is favourable
2 what Christian wants in writing.

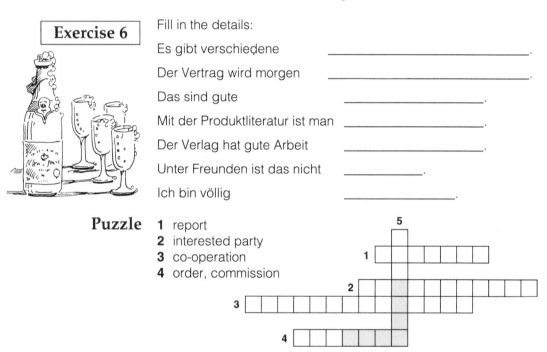

Exercise 6

Fill in the details:

Es gibt verschiedene _____.

Der Vertrag wird morgen _____.

Das sind gute _____.

Mit der Produktliteratur ist man _____.

Der Verlag hat gute Arbeit _____.

Unter Freunden ist das nicht _____.

Ich bin völlig _____.

Puzzle

1 report
2 interested party
3 co-operation
4 order, commission

5 clue: not to be confused with no. 4, this is the one to be signed by all parties

Language structures

Verbs   Imperfect tense

Ich **war** mit meinen Eltern hier.
Wir **hatten** kein Auto.
Meine Schwester **studierte** in London.
Diese Tradition **begann** mit dem Schwert.

The imperfect is often used as an alternative to the perfect tense, particularly in written German. It is the tense commonly used in telling stories and relating incidents and in saying what happened on a regular basis. For a summary of how to form the imperfect tense turn to page 218.

Infinitive with **zu**

Wir freuen uns, Sie an Bord **zu** haben.
Es freut mich, Sie kennen**zu**lernen.
Ich hoffe, bald nach Deutschland **zu** fahren.

These express the content of *what is wished, preferred, hoped for*, etc. The verb in these clauses is placed at the end, and preceded by **zu**. In the case of separable verbs the **zu** is inserted between the separable prefix and the verb.

Adjectives   Towns and cities used as adjectives

Wir fahren in einem London**er** Doppeldecker.
Ich gehe zum Wien**er** Prater.
Trinken Sie gern Dortmund**er** Pils?

The letters **er** are added to the name of a town or city when it is used adjectivally. This ending remains the same in all four cases.

Progress check

1 NVQ S2
In conversation with your German host, how would you express:
a) your particular interest in the sights of Berlin
b) your preference to go by bus
c) your pleasurable anticipation of the trip on the Rhine
d) your enjoyment, as a typical Englishman/woman, in learning German
e) agreement with your host's suggestion to go to Solingen?

2 NVQ W2
As part of a letter, write that as a student you did not have a car and had to go by train. You studied in London and were abroad often.

3 What are:
a) Schneidegeräte?
b) Aufträge?
c) Fachwerkhäuser?

4 NVQ R2
And finally good news! What are the encouraging comments in this extract from a fax?
a) Wir hoffen weiterhin auf gute Zusammenarbeit!
b) Wenn Sie mit diesem Vorschlag zufrieden sind, können wir morgen den Vertrag unterzeichnen.

Summary 10

Language structures overview

Reflexive verbs

ich	interessiere	**mich**	wir interessieren	**uns**
du	interessierst	**dich**	ihr interessiert	**euch**
er			sie interessieren	**sich**
sie	interessiert	**sich**	Sie interessieren	**sich**
es				

The imperfect tense (simple past tense)

This is used particularly for writing in the past, and relating what happened on a regular or prolonged basis.

Regular verbs

Remove **en** from the infinitive and add the appropriate endings.

Studieren:

ich	studier**te** (*I studied*)	wir	studier**ten**
du	studier**test**	ihr	studier**tet**
er		sie	studier**ten**
sie	studier**te**	Sie	studier**ten**
es			

Note: Where the stem ends in **t** or **d**, add **e** between the stem and the ending.

Arbeiten:

ich	arbeit**ete** (*I worked*)	wir	arbeit**eten**
du	arbeit**etest**	ihr	arbeit**etet**
er		sie	arbeit**eten**
sie	arbeit**ete**	Sie	arbeit**eten**
es			

Irregular verbs

These verbs change their stem and show a different pattern of endings from regular verbs.

Kommen:

ich	kam (no ending)	wir	kam**en**
du	kam**st**	ihr	kam**t**
er		sie	kam**en**
sie	kam (no ending)	Sie	kam**en**
es			

Mixed verbs

These change their stem and add regular endings.

Denken:

ich	dach**te**	wir	dach**ten**
du	dach**test**	ihr	dach**tet**
er		sie	dach**ten**
sie	dach**te**	Sie	dach**ten**
es			

All the irregular and mixed verbs occurring in the book are included in the Irregular verbs list on page 221.

Additional exercises

1 Complete each of the following sentences with a reflexive pronoun.

a Langweilen Sie _____?

b Wir machen es _____ bequem.

c Ich interessiere _____ sehr für Geschichte.

d Wir bedanken _____ für Ihr Schreiben.

e Das Kind freut _____ über den Ausflug.

f In der Altstadt befinden _____ viele Restaurants.

g Meine Frau und ich freuen _____ auf die Stadtbesichtigung.

h Der Gast kann _____ an seinen Besuch nicht so genau erinnern.

2 Put the following sentences into the imperfect tense (all the verbs are regular).

a Der Gast bedankt sich für die Stadtbesichtigung.
b Wir tanken an der nächsten Tankstelle.
c Am Montag telefoniere ich mit der deutschen Firma.
d Sie spielen oft Golf, nicht wahr?
e Warum wartet Herr Peters nicht auf mich?
f Sie wohnt nicht weit von Sheffield.
g Viele Leute besuchen den Zoo.
h Endlich lerne ich meine neuen Kollegen kennen.

3 The following sentences use irregular and mixed verbs in the imperfect tense. Put them into the present tense.

Example: Der Zug **kam** um sieben Uhr dreißig an.
          Der Zug **kommt** um sieben Uhr dreißig an.

a Man konnte sich in Recklinghausen kaum langweilen.
b Gab es dort ein paar Fachwerkhäuser?
c Die Damen fanden die Gegend sehr schön.
d Wir fuhren mit dem Bus zum Festspielhaus.
e An Tankstellen mit Kundendienst war ein Bedienungsgeld üblich.
f Frau Clark und Frau Stingl gingen am Rheinufer spazieren.
g Am Abend sahen die Gäste eine Operette von Johann Strauss.
h Ich hatte leider kein Bargeld.
i Mr. Price flog am Freitag nach München.
j Ich mußte noch meinen Kollegen darüber informieren.

Key phrases

Inviting someone to see the town/sights	Möchten Sie die Stadt/Sehenswürdigkeiten besichtigen/sehen?
	Möchten Sie zuerst die Ringstraße sehen?
Expressing acceptance	Ja, gern(e)
	Das wird bestimmt interessant
	Sehr gern(e)

Making a suggestion	Nachher können (könnten) wir ein bißchen spazierengehen
	Dann können (könnten) wir zum Prater fahren
Expressing agreement	Ja, das stimmt
	(Das) meine ich auch
Inviting someone to express a preference	Möchten Sie lieber eine Stadtrundfahrt machen oder ein bestimmtes Stadtviertel kennenlernen?
Confirming an option	Ja, das geht schon
Asking for a recommendation	Was empfehlen Sie?
Welcoming someone	Willkommen in (*town/country*) bei (*company*)

Cultural briefing

Free time and entertainment
Germans are well-known for their capacity for hard work, though decades of high living standards have perhaps reduced this. Expect them to enjoy themselves after work as well, with little of the typical British reserve. There is less reserve also in the directness with which opinions are expressed, that is often wrongly interpreted as impoliteness or abruptness.

When visiting a home, offer flowers (unwrapped) to the hostess. If you don't want to drink a lot, don't empty your glass too quickly; this is often interpreted as a sign that you would like a fill-up. On the other hand, don't forget that **danke** means *no, thank you*, when something is being offered! Be very sure also not to out-stay your welcome – the working day begins early for most Germans! **Prost!** (*cheers*) or **Zum Wohl!** (*good health*) are frequently heard toasts, often accompanied by clinking of glasses.

Pronunciation

s, ß, ss

> Double s and **scharfes s** or **ß** are always pronounced with a hissing sound, as in the English *glass* vergessen, Reisepaß
>
> Single s when at the end of a word or syllable, or before a consonant, is also pronounced as in *glass* Zahnpasta, Erlebnis.
>
> Otherwise s is pronounced as zz in *buzz* versäumen, Setzen Sie sich

Foreign words
Listen carefully to the pronunciation of foreign words, since they don't always follow the rules. Some examples are:

Service, InterCity, Garage, Komfort, Theater, T-Shirt, Parfümerie, Drogerie, Batterie, Energie.

Irregular verbs

The following is a list of the principal parts of irregular verbs occurring in Talking Business German. Irregular verbs which incorporate a prefix are not always included in the list; to see how these are formed look up the main verb or *stem* below, and then add the prefix. For example, **sich befinden** takes the same forms as **finden** – in the present tense **er findet, er befindet sich**.

Past participles that appear in bold take **sein**.

Infinitive	3rd Person Singular Present	3rd Person Singular Imperfect	Past Participle
beginnen	beginnt	begann	begonnen
besitzen	besitzt	besaß	besessen
bieten	bietet	bot	geboten
binden	bindet	band	gebunden
bleiben	bleibt	blieb	**geblieben**
brennen	brennt	brannte	gebrannt
bringen	bringt	brachte	gebracht
denken	denkt	dachte	gedacht
dürfen	darf	durfte	gedurft
empfehlen	empfiehlt	empfahl	empfohlen
erscheinen	erscheint	erschien	**erschienen**
erwerben	erwirbt	erwarb	erworben
essen	ißt	aß	gegessen
fahren	fährt	fuhr	**gefahren**
finden	findet	fand	gefunden
fliegen	fliegt	flog	**geflogen**
geben	gibt	gab	gegeben
gefallen *(+ dat)*	gefällt	gefiel	gefallen
gehen	geht	ging	**gegangen**
gelten	gilt	galt	gegolten
genießen	genießt	genoß	genossen
geschehen	geschieht	geschah	**geschehen**
haben	hat	hatte	gehabt
halten	hält	hielt	gehalten
hängen	hängt	hing	gehangen
heben	hebt	hob	gehoben
heißen	heißt	hieß	geheißen
helfen	hilft	half	geholfen
kennen	kennt	kannte	gekannt
kommen	kommt	kam	**gekommen**
können	kann	konnte	gekonnt
laden	lädt	lud	geladen

Irregular verbs

Infinitive	3rd Person Singular Present	3rd Person Singular Imperfect	Past Participle
lassen	läßt	ließ	gelassen
laufen	läuft	lief	**gelaufen**
liegen	liegt	lag	gelegen
mögen	mag	mochte	gemocht
müssen	muß	mußte	gemußt
nehmen	nimmt	nahm	genommen
rufen	ruft	rief	gerufen
schlafen	schläft	schlief	geschlafen
schlagen	schlägt	schlug	geschlagen
schließen	schließt	schloß	geschlossen
schreiben	schreibt	schrieb	geschrieben
sehen	sieht	sah	gesehen
sein	ist	war	**gewesen**
sinken	sinkt	sank	**gesunken**
sitzen	sitzt	saß	gesessen
sollen	soll	sollte	gesollt
sprechen	spricht	sprach	gesprochen
stehen	steht	stand	gestanden
steigen	steigt	stieg	**gestiegen**
streichen	streicht	strich	gestrichen
tragen	trägt	trug	getragen
treffen	trifft	traf	getroffen
treiben	treibt	trieb	getrieben
trinken	trinkt	trank	getrunken
tun	tut	tat	getan
vergleichen	vergleicht	verglich	verglichen
verlieren	verliert	verlor	verloren
vertreten	vertritt	vertrat	vertreten
waschen	wäscht	wusch	gewaschen
werden	wird	wurde	**geworden**
werfen	wirft	warf	geworfen
weisen	weist	wies	gewiesen
wiegen	wiegt	wog	gewogen
wissen	weiß	wußte	gewußt
wollen	will	wollte	gewollt
ziehen	zieht	zog	gezogen

Vocabulary list

*irregular verb

A

ab (+ dat) from
das **Abendessen, -** supper
aber but
abfahren* (sep) to set off, to leave
die **Abfahrt, -en** departure
abhängen* (sep) **von** (+ dat) to depend on
abheben* to take out (money from bank)
abholen (sep) to meet (at station), to collect
die **Abmessung, -en** dimension
der **Abnehmer, -** customer
absagen (sep) to cancel (a meeting)
der **Abschluß, ¨sse** ending, completion
der **Absender, -** sender
abwaschen* (sep) to wash up
abziehen* (sep) to deduct
die **Adresse, -n** address
ähnlich similar
die **Akte, -n** file
die **Aktentasche, -n** briefcase
akzeptieren to accept
alle all
alles everything
Allerheiligen All Saints' Day
allerlei all sorts of
allgemein general
der **Alkohol, -e** alcohol
alphabetisch alphabetical
als than, as, when
also therefore, well, right, OK
also gut OK then
alt old
der **Amerikaner, -** American (male)
die **Amerikanerin, -nen** American (female)
amüsieren, sich to enjoy oneself
an (+ acc/dat) at, to
die **Ananas, -** pineapple
anbieten* (sep) to offer
das **Andenken, -** souvenir
andere other
der **Anfang, ¨e** beginning
die **Anfrage, -n** enquiry
das **Angebot, -e** offer
angenehm pleasant
der **Angestellte, -n** clerk
die **Anlage, -n** enclosure
das **Anmeldeformular, -e** registration form
ankommen* (sep) to arrive
die **Ankunft, ¨e** arrival
annehmen* (sep) to accept
ansehen* (sep) to look at
antiallergisch anti-allergic
der **Antiquitätenladen, ¨** antique shop
das **Anzeichen, -** indication

der **April** April
das **Apfelkompott** stewed apple
die **Apotheke, -n** dispensing chemist's shop
der **Apotheker, -** chemist
die **Anspruchsbescheinigung, -en** certificate of entitlement
arabisch Arabian
die **Arbeit, -en** work
arbeiten to work
der **Arbeiter, -** worker
der **Arbeitgeber, -** employer
der **Arbeitnehmer, -** employee
das **Appartement, -s** apartment
die **Arbeitsgruppe, -n** working group
der **Architekt, -en** architect
die **Architektur** architecture
ärgerlich annoying
der **Artikel, -** article
der **Arzt, ¨e** doctor
ärztlich medical
atmen to breathe
die **Attraktion, -en** attraction
auch also
auf (+ acc/dat) on, onto
aufbrauchen (sep) to use up
der **Aufenthalt, -e** stay
die **Auffahrt** Ascension Day
die **Aufgabe, -n** task
die **Aufmerksamkeit** attention
aufnehmen* (sep) to accept
der **Auftrag, ¨e** order, commission
das **Auge, -n** eye
der **Augenblick, -e** moment
die **Augentropfen** (pl) eyedrops
der **August** August
aus (+ dat) from, out of
der **Ausbildungsplatz, ¨e** position with on-the-job training
der **Ausdruck, ¨e** expression
die **Ausfahrt, -en** exit
der **Ausflugsbus, -se** excursion bus
die **Ausflugsfahrt, -en** excursion
die **Ausfuhrgüter** (pl) export goods
ausfüllen (sep) to fill in
die **Ausgabe, -n** expenditure
ausgeben* (sep) to spend (money)
ausgezeichnet excellent
die **Auskunft, ¨e** information
das **Ausland** countries abroad
die **Ausnahme, -n** exception
ausreichend sufficient
ausrichten (sep) to pass on (a message)
ausruhen (sep) to rest
ausrüsten (sep) to equip
außer (+ dat) apart from, except, besides

die **Aussicht, -en** view
das **Ausstellungsstück, -e** exhibition item (exhibit)
die **Auswahl, -en** selection
das **Auto, -s** car
mit dem Auto by car
die **Autobahn, -en** motorway
die **Autobahnausfahrt, -en** motorway exit
der **Automat, -en** automatic machine
die **Autoreparatur, -en** car repairs

B

das **Bad, ¨er** bath
die **Bahn, -en** train
mit der Bahn by train
der **Bahnhof, ¨e** station
bald soon
der **Balkon, -s** balcony
die **Bank, -en** bank
die **Banknote, -n** bank-note
die **Banküberweisung, -en** bank credit transfer
die **Bar, -s** bar
das **Bargeld** cash
barock baroque
basteln to do handicrafts
die **Batterie, -n** battery
die **Bauernstube, -n** snug, quaint bar; Tyrolean bar
der **Baum, ¨e** tree
bedanken, sich to express thanks
bedeuten to mean
die **Bedienung** service
die **Bedienungsanleitung, -en** operating instructions
das **Bedienungsgeld, -er** tip
befinden*, sich to be (situated)
beginnen* to begin
das **Begleitschreiben, -** accompanying letter
bei (+ dat) at, near, at the house of
das **Bein, -e** leg
beinahe almost
beinhalten* (insep) to include
das **Beispiel, -e** example
zum Beispiel for example
bekannt familiar
der **Bekannte, -n** acquaintance
beklagen, sich to complain
die **Bekleidung** clothing
bekommen* to get, to have
der **Beleg, -e** slip
die **Belegschaft, -en** staff
Belgien Belgium
der **Belgier, -** Belgian (male)
die **Belgierin, -nen** Belgian (female)
beleidigt offended
beliebt popular

benutzen to use
der **Benzinverbrauch** petrol consumption
bequem comfortable
die **Beratung, -en** advice
der **Berg, -e** mountain
der **Bericht, -e** report
der **Beruf, -e** career, profession
der **Berufskraftfahrer, -** lorry driver
berühmt famous
beschäftigen to employ
die **Bescheinigung, -en** certificate
die **Beschwerde, -n** complaint
beschweren, sich to complain
besichtigen to look round, visit
besonders especially
besprechen* to discuss
die **Besprechung, -en** meeting
besser better
die **Besserung** improvement
bestätigen to confirm
bestehen* to exist
bestehen* aus (+ dat) to consist of
bestellen to order
die **Bestellung, -en** an order
bestimmt certainly
der **Bestimmungsort, -e** destination
der **Besuch, -e** visit
zu Besuch kommen to be (here) on a visit
Besuch haben to have visitors
besuchen to visit
betonen to stress, emphasise
der **Betrag, ⁻e** total, amount
die **Betreuung** care
der **Betrieb, -e** company
die **Betriebsführung, -en** tour of the company, management
das **Betriebsgeheimnis, -se** company secret
der **Betriebsingenieur, -e** works engineer
der **Betriebsrat, ⁻e** works council
das **Bett, -en** bed
der **Beutel, -** bag
bevor before
bezahlen to pay
beziehungsweise or, or rather
das **Bier, -e** beer
das **Bild, -er** picture
die **Bildung** education
die **Bildungsserie, -n** educational series
billig cheap
binden* to bind, tie
der **Binnenmarkt, ⁻e** internal (single) market
die **Birne, -n** pear
bis until, by
bitte please, here you are
bitte schön/sehr it's a pleasure, you're welcome, here you are
blau blue
bleiben* to stay
bleifrei lead-free
die **Bluse, -n** blouse
die **Blume, -n** flower
das **Blumenhaus, ⁻er** flower shop
der **Blumenkohl** cauliflower
an Bord on board
die **Boutique, -n** boutique
die **Branche, -n** branch, area, sector

brauchen to need
breit wide
die **Breite, -n** width
die **Bremse, -n** brake
brennen* to burn
der **Brief, -e** letter
der **Briefeinwurf** letter-box in post office
die **Briefmarke, -n** postage stamp
die **Brieftasche, -n** wallet
der **Briefträger, -** postman
bringen* to bring
der **Brite, -n** British (male)
die **Britin, -nen** British (female)
die **Broschüre, -n** brochure
das **Brot, -e** bread
das **Brötchen, -** bread roll
das **Buch, ⁻er** book
der **Buchhandel** book trade
buchstabieren to spell
der **Bummel, -** stroll
die **Bundesdruckerei** federal printing works
die **Bundeskegelbahn** skittle alley (to official German dimensions)
das **Bundesland, ⁻er** federal state (Germany), federal province (Austria)
das **Bundesparlament** federal parliament
die **Bundespost** federal post office
der **Bundesrat** upper house (parliament)
die **Bundesrepublik Deutschland** Federal Republic of Germany
der **Bundestag** lower house (parliament)
bürgerlich plain, wholesome (cooking)
das **Büro, -s** office
der **Bus, -se** bus
mit dem Bus by bus
die **Butter** butter

C

ca. (circa) approximately
der **Campingplatz, ⁻e** camp-site
das **Café, -s** café
der **Champignon, -s** mushroom
die **Chefsekretärin, -nen** head secretary
die **Chemikalien** (pl) chemicals
chemisch chemical
der **Computer, -** computer

D

da since
Dänemark Denmark
danken (+ dat) to thank
danke schön thank you very much
dann then
darüber across, over, above, about (it, them, etc.)
daß that
das **Datennetz, -e** data network
das **Datum, Daten** date
dauern to last
die **Delikatesse, -n** delicacy
denken* to think
denn because
das **Deutsch** German (language)
der **Deutsche, -n** German (male)
die **Deutsche, -n** German (female)

die **Deutsche Demokratische Republik** the former German Democratic Repblic
der **Dezember** December
dezent subdued, discreet
die **Diät, -en** diet
dieser, diese, dieses this
das **Dienstjahr, -e** year's service (employment)
direkt direct, straight
die **Disko, -s** disco
der **Dolmetscher, -** interpreter
der **Dom, -e** cathedral
der **Doppeldecker, -** double-decker bus
doppelt double
das **Doppelzimmer, -** double room
dort there
dort drüben over there
die **Dose, -n** tin
drei three
dringend urgent
das **Drittel, -** third
die **Drogerie, -n** non-dispensing chemist
drüben over (there)
drücken to press
der **Drucker, -** printer
duftend aromatic
dumm silly
der **Durchfall** diarrhoea
durchgehend non-stop, the whole time
durchschlafen* (sep) to sleep through the night
im Durchschnitt on average
durchsuchen to search (through)
die **Durchwahl** direct dialling
dürfen* to be allowed
der **Durst** thirst
die **Dusche, -n** shower

E

ebenfalls also, likewise
die **Ecke, -n** corner
die **EDV (elektronische Datenverarbeitung) Anlage** electronic data processing system
das **Ei, -er** egg
eigen own
eigentlich schon yes, actually
der **Eigentümer, -** proprietor
eilig quick, hurried
das **Einbahnstraßensystem, -e** one-way system
eingerichtet furnished
einfach single, simple
einführen (sep) to import
der **Einführungspreis, -e** introductory price
der **Eingang, ⁻e** entrance
einholen (sep) to catch up
einige some, several
einkaufen (sep) to buy
das **Einkaufen** shopping
der **Einkaufsleiter, -** chief buyer
die **Einkaufsleiterin, -nen** chief buyer (female)
die **Einkaufsstadt, ⁻e** shopping centre (literally town)
das **Einkaufszentrum, -zentren** shopping centre

das	**Einkommen, -** income	
	einladen* (sep) to invite	
die	**Einladung, -en** invitation	
der	**Einlieferungsschein, -e** certificate of posting	
	einlösen (sep) to cash	
das	**Einmachen** bottling (fruit)	
	einmal once	
	einmalig unique	
das	**Einmarkstück, -e** one-mark coin	
	einnehmen* (sep) to eat, partake of; to take	
	eins one	
	einsteigen* (sep) to get in	
	einteilen (sep) to organise, plan (time)	
	einwerfen* (sep) to put in, to post	
der	**Einwohner, -** inhabitant	
die	**Einwohnerzahl, -en** number of inhabitants	
die	**Einzelheit, -en** detail	
das	**Einzelzimmer, -** single room	
das	**Eis** ice, ice-cream	
das	**Eisen** iron	
	elegant elegant	
	elektrisch electric	
der	**Elektroniker, -** electronics engineer	
	elektronisch electronic	
	elf eleven	
die	**Eltern** (pl) parents	
der	**Empfänger, -** recipient	
	empfehlen* to recommend	
das	**Ende, -n** end	
	eng narrow	
der	**Engländer, -** Englishman	
die	**Engländerin, -nen** English woman	
	englisch English	
das	**Englisch** English language	
	entfernt distant	
	enthalten* to include, to contain	
	entlang (+ acc) along	
	entschuldigen to excuse	
	entspannen, sich to relax	
die	**Entspannung** relaxation	
	entsprechen* to correspond to	
	entweder ... oder ... either ... or ...	
	entwerten to cancel, to stamp	
	er he, it	
die	**Erbse, -n** pea	
die	**Erbsensuppe, -n** pea soup	
das	**Erdgeschoß** ground floor	
die	**Erfahrung, -en** experience	
der	**Erfolg, -e** success	
	erfolgreich successful	
	erfreulich nice, pleasing	
	erhalten* to get, to receive	
	erinnern, sich an (+ acc) to remember	
die	**Erkältung, -en** cold, chill	
	erkennen* to recognise	
das	**Erlebnis, -se** experience	
	erledigen to settle	
die	**Ernte, -n** harvest	
das	**Ersatzteil, -e** spare part	
	erscheinen* to appear	
die	**Erste Hilfe** first aid	
	der, die, das erste first	
	erstklassig first-class	
der, die	**Erwachsene, -n** adult	
	erwarten to expect	
	erwerben* to gain	

	erzählen to tell	
das	**Erzeugnis, -se** product	
	es it	
das	**Essen, -** meal	
	essen* to eat	
	essen gehen* to go out for a meal	
	etwa about, around	
	etwas some, something, somewhat	
	europäisch European	
die	**Europäische Gemeinschaft** European Community	
	evangelisch Protestant	
	eventuell possibly	
der	**Experte, -n** expert	
die	**Expertin, -nen** expert (female)	
die	**Exportabteilung, -en** export department	
	exportieren to export	
der	**Exportleiter, -e** export manager	
die	**Exportleiterin, -nen** export manager (female)	
die	**Exportliste, -n** list of exports	
die	**Exportgüter** (pl) exports	
F		
die	**Fabrik, -en** factory	
der	**Fachhandel** specialist trade	
	fachlich specialist	
das	**Fachwerkhaus, -er** half-timbered house	
	fahren* to go (by transport), to leave	
der	**Fahrer, -** driver	
die	**Fahrkarte, -n** ticket	
die	**Fahrkartenausgabe, -n** ticket office	
der	**Fahrplanauszug, -e** extract from travel timetable	
der	**Fahrpreis, -e** travel cost	
der	**Fahrschein, -e** ticket	
der	**Fahrstuhl, -e** lift	
die	**Fahrt, -en** journey	
das	**Fahrzeug, -e** vehicle	
	falsch wrong	
die	**Familie, -n** family	
der	**Familienname, -n** surname	
	fangfrisch freshly caught	
das	**Farbbild, -er** colour picture	
der	**Farbfernseher, -** colour television	
	fast almost	
der	**Februar** February	
	fehlen to be missing, to be the matter	
der	**Fehler, -** mistake	
	feiern to celebrate	
der	**Feiertag, -e** public holiday	
die	**Feinmechanik** precision engineering	
das	**Fenster, -** window	
die	**Ferienwohnung, -en** holiday flat	
der	**Fernmeldeingenieur, -e** post office engineer	
der	**Fernschreibdienst, -e** telex service	
das	**Fernsehen, -** television	
	fernsehen* (sep) to watch television	
	fertig ready	
das	**Festspiel, -e** festival	
die	**Feuerwehr** fire-brigade	
das	**Fieber, -** fever, (high) temperature	
die	**Filiale, -n** branch office	

der	**Film, -e** film	
	finden* to find	
die	**Firma, Firmen** firm, company	
der	**Firmenwagen, -** company car	
	fix und fertig complete	
die	**Fläche, -n** area	
die	**Flasche, -n** bottle	
das	**Fleisch** meat	
	fliegen* to fly	
	fließend fluent(ly)	
der	**Flug, -e** flight	
der	**Flughafen, -** airport	
	folgend following	
das	**Formular, -e** form	
der	**Fotoartikel, -** photographic accessory	
die	**Frage, -n** question	
der	**Fragebogen, -** or **-** questionnaire	
	fragen to ask	
	Frankreich France	
der	**Franzose, -n** Frenchman	
die	**Französin, -nen** French woman	
	französisch French	
die	**Frau, -en** wife, woman, Mrs (or Miss/Ms in titles)	
	frei free	
die	**Freizeithalle, -n** recreation room	
die	**Fremdsprache, -n** foreign language	
	freuen, sich to be pleased	
	freuen, sich auf (+ acc) to look forward to	
der	**Freund, -e** friend (male)	
die	**Freundin, -nen** friend (female)	
	freundlich friendly	
	frisch fresh	
	frischgepreßt freshly squeezed	
der	**Frisiersalon, -s** hairdresser's	
das	**Frühstück, -e** breakfast	
	frühstücken to have breakfast	
	führen to carry (stock), to lead	
	fünf five	
	funktionieren to work, to operate	
	für (+ acc) for	
der	**Führerschein, -e** driving licence	
der	**Fuß, -e** foot	
	zu Fuß on foot	
die	**Fußgängerzone, -n** pedestrian precinct	
G		
die	**Gabel, -n** fork	
	ganz whole, complete	
	ganzjährig all year round	
der	**Garagenhof, -e** parking area	
	gar nicht not at all	
die	**Garantie, -n** guarantee	
das	**Gartengerät, -e** garden tool	
das	**Gas, -e** gas	
der	**Gast, -e** guest	
der	**Gasthof, -e** pub	
	geben* to give	
das	**Gebäude, -** building	
der	**Gebietsrepräsentant, -en** area representative	
	gebrauchen to use	
	geeignet suitable	
	gefallen* (+ dat) to please	
	gegenüber (+ dat) opposite	
die	**Gegend, -en** area	
die	**Gegenwart** present (time)	
	Gehacktes minced beef	
die	**Gehaltserhöhung, -en** pay-rise	

die **Geheimzahl, -en** secret (PIN) number
gehen* to go (on foot)
gehören (zu) (+ dat) to belong to
gelb yellow
das **Geld, -er** money
der **Geldwechsel, -** bureau de change
das **Gelenk, -e** joint
gelten* to be applicable, valid
die **Gemeinde, -n** community
gemischt mixed
das **Gemüse** vegetable(s)
gemütlich cosy
genau exactly
genauso just as
genießen* to enjoy
das **Genußmittel, -** semi-luxury foods
genußvoll enjoyable
geöffnet open
das **Gepäck** luggage
der **Gepäckträger, -** porter
gepflegt cultivated
geradeaus straight on
das **Gerät, -e** tool, piece of equipment
das **Gericht, -e** dish (food)
gering low, small
gern(e) I'd like to, of course, gladly
gern geschehen it's a pleasure
gesamt entire
der **Gesamtbetrag, -e** total amount
das **Gesamteinkommen, -** total income
das **Geschäft, -e** shop
die **Geschäftsbedingung, -en** condition of trade
der **Geschäftsführer, -** managing director
der **Geschäftsmann, -leute** businessman
die **Geschäftsreise, -n** business trip
geschehen* to happen
das **Geschenk, -e** present
die **Geschichte, -n** history
geschlossen closed
der **Geschmack, -e** taste
die **Gestaltung, -en** layout, design
gesund healthy
die **Gesundheitspflege** health care
gestern abend yesterday evening
die **Getränkekarte, -n** wine list
das **Gewicht, -e** weight
der **Gewinn, -e** profit
gewürzt spiced
gezuckert sweetened
das **Glas, -er** glass
gleich right away, just
gleichfalls likewise
das **Gleis, -e** track, platform
glücklicherweise luckily
golden golden
gratulieren (+ dat) to congratulate
die **Grenze, -n** border
Griechenland Greece
der **Griff, -e** handle
der **Grill** barbecue
die **Grippe** flu
groß large
der **Großbetrieb, -e** large company
Großbritannien Great Britain
die **Größe, -n** size
die **Größenordnung, -en** scale, size
die **Großstadt, -e** city
grün green

der **Grund, -e** reason
die **grüne Versicherungskarte, -n** green card (insurance)
ins Grüne into the country
die **Gruppe, -n** group
günstig reasonable
gut good, well
die **Güteklasse, -n** quality, category
die **Güter** (pl) goods
die **Gymnastik** gymnastics

H

haben* to have
halb half
Halbpension half-board
die **Hälfte, -n** half
die **Halsschmerzen** (pl) sore throat
halt! hold on! stop!
halten* to hold, to stop
die **Hand, -e** hand
das **Handbuch, -er** manual
etwas zur Hand haben to have available
der **Handel** trade
Handel treiben to trade
der **Handelspartner, -** trade partner
die **Handelsstadt, -e** commercial town
die **Haselnußcreme** hazelnut spread
der **Hauptbahnhof, -e** main station
der **Hauptexport -e** main export
das **Hauptgericht, -e** main course
die **Hauptmahlzeit, -en** main meal
hauptsächlich mainly
der **Hauptsitz, -e** head office
die **Hauptstadt, -e** capital city, town
das **Haus, -er** house
zu Hause at home
der **Haushaltsartikel, -** household item
die **Haushaltsgüter** (pl) household goods
der **Heilbutt** halibut
der **Heimarbeiter, -** home worker
heißen* to be called
die **Heizung** heating
helfen* to help
das **Hemd, -en** shirt
herrlich magnificent, splendid
die **Herrenbekleidung** menswear
die **Herrschaften** (pl) ladies and gentlemen
herstellen (sep) to produce
die **Herstellung** production
herunter down
das **Herz, -en** heart
herzlichen Dank thank you very much indeed
heute today
heute früh this morning
heute nachmittag this afternoon
hier here
hierher here (movement)
die **Hilfe, -n** help
hin und zurück there and back, return
hinter behind
hinunter down, along
hinüber across
hoch high
die **Höchstgeschwindigkeit, -en** maximum speed
die **Hochstraße, -n** flyover road

hoffentlich hopefully
Holland Holland
holländisch Dutch
der **Honig** honey
hören to hear
das **Hotel, -s** hotel
das **Hotel garni** bed and breakfast hotel
das **Hotelzimmer, -** hotel room
hübsch pretty
der **Hund, -e** dog
der **Hunger** hunger
der **Husten** cough
der **Hustenreiz** tickling cough

I

ich I
die **Idee, -n** idea
ihr her, its
Ihr your
immer always
immer noch still
importieren to import
in (+ acc/dat) in, into
die **Industrie, -n** industry
industriell industrial
die **Industriestadt, -e** industrial town
der **Ingenieur, -e** engineer
die **Information, -en** information
informieren to inform
inklusive (+ gen) including
innerhalb (+ gen) within
die **Insel, -n** island
installieren to install
das **Instrument, -e** instrument
interessant interesting
das **Interesse, -n** interest
der **Interessent, -en** interested party
interessieren, sich für (+ acc) to be interested in
der **Ire, -n** Irishman
die **Irin, -nen** Irish woman
irren, sich to make a mistake
irisch Irish
Irland Ireland
der **Irländer, -** Irishman
Italien Italy
der **Italiener, -** Italian (male)
die **Italienerin, -nen** Italian (female)
italienisch Italian

J

die **Jacke, -n** jacket
die **Jagd** hunt
das **Jahr, -e** year
das **Jahresende, -n** end of the year
das **Jahrhundert, -e** century
jährlich per year, annually
der **Januar** January
jeder/e/es every
jetzt now
die **Jugendherberge, -n** youth hostel
der **Juli** July
der **Junge, -n** boy
der **Juni** June

K

das **Kabelfernsehen** cable television
der **Kabeljau** cod
der **Kaffee** coffee
das **Kaffeetrinken** coffee break
der **Kalender, -** calendar
die **Kamera, -s** camera

die **Kammer, -n** house, chamber (parliament)
der **Kanadier, -** Canadian (male)
die **Kanadierin, -nen** Canadian (female)
kantonal canton (adj)
die **Karotte, -n** carrot
das **Kartoffelpüree** mashed potatoes
die **Kassette, -n** cassette
katholisch Catholic
kaufen to buy
das **Kaufhaus, -er** department store
der **Kaufmann, -leute** business man
der **Käse** cheese
die **Kasse, -n** cash desk
kaum hardly
die **Kegelbahn, -en** skittle alley
kein, keine no
kennen* to know
kennenlernen (sep) to get to know, to meet
der **Kilometer, -** kilometre
das **Kind, -er** child
die **Kinderbekleidung** children's wear
das **Kino, -s** cinema
die **Kirche, -n** church
die **Kirmes, -sen** fair, funfair
klar obvious
die **Klasse, -n** class
das **Kleid, -er** dress
die **Kleidung** clothing
klein small
das **Kleingeld** loose change
knackig crisp
knapp just under
die **Kneipe, -n** pub
der **Knopf, -e** button
der **Koch, -e** cook
kochen to cook
der **Kofferraum, -e** boot (of car)
der **Kollege, -n** colleague (male)
die **Kollegin, -nen** colleague (female)
der **Komfort** comfort
komfortabel comfortable
kommen* to come
die **Konferenz, -en** conference
die **Kongreßstadt, -e** town where conferences are held
die **Konkurrenz** competition, competitors
konkurrenzfähig competitive
der **Konkurrenzkampf, -e** competition
können* to be able to
die **Konsumgüter** (pl) consumer goods
das **Konto, -s** account
kontrollieren to check
der **Kopf, -e** head
die **Kopfhörer** (pl) headphones
der **Kopfsalat, -e** lettuce
Kopfschmerzen (pl) headache
der **Körper, -** body
kosten to cost
die **Kosten** (pl) costs
der **Kostenvoranschlag, -e** quotation
der **Kraftfahrer, -** motorist, driver
der **Kraftfahrzeugbrief, -e** motor vehicle papers, log book
krank ill
der **Krankenschein, -e** medical insurance record card
das **Krankenhaus, -er** hospital

die **Krankheit, -en** illness
der **Kreisverkehr** roundabout
die **Kreuzung, -en** crossroads
kriegen to get
die **Küche, -n** kitchen
der **Kuchen, -** cake
der **Kunde, -n** customer
die **Kundendatei** customer data-bank
der **Kundendienst** customer service
die **Kundendienststelle, -n** customer service base
die **Kundschaft, -en** customers
kunstvoll artistic(ally)
der **Kurs, -e** exchange rate
kurzfristig at short notice
die **Kurzwaren** (pl) haberdashery

L

die **Ladenkette, -n** chainstore
die **Ladenöffnungszeit, -en** shopping hours
die **Lage, -n** situation
der **Lagerverwalter, -** warehouse manager, supervisor
das **Land, -er** country, province, state
auf dem Land in the country, in farming
die **Landkarte, -n** map
der **Landtag, -e** provincial assembly
der **Landeshauptmann, -er** head of government of a province
lang long
die **Länge, -n** length
langsam slow(ly)
langweilen, sich to be bored
laufen* to run
laufend constantly
leben to live
das **Leben, -** life
lebendig lively
der **Lebenslauf, -e** curriculum vitae
das **Lebensmittelgeschäft, -e** food shop
die **Lebensmittel** (pl) foodstuffs, provisions
der **Lebensmittelautomat, -en** food dispenser
ledig single, unmarried
leger casual
der **Lehrer, -** teacher
der **Lehrling, -e** apprentice
das **Lehrmaterial, -ien** teaching material
leider unfortunately
leisten to achieve
einen Beitrag leisten to make a contribution
leisten, sich to afford
leiten to manage
die **Leitzone, -n** main postal area
lernen to learn
die **Leute** (pl) people
das **Licht, -er** light
das **Lichtbild, -er** photograph
lieb welcome (literally 'dear')
lieber rather
am liebsten preferably, like (doing) best
die **Liebe** love
liefern to deliver
die **Lieferung, -en** delivery
der **Lieferverzug, -e** delay in delivery
liegen* to be situated, to lie

die **Liegewiese, -n** area of grass for sunbathing
das **Lineal, -e** ruler
links on the left, to the left
der **Linksverkehr** traffic on the left
der **Liter, -** litre
der **Lkw-Fahrer, -** lorry driver
der **Löffel, -** spoon
der **Lohn, -e** wage
lokal local
lösen to buy (a ticket)
der **Luftdruck, -e** pressure (in tyres)
Lust haben to want to
Luxemburg Luxembourg
das **Luxushotel, -s** luxury hotel

M

machen to do, to make,
Magenschmerzen (pl) stomach-ache
das **Magenweh** stomach-ache
mager lean
die **Mahlzeit, -en** meal
Mahlzeit! have a good lunch-hour, *bon appétit*
der **Mai** May
das **Mal, -e** time
man one
manchmal sometimes
der **Mangel, -** fault
der **Mann, -er** husband, man
die **Mark, -stücke** mark (currency)
das **Markenheftchen, -** book of stamps
der **Markt, -e** market
der **Marktanteil, -e** market share
die **Marktforschung** market research
die **Marktlücke, -n** gap in the market
der **Marktplatz, -e** market-place
die **Marmelade** jam
der **März** March
die **Maschine, -n** machine, machinery
die **Materialkosten** (pl) materials costs
der **Matjeshering, -e** salted herring
maximal maximum
das **Meer, -e** sea
mehr more
mehrere several
die **Mehrwertsteuer** (MwSt.) value added tax
die **Meile, -n** mile
mein my
meinen to think, have an opinion
die **Meinung, -en** opinion
meist most
meistens mostly
der **Mensch, -en** person
merken to see, to notice
die **Messe, -n** trade fair
das **Messegelände, -** trade fair complex
das **Messer, -** knife
der **Messestand, -e** trade fair stand
die **Metzgerei, -en** butcher's
der **Mietwagen, -** hire car
mild mild, slight(ly)
die **Million, -en** million
das **Mindestalter, -** minimum age
das **Mineralwasser** mineral water
die **Minute, -n** minute
die **Mischung, -en** mixture
das **Mißverständnis, -se** misunderstanding
mit (+ dat) with

der **Mitarbeiter**, - work colleague, employee
mitbringen* (sep) to bring
mitkommen* (sep) to come along
mitnehmen* (sep) to take
das **Mittagessen**, - midday meal
mittags at midday
mittelgroß medium sized
das **Mittelmeer** Mediterranean
mitten in (+ acc/dat) in the middle of
modern modern
die **Möbel** (pl) furniture
die **Mode**, -n fashion
das **Modehaus**, ¨er fashion house
mögen* to like, to want to
die **Möglichkeit**, -en possibility
möglichst if possible
der **Moment**, -e moment
der **Monat**, -e month
monatlich monthly
die **Montage**, -n assembly
das **Motiv**, -e motif, picture
müde tired
der **Mund**, ¨er mouth
die **Münze**, -n coin
der **Münzeinwurf** slot
der **Münzwechsler**, - change machine (money)
das **Museum, Museen** museum
die **Musikabteilung**, -en music department
müssen* to have to
das **Muster**, - sample

N

nach (+ dat) to, after
das **Nachbarland**, ¨er neighbouring country
nachdem after
die **Nachforschung**, -en enquiry
die **Nachfrage**, -n demand
nachfüllen (sep) to top up
nachher afterwards
nachlassen (sep) to abate
der **Nachmittag**, -e afternoon
die **Nachnahme** cash on delivery
die **Nachricht**, -en news
nachsehen* (sep) to check
die **Nachspeise**, -n dessert
nächster/e/es next
die **Nacht**, ¨e night
der **Nachtisch**, e dessert
nachts at night
die **Nähe** vicinity
in der Nähe near here
die **Nahrung** food
der **Name**, -n name
die **Nase**, -n nose
der **Nationalfeiertag**, -e national public holiday
der **Nationalrat** lower chamber (parliament)
natürlich naturally
neben (+ acc/dat) next to, besides
nehmen* to have, to take
der **Nerv**, -en nerve
das **Nettoeinkommen**, - net income
neu new, fresh
das **Neujahr** New Year
neulich recently
neun nine
nicht mehr no longer

nichts nothing
nicht wahr? isn't it? won't they? etc.
nie never
niedrig low
noch even, still
noch etwas? anything else?
nochmals again
noch nie not yet, never before
Nordamerika North America
der **Norden** the north
das **Normal(benzin)** two-star petrol
normalerweise normally
nötig necessary
der **Notruf**, -e emergency telephone number
der **November** November
nützlich useful

O

ob whether
oben upstairs, on top
der **Ober**, - waiter
oberhalb (+ gen) above
obgleich, obwohl although
der **Obstsalat**, -e fruit salad
die **Ochsenschwanzsuppe**, -n oxtail soup
oder or
ofenfrisch oven-fresh
offen by the glass, open
öffentlich public
öffentliche Verkehrsmittel public transport
offerieren to offer
die **Offerte**, -n offer
offiziell official
öffnen to open
die **Öffnungszeit**, -en opening time
die **Ohrenschmerzen** (pl) earache
oft often
das **Ohr**, -en ear
das **Öl**, -e oil
der **Ölstand** oil level
der **Oktober** October
der **Onkel**, - uncle
die **Oper**, -n opera
der **Orangensaft**, ¨e orange juice
örtlich local
der **Osten** the east
das **Ostern** Easter
Österreich Austria
der **Österreicher**, - Austrian (male)
die **Österreicherin**, -nen Austrian (female)
die **Ostsee** Baltic Sea

P

paar few
ein paar ... a few
ein Paar ... a pair
ein paarmal a few times
die **Packung**, -en packet
pädagogisch educational
das **Paket**, -e parcel
die **Panne**, -n breakdown
die **Pannenhilfe** breakdown assistance
das **Papier**, -e paper, documents
das **Parfüm**, -s perfume
die **Parfümerie**, -n perfumery
parken to park
die **Parkgebühr**, -en parking fee

das **Parkhaus**, ¨er multistorey car park
der **Parkplatz**, ¨e car park
das **Parkverbot** 'no parking'
der **Paß, Pässe** passport
das **Passagierschiff**, -e passenger ship, boat
passen to fit
passieren to happen
das **Pauschalangebot**, -e package deal
die **Person**, -en person
das **Personal** staff
der **Personalausweis**, -e identity card
der **Personalchef**, -s head of personnel
persönlich personal
der **Pfannkuchen**, - pancake
das **Pfeffersteak**, -s spicy steak
das **Pfingsten** Whitsuntide
der **Pfirsich**, -e peach
der **Pförtner**, - porter
das **Pfund** pound (sterling)
pharmazeutisch pharmaceutical
das **Pilsener**, - lager
die **Pkw-Unterstellung** accommodation for private cars
das **Plastikgeld**, -er plastic money
der **Po**, -s bottom
die **Polizeiwache**, -n police station
die **Pommes frites** (pl) chips
das **Porto**, -s postage, postal charge
Portugal Portugal
das **Porzellan**, -e porcelain
die **Post** post, post office
das **Postamt**, ¨er post office
der **Postler**, - post office worker (male)
die **Postlerin**, -nen post office worker (female)
die **Postleitzahl**, -en postal code
das **Postwertzeichen**, - postage stamp
das **Prachtexemplar**, -e fine specimen, beauty
der **Preis**, -e price
prima superb
das **Privatzimmer**, - rented room in private house
pro per
die **Probiermöglichkeit**, -en opportunity to sample
das **Produkt**, -e product
die **Produktion** production, manufactured goods
die **Produktionsanlage**, -n production plant
der **Produktionsleiter**, - production manager
die **Produktliteratur** product literature
das **Programm**, -e programme
das **Programmheft**, -e programme booklet
der **Programmierer**, - computer programmer
das **Prozent** per cent
der **Pudding**, -s blancmange
putzen to clean
der **Pullover**, - (Pulli, -s) pullover
der **Punkt**, -e point

Q

der **Quadratkilometer**, - square kilometre
die **Qualität**, -en quality

die **Qualitätsgarantie, -n** quality assurance
die **Quittung, -en** receipt

R
der **Rabatt, -e** regular discount
das **Radio, -s** radio
der **Radiowecker, -** radio alarm clock
rasch quick, speedy
die **Räumlichkeit, -en** capacity, space, premises
die **Rechnung, -en** bill
die **Rechnungsnummer, -n** invoice number
recht haben to be right, correct
rechts on the right
rechtzeitig punctually
der **Redakteur, -** editor
in der Regel in general, as a rule
regelmäßig regular
reichen to hand, pass
die **Reihenfolge, -n** order
der **Reifendruck, ⁻e** tyre pressure
der **Reis** rice
das **Reisebüro, -s** travel agent
die **Reiseländer** (pl) tourist countries
die **Reisende, -n** traveller
der **Reisepaß, -pässe** passport
der **Reisescheck, -s** traveller's cheque
die **Reklamation, -en** complaint
die **Reklame, -n** advertisement
relativ relatively
die **Religion, -en** religion
religiös religious
reparieren to repair
der **Reservekanister, -** spare can
reservieren to reserve
das **Restaurant, -s** restaurant
restlich remaining
das **Rezept, -e** prescription
rheinisch Rhenish
richtig correct, that's right, really
die **Richtung, -en** direction
das **Rindfleisch** beef
die **Rolle, -n** role, part
die **Rolltreppe, -n** escalator
das **Romanisch** Romansch
die **Römerstadt, ⁻e** Roman town
rostfrei stainless
die **Röstkartoffel, -n** roast/fried potato
rot red
der **Rotkohl** red cabbage
der **Rotwein, -e** red wine
der **Rücken, -** back
die **Rückkehr** return
rufen* to call
die **Rufnummer, -n** telephone number
der **Ruhetag, -e** closed (literally 'day of rest'), day off
ruhig quiet, calm, easily
das **Ruhrgebiet** Ruhr area
rund approximately
die **Rundreise, -n** round trip

S
saftig succulent
der **Salat, -e** salad
die **Salzkartoffel, -n** boiled potato
samstags on Saturdays
satt full, satisfied

der **Sauerbraten** stewed pickled beef
die **S-Bahn** local train
schaffen to manage
die **Schallplatte, -n** record
der **Schalter, -** counter
scharf hot, spiced
schauen to look
die **Scheibe, -n** slice
der **Schein, -e** note (money)
der **Schellfisch, -e** haddock
die **Schere, -n** scissors
der **Scherz, -e** joke
schicken to send
das **Schieferdach, ⁻er** slate roof
schiefgehen* (sep) to go wrong
das **Schifahren** skiing
das **Schiff, -e** ship
die **Schiffstour, -en** boat trip
der **Schinken, -** ham
der **Schinkenspeck** bacon
der **Schlaf** sleep
schlafen* to sleep
schlecht bad
schließen* to close
schmal narrow
schmecken (+ dative) to taste
der **Schmerz, -en** pain
das **Schmerzmittel, -** pain-killer
die **Schneidwaren** (pl) cutting implements
schnell quickly
das **Schnitzel, -** cutlet
der **Schnupfen** cold, sniffle
die **Schmucksachen** (pl) jewellery
das **Schneidegerät, -e** cutting implement
schon already
schön good, nice, pleasant, beautiful
die **Schönheit** beauty
schreiben* to write
die **Schreibwaren** (pl) stationery
schriftlich in writing
der **Schuh, -e** shoe
die **Schule, -n** school
schwärmen to be enthusiastic
schwarz black
das **Schweinefleisch** pork
das **Schweineschnitzel, -** pork cutlet
die **Schweiz** Switzerland
der **Schweizer, -** Swiss (male)
die **Schweizerin, -nen** Swiss (female)
schweizerisch Swiss
schwer difficult, heavy
die **Schwerindustrie, -n** heavy industry
der **Schwermaschinenbau** heavy engineering
das **Schwert, -er** sword
das **Schwimmbad, ⁻er** swimming pool
sechs six
sehen* to see
die **Sehenswürdigkeit, -en** sights, places of interest
die **Seife** soap
sein* to be
seit (+ dat) since
seitdem since then
die **Seite, -n** side, page
die **Sekretärin, -nen** secretary
selber, selbst myself, yourself etc.
die **Selbstbedienung** self-service
selbstverständlich of course

die **Sendung, -en** consignment
die **Serie, -n** series
Service inbegriffen service included
setzen, sich to sit down
sicher of course, certainly
Sie you
sie she, it, they
das **Silber** silver
das **Silvester** New Year
sinken* to sink
die **Sitznische, -n** corner seats
die **Sitzung, -en** conference, meeting
der **Sitzungsraum, ⁻e** meeting room
der, das **Skonto, Skonti** cash discount
Slowenien Slovenia
so so
sofort straight away
sogar even
sogenannt so-called
der **Sohn, ⁻e** son
sollen to be (supposed) to
soll ich? should I?
der **Sommer** summer
das **Sonderangebot, -e** special offer
sonst otherwise, apart from that
sonstig other
die **Sorge, -n** worry
die **Sorte, -n** sort
die **Sortieranlage, -n** sorting equipment
sortieren to sort
das **Sortiment, -s** range
die **Sozialversicherung** equivalent of National Insurance contributions
das **Sparbuch, ⁻er** savings book
spät late
spazierengehen* (sep) to go for a walk
der **Spaziergang, ⁻e** walk
die **Spedition, -en** haulage contractor, removal firm
speichern to store
die **Speisekarte, -n** menu
die **Spezialität, -en** speciality
spielen to play
das **Spielzeug** toy
die **Spielwaren** (pl) toys
die **Spirituosen** (pl) spirits
die **Spitze, -n** top, head
der **Sportartikel, -** sports item
der **Sportplatz, ⁻e** sportsground
die **Sprache, -n** language
der **Sprachraum, ⁻e** area where a language is spoken
sprechen* to speak
die **Sprechstundenhilfe, -n** doctor's receptionist
sprühen to spray
der **Staat, -en** state
die **Staatsangehörigkeit, -en** nationality
das **Stadion, Stadien** stadium
die **Stadt, ⁻e** town, city
der **Stadtbereich, -e** the town area
die **Stadtbesichtigung, -en** tour of a town
die **Stadtmitte, -n** town centre
der **Stadtplan, ⁻e** town map
der **Stadtrand, ⁻er** outskirts
die **Stadtrundfahrt, -en** tour of the city

das Stadtviertel, - part of town
das Stadtzentrum, -zentren town centre
der Stahl, -̈e steel
ständig continuously
stattfinden* (sep) to take place
stehen* to stand
die Stelle, -n job, place
stempeln to stamp
die Stenotypistin, -nen shorthand typist
der Stern, -e star
die Steuer, -n tax
die Stichprobe, -n random check
stimmen to be right
der Stock, -werke storey, floor
stören to bother, disturb, interrupt
die Störung, -en interruption
die Stoßzeit, -en rush hour
die Straße, -n street
die Straßenbahnhaltestelle, -n tram stop
der Straßenkünstler, - street artist
der Straßenzustand, -̈e road conditions
der Strauß, -̈e bouquet
streichen* to delete
der Stromanschluß, -schlüsse mains electricity connection
das Stück, -e each, piece, play
der Student, -en student (male)
die Studentin, -nen student (female)
studieren to study
die Stunde, -n hour
suchen to look for
Südafrika South Africa
der Süden the south
südlich (+ gen) to the south
die Summe, -n sum
das Super(benzin) four-star petrol
die Suppe, -n soup
süß sweet
die Süßigkeit, -en sweets
das Symbol, -e symbol

T
die Tabelle, -n (statistical) table
die Tablette, -n pill
der Tafelapfel, -̈ eating apple
der Tag, -e day
am Tag during the day
die Tagesordnung, -en programme for the day
die Tagung, -en conference (few days long)
der Tagungsraum -̈e conference room
tanken to refuel
die Tankstelle, -n petrol station
der Tankwagen, - petrol lorry
der Tankwart, -e petrol pump attendant
das Taschenbuch, -̈er paperback
die Tasse, -n cup
die Tastatur, -en set of push-buttons
die Taste, -n push-button, key
die Tastennummer, -n number of push-button, key
die Tastenreihe, -n row of push buttons, keys
der Taxichauffeur, -e taxi driver
der Taxifahrer, - taxi driver
der Taxi-Ruf number for calling a taxi
der Tee tea

das Teil, -e part, component
der Teil, -e part
die Teillieferung, -en part delivery
teilweise partially
das Telefon, -e telephone
das Telefonat, -e telephone call
das Telefonbuch, -̈er telephone directory
telefonieren (mit + dat) to phone
die Telefonistin, -nen telephonist
die Telefonnummer, -n telephone number
der Telexdienst telex service
die Telexnummer, -n telex number
der Termin, -e appointment
teuer expensive
die Textilien (pl) textiles
die Textilindustrie, -n textile industry
das Theater, - theatre
tiefgekühlt frozen
der Tierfreund, -e animal lover
tippen to type
der Tisch, -e table
das Tischtennis table tennis
der Toast toast
die Tochter, -̈ daughter
die Toilette, -n toilet
die Tomate, -n tomato
die Torte, -n tart, flan
touristisch tourist (adj)
tragen* to take, to carry
trampen to hitchhike
treffen* to meet
die Treppe, -n stairs
das T-Shirt, -s T-shirt
tun* to make, to do
das TÜV (Technischer Überwachungsverein) Zeichen TÜV symbol
typisch typical

U
die U-Bahn underground train
über (+ acc/dat) via, about, over
über Nacht overnight
überall everywhere
übereinstimmen (sep) mit (+ dat) to agree with
übernachten to stay, to spend the night
die Übernachtung, -en overnight stay
der Übernachtungspreis, -e price per night
überprüfen (insep) to check over, to examine
der Übersetzungsdienst, -e translation service
die Überstunde, -n overtime
üblich usual
übrig left over, remaining
übrigens moreover
die Übung, -en practice, exercise
die Uhr, -en clock
die Uhrzeit, -en time
um (+ acc) at, around
die Umrechnungstabelle, -n conversion table
der Umsatz, -̈e turnover
das Umschulungszentrum, -zentren re-training centre
umsteigen* (sep) to change (trains)
der Umtausch exchanged goods, customer services

die Umgebung, -en surrounding region, area
umwechseln (sep) to change (money)
unbedingt certainly
und and
der Unfall, -̈e accident
ungefähr approximately
die Unkosten (pl) expenses
unser our
die Unterhaltung entertainment
die Unterhaltungsmusik light, background music
die Unterkunft, -̈e accommodation
die Unterlage, -n paper, document
das Unternehmen, - firm
unterschreiben* to sign
unterstreichen* (insep) to underline
unterwegs out on a journey
unterzeichnen (insep) to sign
unverheiratet single, unmarried
der Urlaub, -e holiday
usw. (und so weiter) etc.

V
das VDE (Verband Deutscher Elektrotechniker) Zeichen VDE symbol
verabschieden, sich to say good-bye
verantwortlich (für + acc) responsible (for)
verärgert annoyed
verbinden* to connect
die Verbindung, -en connection
verboten prohibited
verbrauchen to consume, to use
verbringen* to spend (time)
verdienen to earn
das Vereinigte Königreich United Kingdom
die Vereinigten Staaten United States
vergleichen* to compare
das Vergnügen, - pleasure
verheiratet married
verkaufen to sell
die Verkaufsbedingung, -en sales conditions
der Verkaufsleiter, - sales manager
der Verkehr traffic
die Verkehrsampel traffic lights
verkehrsgünstig easily accessible
das Verkehrsnetz, -e traffic network
der Verkehrsverein, -e tourist office
das Verlagswesen, - publishing
verlängern to extend
verlegen to postpone
verletzt injured
verlieben, sich (in + acc) to fall in love with
verlieren* to lose
der Verlust, -e loss
der Versand dispatch
versäumen to miss
verschieden various
verschiffen to ship
der Verschluß, -̈sse lock
die Versicherungskarte, -n insurance document
verstehen* to understand

verstopft blocked
versuchen to try
verteilen to distribute
der **Vertrag, ⁻e** contract
vertreten* to represent
der **Vertreter, -** representative
der **Vertrieb, -e** distribution
die **Verwaltung, -en** administration
der, die **Verwandte, -n** relative
verzollen to declare (for customs)
viele many
vielen Dank many thanks
vielleicht perhaps
vielleicht doch perhaps I will after all
vielmals very much (literally many times)
vier four
voll full
vollautomatisch fully automatic
die **Vollpension** full-board
vollständig complete
volltanken (sep) to fill up (with petrol)
von (+ dat) from, of
vor (+ acc/dat) before, ago
der **Vorbehalt, -e** reservation
die **Vorfahrt** right of way
vorgestern the day before yesterday
vorhanden available
vorher beforehand
vorläufig provisionally
der **Vorname, -n** first, Christian name
vorne over there, in front
vorrätig in stock
der **Vorschlag, ⁻e** suggestion
vorschlagen* (sep) to suggest
die **Vorspeise, -n** hors-d'oeuvre
vorwärts forwards
vorziehen* (sep) to prefer

W
der **Wagen, -** car
wählen to choose, to make a choice, to elect
wahr true (see 'nicht wahr')
während (+ gen) during
die **Währung, -en** currency
der **Waliser, -** Welshman
die **Waliserin, -nen** Welsh woman
walisisch Welsh
wann? when?
warm warm
die **Wärmeregulierung** temperature regulation
die **Wartung** servicing
warum? why?
was that, which, what
waschen* to wash
das **Wasser** water
die **Wasserleitung, -en** mains water connection
wechseln to give change, to exchange (money), to change
die **Wechselstube, -n** bureau de change
weg away
wehtun* (sep) to hurt
die **Weihnachten** (pl) Christmas

zweiter Weihnachtstag Boxing Day
weil because
der **Wein, -e** wine
weiß white
der **Weißwein, -e** white wine
weit far
weiter further
weiterfahren* (sep) to continue (by transport)
weitergehen* (sep) to continue (on foot)
weiterzahlen (sep) to continue paying
welcher/e/es? which?
weltbekannt world-famous
wenige a few
weniger less
wenn if
die **Werbekampagne, -n** advertising campaign
das **Werbematerial, -ien** advertising material
die **Werbeschrift, -en** publicity leaflet
der **Werbespot, -s** commercial
der **Werbespruch, ⁻e** advertising slogan
die **Werbung** advertising
werden* to become
die **Werkstatt, ⁻e** garage (for repairing cars), workshop
das **Werkzeug, -e** tool
der **Wert, -e** value
der **Westen** the west
der **Wettbewerb, -e** competition
die **Wette, -n** bet
das **Wetter** weather
der **Wetterbericht, -e** weather report
wichtig important
wie how, as
wieder again
Auf Wiederhören goodbye (on the telephone)
Auf Wiedersehen goodbye
die **Wiedervereinigung** reunification
wiegen* to weigh
das **Wiener Schnitzel** Wiener Schnitzel
wieviel? how much?
wie viele? how many?
das **Wild** game, venison
Willkommen in welcome to
wirklich really
die **Wirtschaft, -en** economy
wissen* to know
wo? where?
die **Woche, -n** week
das **Wochenende, -n** weekend
der **Wochenmarkt, ⁻e** weekly market
wohin? where to?
wohlfühlen, sich (sep) to feel at ease
die **Wohnungsmiete, -n** housing rent
wollen* to want
wunderschön beautiful
der **Wunsch, ⁻e** wish
wünschen to wish
die **Wurst, ⁻e** sausage

Z
zahlen to pay

zählen to count, to include
zahlreich numerous
die **Zahlung, -en** payment
die **Zahlungsmethode, -n** method of payment
die **Zahnpasta, -, Zahnpaste, -n** toothpaste
die **Zahnschmerzen** (pl) toothache
zehn ten
die **Zeichnung, -en** drawing
zeigen to show
die **Zeit, -en** time
die **Zeitschrift, -en** magazine
die **Zeitung, -en** newspaper
das **Zelt, -e** tent
zelten to camp
der **Zentimeter, -** centimetre
die **Zentrale, -n** head office
die **Zentralheizung, -en** central heating
das **Zentrum, Zentren** centre
das **Zeugnis, -se** certificate
das **Ziel, -e** destination
der **Zielbahnhof, ⁻e** destination
ziemlich rather
die **Zigarette, -n** cigarette
das **Zimmer, -** room
der **Zimmernachweis, -e** list of hotels
die **Zimmervermittlung, -en** accommodation bureau
zirka about, approximately
die **Zitrone, -n** lemon
der **Zitronentee** lemon tea
die **Zollauskünfte** (pl) customs information
der **Zollbeamte, -n** customs official
die **Zone, -n** zone, region
zu too, (+ dat) to, at
das **Zubehör, -** accessories
zuerst first of all
die **Zufahrt, -en** access
der **Zufall, ⁻e** coincidence
zufrieden satisfied, happy
zufriedenstellen (sep) to satisfy
der **Zug, ⁻e** train
zuliefern (sep) to supply
zumachen (sep) to close
zunehmend increasingly
zurück back
zurückrufen* (sep) to call back
zurückweisen* (sep) to refuse something
zusammen together
die **Zusammenarbeit, -en** collaboration
zusammenbauen (sep) to assemble
zusätzlich additional
das **Zusatzmaterial, -ien** additional material
zuschicken (sep) to send to
zustimmen (sep) to agree
zwei two
der **Zweigbetrieb, -e** branch (factory or works)
die **Zweigstelle, -n** branch office
der, die, das **zweite** second
die **Zwiebel, -n** onion
zwischen (+ acc/dat) between
zwölf twelve

Unit key

Note: Alternatives are shown in brackets.

UNIT 1

Dialogue 1: **Hello**

Translation

Herr Müller	Hello. Hans Müller from Munich.
Frau Roth	Hello Mr Müller, pleased to meet you. My name is Helga Roth.
Herr Müller	Pleased to meet you too.

Exercise 1

1 *You* Guten Tag Herr Müller, freut mich. Mein Name ist ... (your name).
2 *You* Guten Tag, ... (your name). *You* Freut mich auch.

Dialogue 2: **How are you?**

Translation

Mr Lloyd	Come in!
Receptionist	Mr Lloyd, the visitor from Germany is here.
Mr Lloyd	Oh hello Mrs Kahn. Please come in.
Frau Kahn	Hello Mr Lloyd. How are you?
Mr Lloyd	Well, thank you and how are you?
Frau Kahn	I am well too, thank you.
Mr Lloyd	Would you like a cup of tea or coffee?
Frau Kahn	Yes please, coffee with milk and without sugar.
Mr Lloyd	Mrs Brown, two cups of coffee please.

Exercise 2

You Danke, gut. Und Ihnen? *You* Ja bitte. *You* Ja, ohne Zucker bitte.

Comprehension 1

Transcript
- Guten Tag, Ewald Weidmann und Lotte Meyer aus Mönchengladbach.
- Guten Tag, Herr Weidmann, guten Tag, Frau Meyer. Mr Newby erwartet Sie. (*Phones Mr Newby*.) Er kommt gleich.
- Danke sehr.
- Guten Tag, Frau Meyer, guten Tag, Herr Weidmann. Mein Name ist Michael Newby. Es freut mich, Sie kennenzulernen.
- Guten Tag, Mr Newby, es freut uns auch.

1 Mönchengladbach **2** yes **3** no **4** yes

Exercise 3

Translation
Good morning. My name is Lotte Meyer and I come from Krefeld. I work at Sasshofer's in Mönchengladbach. I am the chief buyer.
Good evening. My name is Ewald Weidmann. I live in Neuß near Düsseldorf and I am the production manager at Sasshofer's.

Mein *Name* ist Lotte *Meyer* und ich *wohne* in Krefeld. Ich *bin* Einkaufs*leiterin*. Ich trinke *Tee* (*Kaffee*) mit *Milch* (*Zucker*).

Ich *heiße* Ewald *Weidmann*. Ich *komme* aus Deutschland. Ich *arbeite* in Mönchengladbach bei der *Firma* Sasshofer. Ich bin Produktions*leiter*. Ich *trinke* Kaffee *ohne* (*mit*) Zucker.

Exercise 4	**1** Ich heiße nicht Ewald Weidmann. **2** Ich komme nicht aus Deutschland. **3** Ich arbeite nicht bei der Firma Sasshofer. **4** Ich bin nicht Produktionsleiter.

Exercise 5	Telefonistin, Ingenieur, Betriebsingenieurin, Elektroniker, LKW-Fahrerin, Geschäftsführer, Betriebsleiterin, Einkaufsleiter, Verkaufsleiterin, Programmierer, Vertreterin, Dolmetscher, Lagerverwalterin, Chefsekretär, Pförtnerin, Empfangsherr.

Exercise 6

Translation

Herr Müller   Hello, my name is Müller. I'm from Duisburg.

Frau Williams   Hello, my name is Williams. I'm pleased to meet you.

Herr Müller   Are you German?

Frau Williams   No, I'm a Scot(swoman).

Herr Müller   Oh I see, that's interesting. Where do you come from?

Frau Williams   I come from Edinburgh. I'm the export manager at Tartan Textiles. And what do you do for a living?

Herr Müller   I'm the sales manager at Edelmetall in Oberhausen near Duisburg.

1 a) false **b)** true **c)** false **d)** false

2 *You*   Guten Tag, freut mich. Mein Name ist …

  You   (Ich komme) aus …

  You   Ich bin … (*your job*) (von Beruf).

Comprehension 2

Transcript

Christian   Guten Tag, Frau Stein. Herzlich willkommen bei uns in der Firma.

Katrina   Guten Tag, Herr Holzhauser. Vielen Dank für die Einladung.

Christian   Bitte schön. Darf ich Ihnen meine Kollegin vorstellen? Frau Herz von unserer Zweigstelle in Wiesbaden.

Katrina   Guten Tag, Frau Herz, es freut mich, Sie kennenzulernen.

Frau Herz   Guten Tag, Frau Stein, es freut mich auch.

Katrina   Also Sie leiten die Vertretung in Wiesbaden?

Frau Herz   Ja, wir haben dort ein kleines Büro.

Christian   Wir möchten Sie gern etwas besser kennenlernen. Darf ich Ihnen einige Fragen stellen, um diesen Fragebogen hier auszufüllen?

Katrina   Aber natürlich.

Christian   Also gut, beginnen wir ganz am Anfang. Ihr Vorname ist Katrina, nicht wahr?

Katrina   Ja, richtig.

Christian   Nachname, Stein. Wohnen Sie hier in Frankfurt?

Katrina   Nicht direkt, etwas außerhalb, nicht sehr weit von hier, in Bad Homburg.

Christian   Kommen Sie ursprünglich aus Hessen?

Katrina   Meine Eltern kommen nicht aus Deutschland, aber seit ich verheiratet bin, wohne ich hier.

Christian   Und Sie arbeiten bei Spieltechnik GmbH hier in Frankfurt. Was sind Sie von Beruf?

Katrina   Ja, meine Stelle … ich bin Auslandsvertreterin, ich bin für die Betreuung unserer Kunden im Ausland verantwortlich.

Christian   Also Sie reisen sehr viel?

Katrina   Das kann man schon sagen. Wir haben auch oft Besuch, aus dem mitteleuropäischen Raum, aber auch aus dem Norden, Skandinavien, aus England, von überall her.

Christian Das klingt interessant.

Translation

Christian Hello, Frau Stein. Welcome to our company.

Katrina Hello, Herr Holzhauser. Thank you for the invitation.

Christian My pleasure. May I introduce you to my colleague? Frau Herz, from our Wiesbaden branch.

Katrina Hello, Frau Herz. I'm very pleased to meet you.

Frau Herz Hello, Frau Stein. It's a pleasure for me too.

Katrina So you run the office in Wiesbaden?

Frau Herz Yes, we have a small office there.

Christian We would like to get to know you better. May I ask you a few questions, in order to fill in this questionnaire?

Katrina But of course.

Christian Alright then. Let's begin right at the beginning. Your forename is Katrina, isn't it?

Katrina Yes, that's right.

Christian Surname – Stein. Do you live here in Frankfurt?

Katrina Not quite. A little outside, not very far from here, in Bad Homburg.

Christian Do you come from Hessen originally?

Katrina My parents aren't from Germany, but I've lived here since I got married.

Christian And you work for Spieltechnik GmbH here in Frankfurt. What's your occupation?

Katrina Oh yes, my job … I represent the company abroad. I'm responsible for looking after our customers abroad.

Christian So you travel a lot?

Katrina You could say that. We often have visitors too, from Central Europe, but also from the North – Scandinavia, from England – from everywhere.

Christian That sounds very interesting.

1 She runs the Wiesbaden office.

2 From central Europe, the North – Scandinavia, from England, from everywhere.

Exercise 7	Stein ● Bad Homburg ● Auslandsvertreterin ● Spieltechnik

Puzzle   **1** willkommen **2** Kunden **3** Besuch **4** leiten **5** Ausland

Progress check

1
a) Guten Tag, guten Morgen, guten Abend.
b) Freut mich. (Es freut mich, Sie kennenzulernen.)
c) Wie geht es Ihnen?
d) Danke, gut.
e) Ich trinke Tee mit Milch.
f) Mein Name ist … Ich heiße …
g) Ich komme aus …
h) Ich bin Verkaufsleiter(in).
i) Ich wohne nicht in Hamburg.

2
a) I am expecting you.
b) I do not work at Edelmetall.
c) Where do you come from?
d) What do you do for a living?
e) I am responsible for general management.
f) Please fill in this questionnaire.

UNIT 2

Dialogue 1:   At the conference

Translation

Delegate A Do you speak German?

Delegate B Yes, I come from Austria. What about you?

Delegate A I'm German and my colleague here is Swiss.

Delegate B   That's inte.esting. I have a Swiss colleague as well. She speaks German, French and Italian and is also learning English with the company. But she isn't here in London.

<table>
<tr><td>Exercise 1</td><td>1 Nein, Britin. 2 Nein, Australier. 3 Nein, Französin. 4 Nein, Österreicher. 5 Nein, Schweizerin. 6 Nein, Kanadier.</td></tr>
</table>

<table>
<tr><td>Exercise 3</td><td>Belgien • Frankreich • Griechenland • Irland • Italien • Österreich • die Schweiz • Spanien</td></tr>
</table>

Dialogue 2: At Anglia Chemicals 2

Translation

David Jones   Hello. I'm pleased to meet you. Are you in England for the first time?

Frau Meyer   Yes, I'm here for the first time but Mr Weidmann often comes to England.

David Jones   I wish you a good stay.

Ewald Weidmann   You speak German very well. Are you learning it here at Anglia Chemicals?

David Jones   No, my wife is German. She comes from Dortmund. We speak German at home.

Frau Meyer   Excuse me, are you perhaps Welsh? Your name is Welsh isn't it?

David Jones   Yes, that's right, but I myself am English.

<table>
<tr><td>Exercise 4</td><td>
Sie Sind Sie Deutscher?
Sie Woher kommen Sie?
Sie Was sind Sie von Beruf?
Sie Sind Sie zum ersten Mal in England?
Sie Ich wünsche Ihnen einen guten Aufenthalt.
</td></tr>
</table>

Comprehension 1

Transcript

Richard Hill   Guten Tag, ich heiße Richard Hill.

Wilhelm Jaeger   Guten Tag, Wilhelm Jaeger aus Hamburg. Woher kommen Sie?

Richard Hill   Ich bin Engländer. Ich wohne in Luton, aber ich arbeite in London.

Wilhelm Jaeger   Bei welcher Firma sind Sie?

Richard Hill   Ich bin Verkaufsleiter bei der Firma Stonecraft. Und Sie?

Wilhelm Jaeger   Ich bin Geschäftsführer der Firma Alsterwerk. Sind Sie zum ersten Mal in Deutschland?

Richard Hill   Nein, ich komme sehr oft nach Deutschland.

Wilhelm Jaeger   Das glaube ich. Sie sprechen nämlich sehr gut Deutsch.

Richard Hill   Danke schön.

1 in Luton 2 in London, at 'Stonecraft' 3 sales manager
4 business manager at 'Alsterwerk' 5 he goes to Germany often

Comprehension 2

Transcript

Katrina   Was für eine gute Idee, die Konferenz in Leipzig abzuhalten. Ich bin zum ersten Mal hier. Es ist sehr schön hier. Was meinen Sie?

Christian   Mir gefällt die internationale Atmosphäre. Schön, daß so viele Teilnehmer aus den osteuropäischen Ländern da sind. Der Übersetzungsdienst ist sehr gut. Es gibt drei Sprachen – Deutsch, Englisch und Französisch.

Katrina   Sehr nützlich, aber ich hatte ein kleines Problem mit den Kopfhörern. Es war viel zu laut, und der Knopf war kaputt, wo man die Lautstärke reguliert.

Christian   Hoffentlich funktioniert es diesmal besser. Der nächste Programmpunkt ist sehr wichtig für uns: eine Diskussion mit dem

Leiter eines englischen Marktforschungsinstituts. Vielleicht verstehen wir das auch ohne Übersetzung. Sie sprechen doch fließend Englisch, nicht wahr?

Katrina Nein, fließend leider nicht, aber es geht. Ich nehme noch Unterricht. „Übung macht den Meister"!

Christian Meine Arbeit bringt mir viel Übung in Englisch. Als Redakteur, im Verlagswesen auf internationaler Ebene, brauche ich Fremdsprachen.

Katrina Das kann ich gut verstehen. Entschuldigen Sie mich bitte, ich komme gleich wieder, ich erwarte ein Telefonat.

Translation

Katrina What a good idea, to hold the conference in Leipzig. It's my first time here. It's very pleasant here – what do you think?

Christian I like the international atmosphere. It's nice that so many participants from the East European countries are here. The translation service is very good. There are three languages – German, English and French.

Katrina Very useful, but I had a little problem with the headphones. They were much too loud, and the button for regulating the volume was broken.

Christian Let's hope it works better this time. The next item on the programme is very important for us: a discussion with the head of an English market research institute. Perhaps we'll understand that even without a translation. You speak fluent English, don't you?

Katrina No, unfortunately not fluently, but I get by. I still have lessons – practice makes perfect!

Christian My work brings me lots of practice in English. As an editor, in publishing at an international level, I need foreign languages.

Katrina I can well understand that. Please excuse me, I'll be back straight away. I'm expecting a phone call.

1 A discussion with the head of an English market research institute.
2 It's not fluent, but she gets by.

Exercise 6

gut ● ist sehr wichtig

Progress check

1 England, Wales, Schottland, Irland.
2 Sind Sie Deutscher, Schweizer oder Franzose?
  Sind Sie Deutsche, Schweizerin oder Französin?
3 Englisch; Deutsch, Französisch, Italienisch, Romanisch.
4 Sind Sie zum ersten Mal in England?
5 Ich wünsche Ihnen einen angenehmen Aufenthalt.

6 Wir sprechen Spanisch zu Hause.
7 Was sind Sie von Beruf?
8 a) plc b) limited company
9 Excuse me, but we do not speak English.
10 a) Market research is very important for us.
   b) The translation service isn't working.

UNIT 3

Exercise 1

1 ist ● verheiratet ● Frau ● Französin ● eine ● Die ● Anneliese
2 Er ● sie ● haben ● Tochter

Exercise 2

Stefan wohnt in Bern und arbeitet als Elektroniker bei der Firma Schmidt AG. Er ist verheiratet. Er hat keine Kinder.

Petra wohnt in Salzburg und ist Sekretärin von Beruf. Sie arbeitet bei der Firma 'Deutsche Textilien GmbH'. Sie ist verheiratet und hat eine Tochter.

Sabine wohnt in Kiel und arbeitet als Geschäftsführerin bei der Firma 'Jung und Sohn GmbH'. Sie ist ledig.

Jürgen wohnt in Mannheim und ist Ingenieur. Er arbeitet bei der Firma 'Schäfer-Autowerke AG'. Er ist verheiratet und hat zwei Söhne.

Comprehension 1

Transcript

Ich heiße Wolfgang Schüßler. Ich bin Student in Berlin und bin noch ledig, also unverheiratet. Ich studiere Architektur, aber ich arbeite auch als Taxifahrer. Meine Mutter und mein Vater wohnen auch in Berlin. Ich wohne also zu Hause.

Mein Name ist Gudrun Schneider. Ich komme aus der Schweiz, aber ich wohne jetzt in Deutschland. Ich bin verheiratet. Mein Mann heißt Karl und ist Deutscher. Wir haben ein Kind. Ich arbeite als Sekretärin bei Nordchemikalien in Hamburg. Die Firma ist französisch. Ich spreche also oft Französisch in der Firma. Ich spreche aber auch Deutsch und lerne Englisch. Mein Mann arbeitet auch bei Nordchemikalien als Vertreter.

1 no 2 yes, as a taxidriver 3 in Berlin, at home with his parents
4 no, he studies architecture 5 no, Swiss 6 German 7 she is a secretary
8 no, she is learning English 9 at 'Nordchemikalien' as a representative

Exercise 4

1 Nein, er studiert Architektur. (Nein, er ist Student und auch Taxifahrer.)
2 Nein, er ist (noch) ledig.
3 Ja, er arbeitet als Taxifahrer.
4 Er wohnt zu Hause, in Berlin.
5 Er heißt Karl.
6 Nein, sie ist Schweizerin.
7 Sie ist Sekretärin (bei der Firma Nordchemikalien).
8 Nein, sie lernt Englisch.

Comprehension 2

Transcript

Christian	Also Ihre Familie kommt aus dem Ausland?
Katrina	Ja, nur mein Mann ist Deutscher. Meine Mutter ist Schweizerin, aus Maloya, bei St. Moritz, in der Nähe von der italienischen Grenze. Und mein Vater ist Italiener.
Christian	Sie haben sich sicher beim Schifahren kennengelernt.
Katrina	Stimmt. Jetzt ist mein Vater schon älter, aber früher hat er jedes Jahr in den Schweizer Alpen Schiurlaub gemacht. Ich fahre selbst auch gern schi, und Sie?
Christian	Ja, es geht. Ich habe Verwandte in Österreich. Sie haben ein Hotel in Tirol, in Lienz, da fahre ich manchmal hin.
Katrina	Ach, was für ein Zufall. Ich habe auch einen Onkel in Linz.
Christian	Nein, nicht Linz, – das ist im Osten. Lienz, L-I-E-N-Z schreibt man das, das liegt in Osttirol. Es ist dort sehr schön.
Katrina	Ach so ... wie lange fährt man da hin?
Christian	Nicht sehr lange ... mit meinem neuen BMW 850 bin ich in vier Stunden dort. Das ist kein Problem für mich.
Katrina	Mein lieber Herr Holzhauser, vier Stunden sind es nach München. So schnell fährt nicht einmal Ihr neuer BMW.
Christian	Meine liebe Frau Stein, das war nur ein Scherz. Es dauert fast doppelt so lang – und mein VW ist schon drei Jahre alt!

Translation

Christian	So your family comes from abroad?
Katrina	Yes only my husband is German. My mother is Swiss, from Maloya, near St. Moritz – near the Italian border. And my father is Italian.
Christian	I'm sure they met each other while skiing.
Katrina	That's right. My father is quite old now, but earlier in life he used to

take a skiing holiday in the Swiss Alps every year. I like skiing myself too. And you?

Christian   Yes, I quite like it. I have relations in Austria. They have a hotel in the Tirol, in Lienz. I sometimes go there.

Katrina   Oh, what a coincidence. I have an uncle in Linz too.

Christian   No, not Linz – that's in the East. Lienz, you spell it L-I-E-N-Z. It's in Eastern Tirol. It's very beautiful there.

Katrina   Really? How long does it take to get there?

Christian   Not very long … in my new BMW 850 I'm there in four hours. That's no problem for me.

Katrina   My dear Herr Holzhauser, it's four hours to Munich. Not even your new BMW goes that fast.

Christian   My dear Frau Stein, that was just a joke. It takes almost twice as long – and my VW is already three years old!

1 They have a hotel in Lienz, Tirol.
2 Eight hours.

| **Exercise 9** | Schweizerin • ist Italiener • Ihr … ist Deutscher |

Puzzle   **1** kennengelernt **2** doppelt **3** stimmt **4** Mutter **5** Zufall **6** schnell

Progress check

1   Ich bin verheiratet/noch ledig.
    Ich habe einen Sohn/eine Tochter (zwei, drei, vier, fünf Söhne/Töchter)/keine Kinder.
2   a) Sind Sie verheiratet? b) Haben Sie Kinder?
3   a) Er ist Schotte und wohnt in Glasgow.
    b) Er ist verheiratet und hat eine Tochter.
    c) Er spricht Französisch und lernt Deutsch.

4   Meine Kollegen sind auch hier in Frankfurt. Sie kommen aus Nordirland und arbeiten bei der Firma *Northern Metal plc* in Bolton bei Manchester.
5   Bitte buchstabieren Sie das.
6   a) I speak a little Italian, but my relatives speak twice as well.
    b) That's no problem, I work near you.

Additional exercises

[1]   **a** sind **b** wohnen **c** kommt **d** arbeitet **e** sprechen **f** lernt **g** bin **h** habe **i** arbeite **j** ist **k** wohnt **l** hat

[2]   **a** der **b** die **c** das **d** die **e** der **f** die **g** der **h** die **i** das

[3]   **a** they **b** you **c** she **d** they **e** she **f** you

[4]   **a** keinen **b** keine **c** keine **d** lernt nicht **e** studiert nicht **f** kommt nicht **g** sprechen nicht

UNIT 4

Comprehension 1   Transcript

1   Wann kommt Herr Schmidt?   Am vierten Mai
2   Wann fliegt Herr Johnson nach Deutschland?   Am neunten Mai
3   Wann besuchen Sie die Firma Sasshofer?   Am zweiten Mai
4   Wann kommen Sie nach Düsseldorf?   Am sechsten Mai
5   Wann fährt Frau Young nach Mönchengladbach?   Am achten Mai
6   Wann kommen Sie zu Besuch?   Am fünften Mai

2 Am neunten Mai **3** Am zweiten Mai **4** Am sechsten Mai **5** Am achten Mai
6 Am fünften Mai

Exercise 1	**1** Sie fliegt am Donnerstag, dem neunten Juni, und möchte fünf Tage bleiben.
	2 Er kommt am Montag, dem ersten Februar, und möchte zwei Tage bleiben.
	3 Sie kommt am Mittwoch, dem sechsten Juli, und möchte eine Woche bleiben.

Exercise 2

1 Vom neunten bis zum vierzehnten Juni.
2 Vom ersten bis zum dritten Februar.
3 Vom sechsten bis zum dreizehnten Juli.

Exercise 3

Transcript
Wann kommen Sie zur Messe?
Am vierten Juli
Am zehnten Mai
Am achten August
Am zwanzigsten März
Am neunundzwanzigsten April
Am siebzehnten Januar
Am dritten Juni
Am zwölften Februar
Am einunddreißigsten Oktober
Am ersten Dezember

4.7. 10.5. 8.8. 20.3. 29.4. 17.1. 3.6. 12.2. 31.10. 1.12.

Exercise 4

1 Tag der Arbeit ist am ersten Mai.
Weihnachten ist am fünfundzwanzigsten Dezember.
Zweiter Weihnachtstag ist am sechsundzwanzigsten Dezember.
Neujahr ist am ersten Januar.
Allerheiligen ist am ersten November.
2 Tag der Arbeit ist im Frühling.
Weihnachten/zweiter Weihnachtstag/Neujahr ist im Winter.
Allerheiligen ist im Herbst.

Comprehension 2

Transcript

Telephonist	Spieltechnik, guten Morgen.
Christian	Holzhauser, Verlag Germania. Guten Morgen. Kann ich bitte Frau Stein in der Exportabteilung sprechen?
Telephonist	Moment bitte, ich verbinde.
Katrina	Stein, guten Tag.
Christian	Guten Morgen Frau Stein, Holzhauser am Apparat. Ich möchte mit Ihnen die Gestaltung der neuen Broschüre für Ihre englischsprachigen Kunden besprechen. Wann hätten Sie Zeit?
Katrina	Diese Woche geht es nicht, ich fliege morgen nach Florenz. Aber nächsten Montag wäre es möglich, am 28.
Christian	Am 28. bin ich leider nicht im Haus. Am 29. fahre ich nach München, zu einer Sitzung am neuen Flughafen. Ich muß bis zum 30. bleiben.
Katrina	Und dann kommt schon der Feiertag, Donnerstag, der 1. Mai, und dann ein verlängertes Wochenende, am Freitag habe ich frei. Am folgenden Montag kommt Besuch aus den Vereinigten Staaten, aber am Dienstag, dem 6. Mai, da geht's. Aber Herr Holzhauser, so lange können wir nicht warten, da muß unser Werbematerial schon fertig sein.
Christian	Ganz meine Meinung. Hätten Sie heute nachmittag kurz Zeit?
Katrina	Eventuell, ich rufe Sie in einer halben Stunde zurück. Geht das?
Christian	Geht in Ordnung. Vielen Dank. Auf Wiederhören.
Katrina	Auf Wiederhören.

Translation

Telephonist	Spieltechnik, Good morning.
Christian	Holzhauser here, Verlag Germania. Good morning. Can I speak to Frau Stein, in the export department please?

Telephonist	One moment, I'm connecting you.
Katrina	Stein. Good morning.
Christian	Good morning Frau Stein. Holzhauser here. I'd like to discuss the layout of the new brochure for your English-speaking customers. When would you have time?
Katrina	This week isn't possible – I'm flying to Florence tomorrow. But it would be possible next Monday, on the 28th.
Christian	Unfortunately I'm not in the office on the 28th. On the 29th I'm going to Munich, to a meeting at the new airport. I have to stay until the 30th.
Katrina	And then there's the bank holiday, Thursday, 1st May, and then an extended weekend. I'm off on the Friday. On the following Monday we have visitors from the United States, but Tuesday, the 6th of May is OK. But Herr Holzhauser, we can't wait as long as that, our promotional material has to be ready by then.
Christian	I agree entirely. Would you have a little time this afternoon?
Katrina	Possibly. I'll phone you back in half an hour. Is that alright?
Christian	That's fine. Many thanks. Goodbye.
Katrina	Goodbye.

1 Because she's flying to Florence tomorrow.
2 Possibly, she will phone back in half an hour.

Exercise 5

Am 28. April ● Am 29. April ● Am 1. Mai ● Am 2. Mai ● Am 6. Mai

Puzzle

1 Exportabteilung **2** besprechen **3** Werbematerial **4** Sitzung **5** Gestaltung **6** fertig

Progress check

1 Hier … (your name) von der Firma … (firm's name). Guten Tag.
2 Ich möchte bitte Frau Blohm sprechen.
3 a) Wann kommt er nach England?
   b) Wie lange bleibt er?
   c) Möchte er eine Woche bleiben?
   d) Bleibt er bis Mittwoch?
4 a) Ich möchte im März kommen.
   b) Ich möchte am Dienstag, dem fünften März kommen.
   c) Ich möchte vom fünften bis (zum) siebten (März) bleiben.

5 a) Am … (your date of birth)
   b) Heute ist der … (the day's date)
6 See Unit 4, Language structures on pages 39–40.
7 zwölf, neunzehn, null vier
   zweiundzwanzig, fünfunddreißig, sechzehn
   siebenundfünfzig, dreiundneunzig, null eins
8 a) We would like to discuss the advertising material at the meeting.
   b) The brochure will possibly be finished the day after tomorrow.

UNIT 5

Exercise 1

1 by air **2** 10 o'clock **3** 11.30 **4** single room with bath

Exercise 2

1c) 2a) 3d) 4b)

Exercise 3

3 Kate Wilson fliegt am Montag von London Heathrow ab.
4 Sue Evans kommt am Dienstag mit der Bahn in Heidelberg an.
5 John Ward kommt am Mittwoch am Flughafen an.
6 Mike Wood fliegt am Freitag nach Berlin.
7 Ann Smith fährt am Samstag mit dem Taxi zur Firma in Goßlar.

Comprehension 1

Transcript

Telefonist	Hotel Bergerhof. Guten Tag.
Mrs. Smith	Guten Tag. Hier Louise Smith von der Firma Dale Stonecraft in

	England. Ich komme nächste Woche nach Düsseldorf und möchte für mich und meine Kollegen Zimmer reservieren.
Telefonist	Ja, gerne. Wie viele Zimmer brauchen Sie denn?
Mrs. Smith	Drei Einzelzimmer mit Dusche bitte.
Telefonist	Wann werden Sie ankommen?
Mrs. Smith	Am Donnerstag, dem 16. März, am Abend.
Telefonist	Und wie lange bleiben Sie?
Mrs. Smith	Eine Woche. Geht das?
Telefonist	Augenblick bitte … bis 23. März, ja, das geht. Kommen Sie mit dem Auto?
Mrs. Smith	Nein, wir fliegen nach Frankfurt und fahren vielleicht mit einem Taxi nach Düsseldorf.
Telefonist	Ja, ich empfehle die Firma PM Taxi. Die Nummer ist Frankfurt 22 17 39.
Mrs. Smith	Vielen Dank für Ihre Hilfe.
Telefonist	Gern geschehen. Auf Wiederhören.
Mrs. Smith	Auf Wiederhören.

1 single rooms with shower **2** three **3** Thursday, 16th March, in the evening **4** one week **5** by air **6** a taxi firm

Exercise 4	*Sie*	Er möchte am vierzehnten Juni kommen und zwei Tage in Winterthur bleiben. Geht das?
	Sie	Ja bitte.
	Sie	Ein Einzelzimmer mit Bad.
	Sie	Ja, er fliegt von Manchester nach Zürich. Dann fährt er mit der Bahn weiter. Er kommt um fünfzehn Uhr dreißig am Flughafen an.

Comprehension 2

Transcript

Telephonist	Verlag Germania, guten Tag.
Katrina	Guten Tag, Katrina Stein, Spieltechnik GmbH. Ich möchte bitte Herrn Holzhauser sprechen.
Telephonist	Augenblick … Ich verbinde Sie mit Frau Koller.
Secretary	Koller, guten Tag.
Katrina	Guten Tag, Frau Koller, Katrina Stein am Apparat, von der Firma Spieltechnik. Herr Holzhauser ist im Moment nicht zu sprechen?
Frau Koller	Er ist leider momentan mitten in einer Betriebsführung. Worum geht es?
Katrina	Es geht um unseren Termin heute nachmittag.
Frau Koller	Kann ich ihm etwas ausrichten?
Katrina	Ja, bitte. Ich hole um vier Uhr einen Besucher vom Flughafen ab. Ich bin also mit dem Wagen unterwegs, und komme vorher kurz zu Ihnen. Es wird so gegen zwei sein. Ich habe dann bis drei Uhr Zeit. Wir müssen die englische Produktliteratur näher besprechen.
Frau Koller	Sie kommen also zwischen zwei und drei zu einer Besprechung. Gut, ich werde das Herrn Holzhauser ausrichten.
Katrina	Wenn alles in Ordnung geht, können Sie den Termin vor zwölf Uhr bestätigen?
Frau Koller	Ja, ich rufe Sie vor Mittag zurück.
Katrina	Vielen Dank. Auf Wiederhören.
Frau Koller	Bitte. Auf Wiederhören.

Translation

Telephonist	Verlag Germania, good morning (or: good afternoon).
Katrina	Good morning. Katrina Stein from Spieltechnik here. I'd like to speak to Herr Holzhauser please.
Telephonist	One moment … I'm connecting you with Frau Koller.

Frau Koller	Koller, good morning.
Katrina	Good morning, Frau Koller. Katrina Stein here, from Spieltechnik. Is Herr Holzhauser not available at the moment?
Frau Koller	Unfortunately he's in the middle of showing someone round the company. What is it about please?
Katrina	It's about our appointment this afternoon.
Frau Koller	Can I give him a message?
Katrina	Yes please. At four o'clock I'm fetching a visitor from the airport, so I'm out in the car, and will come to your firm for a short visit beforehand. It'll be around two. I'll then have until three. We need to discuss the English product literature in more detail.
Frau Koller	So you'll be coming for a meeting between two and three. Fine, I'll pass the message on to Herr Holzhauser.
Katrina	If everything is OK can you confirm the appointment before twelve o'clock?
Frau Koller	Yes, I'll phone back before twelve.
Katrina	Many thanks, goodbye.
Frau Koller	A pleasure. Goodbye.

1 She is fetching a visitor from the airport at 4.00pm.
2 To confirm the appointment.

Exercise 5

2 Uhr ● 3 Uhr ● 2 … 3 Uhr ● 12 Uhr

Progress check

1 Ein Einzelzimmer mit Bad, bitte. (Ich möchte ein Einzelzimmer mit Bad reservieren.)
2 a) Wann kommen Sie auf Besuch?
   b) Fliegen Sie von München?
   c) Wann kommen Sie in London an?
   d) Soll ich ein Hotelzimmer reservieren?
3 a) Er fliegt am zwölften Dezember von Heathrow ab.
   b) Ankunft am Flughafen Zürich um elf Uhr.
   c) Der Zug kommt am Abend in Winterthur an.
   d) Miss Evans holt ihn vom Bahnhof ab.
   e) Sie fahren mit dem Auto zur Firma.

4 Danke für Ihre Hilfe. Auf Wiederhören.
5 Mit freundlichen Grüßen.
6 a) The general manager is on the telephone at the moment and is unfortunately not available.
   b) It is about the room booking.

UNIT 6

Exercise 1

1 Um neun Uhr dreißig (um halb zehn).
2 Um zehn Uhr fünfundvierzig (um Viertel vor elf).
3 Um elf Uhr dreißig (um halb zwölf).
4 Um vierzehn Uhr (um zwei Uhr nachmittags).
5 Um fünfzehn Uhr dreißig (um halb vier).
6 Um fünfzehn Uhr fünfundvierzig (um Viertel vor vier).
7 Um achtzehn Uhr dreißig (um halb sieben).

Exercise 2

1 elf Uhr fünfzehn **2** dreiundzwanzig Uhr fünfundfunfzig **3** dreizehn Uhr fünfunddreißig **4** fünfzehn Uhr fünfunddreißig

Comprehension 1

Transcript

Herr Schneider	Scheider.
Frau Bauer	Guten Tag, Herr Schneider, hier Gerda Bauer. Wie geht es Ihnen?

Herr Schneider	Ach guten Tag, Frau Bauer. Danke gut, und Ihnen?
Frau Bauer	Danke, auch gut. Herr Schneider, ich fahre nächsten Montag nach Düsseldorf zur Messe. Sie auch?
Herr Schneider	Ja, sicher.
Frau Bauer	Also, gut. Ich fliege am Sonntag von München. Wann fahren Sie?
Herr Schneider	Ich fliege am Samstag von Innsbruck. Ich besuche am Wochenende Freunde in Duisburg und fahre dann am Montag mit der Bahn zur Messe.
Frau Bauer	Na, gut, Dann hole ich Sie vom Bahnhof ab. Wann kommen Sie in Düsseldorf an?
Herr Schneider	Um halb neun bin ich in Düsseldorf.
Frau Bauer	Also gut, bis dann. Schönes Wochenende!

1 next Monday **2** by plane and train **3** Frau Bauer on Sunday from Munich and Herr Schneider on Saturday from Innsbruck **4** visiting friends at the weekend **5** by rail **6** at 8.30 **7** at the station

Exercise 3

Sie	Ich fahre am Freitag zur Konferenz in Zürich. Kommen Sie auch?
Sie	Wann fahren Sie?
Sie	Wann kommt Ihr Zug in Zürich an?
Sie	Ich hole Sie vom Bahnhof ab. (Ich werde Sie vom Bahnhof abholen.) Die Konferenz beginnt um elf Uhr und wir werden (noch) rechtzeitig ankommen.
Sie	Um siebzehn Uhr dreißig (um halb sechs).
Sie	Auf Wiedersehen.

Comprehension 2

liegt ● Europa ● sechzehn ● Hauptstadt ● Touristen ● interessant ● Handelspartner ● sind ● Maschinen ● importiert ● Schweiz ● Lebensmittel ● spricht ● auch

Comprehension 3

Transcript

Katrina	Wissen Sie, wie lange die Tagung dauern wird?
Christian	Ich glaube bis spät am Donnerstag Abend. Ich habe hier ein Programmheft mit allen Einzelheiten.
Katrina	Vielen Dank. Ich hoffe, daß ich rechtzeitig ankommen werde. Also sehen wir mal: „Neue Märkte im neuen Binnenmarkt". Tagesordnung … Die Vorträge sind vormittags von halb zehn bis 12.00 und um halb drei beginnen die Arbeitsgruppen.
Christian	Wir präsentieren am Nachmittag unsere neue Serie „Handel in Europa".
Katrina	Werden Sie selbst auch sprechen?
Christian	Ja, ich werde ein Buch über die Geschichte der EG vorstellen und Frau Herz wird ein Referat über „Fremdsprachen in der Wirtschaft" halten.
Katrina	Es gibt zu viel Interessantes, und zu wenig Zeit! Aber vielleicht kann ich zu Ihrem Vortrag kommen.
Christian	Spieltechnik leistet auch einen Beitrag, nicht wahr?
Katrina	Stimmt, wir veranstalten eine kleine Ausstellung im Sitzungsraum. Wir zeigen eine Auswahl unserer Erzeugnisse zum Thema „europäischer Binnenmarkt".
Christian	Sind das nur Muster, oder sagen wir Ausstellungsstücke, oder kann man die Ware auch dort direkt kaufen?
Katrina	Ja also, alles ist im Sonderangebot. Auch der Päda-Computer wird zum Sonderpreis angeboten. Aber man muß die Sachen bestellen.

Translation

Katrina	Do you know how long the conference will last?
Christian	I think until late on Thursday evening. I've got a programme booklet here with all the details.
Katrina	Thanks a lot. I hope I'll arrive in time. So, let's see. 'New Markets in

the New Single Market' Programme … The lectures are in the mornings from half past nine till twelve, and the working groups begin at half past two.

Christian	In the afternoon we're giving a presentation of our new series 'Trade in Europe'.
Katrina	Will you be speaking yourself?
Christian	Yes, I'm going to present a book about the history of the EC, and Frau Herz will give a talk about 'Foreign Languages in Commerce and Industry'.
Katrina	There's too much of interest and too little time! But perhaps I can come to your presentation.
Christian	Spieltechnik is also making a contribution, isn't it?
Katrina	That's right. We're organising a small exhibition in the meeting room. We're showing a selection of our products with the Single European Market in mind.
Christian	Are they just samples, or shall we say exhibition items, or can one also buy them directly there?
Katrina	Well, everything is on special offer. Even the Päda-Computer is offered at a special price. But you have to order the products.

1 Lectures in the mornings, working groups in the afternoons.
2 No, they have to be ordered.

Exercise 4	Handel in Europa ● Europäischen Gemeinschaft ● Fremdsprachen in der Wirtschaft ● Erzeugnisse … „Europäischer Binnenmarkt"

Puzzle 1 Ausstellung 2 Beitrag 3 Erzeugnis 4 Angebot 5 Märkte 6 Präsentieren

Progress check

1 Wie spät ist es bitte? (Wieviel Uhr ist es, bitte?)
2 Zehn Uhr, elf Uhr fünfundfünfzig, zwölf Uhr fünfzehn, zwölf Uhr dreißig, dreizehn Uhr, vierzehn Uhr fünfundzwanzig, zwanzig Uhr dreißig, einundzwanzig Uhr fünfundvierzig. Zehn Uhr, fünf Minuten vor zwölf, Viertel nach zwölf, halb eins, ein Uhr (nachmittags), fünfundzwanzig Minuten nach zwei (fünf Minuten vor halb drei), halb neun (abends), Viertel vor zehn (abends).
3 a) Der Vortrag beginnt am Morgen und dauert zwei Stunden.
 b) Wie lange dauert die Mittagspause?
 c) Wann endet das Nachmittagsprogramm?
 d) Kommt der Produktionsleiter am Abend?
4 a) Um … (time you arrive for work in the morning)
 b) Ja … (time of your lunch break) (eine Stunde/halbe Stunde) (Nein, es gibt keine Mittagspause)
 c) Um … (time you go home in the evening).

5 a) Ich hole Sie vom Bahnhof ab. (Ich werde Sie vom Bahnhof abholen.)
 b) Wir kommen rechtzeitig an. (Wir werden rechtzeitig ankommen.)
 c) Das wird kein Problem sein.
 d) Meine Uhr stimmt nicht.
 e) Ihr Name ist deutsch, nicht wahr?
6 a) My colleague (female) has still to go to the bank today.
 b) Our representatives are going to a conference tomorrow.
 c) See you the day after tomorrow then, and have a nice weekend.
 d) We will discuss the details about the special price later.
 e) Here are the samples, you order the goods directly from us.

Additional exercises

Summary 2

1 **a** hole … ab **b** kommen … an **c** Fliegen … ab **d** kommen … an und fahren … weiter **e** Holen … ab **f** kommen … an **g** fliegt … ab

2 **a** zur **b** vom **c** zum **d** der **e** den **f** das

3 **a** nach **b** nach, zur **c** zum **d** nach **e** nach **f** zur **f** zum

4 **a** Die Konferenz wird um Viertel vor neun beginnen. **b** wird … dauern **c** wird … sein **d** werde … gehen **e** wird … sein **f** werden … bleiben **g** werden … ankommen **h** werde … abholen

5 **a** Ihre Ihr Ihr Ihre Ihre Ihren
b meinem meinen Mein Meine
c unser Unser unserer Unsere unseren

6 **1** ein Doppelzimmer **a 2** für **b 3** eine Telefonnummer **a**, für **b**

UNIT 7

Exercise 1

Sie Entschuldigen Sie, wo fährt die S-Bahn ab?
Sie Danke schön (für die Auskunft).
Sie Wann fährt der nächste Zug zum Hauptbahnhof?
Sie Was kostet das?
Sie Vielen Dank.

Exercise 2

2 Hannover   9.45   **3**   13.10
3 Lübeck   11.24   **6**   16.56
4 Bonn   15.39   **1**   22.16

Exercise 3

1 Eine Fahrkarte **2** Zweiter Klasse **3** DM 72,00 **4** Die Reisende hat nur einen Fünfhundertmarkschein **5** Vierhundertachtundzwanzig Mark

Exercise 4

1 neun Mark sechzig **2** acht Mark achtzig **3** fünf Mark neunundvierzig **4** siebenundzwanzig Mark **5** vierundsiebzig Mark **6** einundfünfzig Mark **7** dreiundsechzig Mark **8** eine Mark

Comprehension 1

Transcript
Wie ist Ihre Nummer bitte?

74	16	25
27	43	02
34	54	88
29	48	65
53	52	44
97	65	21
51	0	93
72	2	28

Exercise 5

1 Zweimal nach Köln, bitte. Zweiter Klasse. Ja.
2 Zweimal zum Hauptbahnhof, bitte. Einfach, erster Klasse. Fünfzig Mark, bitte schön.
3 Entschuldigen Sie, was kostet eine Fahrkarte nach Nürnberg?
Nein, hin und zurück. Erster Klasse. Vielen Dank, einmal, bitte.
4 Dreimal nach Mannheim, bitte. Was kostet das? Zweiter Klasse.
Hin und zurück. Ich habe nur einen Fünfhundertmarkschein. Können Sie wechseln? Danke schön. Auf Wiedersehen!

Comprehension 2   kaufen müssen können

Comprehension 3

Transcript
Ansager Die Schnellbahnverbindung S14 zum Flughafen Frankfurt Rhein-Main fährt in zwei Minuten von Gleis 3 ab. Bitte einsteigen und Türen schließen.
Katrina Wohin fährt denn die S15?
Christian Die S15 fährt auch zum Flughafen.
Katrina Normalerweise, wenn ich nur zwei, drei Tage weg bin, parke ich am Flughafen. Das kostet nur 20 Mark pro Tag.

Christian	Ja, die Parkgebühren sind sehr günstig, was kostet eine Woche?
Katrina	Eine Woche kostet 140 Mark, aber zwei Wochen sind billiger. Zwei Wochen kosten 210 Mark.
Christian	Jetzt fahren wir schon, und die Fahrt dauert nur einige Minuten, es sind nur ungefähr 10 km zum Flughafen.
Katrina	Die Bahn leistet Großartiges, meinen Sie nicht auch? InterCity Züge im Stundentakt mit Verbindungen in alle Großstädte Deutschlands, – und praktisch immer auf die Minute pünktlich.
Christian	Ich kann Ihnen nur zustimmen. Was mir am Reisen mit der Bahn gefällt: es ist bequem, kein Streß, ich kann meine Zahlen überprüfen oder sonst was arbeiten. Ich kann mich gut ausruhen und komme erholt am Ziel an.
Katrina	Hier sind wir schon, am Ziel – Flughafen Frankfurt-Main. Dieser Flughafen imponiert mir. Wie viele Leute hier wohl arbeiten?
Christian	Das weiß ich: circa 50.000. Aber jetzt müssen wir aussteigen. Bitte schön … nach Ihnen.

Translation

Announcer	The fast train connection S14 to Frankfurt Rhein-Main airport departs in two minutes from platform 3. Please board the train and close the doors.
Katrina	Where does the S15 go to then?
Christian	The S15 also goes to the airport.
Katrina	Normally, when I'm only away for two or three days, I park at the airport … It only costs 20 marks a day.
Christian	Yes, the parking fees are very reasonable. What does a week cost?
Katrina	A week costs 140 marks, but two weeks is cheaper. Two weeks costs 210 marks.
Christian	Now we're already leaving, and the journey only takes a few minutes. It's only about 10 km to the airport.
Katrina	The railways really achieve great things, don't you think? Intercity trains hourly, with connections to all cities in Germany – and practically always punctual to the minute.
Christian	I can only agree with you. What I like most about travelling by train is that it's comfortable, stress-free, and I can check over figures, or do some other work. I can have a good rest, and arrive refreshed at my destination.
Katrina	Here we are already, at our destination – Frankfurt-Main airport. I am impressed with this airport. I wonder how many people work here?
Christian	I know that: around 50,000. But now we have to get out. Please – after you.

1 Intercity trains run hourly with connections to all cities and almost always punctual to the minute.
2 It is comfortable, stress-free, he can work, have a rest and arrive refreshed.

Exercise 6   140 Mark ● 210 Mark ● 10 ● 50,000

Puzzle   1 überprüfen 2 Flughafen 3 Parkgebühren 4 unterwegs 5 billiger
6 günstig 7 normalwerweise

Progress check

1 a) Wo ist die Rolltreppe?
  b) Wo fährt die U-Bahn ab?
  c) Wann fährt der nächste Zug zum Hauptbahnhof ab?
  d) Was kostet das?
  e) Einmal zweiter Klasse nach Berlin, hin und zurück, bitte.

  f) Können Sie wechseln?
2 a) Ich habe kein Zweimarkstück.
  b) Ich habe nur einen Zehnmarkschein.
  c) Ich möchte wechseln.
3 Fünf Mark und dreizehn Mark fünfundfünfzig … bitte schön, zwanzig Mark … und eine Mark fünfundvierzig zurück.

4 a) Sie können die Fahrkarte am Fahrkartenschalter kaufen.
      Sie müssen die Fahrkarte vom Automaten kaufen.
   b) Do you want to go by underground or 'S'-rail?
      Why don't you want to go by taxi?
      The information office is over there.

5 a) With British rail you don't always get to your destination
      on time.
   b) I can only agree with you.

UNIT 8

Exercise 1

Sie Wann fährt der nächste Zug nach Berlin?
Sie Fährt der Zug direkt?
Sie Wann kommt der Zug in Hannover an?
Sie Und wann bin ich in Berlin?
Sie Von welchem Gleis fährt der Zug nach Hannover?
Sie Vielen Dank für die Auskunft.
Sie Einmal nach Berlin, bitte.
Sie Hin und zurück, zweiter Klasse.

Exercise 2

1 1.07.92 **2** reverse side **3** 2 **4** Fernrückfahrkarte **5** half price
6 München to Rothenburg **7** Steinach **8** München **9** Hauptbahnhof
10 232 kilometres **11** DM 72,00

Comprehension 1

Transcript

1 • Wann fährt der nächste Zug nach Frankfurt?
   ■ Um 08.30, von Gleis vier.
   • Fährt der Zug direkt nach Frankfurt?
   ■ Nein, Sie müssen in Stuttgart umsteigen.
   • Wann kommt der Zug in Frankfurt an?
   ■ Um 11.45.

2 • Wann fährt der nächste Zug nach Basel?
   ■ Um 10.25 von Gleis 2.
   • Fährt der Zug direkt nach Basel?
   ■ Ja, er fährt direkt.
   • Wann kommt der Zug in Basel an?
   ■ Um 13.08.

3 • Entschuldigen Sie bitte, aber wann fährt der nächste Zug nach Heidelberg?
   ■ Er fährt um 12.45 von Gleis 7.
   • Fährt er direkt nach Heidelberg?
   ■ Nein, Sie müssen in Mannheim umsteigen.
   • Und wann kommt er in Heidelberg an?
   ■ Um 22.15.

4 • Wann fährt der nächste Zug nach Bonn?
   ■ Um 13.37 von Gleis 5.
   • Muß ich umsteigen?
   ■ Ja. Sie müssen in Frankfurt umsteigen.
   • Und wann kommt der Zug in Bonn an?
   ■ Um 16.50.

2 Basel 10.25 Gleis 2 nein 13.08
3 Heidelberg 12.45 Gleis 7 Mannheim 22.15
4 Bonn 13.37 Gleis 5 Frankfurt 16.50

Exercise 3

1 Sie müssen in Köln umsteigen.
2 Nein, das ist ein Inter City Zug.
3 Um zehn Uhr achtundzwanzig.

Comprehension 2 wählen ● drücken ● einwerfen ● zahlen ● nehmen

<table>
<tr><td>

Exercise 4

</td><td>

Er ist ● will ● Er muß ● ihm ● er drückt ● wirft er ● erhält ● Er entwertet ● er ● einsteigt

</td></tr>
</table>

Comprehension 3

Transcript

Flight announcement	Meine Damen und Herren, wir fliegen jetzt über den Südosten der Britischen Inseln und werden in fünfzehn Minuten am Flughafen Birmingham International landen. Das Wetter in Birmingham: stark bewölkt mit Regen und einer Temperatur von plus 3 Grad Celsius. Vielen Dank für Ihre Aufmerksamkeit.
Christian	Das ist typisch englisch.
Katrina	Was?
Christian	Das Wetter natürlich. Gut, daß mich der Verlag Richards & Jones vom Flughafen abholt.
Katrina	Das englische Wetter stört mich nicht. Im Winter ist es recht mild, und im Sommer angenehm kühl. Meine Sekretärin hat einen Mietwagen organisiert, wir machen das immer so.
Christian	Und der Linksverkehr, kompliziertes Einbahnstraßensystem, Stoßzeit frühmorgens und am späten Nachmittag – das alles im Stadtzentrum von Birmingham?
Katrina	Beim Autofahren bin ich Expertin! Aber glücklicherweise muß ich nicht ins Zentrum. Das Unternehmen Educational Electronics liegt direkt an einer Autobahnausfahrt.
Christian	Na ja, ich bleibe bei meinem englischen Chauffeur. Bitte würden Sie mir meinen Mantel reichen, und die Aktentasche, neben Ihnen auf dem Sitz …
Katrina	Gerne, bitte schön.

Translation

Flight announcement	Ladies and gentlemen, we are now flying over the south-east of the British Isles, and will land at Birmingham International Airport in fifteen minutes. The weather in Birmingham: heavy cloud with rain and a temperature of plus 3 degrees Celsius. Thank you for your attention.
Christian	That's typically English.
Katrina	What?
Christian	The weather, of course. It's a good thing that Richards & Jones Publishers are fetching me from the airport.
Katrina	The English weather doesn't bother me. It's nice and mild in winter, and pleasantly cool in summer. My secretary has organised a hire-car for me. We always do it like that.
Christian	And driving on the left, the complicated one-way systems, rush hours in the early morning and late afternoon – all that in Birmingham town centre?
Katrina	I'm an expert at driving! But luckily I don't have to drive into the town centre. The firm, Educational Electronics, lies directly at a motorway exit.
Christian	Well, I'll stick to my English chauffeur. Could you please pass me my coat, and the briefcase next to you on the seat …
Katrina	Of course – here you are.

1 It doesn't bother her, it's mild in winter and pleasantly cool in summer.

2 He thinks driving on the left is difficult, he finds the one-way systems complicated and doesn't like the rush hour. He prefers to have an English chauffeur.

<table>
<tr><td>

Exercise 5

</td><td>

fünfzehn … am ● mit … plus 3 ● im ● am ● einer ● meinem ● mir ● Ihnen

</td></tr>
</table>

Puzzle   **1** typisch **2** Verkehr **3** Mietwagen **4** links **5** Aktentasche **6** Expertin

Progress check

1   a)   Fährt der Zug direkt nach München?
    b)   Muß ich in Frankfurt umsteigen?
    c)   Von welchem Gleis fährt der Zug nach Leipzig?
    d)   Wie komme ich zu den Zügen?
2   a)   Ich möchte eine Fahrkarte kaufen.
    b)   Er muß den Automaten benützen.
    c)   Jetzt müssen Sie das Geld einwerfen (zahlen).
    d)   Dann können Sie die Rückfahrkarte nehmen.
    e)   Mr. Newby ist an der Auskunft.
    f)   Mein Kollege (meine Kollegin) spricht mit dem
         Angestellten (der Angestellten).

3   a)   Danke für die Auskunft.
    b)   Können Sie mir bitte helfen?
4   a)   long distance return ticket
    b)   arrival, departure
    c)   instructions for use
    d)   telephone conversation
5   a)   The traffic in the town centre is very heavy in the rush
         hour.
    b)   Driving on the left-hand side and the one-way system
         always bother me a lot.

Summary 3

Additional exercises

1   **a** muß **b** müssen (muß) **c** muß **d** kann **e** kann **f** können **g** will **h** Wollen **i** wollen

2   **1** vom Geschäftsführer, von der Firma **b**
    2 wünsche + Ihnen **a**
    3 in der Stadt **b**
    4 Wie geht es + *dative*/Ihnen/Ihrer Familie **a**
    5 helfen + *dative*/mir **a**

3   **a** das **b** den **c** der **d** dem, dem **e** der **f** das, dem **g** die **h** den **i** den **j** das **k** die

4   **a** Sie, es **b** Er **c** Er, es **d** ihn **e** ihnen **f** ihr **g** Sie, ihm **h** es **i** ihr

UNIT 9

| Exercise 1 |

1 to fill in a registration form **2** on the first floor **3** the lift **4** around the corner
5 to have the luggage taken upstairs

| Exercise 2 |

Dieses ● diesen ● welchem ● Welche ● diesem ● Welches ● Dieser ● Welcher

Sie   Guten Tag. Ich habe ein Einzelzimmer mit Bad reserviert.
Sie   (your name)
Sie   Ja, stimmt.
Sie   Selbstverständlich. Welche Nummer hat mein Zimmer?
Sie   Wo ist der Fahrstuhl?
Sie   Danke, das geht schon.

Comprehension 1

Transcript
Frau Zimmermann reist am Dienstag, dem achtzehnten März, nach Duisburg und
fährt gleich zum Hotel Arabella. Sie hat im Hotel ein Einzelzimmer mit Bad
reserviert. Heike Zimmermann ist Deutsche und arbeitet und wohnt in Köln. Ihre
Adresse ist Bahnhofstraße 40, 5000 Köln 1. Sie arbeitet bei der Firma Schumann
AG. Sie bekommt Zimmer Nummer 75 im vierten Stock und muß im Hotel ein
Anmeldeformular ausfüllen und unterschreiben. Ihr Paß hat die Nummer F
8206374. Frau Zimmermann hat vor ihrer Abreise am Samstag viel zu tun.

Zimmermann ● Heike ● deutsch ● Bahnhofstraße 40 ● 5000 Köln 1 ● F 8206374
● Dienstag 18.3. ● Samstag 22.3. ● 75 4.Stock ● Schumann AG

| Exercise 4 |

1 *Dame*   Haben Sie (noch) ein Einzelzimmer frei? Vier. Mit Bad.
2 *Herr*   Haben Sie noch Zimmer frei? Ja (stimmt). Für fünf Nächte.
              Mit Dusche, bitte.

3 *Herr*   Guten Abend. Haben Sie noch Zimmer frei?
Für zwei Erwachsene und ein Kind.
Ja, ein Doppelzimmer und ein Einzelzimmer.
Mit Bad, bitte. Für zwei Nächte.

Comprehension 2   Hotel Central

Comprehension 3   **Transcript**

Katrina	Sind Sie mit Ihrer Unterkunft zufrieden?
Christian	Danke, das Hotel ist erstklassig. Es liegt direkt am Messegelände und verfügt über modernsten Komfort. Vor dem Frühstück war ich eine halbe Stunde lang in einem ganz tollen Fitneßraum. Und das englische Frühstück ist ausgezeichnet – eine gute Grundlage für einen Tag harter Arbeit. Aber Sie sehen nicht sehr glücklich aus, ist etwas nicht in Ordnung?
Katrina	Ich habe sehr schlecht geschlafen. Die Engländer haben so weiche Betten, und das Zimmer ist viel zu warm.
Christian	Warum drehen Sie nicht die Heizung ab?
Katrina	Das ist nicht so einfach. Ich bin in einem alten Landhaus untergebracht. Wunderschön renoviert, aber es ist unmöglich, diese altmodischen Fensterverschlüsse zu öffnen. Und die Wärmeregulierung an der Zentralheizung funktioniert auch nicht.
Christian	Und haben Sie sich beschwert?
Katrina	Natürlich. Vor dem Frühstück habe ich bei der Hotelleitung reklamiert.
Christian	Was mich besonders interessiert: war Ihre Beschwerde auf Englisch oder auf Deutsch?
Katrina	Ich war sehr verärgert, auf Englisch oder auf Deutsch, das weiß ich nicht mehr so genau.
Christian	Und was hat die Hotelleitung zu sagen?
Katrina	Wir werden alles sofort überprüfen. Keine Sorge, bis heute Abend ist alles in bester Ordnung, oder Sie bekommen ein anderes Zimmer.
Christian	Na schön, viel Glück! Frau Stein, auf welchem Messestand sind Sie vertreten?
Katrina	Educational Electronics, das ist in der Halle B, Stand Nummer fünf. Am Eingang rechts entlang, da kommen Sie direkt hin.
Christian	Also bis später!
Katrina	Auf Wiedersehen.

Translation

Katrina	Are you happy with your accommodation?
Christian	Yes, thanks. The hotel is first class. It's right next to the trade-fair complex, and offers the most up-to-date amenities. Before breakfast I was in a really great fitness room for half an hour. And the English breakfast is excellent – a good foundation for a day's hard work. But you don't look very happy – is anything wrong?
Katrina	I slept very badly. The English have such soft beds, and the room is much too warm.
Christian	Why don't you turn the heating off?
Katrina	That's not so straightforward. I'm staying in an old country house. Beautifully renovated, but it's impossible to open these old-fashioned window-catches. And the temperature regulation for the central heating doesn't work either.
Christian	And have you complained?
Katrina	Naturally. I complained to the management before breakfast.
Christian	What interests me in particular is: were your complaints in English or German?
Katrina	I was very annoyed. I don't know exactly now whether it was English or German.

Christian	And what did the management have to say?
Katrina	We'll check everything over straight away. Don't worry – by this evening everything will be in perfect order, otherwise you'll have another room.
Christian	Very nice – good luck! Frau Stein, which stand are you represented on?
Katrina	Educational Electronics, in Hall B, stand number 5. Go right along the corridor, and you come straight to it.
Christian	See you later then!
Katrina	Goodbye.

1 He spent half an hour in a fitness room.

2 She complained to the management about her room.

Exercise 5	funktioniert ● beschwert ● reklamiert ● verärgert

Puzzle	**1** Beschwerde **2** Messestand **3** Grundlage **4** Fenster **5** Heizung
	6 erstklassig

Progress check

1
a) Ich möchte ein Doppelzimmer mit Bad für drei Nächte reservieren.
b) Ein Anmeldeformular, bitte.
c) In welchem Stock ist mein Zimmer?
d) Wo ist der Fahrstuhl bitte?
e) Bitte bringen Sie mein Gepäck nach oben.
f) Hier sind die Schlüssel.

2
a) Bitte füllen Sie dieses Formular aus!
b) Bitte unterschreiben Sie hier!
c) Nehmen Sie ein Taxi vom Flughafen zur Firma!
d) Wählen Sie ein Hotel mit einem Parkplatz und einem Restaurant!

3 zehn Einzelzimmer mit Dusche, Toilette, Telefon und TV; zwei Konferenzräume, warme Küche zu Mittag, Tennisplatz

4 Of course we have room for 50 people. Here is our price list for overnight stay. Our recreational facilities are ideal for conferences and conventions. Now I still need the dates of your arrival and departure, and your signature down here, please.

5
a) I understand your complaint, but unfortunately I can't help you.
b) I complained, and now everything is in perfect order.

UNIT 10

Exercise 1	1g) 2h) 3e) 4b) 5f) 6c) 7a) 8d)

Exercise 2	**1** Es **2** es **3** Sie **4** sie **5** er **6** er

Exercise 3	**1** wonderful, onto mountains and lake **2** ten minutes by bus **3** yes **4** ten driving minutes away **5** swimming pool, colourful parks, Roman museum, large zoo, old cathedral **6** phone or write to 'Schneider Appartements'

Exercise 4	**1** Sie werden uns … in der Fabrik besuchen.
	… werden wir Ihnen weitere Information zuschicken.

2 Dear Mrs. Johnson,
We thank you for your letter of 5.5.92 and would like to confirm the following. You are coming to Germany on 3rd July and staying till the 8th. You will visit us here at the factory from the 4th to the 7th. Are you coming by car or by rail or are you flying? There are still rooms available in July at the hotels 'Zum Goldenen Stern' (Golden Star) and 'Sonne' (Sun). Hotel 'Sonne' is more expensive, but better. We can sincerely recommend this hotel. The proprietor, Mr. Lindemann, and his wife are very friendly. (They hardly speak any English, but that does not matter. You know German well now.) The food is good, the rooms are quiet and each has a shower and toilet. The hotel also has car parks. A single room has therefore been provisionally reserved.
Next week I am going on holiday, but my colleague, Herr Braun, and my secretary, Frau Schreiber, are here in the office.

In the next few days we will send you further information about our instruments, prices and sales conditions etc. With kind regards, Karl-Heinz Jeismann, Managing Director.

3 *Sie* Vielen Dank für Ihren Brief an Frau Johnson.

Sie Frau Johnson kommt mit seinem Mann. Bitte reservieren Sie ein Doppelzimmer im Hotel 'Sonne'.

Sie Sie bleiben bis zehnten Juli und reisen mit dem Auto. Also bitte reservieren Sie einen Parkplatz.

Sie Danke schön für Ihre Hilfe. Auf Wiederhören.

Comprehension 1

Transcript

Tourist	Können Sie uns ein nicht zu teures Hotel empfehlen?
Angestellte	Wollen Sie ein Hotel in zentraler Lage?
Tourist	Nein, lieber ein ruhiges Hotel außerhalb der Stadt.
Angestellte	Da gibt es das Parkhotel und den Gasthof Huber. Das Parkhotel ist groß und modern, aber der Gasthof Huber ist billiger.
Tourist	Was kostet ein Doppelzimmer mit Bad im Gasthof?
Angestellte	Eine Übernachtung mit Frühstück, dreißig Mark pro Person.
Tourist	Das geht. Hat der Gasthof einen eigenen Parkplatz?
Angestellte	Ja, hat er – sogar einen großen.
Tourist	Also gut, fahren wir hin. Haben Sie bitte einen Stadtplan?
Angestellte	Ja, bitte schön. Und nehmen Sie auch diesen Zimmernachweis mit.

1 quiet, outside town **2** large, modern **3** 'Huber' is cheaper **4** a large car park **5** street map **6** list of hotels

Comprehension 2

There is a variety of accommodation available in Germany, the right kind for every requirement. Camping is very popular and around a thousand camp sites offer all the usual modern facilities. Youth hostels are the cheapest and very popular with young and old. Hotel accommodation varies from the very comfortable and luxurious to cheaper kinds, such as country inns. Full and half board are available in them all.

Comprehension 3

Transcript

Christian	Ich schlage vor, wir schreiben hier „Allgemeine Geschäftsbedingungen".
Katrina	Aber zuerst kommen die Preise. Die müssen wir auch in den anderen Währungen angeben: zuerst in Mark, dann Schweizer Franken und dann in österreichischen Schillingen. Also machen wir eine kleine Tabelle hier?
Christian	Ja, so ist das ganz übersichtlich. Und jetzt zu den verschiedenen Zahlungsmethoden: Also, per Post mit Scheck, dann am Telefon mit Kreditkarte oder per Telefax. Und dann auch noch per Nachnahme oder mit Banküberweisung ... Habe ich etwas vergessen?
Katrina	Ich glaube nicht. Der nächste Punkt ist die Lieferung: Die hängt von der Größenordnung der Bestellung ab. Also per Bahn oder Spedition, und nach England und in die nordischen Länder wird das in Hamburg verschifft.
Christian	Aber das kommt dann in die englische Übersetzung. Lassen wir das im Moment.
Katrina	Dann bleiben noch Garantie und Reklamation. Zwar dürfen unsere Computer keine Mängel haben, aber es kann ja mal irgendwas schiefgehen. Letzter Punkt: Service oder Wartung.
Christian	Halt, wir haben etwas vergessen – unsere Qualitätsversicherung darf nicht fehlen.
Katrina	Herr Holzhauser, es tut mir leid, aber unsere Zeit ist um. Können wir ein anderes Mal weitermachen?
Christian	Na schön, wenn es sein muß.

Translation

Christian I suggest we write here 'General terms and conditions of business'.

Katrina But first come the prices. We've also got to quote them in the other currencies: first in marks, then in Swiss francs, and then in Austrian schillings. So shall we make a little table here?

Christian Yes, that way it's quite clear. And now to the various methods of payment: so, through the post by cheque, then by telephone with credit-card, or by fax. Then by COD or credit transfer ... Have I forgotten anything?

Katrina I don't think so. The next point is delivery. That depends on the size of the order. So by rail or road haulage, and shipped out of Hamburg to England and the Nordic countries.

Christian But that comes in the English translation. Let's leave that for the moment.

Katrina Then we're left with the guarantee and complaints procedure. True, our computers aren't allowed to have faults, but of course something can occasionally go wrong. Last point: service.

Christian Hold on, we've forgotten something: our quality assurance mustn't be left out.

Katrina Herr Holzhauser, I'm sorry, but our time is up. Can we continue another time?

Christian Yes, alright, if we really have to.

1 In marks, Swiss francs and Austrian schillings.
2 They are to be shipped from Hamburg.

Exercise 5	Scheck ● Kreditkarte

Puzzle **1** Zahlung **2** Währung **3** Bestellung **4** Überweisung **5** Lieferung **6** Garantie

Progress check

1 a) Haben Sie Zimmer frei?
  b) Ich möchte ein Doppelzimmer für zwei Nächte reservieren.
  c) Wann ist Frühstück?
  d) Kann ich ein Zimmer mit Balkon sehen?
  e) Vollpension ist zu teuer.
  f) Wann kann ich die Sehenswürdigkeiten besichtigen?
  g) Wir nehmen die Zimmer, sie sind prima.
2 a) Dieses Gasthaus dort drüben ist größer und billiger.
  b) Ein ruhiges Zimmer ist besser.
  c) Das Hotel hat eine wunderbare Aussicht auf den alten Dom.

  d) Man kann eine Wohnung mit Küche, Bad und zwei Schlafzimmern haben.
  e) Man kann dort auch einen See und einen großen Zoo besuchen.
  f) Im Stadtzentrum ist ein modernes Schwimmbad. Es ist sehr groß. Dort gibt es auch ein Verkehrsbüro. Es ist am Hauptbahnhof.
3 a) proprietor, provisional, sales conditions
  b) list of hotels, tourist information office
  c) electric current, provisions, shops
4 a) I hope nothing goes wrong with the delivery.
  b) The size of our order depends on your terms of trade.

Additional exercises

Summary 4

1 **a** interessanter **b** schöner **c** teurer **d** mehr **e** komplizierter **f** ruhiger **g** älter **h** höher **i** öfter **j** weniger

2 **a** Diese **b** Dieses **c** Diese **d** dieser **e** diesem **f** Diese **g** Dieser **h** diesen

3 **a** der **b** der **c** des **d** der **e** des **f** der **g** des **h** der

4 **a** e, - **b** en, - **c** e, en, - **d** e, e, -, **e** en, en, - **f** -, -, - **g** e, en, e, e, e

UNIT 11

Exercise 1

1c) 2a) 3d) *or* b) 4e) 5b)

Exercise 2

Sie Ich habe gut geschlafen. Ich war sehr müde, aber jetzt geht es mir besser.
Sie Ja, wir haben uns auf einer Konferenz in München kennengelernt.
Sie Es freut mich, Sie wiederzusehen.
Sie Danke, recht gut.
Sie Ja, das stimmt.
Sie Das möchte ich gern. Ich habe so viel über Hamburg gehört.

Exercise 3

Ich habe die Flugkarte bestellt.
Ich habe die Marketing-Zeitschrift gekauft.
Ich habe das Hotelzimmer in Bremen reserviert.
Ich habe mit dem Restaurant Schloßhof gesprochen.
Ich habe einen Tisch für zwei Leute reserviert.
Ich habe die Exportformulare ausgefüllt.
Ich habe den Brief an die Firma Mann GmbH getippt.
Ich habe Hans Schoening vom Bahnhof abgeholt.

Exercise 4

Example: In meiner Freizeit gehe ich gern ins Theater und ich fahre gern ans Meer. Im Sommer reise ich nach Schottland und zelte gern mit meiner Familie. Aber im Winter bleibe ich lieber zu Hause und sehe fern. Ich repariere nicht gern mein Auto, viel lieber spiele ich Tischtennis. Am liebsten bastle ich in meiner Garage.

Comprehension 1

Transcript

Moment bitte, ich lese Ihnen aus dem Prospekt vom Hotel Schultenhof vor:
„Das Hotel ist durchgehend geöffnet, von 11.30 bis 1.00 nachts, warme Küche.
Kein Ruhetag.
Spezialitäten-Restaurant (Wild, Fisch und Balkan-Grill).
Internationale Küche.
Ausreichender Parkplatz am Hause.
Hotelzimmer mit Dusche, WC und Telefon.
Gäste-Garagen und Hofparkplatz.
2 Bundeskegelbahnen im Hause."
Ich kann Ihnen den Prospekt auch durchfaxen, wenn Sie wollen.

1 no, only shower **2** at the hotel **3** yes **4** never

Comprehension 2

1 Von 12.00 bis 15.00 Uhr und von 18.00 bis 24.00 Uhr.
2 Auf der Straße.
3 Weine und Champagner.
4 Ja.
5 Von 06.15 bis 12.30 Uhr.
6 Croissants, mehrere Sorten Brötchen, frischgepreßten Orangensaft und Kaffee.

Comprehension 3

Transcript

Katrina Herr Holzhauser, hier, bitte bedienen Sie sich. Bonbons aus Schleswig.
Christian Oh, vielen Dank. Wie war denn Ihr Urlaub?
Katrina Danke, es war wunderbar. Wir fahren gern ans Meer, und am liebsten in den Süden, ans Mittelmeer. Aber an der Ostsee war es auch sehr schön.
Christian Haben sie sich gut erholt?
Katrina Danke, ich war vorher von der Arbeit sehr müde, aber jetzt bin ich gut ausgeruht. Also – an die Arbeit.
Christian Ja, die Geschäftsbedingungen in dieser Werbeschrift sind noch nicht vollständig.

Katrina	Stimmt, unsere Qualitätsgarantie fehlt noch. Also erst mal das VDE Zeichen.
Christian	Moment – ich stelle mir das anders vor. VDE hier unten links, und das TÜV Zeichen rechts in der Ecke. Was meinen Sie?
Katrina	Ich finde, das ist Geschmacksache, und wir haben nicht viel Platz.
Christian	Aber Sie verkaufen doch nur erstklassige Qualität. Das muß man unterstreichen.
Katrina	Ja, das möchte ich auch betonen.
Christian	Der Markt ist von elektronischen Geräten überschwemmt. Es gibt viele Importe, ja eingeführte, wie auch deutsche Ware von minderwertiger Güte.
Katrina	Wie wär's mit einem Werbespruch?
Christian	Haben Sie einen Vorschlag?
Katrina	„Nur das Beste ist gut genug für Spieltechnik".
Christian	Ja, warum nicht, dann sind wir mit der Broschüre fertig. Ein guter Abschluß.

Translation

Katrina	Herr Holzhauser, help yourself. Sweets from Schleswig.
Christian	Oh, many thanks. How was your holiday?
Katrina	It was wonderful, thank you. We like going to the seaside, and preferably southwards, to the Mediterranean. But it was very pleasant on the Baltic too.
Christian	Did you have a good rest?
Katrina	Yes, thanks. I was very tired from work before, but now I'm well rested. So, down to work.
Christian	Yes, the terms and conditions of trade in this publicity leaflet aren't complete yet.
Katrina	That's right, our quality guarantee is still missing, so, first the VDE symbol.
Christian	Just a moment. I picture that differently. VDE here, bottom left, and TÜV symbol in the right-hand corner. What do you think?
Katrina	I think that is a matter of taste, and we haven't got much room.
Christian	But really, you only sell first-class quality. You have to stress that.
Katrina	Yes, I'd like to emphasise that as well.
Christian	The market is flooded with electronic equipment. There are lots of imports – yes, imported goods as well as German products of lesser quality.
Katrina	How about an advertising slogan?
Christian	Do you have a suggestion?
Katrina	'Only the best is good enough for Spieltechnik'.
Christian	Yes, why not? Then we've finished the brochure. That's a good ending.

1 They went to the Baltic Sea coast.
2 Only the best is good enough for Spieltechnik.

Exercise 5	Qualität ● Güte ● Geschmacksache ● Vorschlag ● Qualitätsgarantie … Werbespruch
Puzzle	**1** viel **2** Ware **3** Geschmack **4** Importe **5** Vorschlag **6** rechts **7** Werbespruch

Progress check

1 Gestern abend war ich sehr müde, aber ich habe sehr gut geschlafen. Jetzt geht es mir besser.
2 a) Das Hotel Restaurant ist nur von zwölf bis vierzehn Uhr geöffnet.
   b) Das Gasthaus (Fisch Spezialitäten) is durchgehend von Mittag bis Mitternacht geöffnet.
   c) Danke für Ihren Besuch.
   d) Ich kann Ihnen später die Sehenswürdigkeiten der Stadt zeigen, wenn Sie wollen.

3 a) Ich habe Herrn und Frau Schwarz von der Firma Rheinland AG kennengelernt.
   b) Ich habe eine Flugkarte nach London bestellt.
   c) Ich habe ein deutsches Buch für meinen Kollegen gekauft.
   d) Ich habe einen Tisch für drei im Restaurant Krone gebucht.

4 a) Ja/nein.
   b) Ich bleibe lieber zu Hause und sehe fern. (Ich fahre lieber in die Stadt und gehe ins Theater.)
   c) Ja/nein.
   d) Ich höre lieber Musik. (Ich repariere lieber mein Auto.)
   e) Am liebsten esse ich … Ich trinke am liebsten …

5 Eating bread rolls fresh from the oven for breakfast, if he/she has time.

6 a) I would like to stress that we are not interested in lesser quality goods.
   b) In Germany, one can apply for VDE and TÜV symbols for imported products.

UNIT 12

Exercise 1

Sie Haben sie einen Tisch für zwei?
Sie Die Speise- und die Getränkekarte, bitte.
Sie Wir haben (schon) gewählt.
Sie Ochsenschwanzsuppe als Vorspeise, und dann Wiener Schnitzel mit Bratkartoffeln, Gemüse und Salat.
Sie Ein Glas Rotwein, bitte.
Sie Ja, einen Pfannkuchen und eine Tasse Kaffee, bitte.

Comprehension 1

Transcript

Kellnerin Bitte sehr, was darf es sein?
Sie   Ich möchte eine Tasse Kaffee bitte.
Er   Eine Tasse Zitronentee für mich bitte.
Kellnerin Sonst noch etwas?
Sie   Ich möchte auch ein Stück Apfelstrudel.
Er   Und ich bekomme ein Vanille-Eis bitte.
           (later) Darf ich bitte die Rechnung haben?
Kellnerin Also, ein Kaffee, das kostet DM 2,00, ein Tee DM 2,00, ein Stück Apfelstrudel DM 2,50 und ein Eis DM 2,20. Alles zusammen macht das acht Mark und siebzig Pfennig.
Er   Also, bitte schön. Stimmt so.
Kellnerin Ich danke Ihnen.

Exercise 3

1 11 2 nein 3 DM 28, - 4 Zigeunerschnitzel 5 einen Eisbecher 6 Wein
7 DM 81, 50 8 die Mehrwertsteuer 9 12.10.92

Exercise 4

Example: Der Kellner hat die Getränkekarte gebracht und ich habe ein Glas Rotwein bestellt. Dann habe ich die Speisekarte bekommen. Die Vorspeise war grüne Erbsensuppe. Sie hat sehr gut geschmeckt. Als Hauptgericht habe ich geräucherte Bockwurst mit Brötchen gegessen. Das war auch nicht schlecht. Als Nachspeise habe ich Schokoladencreme mit Birne gewählt. Dann hat der Kellner die Rechnung gebracht. Es hat nur fünfundzwanzig Mark gekostet.

Comprehension 2

Transcript

Newby   Das ist ein sehr gutes Restaurant. Das Essen schmeckt prima. Kommen Sie oft hierher?
Walter Eigentlich schon. Ich bringe meine Kollegen und Gäste nur hierher.
Newby   Das kann ich gut verstehen. Das Restaurant ist wirklich sehr schön, und es gibt viele interessante Gerichte.
Walter Ich sehe, daß Sie deutsches Essen gut kennen, Mr Newby.
Newby   Ja, ich bin oft auf Geschäftsreise in Deutschland und Österreich gewesen. Wiener Schnitzel habe ich zum ersten Mal in Linz gegessen. Seitdem esse ich sehr oft Wiener Schnitzel. Übrigens, wie schmeckt Ihnen das Essen in England?
Walter Gar nicht so schlecht. Yorkshire Pudding zum Beispiel ist etwas Einmaliges. Aber ich esse lieber deutsche Küche, weil ich gerne gut gewürzt esse.

Weidmann	Ich finde, das schmeckt mir nicht. Ich esse lieber etwas Süßes. Kuchen und Torten mit Sahne schmecken mir sehr, sehr gut.
Meyer	Das merkt man, Ewald. Was ist denn aus Ihrer Diät geworden?
Weidmann	Herr Ober, die Rechnung bitte!

1 It is very nice, the food is superb with an interesting variety.
2 He has been on many business trips in Austria and Germany.
3 It was his first taste of Wiener Schnitzel.
4 He likes food well spiced.
5 Cakes and gateaux with cream.

Comprehension 3

1 Brot mit Butter, Marmelade oder Honig. **2** Fleisch, Gemüse, manchmal auch Suppe und Nachtisch. **3** Brot mit Schinken, Käse, oder Wurst, und Salat.

Comprehension 4

Transcript

Christian	Ich habe Hunger. Möchten Sie vielleicht auch etwas essen?
Katrina	Ja, und vor allem etwas trinken, das war ein hektischer Vormittag. Aber ich habe nur kurz Zeit. Die Firma Vetti stellt um 13 Uhr 30 ihre neue EDV-Anlage vor. Die ist komplett mit Unterrichtsbüchern und mit zusätzlichem Lehrmaterial ausgerüstet.
Christian	Aha, die Konkurrenz!
Katrina	Das kann man wohl sagen. Die Firma Vetti beherrscht den gesamtdeutschen Computermarkt mit einem Marktanteil von 35 Prozent. Wir sind noch neu in dieser Branche.
Christian	Auch wir befinden uns in einer ähnlichen Situation.
Katrina	Im Buchhandel besteht ein starker Konkurrenzkampf, nicht wahr?
Christian	Ja, der Wettbewerb ist sehr lebhaft. Als relativ junges Unternehmen sind wir nur dann konkurrenzfähig, wenn wir Marktlücken füllen. Wir konzentrieren uns auf neue Interessensgebiete und neue Betriebe.
Katrina	Im Ausland haben wir uns einen beachtlichen Marktanteil mit unserer Modellserie „Deutsches Automobil" erworben. Für diese Miniatur-Fahrzeuge mit zerlegbaren Teilen gibt es keine Konkurrenz in derselben Preislage.
Christian	Ich wünsche Ihnen für Ihre high-tech Bildungsserie ebenso viel Erfolg.
Katrina	Das wäre schön, aber im Moment knurrt mir der Magen ...

Translation

Christian	I'm hungry. Perhaps you'd like to eat something too?
Katrina	Yes, and above all I'd like something to drink. That was a hectic morning. But I don't have much time. Vetti is giving a presentation of its new electronic data processing system at 1.30. It comes complete with teaching manuals and additional teaching materials.
Christian	Aha, the competition!
Katrina	You could certainly say that. Vetti dominates the all-German computer market with a market share of 35 %. We're still new to this business-sector.
Christian	We're in a similar situation too.
Katrina	There's strong competition in the book trade, isn't there?
Christian	Yes, the competition is very lively. As a relatively young business, we're only competitive when we're filling gaps in the market. We concentrate on new areas of interest, and new companies.
Katrina	We've gained a significant market share abroad with our model series 'Deutsches Automobil'. There's no competition in the same price category for these miniature vehicles with parts which can be taken apart.
Christian	I wish you just as much success for your high-tech educational series.
Katrina	That would be nice, but for the moment my stomach's rumbling ...

1 An electronic data processing system, complete with teaching manuals and additional teaching materials.

2 That they have a significant market share abroad, that there's no competition in the same price category.

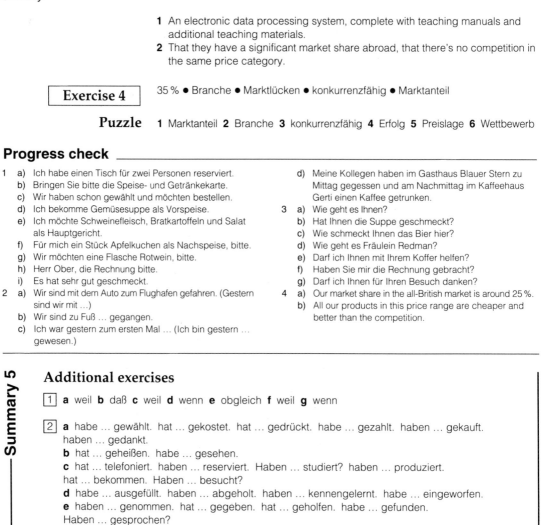

| **Exercise 4** | 35 % ● Branche ● Marktlücken ● konkurrenzfähig ● Marktanteil |

Puzzle   **1** Marktanteil **2** Branche **3** konkurrenzfähig **4** Erfolg **5** Preislage **6** Wettbewerb

Progress check

1
a) Ich habe einen Tisch für zwei Personen reserviert.
b) Bringen Sie bitte die Speise- und Getränkekarte.
c) Wir haben schon gewählt und möchten bestellen.
d) Ich bekomme Gemüsesuppe als Vorspeise.
e) Ich möchte Schweinefleisch, Bratkartoffeln und Salat als Hauptgericht.
f) Für mich ein Stück Apfelkuchen als Nachspeise, bitte.
g) Wir möchten eine Flasche Rotwein, bitte.
h) Herr Ober, die Rechnung bitte.
i) Es hat sehr gut geschmeckt.

2
a) Wir sind mit dem Auto zum Flughafen gefahren. (Gestern sind wir mit ...)
b) Wir sind zu Fuß ... gegangen.
c) Ich war gestern zum ersten Mal ... (Ich bin gestern ... gewesen.)

d) Meine Kollegen haben im Gasthaus Blauer Stern zu Mittag gegessen und am Nachmittag im Kaffeehaus Gerti einen Kaffee getrunken.

3
a) Wie geht es Ihnen?
b) Hat Ihnen die Suppe geschmeckt?
c) Wie schmeckt Ihnen das Bier hier?
d) Wie geht es Fräulein Redman?
e) Darf ich Ihnen mit Ihrem Koffer helfen?
f) Haben Sie mir die Rechnung gebracht?
g) Darf ich Ihnen für Ihren Besuch danken?

4
a) Our market share in the all-British market is around 25 %.
b) All our products in this price range are cheaper and better than the competition.

Additional exercises

Summary 5

☐1 **a** weil **b** daß **c** weil **d** wenn **e** obgleich **f** weil **g** wenn

☐2 **a** habe ... gewählt. hat ... gekostet. hat ... gedrückt. habe ... gezahlt. haben ... gekauft. haben ... gedankt.
b hat ... geheißen. habe ... gesehen.
c hat ... telefoniert. haben ... reserviert. Haben ... studiert? haben ... produziert. hat ... bekommen. Haben ... besucht?
d habe ... ausgefüllt. haben ... abgeholt. haben ... kennengelernt. habe ... eingeworfen.
e haben ... genommen. hat ... gegeben. hat ... geholfen. habe ... gefunden. Haben ... gesprochen?
f ist ... gekommen. ist ... gefahren. sind ... gegangen, nicht wahr? sind ... geflogen? sind ... umgestiegen? bin ... geblieben.

☐3 **a** war (bin gewesen) **b** waren (sind gewesen) **c** war (ist gewesen) **d** Waren (Sind gewesen) **e** waren (sind gewesen) **f** war (ist gewesen) **g** Waren (Sind gewesen)

☐4 **a** hatte (habe gehabt) **b** hatten (haben gehabt) **c** hatte (hat gehabt) **d** hatten (haben gehabt)

☐5 **a** bin gefahren **b** haben gelöst **c** hat reserviert **d** ist abgefahren **e** hat angerufen **f** haben gegessen **g** habe bestellt **h** hat geschlafen

UNIT 13

| **Exercise 1** | *Sie* | Entschuldigen Sie, ich möchte für meine Familie in England Geschenke kaufen. Können Sie mir ein Geschäft empfehlen? |

Sie Ich weiß nicht genau, vielleicht Bücher, Parfüm oder T-Shirts.
Sie Ja, ich weiß, aber die (sie) sind ziemlich teuer.
Sie Wie komme ich am besten dahin?
Sie Vielen Dank für Ihre Hilfe.

Exercise 2

1 rechts **2** geradeaus Kreuzung links zweite rechts **3** geradeaus Hamburger Straße entlang die erste **4** Gehen Sie hier geradeaus bis zur Kreuzung. Die Straße rechts ist der Dortmunder Weg. (Gehen Sie hier geradeaus und dann die zweite Straße rechts. Das ist der Dortmunder Weg.)

Comprehension 1

Transcript

Normalerweise sind deutsche Geschäfte und Postämter montags bis freitags zwischen 08.00 oder 09.00 und 18.30 offen. Samstags müssen alle Geschäfte um 14.00 schließen, aber am ersten Samstag im Monat dürfen sie bis 18.00 offen bleiben (sogenannter „langer Samstag").

1 zwischen 08.00 oder 09.00 und 18.30 **2** um 14.00 **3** bis 18.00
4 der erste Samstag

Exercise 3

1 Dann gehen Sie am besten zur Stadtparfümerie Pieper.
2 Dann gehen Sie am besten zur Buchhandlung Grauert.
3 Beim Weinmann Tscharke.
4 Dann gehen Sie am besten zur Engel-Drogerie.
5 Gehen Sie zum Uhren- und Schmuckfachgeschäft Mössing.
6 Dann gehen Sie am besten zum Foto Goertz.

Exercise 4

1 Im ersten Stock **2** Im Erdgeschoß **3** Im zweiten Stock **4** Auch im zweiten Stock **5** Im Erdgeschoß **6** Auch im Erdgeschoß **7** Auch im Erdgeschoß **8** Auch im Erdgeschoß.

Comprehension 2

1 small village, 2200 inhabitants, in the southern Odenwald, surrounded by beautiful countryside **2** good air **3** hiking **4** beautiful church in the middle of the village **5** bakeries, butchers, supermarkets, greengrocer, stationery, hairdressers **6** entertainment can be found in the next town **7** doctor, dentist, chemist

Comprehension 3

Transcript

Katrina	Guten Tag, Herr Holzhauser wie geht es Ihnen heute?
Christian	Ganz ausgezeichnet, danke, und Ihnen?
Katrina	Auch sehr gut, vielen Dank. Also kommen wir gleich zur Sache. Diese Rechnung von Ihnen bereitet mir ein wenig Kopfzerbrechen. Rechnungsnummer zwohundertdreizehn, vom 31. März.
Christian	Einen Moment bitte, hier sind meine Unterlagen … Nummer 213 0C, also gemäß Ihrer Bestellung vom 28. November haben wir Ihnen ab Januar monatlich eine Teillieferung von je eintausend Broschüren und fünfhundert Handbüchern geschickt.
Katrina	Das stimmt. Laut Ihrer Offerte vom 10. November war der Preis auf 50 Pfennig pro Stück für die Farbbroschüren, und 2 Mark für die Handbücher festgesetzt.
Christian	Das ergibt einen Betrag von sechstausend Mark. Das beinhaltet die gesamten Materialkosten. Dann bekommen Sie von uns 2 Prozent Rabatt, der wird abgezogen. Dazu kommt noch die Mehrwertsteuer, und hier ist der Gesamtbetrag.
Katrina	Ja, aber Sie haben uns in einem Telefongespräch am 25. November eins Komma fünf Prozent Skonto für prompte Zahlung zugesagt.
Christian	Was? Daran kann ich mich nicht erinnern.
Katrina	Nein, das waren auch nicht Sie persönlich, Herr Holzhauser. Ihr Herr Dr. Großmut hat mit unserem Einkaufsleiter darüber gesprochen.
Christian	Ja, davon weiß ich nichts. Das tut mir sehr leid, Frau Stein. Da haben wir offensichtlich einen Fehler gemacht. Bitte entschuldigen Sie, ich schicke Ihnen sofort eine neue Rechnung.
Katrina	Ach, das kann schon mal passieren, es hat keine Eile.

Translation

Katrina   Hello, Herr Holzhauser. How are you today?

Christian   Absolutely excellent, thanks. And you?

Katrina   Also fine, thank you very much. So, let's get straight down to business. This bill from you is puzzling me a little. Invoice number 213, of 31st March.

Christian   One moment please, here are my papers … number 213 0C. So following your order of 28th November we have sent you from January a monthly part-delivery of one thousand brochures and five hundred manuals.

Katrina   That's right. According to your offer of 10th November the price was fixed at 50 pfennigs each for the colour brochures, and 2 marks for the manuals.

Christian   That makes a total amount of 6,000 marks. That includes all material costs. Then you get a 2 % regular discount, that's deducted. Then comes the VAT, and here's the final amount.

Katrina   Yes, but in a telephone conversation on 25th November you promised us a l. 5 % cash discount for prompt payment.

Christian   What? I can't remember that.

Katrina   No, it wasn't you personally, Herr Holzhauser. Your Dr Großmut spoke to our chief buyer about it.

Christian   Ah, well I didn't know anything about that. I am sorry, Frau Stein. We've obviously made a mistake here – please accept our apologies. I'll send you a new invoice immediately.

Katrina   Oh, it can easily happen. There's no hurry.

1 Dr Großmut arranged it with Spieltechnik's purchasing manager.
2 Christian will send a new invoice immediately.

Exercise 5

213 0C ● 28. November ● 1000 ● 50 Pfennig ● 500 ● DM 6 000 ● 2 %
● 25. November ● 1.5 %

Puzzle   **1** Handbuch **2** Teillieferung **3** Materialkosten **4** Rabatt **5** Fehler **6** Skonto
7 Unterlagen

Progress check

1 a) Ich suche das Verkehrsbüro.
   b) Gehen Sie geradeaus.
   c) Nehmen Sie die zweite (Straße) links.
   d) Gehen Sie die Steinstraße entlang.
   e) Das Kaufhaus ist rechts.
   f) Die Altstadt liegt links.
2 a) Können Sie mir ein Andenkengeschäft empfehlen?
   b) Wie komme ich am besten dahin?
   c) Wo kann ich Geschenke für meine Familie kaufen?
   d) Ist der Friseur im Erdgeschoß?
   e) In welchem Stock ist die Musikabteilung?
   f) Wann ist das Postamt offen (geöffnet)?
   g) Ist die Buchhandlung zu Mittag geschlossen?

   h) Kennen Sie meinen Kollegen?
   i) Wissen Sie, wo die Toiletten sind?
3 **Apotheke** is a dispensing chemist, **Drogerie** is a 'drugstore' type chemist.
4 I'm sorry, but I don't know. I don't know this town either, I'm only here for a few days' visit. Yes, I know a good food shop. Do you know where the fashion house Heinemann is? Turn left at the crossroads there, then you come directly to a big Spar shop. There is also a bakery and a butcher's there.
5 a) You can deduct a 2 % cash discount from the total amount for prompt payment.
   b) This mistake must never happen again.

UNIT 14

Exercise 1

1 In der Parfümerie, im ersten Stock.
2 Ob ihr Sohn lieber ein T-Shirt oder Spielzeug möchte.
3 Sechs Jahre alt.
4 Das Micky Maus-Motiv gefällt ihm sicher.
5 DM 17,90.
6 65 cm.

7 26 inches.

8 Sie sucht die Musikabteilung (sie möchte eine Kassette für ihre Tochter kaufen).

Exercise 2

1 gefällt mir **2** es paßt … nicht **3** gefällt mir gut **4** sie passen … nicht
5 geht … gut **6** er … mir nicht

Exercise 3

Sie Ich möchte ein T-Shirt für meine Tochter kaufen.
Sie Sie wird dieses Jahr dreizehn Jahre alt.
Sie Das rote gefällt mir.
Sie Einundachtzig Zentimeter, bitte. Was kostet das?
Sie Wo kann ich (denn) ein Spielzeug für meinen Sohn kaufen?
Sie Danke schön. Auf Wiedersehen.

Exercise 4

1 *Example:*
Verkäufer Guten Tag. Kann ich Ihnen helfen?
Kunde Ich möchte eine Flasche Orangensaft.
Verkäufer Bitte sehr. Sonst noch etwas?
Kunde Ja, zwei Schweineschnitzel, bitte.
Verkäufer Zwei Schnitzel … fünfhundert Gramm. Sonst noch etwas?
Kunde Nein, danke, das ist alles.
Verkäufer Eine Flasche Orangensaft, fünfhundert Gramm Schweineschnitzel,
    … das macht fünf Mark achtundsechzig.
Kunde Bitte schön (*handing over ten marks*).
Verkäufer Und vier Mark zweiunddreißig zurück. Vielen Dank.
Kunde Bitte. Auf Wiedersehen.

2 a) mild and lean **b)** deep frozen **c)** slightly salted **d)** mixed **e)** ten pack
f) with sugar **g)** 236 ml tin

Comprehension 1

Transcript

Gast A Also, gehen Sie die Donaustraße entlang, bis Sie zur Hochstraße kommen. Hier gehen Sie nach links. Auf der rechten Seite sehen Sie dann das Büro. Sehr modern ist es. Dort finden Sie einen Stadtplan und andere Auskünfte über unsere Stadt. Es ist gar nicht weit.

Gast B Ja, also gegenüber dem Hotel ist die Steinstraße. Gehen Sie diese Straße entlang bis zur Kreuzung. Dort müssen Sie dann nach links und dann die zweite Straße rechts nehmen. Sie sehen dann rechts die Firma. Der Geschäftsführer heißt Herr Lange. Er spricht bestimmt Französisch, weil er mit Frankreich und Belgien Geschäftsverbindungen hat.

Gast C Ja, das ist ganz einfach. Vom Hotel sind das nur fünf oder sechs Minuten. Gehen Sie hier links geradeaus bis zur Kreuzung. Dort geht es rechts weiter in die Berliner Allee. Das Geschäft liegt auf der rechten Seite. Wenn sie sehr moderne Bekleidung suchen, kann ich Ihnen ein zweites Geschäft empfehlen. Es heißt Chic. Gehen sie die Berliner Allee hinunter und dann links in den Bonner Weg. Das Geschäft ist dort links an der Ecke.

Gast D Das ist hier im Zentrum. Sehen Sie den Fußgängerüberweg dort drüben? Gehen Sie darüber und dann in die Sankt-Pauli-Straße. Dort geht es rechts weiter bis in die Hochstraße. Gehen Sie dann links noch 200 Meter weiter. Bis der Zug fährt, haben Sie bestimmt noch zwanzig Minuten.

Gast E Einzelzimmer haben wir frei, aber leider keine Doppelzimmer. Ich empfehle Ihnen den Sonnenhof in der Steinstraße auf der linken Seite. Der Inhaber heißt Herr Weismann. Dort sind noch Zimmer frei.

Gast B 3, Firma ● *Gast C* 5, 4 Geschäfte ● *Gast D* 2, Bahnhof ● *Gast E* 6, Hotel Sonnenhof

Comprehension 2

1 ungefähr 26 Prozent **2** ungefähr 16 Prozent und 8 Prozent **3** Nahrungsmittel sind teurer **4** Strom, Gas und Brennstoffe sind billiger **5** nicht viel

Comprehension 3

Transcript

Katrina	Wir müssen noch ein paar Minuten auf Frau Haider warten. Darf ich Ihnen inzwischen eine persönliche Frage stellen?
Christian	Gerne, worum handelt es sich denn?
Katrina	Ich weiß, man kann nie direkt vergleichen, aber es würde mich interessieren, ob eine relativ junge Gesellschaft wie Ihr Verlag auch so gut bezahlt wie unser Betrieb … Ich meine, ob Sie ein gutes Gehalt kriegen.
Christian	Ja Frau Stein, eine sehr delikate Frage. Ich würde sagen, daß ich eine Gehaltserhöhung nie zurückweisen würde.
Katrina	Nein, ich auch nicht … Unter Kollegen kann man ja einmal über solche Dinge sprechen. Unsere Firma zum Beispiel zahlt prinzipiell keine Überstunden. Ist das bei Ihnen auch so?
Christian	Überstunden? Darüber spricht man bei uns nicht. Wir müssen uns die Zeit einfach besser einteilen. Mein Gehalt – na ja, sagen wir das liegt so zwischen DM 5 000 und DM 10 000, so wichtig ist das ja nicht. Die genaue Summe, die bleibt ein Betriebsgeheimnis.
Katrina	Und wenn man die Steuern und Sozialversicherung bedenkt … aber trotzdem, Sie verdienen bestimmt besser als ich.
Christian	Das möchte ich gar nicht sagen, Sie haben ja mehr Dienstjahre hinter sich.
Katrina	Ich kann Sie ja noch einholen, Sie werden schon sehen. Was wetten wir?
Christian	Eine Wette kann ich mir nicht leisten.

Translation

Katrina	We still have to wait a few minutes for Frau Haider. May I ask you a personal question in the meantime?
Christian	Of course. What is it about?
Katrina	I know you can never compare directly, but it would interest me (to know) whether a relatively new company like your publishing house pays as well as our firm … I mean, whether you receive a good salary.
Christian	(laughing) Yes, Frau Stein, a very delicate question. I would say that I'd never refuse a pay rise.
Katrina	No, neither would I. But between colleagues one can occasionally speak about such things. Our firm, for example, pays no overtime on principle. Is it the same with you?
Christian	Overtime? You don't even talk about that in our company. We just have to organise our time better. My salary – well let's say it's between 5 000 and 10 000 marks – it's not so very important. The exact figure remains a company secret.
Katrina	And when one considers tax and national insurance … but nevertheless, you certainly earn more than me.
Christian	I wouldn't (like to) say that. After all, you have more years of service behind you.
Katrina	I can still catch up with you, you'll see. Want to bet?
Christian	I can't afford to bet.

1 Christian.
2 He can't afford one.

zurückweisen ● Überstunden ● Betriebsgeheimnis ● einholen ● leisten

Puzzle **1** vergleichen **2** Steuern **3** Geheimnis **4** Überstunden **5** prinzipiell **6** verdienen

Progress check

1   **a)**   Dieses T-Shirt gefällt mir.
    b)   Welche Farben haben Sie?
    c)   Ich nehme das blaue.
    d)   Haben Sie eine Umrechnungstabelle?
    e)   Diese Größe wird meinem Sohn passen.
    f)   Ich möchte für meine Tochter ein Spielzeug kaufen.
2   **a)**   eine Flasche Orangensaft.

    b)   eine Dose Ananas.
    c)   250g Käse.
3   Pedestrian crossing.
4   **a)** D **b)** G **c)** A **d)** C **e)** E **f)** H **g)** F **h)** B
5   **a)**   We pay no overtime on principle.
    b)   We can only afford a pay-rise next year.

Summary 6

Additional exercises

☐1 **1a 2b 3c 4c 5a 6a**

☐2 **a** wird **b** Werden **c** wird **d** geworden **e** werden **f** werde

☐3 **a 1** I like the old part of the town very much.
     2 How do you like this toy?
     3 I do not like these colours here at all.
     4 Do you like these German magazines?
     5 Which T-shirt do you prefer, the red one or the blue one?
     6 The English visitors do not like the food shop in the main street.
   b 1 Gefällt Ihnen dieses Buch?
     2 Wie gefallen Ihnen die Geschäfte in Mönchengladbach?
     3 Wie gefallen Frau King die kleinen Dörfer im Odenwald?
     4 Gefällt den Kunden unsere neue Ware (unser neues Produkt/Erzeugnis)?
     5 Dieses Andenkengeschäft gefällt mir.
     6 Unseren Gästen gefällt das Abendprogramm. (Das Abendprogramm gefällt unseren Gästen.)
     7 Herrn Newby gefallen diese Schuhe nicht.
     8 Diese Zeitung gefällt mir gar nicht.
     9 Warum gefällt Ihnen die Firma nicht?

☐4 **a** zweihundertzwanzig   **b** hunderzweiundsiebzig
     c dreihundertzehn   **d** neunhundertachtundsiebzig
     e fünfhunderteinundsechzig   **f** vierhundertsechsunddreißig
     g sechshundertsiebenundsiebzig **h** siebenhundertneunundachtzig

☐5 **a** Welches **b** Welche **c** Welchen **d** Welche **e** Welche **f** Welchen **g** Welches

UNIT 15

Exercise 1

1 11.20 a.m. **2** to spell it **3** medical insurance record card **4** headache and stomach pains **5** last night **6** could not sleep at all **7** flu **8** to go to bed immediately **9** he is annoyed **10** round the corner **11** receptionist

Exercise 2

Sie   Ich möchte einen Termin für heute.
Sie   Ja, das geht.
Sie   Ich heiße (mein Name ist) … Ich bin Engländer-in.
Sie   …
Sie   Ich habe einen internationalen Krankenschein.

Exercise 3

Example:
■ Wie geht es Ihnen?   ■ Am besten gehen Sie zum Arzt.
● Leider schlecht.   ● Ja, das mache ich.
■ Was fehlt Ihnen?   ■ Also, gute Besserung.
● Ich habe Magenschmerzen.   ● Danke.
■ Seit wann haben Sie diese Schmerzen schon?
● Seit heute morgen.

Comprehension 1

Transcript

Wenn ein Arbeitnehmer in der Bundesrepublik krank ist, muß er am dritten Tag zum Arzt gehen. Wenn er wirklich nicht arbeiten kann, bekommt er vom Arzt eine Arbeitsunfähigkeitsbescheinigung. Diese Bescheinigung muß der Arbeitnehmer dann seinem Arbeitgeber geben. Der Arbeitgeber muß den Lohn für sechs Wochen weiterzahlen, wenn der Arbeitnehmer so lange krank ist.

1 two days **2** give it to the employer **3** 6 weeks

Comprehension 2

1c) 2a) 3b) 4g) 5f) 6d) 7e)

Comprehension 3

Transcript

Katrina	Also, Begleitschreiben an die Firma Liebmann, das muß heute noch abgehen, es ist dringend.
Frau Kirchhof	Ja, die Anfrage und der Kostenvoranschlag sind noch im Finanzbüro. Ich werde die Akte holen und die Adresse in der Kundenatei speichern.
Katrina	Ja, hoffen wir, daß es zu einer Bestellung kommt. Also, „Wir bedanken uns für Ihr Interesse und senden Ihnen als Anlage unseren Kostenvoranschlag für die gewünschten Artikel. Darf ich darauf hinweisen, daß wir den Päda-Computer mit Drucker, Handbuch und Lehrmaterial zu äußerst günstigen Einführungspreis anbieten. Dieses Pauschalangebot gilt nur bis Jahresschluß und kann nicht verlängert werden". Nein, bitte streichen Sie das, die letzten fünf Worte sind nicht notwendig. *(Telephone rings)*
Frau Kirchhof	Moment bitte, … Kirchhof am Apparat … werde ich ausrichten. Vielen Dank.
Katrina	Das war doch der Verlag Germania nicht wahr?
Frau Kirchhof	Stimmt. Frau Koller möchte sich für Herrn Holzhauser entschuldigen. Er ist krank und muß die Besprechung am Nachmittag leider absagen.
Katrina	Was fehlt ihm denn?
Frau Kirchhof	Er hat sich anscheinend den Rücken verletzt.
Katrina	Hoffentlich ist es nichts Ernstes. Können Sie morgen versuchen, das Meeting auf nächsten Donnerstag zu verlegen, zur gleichen Zeit?
Frau Kirchhof	Geht in Ordnung. Wie war der letzte Satz Ihres Briefes, könnten Sie das bitte wiederholen?

Translation

Katrina	So, accompanying letter for Liebmann's. It's got to go off today, it's urgent.
Frau Kirchhof	Yes, the enquiry and the quotation are still in the finance office. I'll fetch the file and store the address in the customer databank.
Katrina	Yes, let's hope that an order comes of it. So, 'We thank you for your interest, and enclose our quotation for the items required. May I point out that we are offering the Päda-Computer with printer, manual and teaching material, at an extremely favourable introductory price. This package deal is valid only until the end of the year, and can not be extended.' No, please delete that. The last five words aren't necessary. *(Telephone rings)*
Frau Kirchhof	Just a moment please … Frau Kirchhof here … I'll pass on the message. Many thanks.
Katrina	That was Verlag Germania, wasn't it?
Frau Kirchhof	That's right. Frau Koller sends Herr Holzhauser's apologies. He's ill and regrets that he must cancel the meeting this afternoon.

Katrina	What's wrong with him?
Frau Kirchhof	Apparently he's injured his back.
Katrina	I hope it's nothing serious. Tomorrow could you try to postpone the meeting to next Thursday at the same time?
Frau Kirchhof	Yes, that's fine. What was the last sentence of your letter? Could you repeat it please?

1 It is offered at an extremely favourable introductory price lasting till the end of the year.

2 Frau Kirchhof will try to postpone it until next Thursday at the same time.

Exercise 4	Begleitschreiben ● Anfrage ● Kostenvoranschlag ● Einführungspreis ● Pauschalangebot

Puzzle　**1** Einführungspreis **2** Begleitschreiben **3** Kostenvoranschlag **4** Pauschalangebot **5** Anfrage

Progress check

1　a) Ich möchte einen Termin für heute.
　b) Seit gestern abend habe ich Kopfschmerzen.
　c) Ich habe meinen Krankenschein mitgebracht.
　d) Schicken (Werden) Sie mir die Rechnung (schicken)?
2　Ich habe Halsschmerzen und einen Husten und mein linkes Ohr tut weh. Ich habe Fieber und gestern habe ich gar nicht geschlafen.

3　Holen Sie bitte meine Ohrentropfen, Hustenmedizin und Halsschmerztabletten ab!
4　a) employee b) employer c) salary
5　a) Please store the quotation, the printer is not working.
　b) We are offering you the products at a favourable introductory price, but this offer can only apply until the end of the month.

UNIT 16

Exercise 1	*Sie*　Guten Morgen. Ich war gerade beim Arzt. Ich habe ein Rezept. Bitte sehr.
	Sie　Wie oft muß ich die (ein)nehmen?
	Sie　Vor oder nach dem Essen?
	Sie　Wie lange muß ich die einnehmen?
	Sie　Ich danke Ihnen. Was kosten die Tabletten?

Exercise 2	*Example:*
	Sie　Frau Kröger, Herrn Norwak geht es nicht sehr gut.
	Sie　Er hat Magenschmerzen und Kopfschmerzen.
	Sie　Ja, es tut ihm sehr weh.
	Sie　Ja, das mache ich sofort.

Exercise 3	Sie ● Kreuzung ● Unfall ● verletzt ● Krankenhaus ● Polizei ● Arzt (Doktor) ● Frau ● Jungen ● Krankenwagen

Comprehension 1　**Transcript**

Ja, guten Tag. Hier Wagner, Herrn Dr Bennings Sekretärin, von den Wiener Stahlwerken. Gespräch vom achten Januar, acht Uhr zehn. Ich muß Ihnen leider mitteilen, daß Herr Dr Benning krank ist, und deshalb kann er morgen nicht nach England fliegen. Da er eine Grippe hat, dauert es bestimmt ein paar Tage, bis er wieder gesund ist. Wenn es ihm nächste Woche besser geht, werden wir Sie noch einmal anrufen. Vielleicht können wir dann einen Termin für den 16. oder 17. ausmachen, wenn das Herrn Hall und seinen Kollegen paßt. Wenn das nicht paßt, besucht Dr Benning am Ende des Monats die Automesse in London und kann dann direkt danach Ihre Firma besuchen, also am 29. oder am 30. Januar. Als Bestätigung dieses Anrufs schicke ich Ihnen auch heute noch ein Fernschreiben. Ich komme dann in zwei Tagen zurück, wenn ich weiß, wie es Dr Benning geht. Dr Benning läßt Mr Hall grüßen und bedauert sehr, daß er diese Woche nicht kommen kann.

1 Call from Dr Benning's secretary at **Wiener Stahlwerke** on 8.1., 8.10 a.m. Dr Benning is ill and has to cancel his visit tomorrow. Would it be possible to arrange a visit for next week, on the 16th or 17th, if he is better? If not, he will be at the motor show in London at the end of the month and could visit us on the 29th or 30th. His secretary will ring back in two days to fix the visit. Dr Benning sends his apologies, and very best wishes.

2 BESUCH VON DR BENNING

HOFFENTLICH GEHT ES DR BENNING BESSER.

16., 17. JANUAR IST HERR HALL NICHT IM BUERO, EIN BESUCH PASST ALSO NICHT. 29. ODER 30. JANUAR PASST GUT.

BITTE INFORMIEREN SIE MICH UEBER DR BENNINGS PLAENE. DANN KANN ICH EIN HOTELZIMMER BUCHEN UND MEINE KOLLEGEN UEBER DEN TERMIN INFORMIEREN.

Comprehension 2

1 Austria is a small, sparsely populated state with a population of 7.5 million, 90 per cent of which is Roman Catholic. Situated at 'the heart of Europe' it borders onto Switzerland, Germany, Czechoslovakia, Hungary, Slovenia and Italy. It is divided into nine federal provinces with their own provincial government. Parliament consists of two chambers with just over 200 members. The capital is Vienna, renowned international city and industrial centre.

2 a) Eisen, Stahl, Kameras, Mikroskope, Papier, Kraftfahrzeuge, Textilien, Elektrizität.

   b) Zur Feinmechanik.

   c) Tourismus und Elektroindustrie sind sehr wichtig.

   d) Elektrizität ist wichtig für den Export.

Comprehension 3

Transcript

Christian	Frau Stein, schönen guten Morgen. Darf ich Ihnen Herrn Suchanek aus Graz vorstellen?
Katrina	Guten Tag, Herr Suchanek, es freut mich sehr, daß Sie uns besuchen.
Herr Suchanek	Guten Tag, Frau Stein, vielen Dank, daß Sie Zeit für mich haben. Ich interessiere mich sehr für Ihre Firma und Ihre Erzeugnisse. Bitte erzählen Sie mir etwas mehr.
Christian	Entschuldigung, ich werde mich gleich verabschieden. Ich hole Sie in einer Stunde wieder ab. Auf Wiedersehen Herr Suchanek, auf Wiedersehen, Frau Stein.
Katrina	Also wir sind ein mittelgroßes Unternehmen mit einer Belegschaft von ungefähr 70 Mitarbeitern. Unsere Zentrale ist hier in Frankfurt, aber die Produktionsanlage haben wir vor kurzem nach Erfurt verlegt. Dann haben wir auch noch eine Filiale in Hamburg.
Herr Suchanek	Sind Sie auch im Ausland vertreten?
Katrina	Verschiedene Ladenketten in anderen europäischen Ländern führen unsere Produkte in ihrem regulären Sortiment. Eigene Büros haben wir bislang noch nicht. Allerdings haben wir vor, im nächsten Jahr in England eine Kundendienststelle zu eröffnen. Es bestehen Pläne für Warrington, das ist in der Nähe von Manchester.
Herr Suchanek	Sehr interessant. Wie alt ist denn der Betrieb schon?
Katrina	Vor zehn Jahren haben wir mit unserer „Deutsches Automobil" Serie begonnen. Sie war sehr erfolgreich, ja, das war der Anfang.
Herr Suchanek	Und diese Serie läuft noch?
Katrina	Ja, diese Miniatur-Fahrzeuge sind nach wie vor sehr beliebt. Sie bestehen aus zerlegbaren Teilen. Man kann sie selbst zusammenbauen. Hier ist ein Prospekt, der zeigt die verschiedenen Modelle.
Herr Suchanek	Danke schön, sehr hübsch. Stellen Sie auch elektronisches Spielzeug her?
Katrina	Unser neuestes Produkt ist der sogenannte „Päda-Computer". Die

Elektronik Hardware lassen wir uns zuliefern, aber die Montage, Design, Programme und Zubehör stammen von uns. Hier ist ein Informationsblatt.

Translation

Christian	Frau Stein, a very good morning to you. May I introduce you to Herr Suchanek, from Graz?
Katrina	Hello, Herr Suchanek. I'm very pleased that you're visiting us.
Herr Suchanek	Hello, Frau Stein. Thank you very much for having the time to see me. I'm very interested in your company and your products. Please tell me a little more.
Christian	Excuse me, I'll say goodbye straight away. I'll pick you up again in an hour, Herr Suchanek. Goodbye. Goodbye, Frau Stein.
Herr Suchanek	Many thanks, Herr Holzhauser. Goodbye.
Katrina	So, we're a medium-sized firm with a staff of about seventy employees. Our head office is here in Frankfurt, but we've recently moved the production plant to Erfurt. And then we also have a branch office in Hamburg.
Herr Suchanek	Are you also represented abroad?
Katrina	Various chain stores in other European countries carry our products in their regular range. As yet we don't have our own offices. We do intend, though, to open a customer service base in England next year. Plans exist for Warrington. That's near Manchester.
Herr Suchanek	Very interesting. How old is the business?
Katrina	We began ten years ago with our 'Deutsches Automobil' series. That was very successful. Yes, that was the beginning.
Herr Suchanek	And that series is still going.
Katrina	Yes, these miniature vehicles are just as popular now as then. They consist of parts which can be disassembled. One can assemble them oneself. Here's a brochure which shows the various models.
Herr Suchanek	Thank you, very nice. Do you produce electronic toys as well?
Katrina	Our latest product is the so-called 'Päda-Computer'. We have the electronic hardware supplied to us, but assembly, design, programs and accessories are our own. Here's an information leaflet.

1 They want to open a customer service base in Warrington near Manchester next year.
2 The 'Deutsches Automobil' series was very successful, and is still as popular as ever. The miniature vehicles can be taken apart and re-assembled.

Exercise 4   mittelgroß ● 70 ● Frankfurt ● Erfurt ● Hamburg ● Kundendienststelle ● Deutsches ● Automobil ● Päda-Computer

Puzzle   1 Sortiment 2 Belegschaft 3 beliebt 4 Mitarbeiter 5 Zentrale 6 Zubehör 7 Filialen

Progress check

1 a) Ich habe hier ein Rezept.
   b) Wie viele Tabletten? Vor oder nach dem Essen, und wie lange?
   c) Wieviel kosten die Tabletten?
2 a) Take two tablets three times a day, one before and one after meals.
   b) An accident has happened here. Quickly call an ambulance.

c) If the pains don't stop, go back to the doctor.
d) Please confirm this appointment, when you know how Mr. Renner is.
3 a) Ich hoffe, daß es Ihnen besser geht. (Ich hoffe, es geht Ihnen besser.)
   b) Ich möchte für nächste Woche einen Termin ausmachen.

4 a) federal province b) precision engineering c) vehicle
   d) world famous
5 a) Tell me some more about your planned customer service
      base abroad.

b) We will carry your product in our regular range, but you
   should take on (over) the assembly yourselves.

Additional exercises

1 **a** muß, kann, will **b** muß, kann, will, möchte **c** kann, darf, kann, darf

2 **a** Seit letzter Woche. **b** Seit heute morgen. **c** Seit Mittwoch. **d** Seit gestern. **e** Seit zwei Wochen. **f** Seit drei Tagen.

3 **a** Fahren Sie zur Stadtmitte weiter.
   b Holen Sie Herrn Müller vom Bahnhof ab.
   c Sehen Sie den Arzt in einer Woche wieder.
   d Werfen Sie das Fahrgeld in den Automaten ein.
   e Steigen Sie in Köln um.

UNIT 17

| Exercise 1 | 1 Können Sie bitte diesen Hundertmarkschein in einen Fünfzigmarkschein und fünf Zehnmarkscheine wechseln?
2 Können Sie bitte dieses Fünfmarkstück in vier Markstücke und zwei Fünfzigpfennigstücke wechseln? |

Exercise 2

Sie Kann ich hier Reiseschecks einlösen?
Sie Selbstverständlich. Bitte schön.
Sie Ich habe hier fünfzig Pfund. Wie steht der Wechselkurs im Moment?
Sie Zwei Fünfzigmarkscheine und etwas Kleingeld, bitte.
Sie Vielen Dank. Auf Wiedersehen.

Exercise 3

1 DM 2 800, - 2 when the banks are closed, i.e. in the evening or at weekends
3 personal account 4 in many European tourist countries

Exercise 4

Sie Guten Morgen. Ich möchte bitte zwei Briefmarken zu einer Mark. Ich möchte die Briefe nach England schicken.
Sie Ich möchte ein Paket schicken.
Sie Ins Ausland, ich möchte es nach London schicken. Wieviel kostet das?
Sie Kann ich einen Einlieferungsschein haben?
Sie Nein danke, das ist alles. Wo kann ich meine Briefe einwerfen?
Sie Danke schön. Auf Wiedersehen.

Exercise 5

Example:
WIR HABEN GESTERN EIN PAKET MIT 20 KALENDERN UND LINEALEN GESCHICKT. WENN DAS PAKET NICHT ANKOMMT, BITTE ANRUFEN. WIR HABEN EINEN EINLIEFERUNGSSCHEIN.

Exercise 6

1 stamps 2 to buy a few spare stamps 3 automatic machine

Comprehension 1

Transcript

Angestellte	Guten Tag. Kann ich Ihnen helfen?
Tourist	Ja, bitte. Ich möchte englisches Geld in D-Mark umwechseln. Wie ist denn der Wechselkurs im Moment?
Angestellte	DM 2,92.
Tourist	Ach, das Pfund sinkt ständig! Vor zwei Jahren war es noch auf DM 3,38. Also, geben Sie mir D-Mark für hundert Pfund. Ich habe fünfzig Pfund Bargeld, und ich will auch fünfzig Pfund Reiseschecks einlösen. Geht das?

Angestellte	Ja. Darf ich Ihren Paß sehen?
Tourist	Bitte schön.
Angestellte	Danke schön. Wollen Sie das Geld in großen Scheinen?
Tourist	Ich möchte fünf Fünzigmarkscheine, drei Zehnmarkscheine und etwas Kleingeld, bitte.
Angestellte	Unterschreiben Sie hier, bitte. So, bitte schön. Den Wechselkurs finden Sie auf der Quittung.
Tourist	Vielen Dank. Auf Wiedersehen.
Angestellte	Auf Wiedersehen.

1b) 2e) 3f) 4g) 5i) 6c) 7h) 8d) 9j) 10a)

Comprehension 2

1 falsch **2** falsch **3** richtig **4** richtig **5** richtig **6** richtig **7** falsch

Comprehension 3

Transcript

Christian	Guten Tag, Frau Stein, pünktlich wie immer.
Katrina	Guten Tag Herr Holzhauser, wie geht's?
Christian	Danke, aber ich habe im Moment ein kleines Problem. Bitte nehmen Sie Platz. Mir ist etwas ganz Dummes passiert. Ich habe meine Brieftasche verloren und muß Frau Koller bitten, einige Nachforschungen anzustellen.
Katrina	Das tut mir sehr leid, war viel Geld drin?
Christian	So circa 50 Mark, aber noch wichtiger, meine Kreditkarte und einige Reiseschecks von meiner letzten Englandreise. Ach, hier kommt Frau Koller. Möchten Sie einstweilen diese Zeichnungen ansehen? Das sind unsere Vorschläge für die graphische Gestaltung des englischen Handbuches.
Katrina	Ach, wie interessant.
Christian	Bitte entschuldigen Sie mich kurz. Frau Koller, ich kann meine Brieftasche nicht finden. Darf ich Sie bitten, einige Nachforschungen für mich anzustellen?
Frau Koller	Natürlich, was kann ich tun?
Christian	In der Mittagspause war ich auf der Deutschen Bank im Stadtzentrum und habe 50 Mark vom Geldautomaten abgehoben. Dann habe ich die Parkgebühren bezahlt. Also da war die Brieftasche auch noch da.
Katrina	Kamen Sie dann gleich in Ihr Büro zurück?
Christian	Nein, hier in der Firma mußte ich zuerst in die Versandabteilung, um eine dringende Sendung nach Erfurt zu überprüfen. Dann war ich eine Viertelstunde in der Verwaltung, zuerst beim Chef, und dann bei Herrn Klammer.
Frau Koller	Es ist immerhin möglich, daß die Brieftasche aus der Jacke gefallen ist. Noch besteht kein Grund zur Aufregung.
Christian	Vielen Dank, Frau Koller. Und nun an die Arbeit, Frau Stein.
Katrina	Diese Zeichnungen gefallen mir recht gut, mit einigen Vorbehalten. *[telephone rings]*
Christian	Schon wieder eine Störung, wie ärgerlich. Holzhauser.
Frau Koller	Herr Holzhauser, Frau Filz hat Ihre Brieftasche auf dem Firmenparkplatz gefunden. Sie können sie im Empfangsbüro abholen.
Christian	Ach, sehr erfreulich. Vielen Dank. Also jetzt ist alles in Ordnung. Nun aber wirklich an die Arbeit.

Translation

Christian	Hello, Frau Stein, on time as always.
Katrina	Hello, Herr Holzhauser, how are you?
Christian	Thanks for asking, but I've got a little problem at the moment. Please sit down. Something really silly has happened to me. I've lost my wallet and I must ask Frau Koller to make some enquiries.
Katrina	I'm very sorry. Was there a lot of money in it?

Christian	About 50 marks, but more important than that my credit card and some traveller's cheques from my last trip to England. Ah, here comes Frau Koller. Would you like to examine these drawings while you're waiting? They're our suggestions for the graphic layout of the English handbook.
Katrina	Oh, how interesting.
Christian	Please excuse me for a moment. Frau Koller, I can't find my wallet. Can I ask you to make a few enquiries for me?
Frau Koller	Of course. What can I do?
Christian	In the lunch break I was at the Deutsche Bank in the town centre, and drew out 50 marks from the cash machine. Then I paid the parking fee, so I still had the wallet then too.
Frau Koller	And then did you come straight back to your office?
Christian	No, here in the firm I first had to go to the dispatch department to check over an urgent consignment for Erfurt. Then I was in administration for a quarter of an hour, first with the boss, then with Herr Klammer.
Frau Koller	Anyway, it's possible that the wallet fell out of your pocket. There's no need to panic yet.
Christian	Thanks a lot, Frau Koller. And now to work, Frau Stein.
Katrina	I like these drawings a lot, with one or two reservations. [*telephone rings*]
Christian	Yet again an interruption. How annoying! Holzhauser here.
Frau Koller	Herr Holzhauser, Frau Filz found your wallet on the company car park. You can fetch it from reception.
Christian	Ah, I'm delighted. Many thanks. So, now everything's alright. It's really time for work!

1 She is looking at proposed drawings for the English manual.
2 First he was in the dispatch unit, checking an important consignment for Erfurt, then in administration, first with his boss, then with Herr Klammer.

Exercise 7　　50 Pfund ● bezahlt ● verloren ● gefallen ● gefallen ● gefunden

Puzzle　1 Sendung　2 Verwaltung　3 Vorbehalt　4 Versand　5 Störung

Progress check

1 a) Kann ich hier Reiseschecks einlösen?
　b) Wie steht der (Wechsel)kurs im Moment?
　c) Ich möchte für achtzig Pfund Mark, bitte.
　d) Wo bekomme ich das Bargeld?
　e) Möchten (wollen) Sie meinen Reisepaß/Personalausweis sehen?
　f) Wo ist der Geldwechsel?
　g) Können Sie bitte diesen Hundertmarkschein in einen Fünfzigmarkschein, einige Zehnmarkscheine und etwas Kleingeld wechseln?

2 a) Ich möchte ein Paket ins Ausland schicken.
　b) Können Sie bitte diesen Brief wiegen? Wieviele Marken brauche ich?

　c) Wo kann ich Briefe einwerfen?
3 a) certificate of posting
　b) receipt
　c) post code
　d) recipient
　e) three marks and three stamps
4 a) I will make enquiries in the dispatch department immediately.
　b) Your suggestion is excellent, with one or two small reservations.

Additional exercises

1 **a** keine **b** keinen **c** keine **d** keinen **e** keine **f** keine **g** kein **h** keinen **i** kein

2 **a** nichts Neues **b** etwas Billiges **c** etwas Heißes **d** viel Interessantes

3 **a** der siebte Juni (der siebte sechste) **b** der zwanzigste September (der zwanzigste neunte)
c der fünfzehnte Januar (der fünfzehnte erste) **d** der neunte November (der neunte elfte)
e der einundzwanzigste August (der einundzwanzigste achte) **f** der dritte Mai (der dritte fünfte)

Summary 8

UNIT 18

Exercise 1	**1** an der Zollgrenze **2** von Budapest **3** Paß, Führerschein, Versicherungskarte **4** nach Wien **5** ungefähr 400 Kilometer **6** nein **7** er muß Stichproben machen **8** höchstens zehn Minuten **9** um elf Uhr

Exercise 2 1e) 2c) 3g) 4j) 5a) 6b) 7h) 8i) 9d) 10f)

Exercise 3 **1** richtig **2** falsch **3** falsch **4** richtig **5** richtig **6** falsch **7** falsch **8** falsch **9** falsch **10** richtig

Exercise 4
Sie Ja, Bleifrei, bitte, und prüfen Sie bitte den Reifendruck.
Sie Ja, und prüfen Sie bitte auch den Wasserstand.
Sie Vielen Dank, das ist alles. Was macht das?

Exercise 5 **1** 3rd February 1992 **2** 7 litres **3** DM 54, 49

Exercise 6 **1** Der Opel Corsa kostet ungefähr DM 15 305, -. Er hat eine Höchstgeschwindigkeit von 153 Stundenkilometern und verbraucht 4, 7 Liter Superbenzin pro 100 Kilometer. Er wiegt 772 Kilo und hat eine Länge von 3, 62 Metern und eine Breite von 1, 53 Metern.
2 Der BMW ist (viel) teurer als der VW, und er fährt (viel) schneller. Er verbraucht auch mehr Benzin als der VW. Aber Benzin für den BMW ist teurer als für den VW. Der BMW ist mehr als zweimal so schwer wie der VW, und mehr als einen Meter länger. Er ist auch etwas breiter.

Exercise 7 This is an advert for a trainee position as a professional driver. The firm (**Lohmann Spedition**) is a successful and modern haulage firm covering Western Europe. Quality and service have made them internationally well known. Now they need young people for interesting posts from January 1st. The minimum age is 21. Anybody interested should send their curriculum vitae complete with photo and training reports to the firm's address in Münster.

Comprehension 1

Transcript

Polizist	Guten Tag, was machen Sie denn hier? Sehen Sie denn nicht, in der Grünstraße ist Parkverbot.
Herr Kramer	Guten Tag. Ja, ich weiß. Es tut mir leid, aber ich habe eine Panne.
Polizist	Darf ich bitte Ihre Papiere sehen? ... So, Herr Kramer, was ist denn los?
Herr Kramer	Das weiß ich nicht. Die Batterie ist es bestimmt nicht, weil das Licht noch funktioniert. Benzin ist es auch nicht, weil ich gerade vollgetankt habe.
Polizist	Also, was wollen Sie machen? Wollen Sie den ADAC rufen, oder zur nächsten Werkstatt gehen, oder können Sie es selbst reparieren?
Herr Kramer	Wo gibt es hier in der Nähe eine Werkstatt?
Polizist	Also, gehen Sie bis zur Kreuzung, dann links. Nach ungefähr 30 Metern nehmen Sie wieder die erste Straße links. Aber machen Sie schnell. Die Werkstatt macht um fünf Uhr dreißig zu. Dann ist kein Mensch mehr da. Kommen Sie innerhalb von dreißig Minuten zurück, sonst bekommen Sie eine Strafe von 25 Mark.

1e) 2d) 3a) 4f) 5b) 6c)

Comprehension 2 **1** 6, 4 Millionen **2** Deutschland, Österreich, Italien und Frankreich **3** Maschinen, Filmapparate, chemische und pharmazeutische Produkte, Textilien, Uhren und Lebensmittel **4** klein **5** es verbindet die Gemeinden und Städte miteinander und mit den Flugplätzen **6** mit dem Auto, mit der Bahn oder

mit dem Flugzeug **7** Deutsch, Französisch, Italienisch und Romanisch
8 katholisch und evangelisch **9** die Schweiz ist zweihundertzwanzig Kilometer lang und dreihundertachtundvierzig Kilometer breit
10 einundvierzigtausendzweihundertdreiundneunzig Quadratkilometer

Comprehension 3

Transcript

Katrina	Sind Sie mit Ihrem Wagen hier?
Christian	Ja, warum?
Katrina	Darf ich Sie bitten, mich bis zum Bahnhof mitzunehmen? Mein Auto wollte heute mittag plötzlich nicht anspringen. Ich habe den ADAC angerufen, und jetzt ist der Wagen in der Werkstatt, der Motor war kaputt.
Christian	So ein Pech. Aber ich nehme Sie gerne mit.
Katrina	Das ist sehr nett von Ihnen, vielen Dank. Morgen nehme ich einen Firmenwagen. Ich muß auf eine Geschäftsreise in die Schweiz.
Christian	So? Gibt's Probleme mit der Kundschaft?
Katrina	Nein, wir müssen unseren Umsatz vergrößern. Die Firma führt im Augenblick eine intensive Werbekampagne durch. Im schweizer Fernsehen läuft sogar ein Werbespot von Spieltechnik.
Christian	Das wird Ihnen sicher viele neue Abnehmer bringen. Unsere beste Werbung sind unsere Bücher, – zumindest die erfolgreichen. Aber auch wir sind ständig auf der Suche nach neuen Märkten. Zum Beispiel machen wir Reklame im *Deutschen Handelsblatt* – jeden Monat haben wir ein anderes Buch im Angebot.
Katrina	Und bringt Ihnen das einen Gewinn?
Christian	Ja, wir verkaufen die Bücher zwar billiger, aber die Nachfrage steigt, und damit der Gewinn.
Katrina	Das klingt so einfach. Verluste kennen Sie also nicht?
Christian	Verluste müssen wir auch in Kauf nehmen, – das ist ganz klar. Aber ich beklage mich nicht. Unser Geschäft läuft zur Zeit bestens.

Translation

Katrina	Have you got your car here?
Christian	Yes, why?
Katrina	May I ask you to take me as far as the station? Suddenly this lunchtime my car wouldn't start. I phoned the ADAC, and now the car's in the garage. The engine wouldn't work.
Christian	What bad luck. But I'll gladly give you a lift.
Katrina	That's very nice of you, thanks a lot. Tomorrow I'll take a company car. I've got to go on a business trip to Switzerland.
Christian	Really? Are there problems with customers?
Katrina	No. We have to increase our turnover. At the moment the company's carrying out an intensive advertising campaign. There's even a Spieltechnik commercial on Swiss television.
Christian	That'll certainly bring you lots of new customers. Our best publicity is our books – at least the successful ones. But we're also always searching for new markets. For example, we advertise in the *Deutsches Handelsblatt*. We have a different book on offer every month.
Katrina	And does that bring you in a profit?
Christian	Yes. We sell the books cheaper, true, but the demand rises, and with it the profit.
Katrina	That sounds so simple. So you don't experience losses?
Christian	We have to put up with losses too, of course. But I'm not complaining. Our business is flourishing at the moment.

1 Spieltechnik has embarked on an intensive advertising campaign.
2 Although the books are sold more cheaply, demand rises and with it the profit.

Summary 9

Exercise 8	Umsatz ● Kampagne ● Abnehmer ● Märkte ● Reklame ● Verluste

Puzzle   **1** Werbespot **2** Gewinn **3** Umsatz **4** Verluste **5** Abnehmer

Progress check

1 a) Ich habe nichts zu verzollen.
   b) Mein Paß, Führerschein und die grüne Versicherungskarte sind im Auto.
   c) Wie ärgerlich!
   d) Es dauert nur fünf Minuten.
   e) Ich fahre schon seit fünf Stunden.
2 a) Volltanken bitte, Super, bleifrei.
   b) Bitte waschen Sie das Auto.
   c) Füllen Sie das Wasser nach.
   d) Prüfen Sie den Reifendruck.
   e) Kann ich eine Quittung haben?
3 Ich habe die technischen Daten geprüft. Das neue Auto ist länger, breiter und etwas schwerer als das alte. Es fährt

schneller und Preis und Benzinverbrauch sind ungefähr so hoch wie vorher. Wo bekomme ich den Schlüssel und wohin sollen wir zum Mittagessen fahren?
4 If you are looking for a new work- or training position, send your curriculum vitae with a photograph and school/training reports directly to the head office of the Lohman haulage firm.
5 a) We are advertising in newspapers, magazines, on radio and TV, in fact in almost all the mass media.
   b) Customers are complaining, profits are sinking, losses are rising … we must mount an urgent advertising campaign.

Additional exercises

1 **a** als **b** wie **c** als **d** als **e** wie **f** als

2 **a** Wenn das geht, möchte ich … **b** Wenn Sie … wollen, gehen Sie …
c Wenn Sie müde sind, können wir … **d** Wenn man … hat, muß man …
e Wenn wir … haben, muß ich … **f** Wenn Sie möchten, können wir …

3 **a** Ich habe … gegeben. **b** Mein Kollege hat … geprüft. **c** Wir haben … gewechselt.
d Der Wagen ist … geblieben. **e** Der Zollbeamte hat … gemacht. **f** Es hat … gedauert.
g Die Besucher sind … zurückgekommen. **h** Ich habe … eingelöst. **i** Wir haben … gebraucht.
j Er hat … bekommen.

UNIT 19

Exercise 1	**1** Sie ist zum ersten Mal in Düsseldorf.

2 Sie ist Düsseldorfs bekannteste und eleganteste Straße.
3 In Spezialgeschäften und Antiquitätenläden.
4 Sie gehen spazieren, und später machen Sie am Rheinufer einen Spaziergang.
5 Düsseldorf soll eine der schönsten Städte Europas sein.
6 Düsseldorf liegt am Rhein.

Exercise 2	*Sie* Ja, ich bin zum ersten Mal hier.

Sie   Ja, (das möchte ich) gern.
Sie   Ja und dann möchte ich die Donau besichtigen.
Sie   Es ist sehr imposant (schön). Ich habe es im Film „Der dritte Mann" gesehen.

Exercise 3	befinden sich ● setzen Sie sich ● sich bequem ● langweilen Sie sich ● sich …

freuen ● sich … interessieren ● sich … wohlfühlen ● verliebt sich ● freue mich ●
euch … amüsieren ● euch … gut unterhalten ● uns … entspannen ● bedanke
mich

Exercise 4	*Examples:*

1 *Sie*   Guten Tag. Ich bin hier fremd. Können Sie mir bitte helfen?
Angestellte   Ja, gern.
Sie   Wie komme ich am besten zum Schwimmbad?
Angestellte   Ach, das ist ganz einfach. Gehen Sie zu Fuß?
Sie   Nein, ich bin mit dem Auto hier.
Angestellte   Also fahren Sie hier links bis zur Verkehrsampel und dann

wieder links. Dann fahren Sie wieder links, die Berliner Allee entlang bis zum Kreisverkehr. Dort fahren sie (nach) rechts, direkt zum Schwimmbad.

2 *Sie* Wo kann man hier gut parken?

Angestellte Es gibt einen großen Parkplatz in der Nähe vom Markt. Fahren Sie vom Schwimmbad geradeaus um den Kreisverkehr. Dann fahren Sie geradeaus bis zur zweiten Kreuzung. Dort fahren Sie (nach) rechts, und an der nächsten Kreuzung links. Fahren Sie diese Straße entlang, und der Parkplatz ist auf der linken Seite.

3 *Sie* Wie komme ich vom Parkplatz zum Museum?

Angestellte Gehen Sie links aus dem Parkplatz und nehmen Sie die erste Straße links. Gehen Sie dann geradeaus bis zum Museum auf der linken Seite.

4 *Sie* Und wie komme ich vom Museum zur St. Pauli Kirche?

Angestellte Da fragen Sie am besten im Museum!

Comprehension 1

Transcript

1 Sie ist in der Steinstraße. Dort sehen Sie viele Bilder, besonders von Nolde.
2 Es liegt in der nächsten Straße. Im Moment ist eine sehr gute Ausstellung von Antiquitäten zu sehen.
3 Ja, gleich hier um die Ecke. Es ist von acht Uhr morgens bis zehn uhr abends geöffnet. Der Eintritt is nur drei Mark 50, und das Wasser ist warm.
4 Das finden Sie in der Münchener Straße. Der Film soll sehr interessant sein, und die Musik ist auch sehr gut, glaube ich.
5 Es ist gegenüber dem Stadtpark. Diese Woche können Sie ein Stück von Shakespeare auf Deutsch sehen.

1 Kunstgalerie **2** Museum **3** Schwimmbad **4** Kino **5** Theater

Comprehension 2

1 no, from Easter till the end of September **2** comfortable **3** there are bars and restaurants on board **4** children as well as adults **5** the last sentence expresses that one is very welcome **6** yes, there are various different trips on offer

Comprehension 3

Transcript

Katrina Die Firma Educational Electronics hat den Vertrieb in England.

Enquirer Und wie steht es mit der Lieferung?

Katrina Ja, die haben den Päda-Computer auf Lager, Ersatzteile und gesamtes Zubehör. Educational Electronics kann auch kurzfristig liefern. Keine Sorge – Lieferverzug gibt es bei dieser Firma nicht.

Enquirer Meine Erfahrung hier in England ist anders. Aber wer weiß, die Ausnahme bestätigt die Regel. Vielen Dank, und viel Glück! Good bye.

Katrina Good bye. Wir sehen uns bestimmt nicht wieder.

Christian Hello, Mrs. Stone, how is business?

Katrina Mr Woodhauser, was machen Sie denn hier in London?

Christian Ein wenig Marktforschung betreiben. Das kann nie schaden.

Katrina Ja, darf ich Ihnen unser neuestes Erzeugnis vorstellen, komplett mit englischsprachigem Handbuch und Informationsmaterial?

Christian Nein danke, darüber können Sie mir nichts Neues sagen. Ich weiß schon alles.

Katrina Sie irren sich, mein lieber Herr Holzhauser. Wir haben soeben ein prima Geschäft abgeschlossen. Wollen Sie nicht Genaueres wissen?

Christian Also gut.

Katrina Zehn Stück unserer Päda-Prachtexemplare werden nächsten Monat in einem Umschulungszentrum in Newcastle installiert.

Christian Das muß ein Mißverständnis sein.

Katrina Nein, Sie haben ganz richtig gehört. Und heute abend feiern wir das. Kommen Sie mit? Frau Haider, Udo und ich laden Sie zu einem Glas Wein ein.

Christian Das nehme ich gerne an. Ich gratuliere!

Translation

Katrina	Educational Electronics have the agency in England.
Enquirer	And what about delivery?
Katrina	Yes, they have the Päda-Computer in stock, replacement parts and all accessories. Educational Electronics can deliver at short notice too. No need to worry, there are no delays in delivery with this firm.
Enquirer	My experience here in England is different. But who knows? The exception proves the rule. Thanks a lot, and good luck! Good bye.
Katrina	Good bye. We won't be seeing each other again, that's certain!
Christian	Hello, Mrs. Stone, how is business?
Katrina	Mr Woodhauser, what are you doing here in London?
Christian	Doing a little market research, no harm in that.
Katrina	Yes, well, may I introduce our latest product, complete with English language manual and information material?
Christian	No thanks, you can't tell me anything new about that. I already know everything.
Katrina	You're wrong, my dear Herr Holzhauser. We've just clinched a first-class deal. Don't you want to know more about it?
Christian	Alright then.
Katrina	Ten sets of our top specimens will be installed next month in a retraining centre in Newcastle.
Christian	That must be a misunderstanding.
Katrina	No, you heard correctly. And this evening we're celebrating it. Are you coming along? Frau Haider, Udo and I invite you to a glass of wine.
Christian	I'll gladly accept that. Congratulations!

1 Educational Electronics have the distribution agency. They have a complete range of spare parts and accessories in stock, and can deliver at short notice.

2 They've just clinched an excellent deal.

Exercise 5	übernommen ● liefern ● vorstellen ● sagen ● abgeschloßen ● sein ● gehört

Progress check

1. a) Kann ich die Stadt sehen?
   b) Wie heißt die bekannteste Straße?
   c) Haben wir Zeit für einen Spaziergang am Rhein?
   d) Finden Sie alte Gebäude interessant?
2. a) Setzen Sie sich und machen Sie es sich bequem.
   b) Ich freue mich auf einen Spaziergang in der Altstadt.
   c) Ich bedanke mich für Ihre Aufmerksamkeit.
3. Fahren Sie geradeaus, und dann rechts am Kreisverkehr. Dann nehmen Sie die zweite Straße links. Das Krankenhaus ist gegenüber dem Schwimmbad.

4. a) Under no circumstances must we miss the exhibition at the exhibition centre.
   b) Before your return to England you really must take part in an excursion on the Rhine.
   c) The afternoon at the art gallery was the greatest pleasure.
5. a) We do not have our own office in the Netherlands, but Van der Bloom has the agency for our products.
   b) We can deliver spare parts at any time at short notice. You will find details in our product literature.

UNIT 20

Exercise 1	**1** als Kind **2** nein **3** er möchte die City sehen, weil er Geschäftsmann ist **4** den ganzen Tag **5** weil man vom Bus aus viel besser sehen kann **6** einen Doppeldecker

Exercise 2	
Sie	Sind Sie zum ersten Mal hier?
Sie	Dann müssen Sie unbedingt die Stadt besichtigen. Haben Sie Lust dazu?
Sie	Möchten Sie lieber eine Stadtrundfahrt machen, oder die Sehenswürdigkeiten besichtigen?
Sie	Möchten Sie mit dem Bus fahren, oder mit dem Auto, oder lieber zu Fuß gehen?

Exercise 3

Transcript

Herrn Georg Schmidt
International Computers AG
Postfach 30 47 56
D-8000 München 4

Sehr geehrter Herr Schmidt,
Ich danke Ihnen für Ihr Schreiben vom siebzehnten Mai und freue mich, daß so viele Ehepartner Ihrer Kollegen und Kolleginnen auch zur Tagung mitkommen. Sie sind bei uns hier in England herzlich willkommen.
Während der dreitägigen Konferenz versuchen wir, den Damen und Herren ein abwechslungsreiches und interessantes Programm zu bieten. Das Programm ist noch nicht fertig, aber für Folgendes werden die Damen und Herren sich bestimmt interessieren: Busausflüge, Stadtbesichtigung, Führung durch eine Modefabrik, Theaterbesuch, Zeit zum Einkaufen und so weiter. Unsere Dolmetscher und Dolmetscherinnen werden natürlich immer zur Hand sein. Genauere Informationen schicken wir Ihnen in zwei bis drei Wochen zu.
Ich bin sicher, daß unsere Gäste diese Gegend sehr schön finden werden. Langweilen werden sie sich bestimmt nicht.
Mit freundlichen Grüßen

Richard Wood

Exercise 4

Translation

Tourist information can be obtained on number 120, the weather forecast on number 162. Also teletext and videotext keep you constantly informed about the latest news. Useful numbers: breakdown service 140, police 117, fire brigade 108, road condition 163. These and further numbers you can find in the blue pages of all official phone books. Shop opening times: Monday to Friday as a rule from 8am to 6.30pm, Saturdays usually till 4pm. At important stations snack-machines have been installed. Public holidays: New Year's Day, Easter, Ascension, Whitsun and Christmas. 1st August is the National Holiday. Local tourist offices give information about holidays in cantons and local areas. In all restaurants a service charge is included in the price. A tip is customary for porters, at petrol stations with customer service and for taxi drivers in some towns.

Exercise 5

1 in dem/im, auf der **2** in der **3** auf dem, vor dem **4** an der **5** vor dem
6 gegenüber dem **7** hinter dem

Comprehension 1

Transcript

Gastgeber	Willkommen in Recklinghausen. Sind Sie zum ersten Mal hier?
Vertreterin	Im Ruhrgebiet war ich schon viermal, aber in Recklinghausen selbst noch nie.
Gastgeber	Möchten Sie heute nachmittag Sehenswürdigkeiten besichtigen?
Vertreterin	Sehr gerne. Recklinghausen soll eine schöne Stadt sein.
Gastgeber	Ja, es ist heute eine moderne Stadt mit vielen interessanten Gebäuden. Als Handels-, Einkaufs-und Kongreßstadt ist es nicht mehr die typische Industriestadt von früher.
Vertreterin	Gibt es noch alte Gebäude?
Gastgeber	Eigentlich nur wenige. Recklinghausens ältestes Gebäude ist die Kirche St. Peter. Sie ist aus dem zwölften Jahrhundert. Die barocke Engelsburg ist jetzt ein Hotel. Auch gibt es hier ein paar Fachwerkhäuser. In einem davon befindet sich eine interessante Kunstgalerie.
Vertreterin	Ich habe gehört, daß Recklinghausen dem Besucher viel zu bieten hat.
Gastgeber	Ja, das stimmt. Wir haben außer Museen und Kunstgalerien das Ruhrfestspielhaus. Hier finden die berühmten Ruhrfestspiele statt.

	Das Planetarium ist auch eine große Attraktion. 40 000 Personen besuchen es jährlich. Und für Tierfreunde gibt es den Zoo.
Vertreterin	Eine lebendige Stadt, also. Ich glaube, daß man sich hier kaum langweilen kann!
Gastgeber	Meine ich auch. Ich hoffe, Sie werden Ihren ersten Besuch in unserer Stadt so richtig genießen.

1 never before **2** St. Peter's church **3** half-timbered house **4** Ruhr festival hall, planetarium, zoo

Comprehension 2

1 seit dem dreizehnten Jahrhundert **2** nicht ganz eine halbe Stunde **3** zu Hause in ihren eigenen Werkstätten **4** ja, weltbekannt **5** ungefähr fünfzig Prozent **6** alt und neu, traditionell und modern

Comprehension 3

Transcript

Christian	Also der Päda-Computer hat das Vereinigte Königreich im Sturm erobert?
Katrina	Das ist etwas übertrieben, aber der britische Markt hat ihn gut aufgenommen.
Frau Haider	Es gibt verschiedene Interessenten, unter anderem eine Pädagogische Hochschule in Nordirland. Und der Vertrag mit MCK in Newcastle wird morgen unterzeichnet. Das sind gute Anzeichen, als Verkaufsleiterin kann ich das beurteilen.
Udo Kralle	Pädagogische Hochschule, da paßt er gut hin unser pädagogischer Computer.
Christian	Und mit der englischen Produktliteratur ist man zufrieden?
Frau Haider	Ja, sie kommt sehr gut an. Ihr Verlag hat gute Arbeit geleistet. Später brauchen wir sicher noch verschiedene Zusatzmaterialien.
Christian	Ist das der nächster Auftrag? Kann ich das bitte schriftlich haben?
Katrina	Aber Herr Holzhauser, unter Freunden ist das doch nicht nötig.
Frau Haider	Wie meinen Sie das, Frau Stein?
Katrina	Nun ja, Christian Holzhauser und ich haben so gut zusammengearbeitet, daß wir wirklich zum 'Du' kommen sollten. Was meinen Sie, Herr Holzhauser?
Christian	Sie können ruhig Christian zu mir sagen. Da bin ich völlig einverstanden.
Udo Kralle	Da muß ich mitmachen. Wir kennen uns doch auch schon länger, nicht wahr? – Udo –
Frau Haider	Und ich möchte auch nicht fehlen. Wir arbeiten schon seit Jahren zusammen, nicht wahr, Katrina? Und Udo war schon vor mir bei Spieltechnik. Also zum Wohl allerseits!
Udo	Zum Wohl, auf Ursula, Katrina, Christian und Udo.
Christian	Weiterhin viel Erfolg! Prost!
Katrina	Auf Ihr Wohl – auf gute Zusammenarbeit in der Zukunft!
Christian	Sehr schön, aber ich muß mich bald verabschieden. Ich muß heute noch einen Bericht schreiben. Also, Katrina bitte ruf' mich an, wenn die nächste Besprechung festgelegt wird. Euch allen noch einen schönen Abend! Auf Wiedersehen.

Translation

Christian	So, the Päda-Computer has taken the UK by storm?
Katrina	That's a slight exaggeration, but the British market did accept it well.
Frau Haider	There are various interested parties, amongst others a College of Higher Education in Northern Ireland. And the contract with MCK in Newcastle will be signed tomorrow. Those are good indicators. As a sales director I can tell that.
Udo Kralle	College of Higher Education. In German Pädagogische Hochschule – the Päda-Computer is well placed there!
Christian	And are people satisfied with the product literature in English?

Katrina	Yes, it's very well received. Your publishing house did some good work there. Later on we'll certainly still need various additional materials.
Christian	Is that the next order? Can I have that in writing please?
Katrina	But Herr Holzhauser, surely that's not necessary between friends.
Frau Haider	What do you mean by that, Frau Stein?
Katrina	Well, Christian Holzhauser and I have done such good work together that we really should use 'du' with each other. What do you think, Herr Holzhauser?
Christian	Have no hesitation in calling me Christian. I agree completely.
Udo Kralle	I must play my part in this. We've known each other for quite a while too, haven't we? Call me Udo.
Frau Haider	And I don't want to be left out. We've been working together for years, haven't we Katrina? And Udo was with Spieltechnik even before me. So, cheers everybody!
Udo Kralle	Good health to Ursula, Katrina, Christian and Udo.
Christian	To much success to come! Cheers!
Katrina	Good health – to good collaboration in the future!
Christian	Very nice, but I must say cheerio soon. I've still got a report to write today. So, Katrina, please phone me when the next meeting's arranged. A lovely evening to everyone! Goodbye!

1 There are various interested parties, amongst others a college of higher education in Northern Ireland. The contract with MCK in Newcastle is going to be signed tomorrow.

2 He jokingly enquires whether Katrina's comment indicates a new order from Spieltechnik. If so, he'd like it in writing.

Exercise 6	Interessenten ● unterzeichnet ● Anzeichen ● zufrieden ● geleistet ● nötig ● einverstanden

Puzzle   **1** Bericht **2** Interessent **3** Zusammenarbeit **4** Auftrag **5** Vertrag

Progress check

1 a) Ich interessiere mich besonders für die Sehenswürdigkeiten in Berlin.
   b) Ich fahre lieber mit dem Bus.
   c) Ich freue mich auf eine Fahrt auf dem Rhein.
   d) Als typischer Engländer/typische Engländerin lerne ich gern Deutsch.
   e) Also gut. Fahren wir nach Solingen.
2 Als Student(in) hatte ich kein Auto und mußte mit dem Zug fahren. Ich studierte in London und war oft im Ausland.

3 a) cutting tools
   b) orders
   c) half-timbered houses
4 a) We hope for good collaboration in the future too!
   b) If you are happy with this proposal, we can sign the contract tomorrow.

–Summary 10

Additional exercises

1   **a** sich **b** uns **c** mich **d** uns **e** sich **f** sich **g** uns **h** sich

2   **a** bedankte **b** tankten **c** telefonierte **d** spielten **e** wartete **f** wohnte **g** besuchten **h** lernte

3   **a** kann **b** gibt **c** finden **d** fahren **e** ist **f** gehen **g** sehen **h** habe **i** fliegt **j** muß